NEW DIRECTIONS IN ROYAL COMMISSIONS & PUBLIC INQUIRIES

Do we need them?

EDITED BY SCOTT PRASSER

connorcourt
PUBLISHING

Published in 2023 by Connor Court Publishing Pty Ltd

Connor Court Publishing Pty Ltd
PO Box 7257
Redland Bay QLD 4165
sales@connorcourt.com
www.connorcourt.com

Printed in Australia

ISBN: 9781922815255

Cover by Ian James.

This volume is dedicated to the late Dietrich H Borchardt AM, foundation librarian at La Trobe University, Australia. His long standing research and series of publications, *Checklists of Royal Commissions, Select Committees and Boards of Inquiry,* laid the basis for the study of public inquiries, especially in Australia.

All chapters in this volume were blind refereed.

Contents

Introduction

Why another book on public inquiries?

Scott Prasser

Introduction

This new book has been developed because governments in Australia and overseas continue to appoint public inquiries in great numbers, often into important topics that gain considerable interest from stakeholders, the public, and the media. Most importantly, inquiries often have major impacts on public policy and politics.

To clarify, public inquiries are those temporary, ad hoc, external, independent, advisory and investigatory bodies appointed by executive government. They are required to report on a wide variety of issues and topics – from scandals to many complex policy issues. Public inquiries take a variety of forms. Some are statutorily based royal commissions or commissions of inquiry with coercive powers of investigation. Others are non-statutory without any formal powers. Their status and impact are determined by the appointing government and the nature of their membership. Inquiries work under many different nomenclatures such as: royal commissions, commissions, special commissions, committees, boards of inquiry, independent reviews, taskforces, working parties and advisory committees.

In summary, for the purpose of this publication, and to distinguish public inquiries from other more permanent advisory and investigatory bodies, public inquiries have the following characteristics:

- appointed by executive government (not by a government

department, statutory body or other permanent government agency);

- are non-permanent, ad hoc and temporary bodies, disbanding once their report has been submitted;
- their members are drawn mostly from outside of government but may include former public servants and elected officials;
- have clear public terms of reference;
- have public processes in the conduct of their inquiries (these may be informal meetings or more formal public hearings);
- their reports are released to the public within a reasonable specified timeframe;
- only make recommendations – they exercise no decision-making powers – it is up to governments to decide what to do with their recommendations;
- some inquiries are statutorily based with coercive powers of investigation, but most (in Australia) are not;
- perceived to be independent from executive government although appointed by it.

Importantly, although some public inquiries like royal commissions or their equivalents are sometimes chaired by current or former members of the judiciary, in the Australian system of government with its clear formal constitutional separation of powers, they are not in any way a 'judicial inquiry'. The judiciary does not appoint public inquiries. Rather, it is executive government alone that appoints public inquiries as defined in this volume. Unfortunately, many commentators and even appointing governments, sometimes inaccurately refer to inquiries as such.

In summary, public inquiries excludes a host of other bodies which although having certain 'public inquiry' elements are not public inquiries. For instance, parliamentary committees conduct inquiries and hold public hearings, collect evidence and release their reports, but are excluded as they are dominated by partisan parliamentarians and often not perceived as independent. Also, they are formally established by parliament rather than by executive government. In Australia, permanent advisory bodies such as the Productivity

Commission and the Australian Law Reform Commission and a host of other policy advisory bodies in and around government, are also excluded given their permanent nature and the fact that they often set their own research agendas. Similarly, permanent anti-corruption bodies that now exist across all Australian jurisdictions, although often proclaimed as "standing royal commissions" are also excluded given their permanence and other factors.

As discussed later (**Chapter 1**), public inquiries have a long history in Australia and in many other countries (**Chapters 14-17**). Indeed, in Australia and other jurisdictions, hardly a day passes without someone calling for a public inquiry, one being appointed or an inquiry releasing its report. Their ubiquity, the range of issues they investigate, the constant public demand for inquiries and the willingness of governments to accede to those demands, have made public inquiries one of the consumer items of modern government. They have become a part of the architecture of modern government, though exactly what part is open to debate. It is an issue pursued in this volume.

Why this new volume?

Several factors have prompted this new volume.

In Australia, the Commonwealth (national government), after a lull in their use for the preceding decade, has established at the time of writing ten royal commissions since 2013 – one every year until 2022. Commentators like Paul Kelly, believe that in the last decade there has developed the "cult of the royal commission" whereby governments have too easily resorted to royal commissions in the hope they will resolve both the policy and political problems concerning complex and difficult issues, rather than seeking to do so through the normal processes of government.[1] That the new federal Labor Albanese Government elected in May 2022 has kept their promise to appoint a royal commission into the Robodebt scheme, a major failed program of the previous administration (Morrison Government), highlights the continuation of this trend at the national level in Australia.[2] In addition, many other non-statutory public inquiries have been appointed by the successive Coalition governments under prime ministers Abbott, Turnbull and Morrison.

So too, during the last decade have Australian States been busy in appointing a host of royal commissions, special commissions, and other public inquiries into issues such as: mental health, domestic violence, police informants, the Murray-Darling Basin, drugs, child abuse, the nuclear fuel cycle, education, legal issues, natural disasters, quarantine matters, integrity arrangements, and maladministration.

In addition, new legislation covering public inquiries has emerged in some Australian jurisdictions. The 2009 federal Australian Law Reform Commission[3] (ALRC) review of the Commonwealth's *Royal Commission Act 1902* recommended that legislation be changed to cover both royal commissions and more general policy inquiries, but this has been ignored by all subsequent federal governments. However, the Victorian State government enacted new legislation in 2014 that largely reflected those recommendations. Given that Victoria has now appointed several inquiries under its new legislation, one of issues examined in this volume (**Chapter 4**) is how that legislation has impacted on inquiry operations. Similar changes are being proposed to South Australian legislation.

Further, as in the past, there have been in Australia several recent joint Commonwealth-State public inquiries during the last decade such as: *Royal Commission into Institutional Responses to Child Sexual Abuse* (2013); *Royal Commission into the Protection and Detention of Children in the Northern Territory* (2016); *Royal Commission into Violence, Abuse, Neglect and the Exploitation of People with Disability* (2019); and the *Royal Commission into National Natural Disaster Arrangements* (2020).

Despite this seemingly easy predilection to resort to public inquiries it is also, important and revealing to note where governments have been reluctant to heed public demands for particular inquiries. Such has been the case in Australia where calls from several political leaders and academics for some type of inquiry into Commonwealth and State government responses to the recent pandemic have been ignored to date.[4] By contrast, the United Kingdom (UK) Sweden and more recently, New Zealand, have initiated major independent public inquiries into this issue.

There have also been important developments overseas concerning publix inquries which is another reason for this new volume.

In New Zealand new legislation (*Inquiries Act 2013*) finally came into force in 2013 following a review by the New Zealand Law Commission five years earlier. Several major royal commissions have since been appointed under this new legislation, the most recent being the *Royal Commission of Inquiry (COVID-19 Lessons)* appointed in December 2022. Many other more general public inquiries have also been appointed under this new legislation (see **Chapter 15**).

So too in the UK has new legislation been passed in 2005 (*Inquiries Act 2005*) governing public inquiries. This has at last clarified their investigatory powers and appointment processes and brought consistency in how public inquiries are employed, their powers and processes. Extensive parliamentary reviews and debate have subsequently ensued about the operations of inquiries appointed under this new legislation and the role, length and costs of inquiries (**Chapter 14**). Although the UK is the home for public inquiries for Westminster democracies like Australia, there are many differences in how they operate, their membership and even nomenclatures. For instance, while royal commissions continue to be appointed and demanded in Australia, they have become largely defunct in the UK.[5] Nevertheless, other inquiries under the new legislation continue to be appointed. At the time of writing a new one had been established to review the UK's response to the COVID-19 pandemic.[6]

In the United States (US) presidential commissions, the equivalent in many ways to the Westminster royal commission, have continued to be appointed by successive Democrat and Republican administrations into issues of national importance and controversy. At the same time, as is explored in this volume (**Chapter 16**), the American advisory system is complex, and often bewildering to outsiders and played against a background of presidential-congressional politics and rivalries in a way that does not occur elsewhere to the same degree.

Meanwhile, across the Nordic countries commissions of inquiry have long been an integral part of the decision-making and advisory processes, and have served an additional role in brokering agreements with interest groups in ways different from Westminster systems. Nevertheless, there have been changes in recent years among several Nordic countries affecting the number of inquiries being appointed, the composition of their memberships and their roles. These developments are discussed later in this volume (**Chapter 17).**

Issues about public inquiries

Regardless of jurisdiction, particular inquiry under review or what aspect about inquiries that each chapter in this volume addresses, there are common issues about public inquiries relevant to all jurisdictions and the different case studies in this volume. These include:

Why are inquiries appointed?

First and foremost, relevant to all public inquiries, is why do governments appoint them? Afterall, modern government has a large permanent public bureaucracy and an extensive array of other advisory mechanisms at its disposal. Moreover, appointing an inquiry is not without risks – their findings may embarrass the appointing government, their reports may be inadequate, their recommendations impractical, and their costs excessive. Whether the continued resort to public inquiries reflects declining capabilities of the public service[7] or public trust in existing institutions is another issue that needs to be explored.

Of course, all public inquiries are bespoke instruments established at the discretion of executive government. Consequently, the exact reasons for their appointment are made by decision makers behind closed doors which makes an accurate assessment of why they were appointed hard to fully verify. This is particularly the case in Westminster systems where public inquiries are not an integral part of the decision-making process as in Nordic countries.

The fundamental issue concerning every inquiry is whether it was established for legitimate reasons to discover the facts about an issue and to provide expert advice; or was it appointed for more covert political goals – to delay decisions, manage the agenda, and show concern with little intention to implement the recommendations?

What is their impact?

If there are concerns about why inquiries are appointed, there is even greater interest in their impact – what happens to their reports and recommendations? As one scholar once said the "greatest degree of dissatisfaction with royal commissions" concerns the lack of implementation of their recommendations.[8] Compounding this concern about non-implementation is the high costs of some inquiries, making their appointment seem not only questionable, but also wasteful. As one commentator lamented, public inquiries seem a "wilful waste of public money and private time".[9] Just how valid is this view is another issue pursued across the chapters in this volume (**Chapters 9-13**). Indeed, contrary to some popular perceptions, many inquiries have had positive impacts, with their recommendations not just being accepted, but more importantly, implemented – an important distinction. So, as is discussed in this volume, there needs to be careful consideration of how public inquiry impacts may be measured, over what timeframes and in what ways.

Are inquiries appropriate mechanisms to give expert policy advice?

A related issue concerns whether inquiries, especially royal commissions, chaired as they often are by sitting or former judges and with their panoply of legal procedures and public hearings, are appropriate to tackle complex policy issues? While royal commissions might be suitable to establish the facts about an issue or to allocate responsibility for some incident, are they capable making broader policy recommendations involving proposals for large increases in public expenditure with little regard to wider concerns and priorities.[10] How inquiries manage the complex and often conflicting information and evidence they receive is a related issue. These concerns are discussed in this volume in relation to both Australia and international jurisdictions (**Chapters 4-8; 14-17**).

Powers and legal status of inquiries

Another theme is that some inquiries like statutorily based royal commissions as in Australia, have been seen to exercise too much power, and have open hearings that adversely impact on citizens' rights. At the same time, it has been argued that general policy inquiries that currently lack a statutory base in many jurisdictions, should in future have a more defined legislative base. As noted above, such proposals have been recommended by the ALRC but have only gained acceptance in some State jurisdictions.

What makes for successful inquiries?

With so many inquiries being appointed, there is the issue of what constitutes a 'good' or 'successful' inquiry? These terms require definition and debate. Certainly, many of the contributions to this volume show, that inquiry 'success' can be assessed in many ways. For instance, considerations may include: their processes and levels of engagement with stakeholders. Too often whether recommendations are accepted and implemented has been used as the sole criterion for gauging inquiry success. More qualitative judgements are needed to assess the soundness of an inquiry's report and whether it has served the public interest by properly informing debate, clarifying facts, promoting some consensus about what must and can be done, or to improve the quality of life.[11]

Where do inquiries fit in modern government?

Lastly, there remains the issue as to where public inquiries, which in many jurisdictions lack any formal constitutional standing, fit in the architecture of modern government with its increasingly complex web of advisory and investigative bodies. The durability of the public inquiry instrument as indicated by their continued appointment, suggests that inquiries serve particular purposes and have certain characteristics that more permanent bodies are unable to match.

What this volume covers

Section 1: Inquiries – their place in Australian history: provides an historical overview of the use of public inquiries in Australia and overseas (**Chapter 1**). The subsequent chapter (**Chapter 2**) examines royal commissions during the Coalition Bruce Government of the 1920s and is followed by the role of public inquiries in progressing tax reform from the 1920s and over almost the next 100 years (**Chapter 3**). These historical perspectives highlight why public inquiries were deployed, their memberships and processes, and their impacts.

Section 2: Inquiries in action: how inquiries work in terms of collecting evidence, dealing with complex problems and grappling with large amounts of data, is affected by legislation and the interactions with the political environment that spawned their appointment is considered in these chapters (**Chapters 4-8**).

Section 3: Impacts of inquiries: the five chapters in this section (**Chapters 9-13**) attend to the impact of public inquiry reports. Consideration is given in two chapters as to how success may be measured (**Chapters 9-10**); then in another, the unforeseen fiscal impacts of some inquiries are assessed (**Chapter 11**). Another chapter examines the impact of inquiries into child abuse in the UK (**Chapter 12**). The concluding **Chapter 13** analyses whether royal commissions – given their particular membership, expertise and processes – are an appropriate mechanism to make wide-ranging recommendations on complex policy issues.

Section 4: Other countries' inquiries: **Chapters 14-16** provide an update on the use of public inquiries in several Westminster democracies like the UK and New Zealand, and related ones like the United States. It then looks further afield by examining trends in public inquiry use and form across the Nordic countries (**Chapter 17**). While there are certain issues considered that reflect the jurisdictions in which they operate, these chapters raise many common concerns about inquiries. These include: reasons for appointment; suitability of the inquiry instrument and their processes; costs; memberships; and of course, their impact. All this just shows how despite the constitutional, political and cultural differences across these different jurisdictions, there are shared issues and much to learn from other countries' experiences.

Section 5: Conclusions: this last section reflects on previous chapters and argues that public inquiries should cease to be seen as an aberration loosely appended to executive government and be accepted as an integral, though unspecified part of modern government as their continued extensive use suggests. Moreover, because of a host of other trends in modern government they are still wanted by the public, will continue to be appointed by government and are needed to support the development of better policies.

Notes

1 Paul Kelly, "The cult that won false hopes in 2020", *The Australian*, 23 December 2020.

2 Scott Prasser, "Labor should be careful what it wishes for", *Canberra Times*, 8 June 2022.

3 Australian Law Reform Commission, *Making Inquiries: A New Statutory Framework*, Report 111, Commonwealth of Australia, Sydney, 2009.

4 George Williams, "COVID mistakes? We made a few … so let's take a look", *The Australian*, 22 March 2022.

5 House of Commons Library, *Statutory Commissions of Inquiry, The Inquiries Act 2005*, Briefing Paper Number 064110, 8 September 2020.

6 This is the *UK COVID-19 Inquiry* originally announced by the Johnson Government in early 2021. Its chair, Baroness Heather Hallett, a retired judge, was not appointed until December 2021 and its terms of reference only resolved in May 2022 after extensive consultation.

7 Gary Banks, "The public service needs to pick up its game in policymaking", *Australian Financial Review*, 22 November 2011.

8 Martin Bulmer, "Increasing the Effectiveness of Royal Commissions: A Comment", *Public Administration* (London), Vol 61, 1983, p. 441.

9 Ross Gittins, "Would you head a government inquiry", *Sydney Morning Herald*, 22 January 1981.

10 Dominque Hogan-Doran, "Responding to Crisis; Royal Commissions in Australia", Paper for University of New South Wales Master of Laws Course, 27 September 2013.

11 Scott Prasser and Helen Tracey, "Public inquiries – living up to their potential", in Scott Prasser and Helen Tracey, (eds), *Royal Commissions and Public Inquiries: Practice and Potential*, Connor Court Publishing, Ballarat, 2014, pp. 372-95.

Section 1: Inquiries –
their place in Australian history

Introduction

Scott Prasser

The three chapters in this section focusses on the Australian experience of public inquiries.

Chapter 1 provides a historical overview from before federation when the six colonies appointed numerous public inquiries through to present day. The peaks and troughs of public inquiry use are outlined and attention is given to the increasing preponderance of non-statutory public inquiries from the 1940s onwards though royal commissions continue to be appointed. Attention is given to the upsurge in public inquiry numbers and the areas they covered with the election of the short-lived Whitlam Labor Government (1972-75). While there were reasons for this increase closely associated with that government, subsequent Coalition and Labor federal governments have continued to appoint inquiries in numbers far greater than had been the case previously, emphasising how inquiries have become an integral part of the Australian political system.

Chapter 2 David Lee gives attention to the Bruce Coalition Government's (1923-29) use of royal commissions. This period was chosen because of the many royal commissions appointed (some 21), the importance of their topics, and because some critics have argued that most were appointed for politically expedient reasons of showing activity with little action on their recommendations – one of the core complaints about inquiries. The chapter's analysis of several of the major royal commissions of this period concludes that such assessments are simplistic and ignores their many long term impacts. For instance, although the 1925 *Royal Commission on Health's* far reaching recommendations were not fully or immediately implemented because of constitutional arrangements and the subsequent Great Depression, its impacts were to be long lasting and significant. The chapter also highlights that the appointment of so many royal commissions during this period partly reflected the limited capabilities of the then small, and still developing Commonwealth Public Service. This has certain parallels with current concerns that declining public service policy capabilities are seen by some as driving governments to resort to the public inquiry instrument today.

Paul Tilley in **Chapter 3** provides a nearly hundred year study of public inquiries from the Commonwealth's 1920 *Royal Commission on Taxation* through to the State *NSW Review of Federal Financial Relations* in 2019. The chapter goes beyond a descriptive historical narrative. Rather, it gives attention to the value of the public inquiry instrument, and the drivers that led to the appointment of taxation inquiries. In tracing what happened to the different tax inquiry reports over such a long period Tilley makes important observations that are relevant to all public inquiries. First, the interplay between the political arena and the expert public inquiry is highlighted. The inquiry report might be right on technical and economic grounds, but the political environment could not immediately sustain it. The *Asprey Tax Review* is an example. It received scant attention when it reported in 1975. It was ignored by subsequent governments. Nevertheless, it became "the foundational review that established the tax reform blueprint" that was eventually implemented with the introduction of the Goods and Services Tax (GST) in 1999. This highlights how inquiry reports can over the long term "filter through to decision makers" and be adopted and has important implications in appreciating the impact of inquiries which is explored in more detail in Section 3 of this volume.

Overall, these chapters give attention to the extensive use of public inquiries in Australia and the important areas they have covered. Public inquiries are not a new phenomenon. They have been used consistently in Australia and elsewhere for a considerable period, though their form and processes have, as will be discussed in the next section, changed with new technology and the growing complexity of many policy issues.

1

Trends in public inquiries in Australia

Scott Prasser

Introduction

This chapter provides an overview of trends in their use with particular emphasis on national developments in Australia.

Where did public inquiries come from – the British connection

Australia as a Westminster democracy clearly inherited its use and form of public inquiries, including royal commissions, from the United Kingdom (UK). Public inquiries have a long history in the UK that can be traced back to Tudor and Stuart times becoming particularly significant in the nineteenth century in mapping out reforms across a wide range of areas.

This practice of appointing public inquiries was soon duplicated in the colonies settled by Britain around the world. Canada had legislation for appointing inquiries prior to confederation (1867) with the passing in 1846 of the *Act to Empower Commissioners for Inquiring into Matters Connected with Public Business to Take Evidence on Oath*. National legislation subsequently followed. Canada now has the national *Inquiries Act 1985*. Canadian provinces have similar legislation. New Zealand passed the *Commission Powers Act* in 1867, that became the *Commissions of Inquiry Act 1908*. The six Australian colonies also adopted legislation for royal commissions which was copied by the Commonwealth in 1902. It is interesting to note that since independence Papua New Guinea has followed in this tradition and developed the *Commission of Inquiry Act 1951* so it can appoint royal commissions – an important one reported in 2022.[1]

Although Westminster democracies share a common political and institutional heritage, quite early on there were divergences across these different jurisdictions in how they used and developed public inquiries, just as they have modified other institutions such as parliament also inherited from Westminster. For instance, royal commissions in the United Kingdom, unlike in Australia, Canada or New Zealand, were not established under any legislation and therefore operated with limited powers of investigation. Inquiries with such powers were limited in the United Kingdom to those very small number established under the *Tribunal of Inquiry (Evidence) Act 1921*. While there has been new legislation in Canada (1985) and New Zealand (2013) and more recently in Victoria (2014) allowing for the appointment of a two-tier system of inquiries this has not occurred in Australia at the national level as noted in the Introduction to this volume.

Early experiences of inquiries among the Australian colonies prior to federation

It is estimated that some 78 royal commissions were appointed by the colonies prior to federation in 1901. Topics included: native police, charities, civil service (New South Wales); defence, local government, sugar industry, mining accidents (Queensland); education, factory regulation, the River Murray (Victoria); shipping losses, sanitation, lunatic asylums (South Australia); public education, railways (Tasmania); treatment of native prisoners, the penal system (Western Australia); and public service reform across most jurisdictions. After federation, the States, as the colonies had become, continued to appoint royal commissions and other forms of statutory and non-statutory public inquiries.

Inquiries and the new Commonwealth Government

Following federation, the new Commonwealth Government was quick to appoint its own public inquiry in the form of an inquisitorial royal commission concerning the death of soldiers on a ship returning from the Boer War.[2] It was quickly appreciated that although the Governor-General could under his prerogative powers, issue *Letters Patent* for a royal commission, a royal commission had no powers conferred by parliament to conduct its investigations. Consequently, two weeks after the announcement of the royal commission the *Royal Commissions Act 1902* (Cth) was hastily passed, so the commission had adequate powers to call witnesses and impose penalties. It was largely copied from State legislation, as the then Commonwealth Attorney-General, Alfred Deakin admitted during the parliamentary debates.

Commonwealth trends

Royal commissions 1902-1972

Trends in Commonwealth public inquiries appointed since federation at a national level showed a gradual increase in the appointment of royal commissions until the end of the 1920s. From 1910-29, 54 royal commissions were appointed. This was their peak. Subsequently, royal commission numbers declined. Twelve royal commissions were appointed from 1929-40, five from 1940-49, and during the long period of uninterrupted Coalition governments from December 1949-72, only seven were established. Of these seven, four were inquisitorial including the controversial 1954 *Royal Commission on Espionage* (Petrov Royal Commission) and the two into the 1964 HMAS Voyager disaster (one in 1964, the other in 1967), and one into corruption in the Victorian offices of the Post Office (1962). Three were policy advisory inquiries on: transport, the introduction of television and on issues concerning the Great Barrier Reef.

Non-statutory policy inquiries early trends

Most importantly, from the 1940s onwards non-statutory, mostly policy public inquiries, became the dominant inquiry form. However, they were used relatively sparingly during the Coalition period from 1949-72 when just 57 were appointed, covering areas such as: tertiary education, taxation, economic policy, decimal currency, poverty, taxation, administrative law, and population issues. Some of these were especially important such as the Murray *Committee on Universities* (1956) and the Martin *Committee on the Future of Tertiary Education in Australia* (1961), which resulted in increased Commonwealth involvement and spending in tertiary education in what was and is a State constitutional responsibility.

The impact of the Whitlam Labor Government on inquiries

The real watershed in the use of public inquiries in Australia occurred under the brief three year term of the Whitlam Labor Government (1972-75). It needs to be appreciated that the Labor Party had been out of office for 23 years (1949-72), had a large pent-up policy program to implement, and was naturally suspicious of the Commonwealth Public Service and its senior ranks given their long service to Coalition governments. Consequently, appointing external public inquiries with many members drawn from outside the government was seen as a means to promote faster policy development, overcome any suspected resistance from the public service, and to connect through the open inquiry process more directly with the Australian people.

Consequently, public inquiry numbers of all types increased dramatically under Whitlam. Some 73 non-statutory mainly policy advisory inquiries were appointed across areas including: school funding, manufacturing, child care, museums and national superannuation to name a few. In addition, 13 royal commissions were established. Most of the royal commissions were policy inquiries covering issues like: Aboriginal land rights; review of the Post Office; land tenures; human relationships; and FM radio – only two were inquisitorial.[3] Whitlam provided an overarching rationale for the deployment of so many public inquiries such as: the need for external outside expert advice; providing a means to consult with the public; developing policies in new areas; and relieving the public service of the burden and strain of such work so it could better focus on implementation of Labor's detailed policy program and administrative reforms.[4]

Despite criticism from the then Liberal-National Party Coalition Opposition about this proliferation of inquiries, their costs, and their usurping the roles of the public service, the public inquiry genie was out of the bottle and the Coalition once they regained office in 1975, and subsequent governments, have continued to appoint public inquiries at a far greater rate than had occurred previously. Here is a summary of trends since 1975:

- Fraser Coalition Government (1975-83) appointed 84 public inquiries plus eight royal commissions – a total of 92 inquiries;

- Hawke–Keating Labor governments (1983-96) appointed 189 public inquiries plus 12 royal commissions – a total of 201 inquiries;

- Howard Coalition Government (1996-2007) appointed 84 public inquiries plus four royal commissions – a total of 88 inquiries.

The Rudd and Gillard Labor governments (2007-13) established just one royal commission during six years in office – though a particularly important one, namely the inquisitorial 2013 *Royal Commission into*

Institutional Responses to Child Sexual Abuse. It was appointed jointly with the States and Territories and became Australia's most expensive inquiry. Numerous policy non-statutory inquiries were also appointed into: regional telecommunications, the automotive industry, quarantine arrangements, overseas aid, aged care, the public service, human rights, higher education funding, school funding, defence, asylum seekers, drought policy, and media regulation to name but a few. There is no reliable, comprehensive list of these inquiries so only an approximate assessment of their numbers can be made amounting to somewhere between 60 and 80 inquiries.[5]

The return of the Coalition in September 2013, (first under prime ministership of Abbott, then Turnbull and finally Morrison) also saw the appointment of numerous public inquiries including eight royal commissions by 2021. Clearly, this was more than its immediate Labor predecessor (with just one royal commission) and the four appointed by the Howard Coalition Government. All the royal commissions appointed by the Coalition governments since 2013 have been of the inquisitorial type, though several of these, such as the *Royal Commission into Aged Care Quality and Safety*, produced important policy recommendations. At the time of writing two royal commissions have yet to report – the *Royal Commission into Violence, Abuse, Neglect and Exploitation of People with Disability* and the *Royal Commission into Defence and Veteran Suicide*. In addition, more than 40 non-statutory policy inquiries were appointed into: higher education, the arts, energy, financial deregulation, welfare benefits, teacher education, nursing education, regional telecommunications, defence, refugees, sports integrity, and again, the public service.

State inquiry trends

Since federation State and Territory governments have also been active in appointing many public inquiries including statutory based royal commissions, commissions, special commissions, boards of inquiry, and other non-statutory reviews and committees. While many royal commissions were inquisitorial investigating allegations of corruption, scandals or maladministration, others covered a wide range of policy and public administration issues.

In more recent times, there has been little abatement in inquiry use by State and Territory administrations. For instance, between 1960-2021: New South Wales alone appointed 13 royal commissions or similar type bodies; Queensland, 15; South Australia, 9; Tasmania, 3; Victoria, 12; and Western Australia 6. The most recent of these were the two royal commissions appointed in 2021 by the Victorian and Western Australian governments into the operations of Crown Casino in their respective States.

The States have also appointed other inquiries into broader policy areas including: education, lands administration, the coal industry, primary industry, health, gambling, local government, status of women, law, legal issues, and environmental matters to name just a few.

During the late 1980s to the early 1990s there was a spate of State public inquiries – primarily royal commissions – into State financial collapses, police corruption, organised crime, allegations of bribery, and ministerial improprieties. Perhaps the most noted of these was the Fitzgerald Commission of Inquiry appointed by the Queensland National Party Government in 1987, which reported in 1989.[6] Given that these royal commissions caused several administrations to lose office,[7] State governments became wary of appointing such bodies for some time. There was also the expectation that the new permanent anti-corruption bodies that those royal commissions spawned would lead to less need for ad hoc royal commissions. Such expectations have only partially been met given the numerous problems that subsequently enveloped these new anti-corruption bodies concerning their memberships, powers, costs and processes. Consequently, one-off commissions of inquiry continue to be demanded by the public to which governments have accordingly responded.

Historically, State and Territory governments have not been as enthusiastic as the Commonwealth in appointing many non-statutory policy advisory inquiries to address different policy issues. Certainly, some have been established, but State policy development remains a more 'in-house' affair compared to the Commonwealth. State governments and ministers have relied more heavily on their departments as the prime source of their advice.[8] Recent trends in State public administration such as the increased centralisation of decision making in the hands of the premier with the concomitant expansion of departments of premier and cabinet, have also mitigated against the appointment of such policy inquiries.

Public inquiry numbers and partisanship

There was once a correlation between government partisanship and inquiry numbers with Coalition governments being less enthusiastic in appointing public inquiries than their Labor counterparts. Explanations for this difference used to be that Coalition governments were less active in supporting intervention in society and therefore had a less programmatic policy agenda. Following the Whitlam period, Coalition governments have embraced the public inquiry instrument more enthusiastically, though they tend to appoint inquiries at a slower rate than Labor – that is fewer inquiries over longer periods of time.

The reasons for this change and indeed the increased use of public inquiries reflects several drivers.

One has been the expansion of Commonwealth Government intervention in society pushed by rising public expectations of government. Governments are expected to provide 'solutions' to an increasing array of policy 'problems' and the appointment of 'expert' public inquiries is one way they seek to do so.

Further, the increased demand for public participation in government decisions can be accommodated easily by the public inquiry instrument given their open processes and promotion of public participation in their proceedings.

Another driver is the current political environment of continuous campaigning whereby governments must be seen to respond instantly to public and media demands for action – and appointing an inquiry is something governments can easily and quickly be seen to do! Public inquiries are now one of the appurtenances of modern government reached for eagerly by whichever party is in office. The decline in trust in government and its related institutions like the public service because of its increasingly politicisation has also made public inquiries a preferered choice.[9] Increasingly, the resort to public inquiries is less to do with a government's partisanship or its programmatic 'reformist' policy agenda, or even in seeking ways to be better informed. It is more and more about their value in stage managing debates, and being seen to be 'informed' by independent sources.

Conclusions

Public inquiries have a long history of sustained use in Australia at both national and state levels. Inherited from the United Kingdom they are enthusiastically appointed in Australia these days regardless of who is in office. While royal commissions are not used as frequently as during the first three decades of federation, the federal Coalition Government's appointment of eight royal commissions between 2013 and 2022 highlights just how important this form of inquiry still is. Indeed, the incoming federal Albanese Labor Government's announcement in 2022 of a royal commission into the Robodebt scandal reinforces this even further. Public inquiries in all their forms are now an integral part of the architecture of modern Australian government even though their use has been frequently overlooked by commentators and academics.

Notes

1   The *Royal Commission of Inquiry into the Purchases and Procedures Followed by the Government of Papua New Guinea in Obtaining the Off-Shore Loan from the Union Bank of Switzerland and Related Transactions* was appointed in 2019 under the *Commission of Inquiry Act 1951* and reported in April 2022.

2   *Royal Commission on the Transport of Troops from Service in South Africa in the SS Drayton grange and the Circumstances under which Trooper H Burkitt was not landed at Adelaide from SS Norfolk* - was appointed in August 1902.

3   For a detailed list of all public inquiries appointed by the Whitlam Government see Scott Prasser, *Royal Commissions and Public Inquiries in Australia*, 2nd ed, LexisNexis, Chatswood, 2021, Appendix 6, pp. 330-40.

4   Edward G. Whitlam, PM, "Australian Public Administration under a Labor Government", *The Sir Robert Garran Memorial Oration*, 12 November 1973.

5   See Prasser, *Royal Commissions and Public Inquiries*, Appendices 7-9, pp. 341-86.

6   Its correct title was: *Commission of Inquiry into Possible Illegal Activities and Associated Policy Misconduct*.

7   For instance, the Queensland National Party Government fell in 1989 following the release of the Fitzgerald Commission of Inquiry into police corruption. Other State governments that also lost office included: Labor governments in Victoria, South Australia and Western Australia while in Tasmania a Liberal premier stood down following a royal commission into an alleged bribery. For list of State inquiries into corruption see Prasser, *Royal Commissions and Public Inquiries*, Appendix 10, pp. 387-91.

8   John Phillimore and Tracey Arklay, "Policy and policy analysis in Australian states", in Brian Head and Kate Crowley, (eds), *Policy Analysis in Australia*, Policy Press, Bristol, 2015, pp. 87-104.

9   Gary Banks, "Truth losing out to the new 'Yes Minister' mob", *The Australian*, 29 September 2020.

2

Royal commissions of the Bruce-Page Government, 1923-29

David Lee

Introduction

The government led by Stanley Melbourne Bruce, known as the Bruce-Page Government, was well known for making extensive use of royal commissions and other commissions of inquiry. The numerous royal commissions were widely criticised at the time as a waste of money serving little purpose.[1] This view was exemplified by Frank Anstey, a member of the Labor Opposition. In 1927 Anstey asked Bruce whether he would establish a royal commission to inquire into the necessity for "royal commissions, commissions and boards".[2] Some historians, too, have seen Bruce's use of royal commissions as cynical. Stuart Macintyre argued that between 1923 and 1929 Bruce appointed twenty-one royal commissions "without any intention of acting on their recommendations".[3] In the same vein, Michael Roe observed that Bruce "delighted to establish" royal commissions "thereby appearing and aspiring to tackle major problems, without in the event doing much".[4]

These views, perhaps valid in some cases, are unduly harsh when looking at the larger picture. In the 1920s using the royal commission technique compensated for an undeveloped public service. Commissions played an important role in assembling information, airing, and informing public opinion and pointing to directions which policy might take when circumstances were propitious. Some of the commissions were designed to provide the basis for longer-term action on questions of social and economic policy. While the Bruce-Page Government did not actively pursue all their recommendations, the work of these commissions fed into the political process leading to establishment of Australia's welfare state in the 1930s and 1940s. Other royal commissions were established to help to clarify important constitutional questions or matters where Commonwealth involvement was desirable.

While the extent to which Bruce-Page Government acted on their recommendations was limited, the longer-term effects can be seen in such institutions as the Commonwealth Grants Commission established in 1933. They can also be seen in incremental insertion of the Commonwealth into such fields as health, social welfare, housing and education in the 1940s.[5] A third category of commissions included inquiries on matters that were the subject of political criticism or controversy. In some cases, commissions were established to respond to criticism of areas of public policy, in others to investigate political allegations and in others again to defuse intractable political problems. While some of the commissions in this third category were non-productive, others, such as the inquiry into the coal industry, laid the basis for effective public policy towards one of Australia's major industries.

Royal commissions on issues of economic and social policy

The Bruce-Page Government's royal commissions on economic and social policy on the 1920s had their origins in earlier political developments. The *Royal Commission on Child Endowment or Family Allowances*, for example, was a legacy of the policies of Bruce's predecessor as prime minister, William Morris (Billy) Hughes. Hughes was prime minister in 1918 when Bruce won a by-election for the seat of Flinders.[6] By that time, there was widespread concern that as a consequence of the Great War Australian living standards had been eroded. Responding to these concerns, Hughes promised an inquiry into wages and living costs during the campaign for the 1919 federal election. In 1920 he fulfilled his promise by appointing a royal commission chaired by Albert Piddington and consisting of three representatives each for employers and employees. The *Royal Commission on the Basic Wage*, as the inquiry was known, heard many witnesses and, as a measure of its sympathy for working families, proposed £5 16 shillings as a reasonable household wage. The proposal excited considerable controversy since the existing federal wage was then more than one pound lower than £5 16 shillings a week.[7]

While trade unions were supportive of Piddington's proposal, employers protested that such a large change would be unaffordable. The Commonwealth Statistician, Sir George Knibbs, endorsed the concern of employers by advising Hughes that industry would simply be unable to pay the proposed federal wage to all workers. Accepting Knibbs's advice, Hughes asked Piddington to reconsider his proposal. Piddington responded on 22 November 1920 by accepting that each worker should achieve a lower basic wage of at least £4, that being sufficient to maintain a couple, but that the basic wage should be supplemented by a system of federal child endowment. He envisaged that the Commonwealth Government would pay a family twelve shillings a week extra for each child aged fourteen and under.[8]

Hughes' Nationalist Government found it difficult to adopt the Piddington Commission's recommendation. This was because of continuing disagreement about both the merits of child endowment and how child endowment, if established, would interact with the basic wage.[9] Hughes had made no progress on child endowment when he resigned as Prime Minister in 1923. In place of Hughes's Nationalist Government, a composite Nationalist–Country Party ministry led by

Stanley Bruce as Prime Minister and the Country Party leader, Earle Page as Treasurer, took office. Bruce provided continuity between the governments, having served as Hughes's Treasurer from 1921 to 1923.

The Bruce–Page Government regarded some form of child endowment as vital for the success of its economic and industrial relations policy. But Bruce was disinclined to implement a Commonwealth child endowment scheme when the States shared responsibility over industrial relations with the Commonwealth. He had doubts, moreover, about financing the scheme by raising taxation. This, he feared, would involve doubling the Commonwealth's income taxation. Bruce's proposal for the Commonwealth to assume full power over industrial relations was defeated in a referendum held in 1926, leaving industrial matters and wages as a divided responsibility between the Commonwealth and States.[10] In 1927 Bruce convened a meeting of State premiers and tried to convince them to agree to a voluntary scheme of child endowment. They were not attracted to the idea and urged the Commonwealth to finance the scheme. Matters were further complicated when the Labor ministry led by Jack Lang in New South Wales introduced its own scheme of child endowment funded by a payroll tax.[11]

It was in these circumstances that Bruce set up the *Royal Commission on Child Endowment or Family Allowances* on 28 September 1927. The Commission was chaired by Thomas O'Halloran, an Adelaide barrister. Other members were John Curtin, editor of the *Westralian Worker* who would be elected to the federal seat of Fremantle in 1928 and later become prime minister; Iver Evans, a member of the firm Briscoe and Co. Ltd; Stephen Mills, formerly Comptroller-General of Customs and a member of the short-lived Inter-State Commission, 1913–20; and Mildred Muscio, Vice-President and Secretary of the National Council of Women.[12]

The *Royal Commission on Child Endowment* heard evidence from a wide range of individuals and groups.[13] Business and rural organisations generally opposed the scheme.[14] The evidence of groups such as these pointed to the harmful effects of a system of child endowment on the economy and its inhibiting effect on the willingness of individuals to better their circumstances. Others were more sympathetic. Jock Garden, Secretary of the Labour Council of New South Wales, supported child endowment in principle but insisted that it should be separate and independent from determination of the basic wage.[15] William Holman, the former premier of New South Wales, who had himself proposed a State scheme of child endowment in 1919, regarded endowment as an adjunct to the basis wage, the endowment to disappear when a certain wage was reached.[16]

Given its varying composition and the diversity of evidence, it was no surprise that the *Royal Commission on Child Endowment* was split in its recommendations. The majority, O'Halloran, Mills and Evans, rehearsed all the arguments against child endowment, including the contention that current wages were sufficient for the maintenance of children, that an employer levy to finance the scheme would have negative consequences for industry and that a scheme financed from general revenue would have a disastrous effect on the level of Australian taxation. In the view of the majority, a Commonwealth scheme was the only real option and strikes would be larger and more frequent unless the Commonwealth was responsible for both wage fixing and child endowment. It concluded that the best kind of Commonwealth action was a purely voluntary scheme. Curtin and Muscio dissented. It was their view that for workers in industry, some system of family allowances was the logical corollary of the living wage doctrine.[17]

The *Royal Commission on Child Endowment* followed an earlier *Royal Commission on National Insurance*. Some sort of scheme for national insurance had been mooted earlier by Prime Minister Alfred Deakin, but serious consideration of the matter had been shelved during the Great War. In the intervening time, schemes for national insurance were established in other countries such as Britain and Germany.[18] In 1923

Bruce appointed the Nationalist Tasmanian Senator, John Millen, to chair the *Royal Commission on National Insurance*. Other commissioners, reflecting a blend of representatives from the Nationalist Party, the Country Party and the Labor Party, were Albert 'Texas' Green, Labor Member for Kalgoorlie, William Mahony, Labor Member for Dalley, New South Wales, Senator John Grant, Deputy Leader of the Labor Party in the Senate, Roland Green, Country Party Member for Richmond, and Jos Francis, Nationalist Member for Moreton.[19]

The *Royal Commission on National Insurance*, which ran from 7 September 1923 to 5 October 1927, issued four reports, the first dealing with casual sickness, invalidity and old age; the second devoted to unemployed people; the third on destitute allowances; and the fourth dealing with membership, finance and administration.[20] The recommendations were far-reaching. They embraced the establishment of a national insurance fund that promised financial security for the ill, disabled, and unemployed, and a national health scheme that promoted public health and that would be directed by the Commonwealth Department of Health.[21] Bruce introduced legislation for National Insurance in 1928 and promised to discuss the matter fully at a meeting of Commonwealth Ministers in 1929. His project lapsed, however, in the dramatic period leading to the fall of the Bruce–Page Government in September 1929.

The royal commissions on child endowment and national insurance nonetheless fed into the longer-term and incremental development of the welfare state. In 1938, Prime Minister Joseph Lyons introduced the *National Health and Pensions Insurance Act*, providing disability, sickness and medical benefits as well as old-age and widows' pensions for workers and their dependents based on contributions by government, employers and employees.[22] Under pressure from the Country Party, the scheme was shelved in 1939. In the 1940s Labor governments established such welfare payments as schemes financed from Commonwealth revenue, which was substantially bolstered by the uniform taxation of incomes after 1942.[23] Before that, the wartime Menzies Government in 1941 established child endowment as a non-means tested uniform allowance for all but the first child.

Royal commissions on constitutional matters and issues related to the federation

Other royal commissions established by the Bruce-Page Government were concerned with constitutional matters or matters which fell within the responsibilities of the States but were felt to have federal implications. One of these was the *Royal Commission on Health*.

Royal Commission on Health

The Constitution had given the Commonwealth power to legislate on quarantine but not on health. Commonwealth legislation in 1908 had established a Federal Quarantine Service. During the Great War this Quarantine Service did well in checking the spread of disease from returned servicemen. The aftermath of the Great War brought with it increasing support for the Commonwealth to extend its responsibilities beyond quarantine to health. The year 1919 also saw the influenza pandemic in which, again, the Federal Quarantine Service performed well. It helped to keep the death rate from the pandemic lower than in other countries such as South Africa and New Zealand.[24]

In 1921 the Hughes Government responded to the success of the Quarantine Service and the Commonwealth's tentative forays into health matters by establishing a Federal Department of Health. Hughes appointed the Western Australian John Howard Lidgett Cumpston as Director-General of Health and Director of Quarantine. While quarantine remained the core work of the new department, it also worked on, among other matters, tropical medicine, industrial hygiene, sanitary engineering and laboratories and sera.[25]

Throughout 1924, Neville Howse, a medical doctor who had overseen medical services for the Australian Imperial Force and had been elected to the seat of Calare in 1922 as a Nationalist, and who became Minister for Health (1925-7), urged the Bruce–Page Government to establish a royal commission to investigate the question of public health and recommend better measures for prevention of disease.[26] The acknowledged limitation of such a commission was that health fell entirely within the jurisdiction of the States. Bruce agreed, nonetheless, to establish a *Royal Commission on Health* in 1924. In his view a royal commission was necessary because of the limitation of expertise on health available within the Commonwealth Government. He selected Sir George Syme, a recently retired surgeon, as chairman. Sitting with Syme were Frank Hone, consulting physician in Adelaide, Jean Greig, chief medical adviser of the Education Department of Victoria, Robert Todd, a qualified medical practitioner and barrister and solicitor of the Supreme Court of New South Wales, and Sydney Innes-Noad, President of the Royal Society for the Welfare of Mothers and Babies of New South Wales.[27]

Commencing in January 1925, the *Royal Commission on Health* held 88 public sittings at 22 centres in each of the six States and examined 319 witnesses.[28] It recommended that the new Commonwealth Department of Health should take control of medical services in all Australian territories and encourage research activities, especially around matters such as venereal disease, maternity, child welfare and industrial hygiene.[29] It also suggested that the department should co-ordinate the health work of the States through a Federal Council.[30]

A Federal Health Council, according to historian Michael Roe, was chief among the *Royal Commission on Health's* 'ambiguous gains'.[31] Following endorsement by a meeting of health ministers, the Council met for the first time in January 1927 with Cumpston as Chairman and the heads of State health offices. Thereafter, the Council, meeting annually, discussed issues such as venereal disease, tuberculosis, and the health of children. The Council failed, however, to live up to the promise of taking a directive role of the State health offices except in relation to cancer. In 1927–28 the Department of Health purchased ten grammes of radium for experimental use and convened the first annual cancer conference in Canberra in 1930. Another initiative, foreshadowed by Cumpston at the royal commission was the establishment, under the aegis of the University of Sydney, of the School of Public Health and Tropical Medicine.

Royal Commission on the Commonwealth Constitution

The *Royal Commission on Health* reported on 14 January 1926, more than a year before another commission, the *Royal Commission on the Commonwealth Constitution*, was established. The latter commission was appointed in the wake of significant constitutional developments during the 1920s. At the beginning of the decade, the High Court gave Commonwealth powers the widest potential construction they had ever received.[32] In the *Engineers' Case* in 1920, the High Court reviewed its previous practice of following the United States jurisprudence of intergovernmental immunity, namely that neither the Commonwealth nor the State parliaments could be affected by the laws of the other. The practical effect of *Engineers' Case* was:

> … to expand greatly the potential scope of Commonwealth power, because the Constitution operates by way of gift of power to the Commonwealth, not to the States, and the decision requires that powers so granted should be given the fullest amplitude of meaning possible before one can speak of the powers left to the States.[33]

Paradoxically, interpretation of the Constitution by the High Court had more effect in expanding the powers of the Commonwealth than formal constitutional amendment; this was evidenced in 1926 when a referendum to expand the Commonwealth's powers on industry and commerce and essential services failed. Another major constitutional development was the 1927 *Commonwealth–State Financial Agreement*, which discontinued the system of per capita Commonwealth payments to the States that had existed since 1910. It established a Commonwealth–State body, the Loan Council, to coordinate Commonwealth and State loan raisings to avoid competition between governments on domestic and foreign capital markets. The agreement subjected the borrowing of the States to decisions of the Loan Council and provided for Commonwealth assistance to the States in debt reduction. The agreement, ratified by all jurisdictions in 1928, was put beyond constitutional doubt when majorities in all States supported insertion of a new provision, Section 105A, into the Constitution.[34]

In 1926, grants by the Commonwealth to the States for the building of roads constituted the first significant use of Section 96 of the Constitution to provide Commonwealth assistance for a specific purpose.[35] The High Court cursorily dismissed a challenge to the validity of the act in 1926.[36] In the realm of external affairs, there had also been significant developments in the 1920s. The Balfour Report of 1926 defined Great Britain and the self-governing Dominions to be:

> ... autonomous Communities within the British Empire, equal in status, in no way subordinate one to another in any aspect of their domestic or external affairs, though united by common allegiance to the Crown, and freely associated as members of the British Commonwealth of Nations.[37]

Domestically, unhappiness with Western Australia's position in the federation saw emergence of a secessionist movement in that State. In 1924, to alleviate discontent in Western Australia, Bruce had set up a *Royal Commission on the Finances of Western Australia* to inquire into the effects of federation.[38] He established another royal commission in 1928 to examine the effect of federation on the finances of South Australia.[39] The reports of both these royal commissions highlighted how the Commonwealth's protective tariff and the *Navigation Act* had tended financially to disadvantage these two smaller States. Following these royal commissions, the unhappiness of Western Australians with the federation increased to the point where, in 1933, the people of Western Australia voted in a plebiscite to secede from the Commonwealth of Australia. Partly to alleviate discontent in Western Australia and the smaller States, the Lyons Government in 1933 established the Commonwealth Grants Commission to advise on financial assistance to the States under Section 96 of the Constitution.

On 18 August 1927 Bruce established the *Royal Commission on the Commonwealth Constitution* to inquire into how well the Constitution was working and how it might be improved.[40] Sir John Peden, Dean of the Faculty of Law at the University of Sydney and President of the New South Wales Legislative Council, was appointed chairman. The membership was: Senator Percy Abbott, a lawyer and former member of the House of Representatives; Thomas Ashworth, President of the Victorian Employers' Federation; Eric Bowden, a lawyer in New South Wales and the Minister for Defence from 1923 to 1925; Sir Hal Colebatch a former premier of Western Australia and Agent-General in London; M. B. Duffy, associated with the Labor Party in Victoria; and Daniel McNamara, General Secretary of the Federal Labor Party.[41] Harold Nicholas (afterwards Justice of the Supreme Court of New South Wales) was counsel assisting the Commission. All had experience in the working of the federation but only Peden had taken a prominent part in study of the Constitution.

The *Royal Commission on the Commonwealth Constitution* held 198 meetings at which witnesses were examined and exhibits discussed.[42] Among the witnesses were the Victorian barrister, Owen Dixon (shortly to be appointed a Justice of the High Court), leading public servants, including the Solicitor-General, Sir Robert Garran, financial authorities and economists.[43] Opinion in the smaller States was often against centralisation of Commonwealth power. In Western Australia, for example, the historian, Professor Edward Shann, argued that federal powers should be restricted to those set out by the framers of the Constitution, while Alfred Chandler, on the editorial staff of Perth's *Sunday Times*, argued the case for Western Australia's secession from the Commonwealth of Australia. Sir James Mitchell, the former premier of Western Australia and leader of the opposition in the Legislative Assembly, saw three courses open to Australia: the first was for the Commonwealth to observe the letter and spirit of the Constitution; the second was unification, which he feared was imminent; and the third course was for the smaller States to pursue secession.[44]

One question that recurred throughout the Royal Commission was whether the federal system of government should be preserved. In the end, a majority of the Commissioners (Peden, Abbott, Bowden and Colebatch) recommended not only retention of the federal system but that it should be one "in which not only are the powers of the local and central legislatures defined by a charter but the powers of the local legislatures and executive governments are substantial and significant".[45] The majority also concluded that the arbitration power should not be exercised by two authorities and should be in the hands of the States rather than the Commonwealth. This provided grist to the mill for Bruce's 1929 initiative for the Commonwealth to vacate the field of industrial relations.[46] A minority (Ashworth, Duffy and McNamara) made recommendations favouring unification, arguing that "full powers such as those embodied in the Constitutions of Great Britain and New Zealand and South Africa, be vested in the Commonwealth Parliament".[47]

The *Royal Commission on the Commonwealth Constitution* in the event reported to the Scullin Labor Government following its victory in the 1929 federal election. Ironically, the Federal Labor Party had declined an invitation of representation on this royal commission. Consequently, the Commission produced little of practical consequences; for Geoffrey Sawer it was "a useful student's textbook and a minor alteration of the Judiciary Act".[48] Under Scullin, constitutional reform proceeded towards a unitary system of government although with a similar lack of success.[49] Nonetheless, Bruce's constitutional royal commissions pointed to problems of the smaller States in the federation, influenced development of the Commonwealth Grants Commission and laid the ground for extension of Commonwealth power in fields such as health and social welfare.

Royal commissions and politics

Many royal commissions appointed by the Bruce-page Government were designed to help to manage criticism of public policy or to defuse political controversy. For example, early in the Bruce Government, an allegation was made that the Secretary of the Prime Minister's Department, Percy Deane, had received a gift of £1,000 in return for the Commonwealth's purchases of sugar from a private company in 1920.[50] Bruce immediately set up an inquiry to investigate the matter while Deane stood aside from his position. The Royal Commission[51], conducted by the Melbourne barrister Edward Mitchell, cleared Deane of any impropriety and he returned to his position.[52] A similar royal commission investigated an allegation that bribery had played a part in former Queensland premier, Edward Theodore, winning a seat in the House of Representatives in 1927.[53] Other royal commissions were established to deal with criticism of joinery supplied to War Service Homes (1923–24), assessment of War Service disabilities (1924–25) and Labor MHR James Scullin's discussion of land tax matters in the House of Representatives (1924–25).

Royal Commission on the Navigation Act

The readiness of Bruce and previous prime ministers to set up royal commissions on a range of such questions led Western Australian historian Fred Alexander in 1928 to describe the first 'golden rule' relating to royal commissions as: "When in doubt or serious difficulty, appoint a royal commission".[54] An example he adduced was the *Royal Commission on the Navigation Act*. Passed in 1912, the *Navigation Act* established that the coastal trade of the Commonwealth should be reserved for ships conforming to Australian conditions and licensed to trade on the Australian coast. Although enacted in 1912 the act was shelved during the war and its coastal provisions only took effect in 1921.[55] Generally supported by the union movement, the legislation was widely criticised, including by Tasmania, Western Australia and the Lieutenant-Governor of Papua, Sir Hubert Murray.[56]

Responding to conflicting views about the effect of the legislation, on 7 November 1923 Bruce remitted the matter to a royal commission. The membership was entirely parliamentary. John Prowse (Farmers and Settlers Member for Swan) the Chairman, sat with three Senators, Walter Duncan (Nationalist, New South Wales), Harold Elliott (Nationalist, Victoria) and Charles McHugh (Labor, South Australia) and three members of the House of Representatives, Frank Anstey (Labor Member for Bourke), Alfred Seabrook (Nationalist Member for Franklin) and George Yates (Labor Member for Adelaide).57 As only four of its members were from the government parties, the commission was bound to reflect partisan differences.

In this case, however, the report of the *Royal Commission on the Navigation Act* split three ways. Prowse and Seabrook concluded that the *Navigation Act* had failed in its main purpose to establish an Australian mercantile marine.[58] They added that the legislation had been particularly injurious to Tasmania, affecting its tourist traffic and timber and fruit industries, and had made Western Australia's trade relations with the eastern States 'almost impossible'.[59] In their view, the solution was to delete entirely the coastal trade provisions from the Navigation Act. This recommendation stood in stark contrast to that of the commissioners from the Labor Party, Anstey, Yates and McHugh. The Labor members were wholehearted in their insistence that the *Navigation Act* should be retained in its current form and that the only improvement to be made was in its administration. The recommendations of Duncan and Elliott was situated between the two extremes. Duncan and Elliott agreed with Prowse and Seabrook that the coastal trading provisions of the Navigation Act should be repealed, but they also advised that these be replaced by protection with tariffs against foreign shipping under the *Customs Tariff Act*.[60]

The Bruce Government received the Royal Commission's first report in August 1924. For some time, Bruce seemed to treat the recommendations of the Royal Commission in accordance with Fred Alexander's second golden rule of royal commissions: "when immediate difficulties are past, pigeon-hole the report". But that was not the end of the story. During the 1928 election, Bruce resurrected the recommendations of Senators Duncan and Elliott by promising that the coastal trade provisions of the *Navigation Act* would be repealed and replaced by tariff protection, which would be given to vessels complying with Australian standards of wages and living conditions.[61]

Royal Commission on the Coal Industry

Another royal commission established to deal with an intractable political problem was the 1929–30 *Royal Commission on the Coal Industry*. The circumstances arose from the New South Wales black coal industry's precipitate decline in the late 1920s. The Premier of New South Wales, Thomas Bavin, approached Bruce in 1929 advising him that the industry was in serious trouble with markets being lost due to the high price of coal and the unemployment rate steadily rising on the coalfields. Bruce and Bavin assembled a package under which the Commonwealth would offer a bounty of one shilling per ton on inter-state and overseas exports provided that the price of coal produced for local consumption could be reduced by four shillings per ton.[62] This would enable the price of coal exported to other States or abroad to be reduced by five shillings per ton. But the Commonwealth's offer was conditional on the miner-owners agreeing to reduce their profits and the workers voluntarily agreeing to accept lower wages.[63]

With the unions resisting wage cuts, mine-owners started to take matters into their own hands. The northern colliery owners closed their pits on fourteen days' notice and they remained closed from March 1929 to June 1930. The high point of the lockout came in December 1929 when New South Wales Police drew their revolvers and shot into a crowd of locked-out miners in Rothbury, New South Wales, killing a young miner and injuring many others. Not long after the closing of the northern mines, the Commonwealth and New South Wales governments appointed a royal commission after the miners had finally rejected the Bavin-Bruce rationalisation plan.

The *Royal Commission on the Coal Industry* consisted of the New South Wales Supreme Court Judge, Justice (later Sir Colin) Davidson as chairman, together with Herbert W. (later Sir Herbert) Gepp and Leonard Keith Ward, Government Geologist of South Australia.[64] The three were commissioned by Commonwealth and State governments to report on everything connected with the coal industry, including production, carriage, export, distribution and sale of coal.[65] There were twelve subsidiary items of investigation, including capitalisation of collieries, profits and losses, conservation of coal, industrialisation, the practicability of collective contracts, the economic value of coal, reorganisation of the industry and the interests of the industry and the general community.[66] The *Royal Commission on the Coal Industry* commenced its work in Darlinghurst on 10 June 1929 and concluded on 19 December.[67] By the time that it finished, the Bruce–Page Government had lost office. The Davidson Royal Commission issued a preliminary report on 13 January 1930 and a final one containing recommendations on 29 March to the Scullin Labor Government about a year after the northern mines closed.

Its main conclusion was that a three-person board, endowed with federal and state powers, should be established to control the coal industry.[68] The commissioners argued that the board should have the power to inquire into and fix the selling price of coal and to fix all rates of payment, hours and economic conditions of employment.[69] It would issue licenses to all mine workers in a reorganised industry and assess compensation to owners of closed mines. They envisaged that the board would also act as a tribunal of conciliation and arbitration. In case of a strike, it would have power to order a resumption, impose fines on persons responsible and to withhold from employees refusing to work their licenses to remain in the industry. Coal owners were highly critical of the recommendations of the Royal Commission, arguing that the powers of the proposed board exceeded those of bodies set up to regulate the coal industry in Britain and Australia during the Great War.[70]

The Royal Commission's recommendations were, indeed, so far ahead of their time that neither the Scullin Government (1929–31) nor the Lyons Government (1931–39) acted on them. However, the Commission provided invaluable experience for Davidson, who was in 1945 appointed by the Curtin Labor Government as chairman of another Commonwealth commission (Board of Inquiry) into the coal industry.[71] As a result of this later inquiry, the New South Wales coal industry was totally reorganised, along lines adumbrated in the 1930 report through appointment of a Joint Coal Board, endowed with federal and State powers, and a special arbitral tribunal for the industry.[72]

Royal Commission on the Moving Picture Industry in Australia

Still another royal commission was established at around the same time to respond to public feeling that the motion picture industry in Australia was becoming dominated by American films of questionable morality.[73] The issue was politically important with more than 100 million visits to cinemas at one thousand theatres across Australia each year.[74] Bruce sought to deflect criticism by referring it to a joint parliamentary committee in 1927–28, but the Picture Distributors' Association petitioned Bruce to appoint a royal commission to "probe every aspect from production to actual exhibition of films in theatres".[75]

Bruce eventually agreed and in 1928 appointed a royal commission chaired by Walter Marks, Nationalist Member for Wentworth, with five other members dawn from the Senate and House of Representatives.[76] The Royal Commission recommended establishment of a board of film censors and establishment of a quota for films of British empire origin.[77] Sir Victor Wilson, a former minister in Bruce's Government who was also President of the Motion Picture Distributors' Association, defended the Australian industry against partiality to American films and against the allegation that receipts from the Australian box office unduly enriched Americans.[78] There were two consequences of the Royal Commission that were unfortunate for Bruce. One was that Marks, the Chairman of the Commission, became so alienated from Bruce that he joined dissident backbenchers critical of Bruce's 1929 *Maritime Industry Bill*. Another was that an amusements tax imposed on the film industry in the wake of the royal commission was so unpopular that it contributed to decisive defeat of the coalition parties in the general election of 1929.[79]

Conclusion

In response to criticism of the plethora of royal commissions and other commissions of inquiry established between 1923 and 1929, Bruce insisted in 1929 that he was "unrepentant".[80] Some of his commissions were established for partisan purposes and many did not bear fruit during the life of the Bruce–Page Government. But, in the longer term, the economic and social royal commissions fed into the policy process leading to establishment of the welfare state. The royal commissions on various constitutional matters provided valuable evidence and information that helped the Commonwealth to navigate a period of extraordinary constitutional change. They also bore practical fruit in the 1930s and 1940s in efforts to remedy the financial position of the smaller States and in steady extension of Commonwealth involvement in health, education and social welfare in particular. Of other commissions, the *Royal Commission on the Motion Picture Industry* had particularly negative consequences for Bruce's Government. But another with perhaps the most lasting implications was the *Royal Commission on the Coal Industry*, which laid the foundations for the radical reforms to the New South Wales coal industry that took place after 1946.[81]

Public inquiries mentioned in this chapter[82]

Royal Commission on National Insurance (Millen, 1923)

Royal Commission on the Navigation Act (Prouse, 1923)

Royal Commission on the Finances of Western Australia as affected by Federation (Higgs, 1924)

Royal Commission on Health (Syme, 1925)

Royal Commission on Child Endowment or Family Allowances (O'Halloran, 1927)

Royal Commission on the Motion Picture Industry in Australia (Marks, 1927)

Royal Commission on the Commonwealth Constitution (Peden, 1927)

Royal Commission on the Coal Industry (Davidson, 1929)

Notes

1   For example, "The Cost of Federal Royal Commissions", *The Advertiser* (South Australia), 5 March 1929; Prime Minister James Scullin revealed the cost of these royal commissions as £107,765, "Parliamentary Topics", *Chronicle* (Adelaide), 31 July 1930.

2   "Trouble on the Waterfront. Royal Commissions", *The Telegraph* (Brisbane), 30 November 1927.

3   Stuart Macintyre, *Winners and Losers: The Pursuit of Social Justice in Australian*

History, Allen & Unwin, Sydney, 1985, pp. 63-4.

4 Michael Roe, *Nine Australian Progressives: Vitalism in Bourgeois Social Thought 1890–1960*, University of Queensland Press, St Lucia, 1984, p. 137.

5 Stuart Macintyre, *Australia's Boldest Experiment: War and Reconstruction in the 1940s*, NewSouth Publishing, Sydney, 2015.

6 David Lee, *Stanley Melbourne Bruce: Australian Internationalist*, Continuum, London and New York, 2010, pp. 17-18.

7 Roe, *Nine Australian Progressives*, pp. 227-8.

8 Ibid. See also *Report of the Royal Commission on the Basic Wage Together With Evidence*, Government Printer for the State of Victoria, Melbourne, 1920.

9 Laurie Fitzhardinge, *The Little Digger 1914-1952. William Morris Hughes: A Political Biography. Volume II*, Angus & Robertson, Sydney, 1979, pp. 445-6.

10 Aaron Wildavsky, *The 1926 Referendum*, Cheshire, Melbourne, 1958.

11 Bede Nairn, *The "Big Fella": Jack Lang and the Australian Labor Party 1891–1949*, Melbourne University Press, Carlton, 1986, pp. 157-8.

12 "Child Endowment. Federal Royal Commission", *Worker* (Brisbane), 14 September 1927; "Child Endowment Royal Commission", *The Telegraph* (Brisbane), 6 September 1927.

13 *Report of the Royal Commission on Child Endowment or Family Allowances*, Government Printer, Canberra, 1928.

14 Julie Smith, "Paying for Care in Australia's 'Wage Earners' Welfare State': The Case of Child Endowment", in Miranda Stewart, (ed), *Tax, Social Policy and Gender: Rethinking Equality and Efficiency*, ANU E Press, Canberra, 2017, pp. 161-205.

15 "Child Endowment. Evidence Before the Royal Commission", *The Australian Worker* (Sydney), 9 May 1928.

16 Herbert Evatt, *Australian Labour Leader: The Story of W.A. Holman and the Labour Movement*, Angus & Robertson, Sydney, 1942, pp. 488-9, 491.

17 "Child Endowment. Royal Commission's Findings. Voluntary Scheme Suggested", *Sydney Morning Herald*, 19 March 1929.

18 "National Insurance. Royal Commission Appointed", *Truth* (Brisbane), 21 October 1923.

19 "Members of the Royal Commission on National Insurance", *Sunday Times* (Perth), 7 March 1926.

20 "National Insurance. Royal Commission's Recommendations", *Nambour Chronicle and North Coast Advocate* (Queensland), 16 December 1927; *Minutes of Evidence/Royal Commission on National Insurance*, Government Printer, Melbourne, 1926.

21 Roe, *Nine Australian Progressives*, p. 137; "Compulsory National Insurance. Royal Commission's Last Report", *The Great Southern Advocate* (Victoria), 28 April 1927.

22 Rob Watts, *The Foundations of the National Welfare State: The Australian Experience*, Allen & Unwin, Sydney, 1987, pp. 7-24; John Murphy, *A Decent Provision: Australian Welfare Policy, 1870 to 1949*, Ashgate Publishing, Farnham, 2011.

23 Allan Martin, *Robert Menzies: A Life. Volume 1 1894–1943*, Melbourne University Press, Carlton, 1993, pp. 250-1.

24 Roe, *Nine Australian Progressives*, pp. 127-9.

25 Ibid., pp. 133-5.

26 "Royal Commission for Public Health", *The Albury Banner and Wodonga Express*, 18 July 1924.

27   "National Health. Personnel of the Royal Commission", *The Katoomba Daily*, 3 December 1924.

28   *Minutes of Evidence. Royal Commission on Health*, Government Printer, Melbourne, 1925; Ann Waters, "Health Welfare and the State: A Study of the 1925 Royal Commission on Health", PhD Thesis, University of Sydney, 2014.

29   "Public Health. Royal Commission's Report. Important Recommendations", *The Kalgoorlie Miner*, 31 December 1925; *Report of the Royal Commission on Health Together with Appendices*, Government Printer for the State of Victoria, Melbourne, 1925-1926; and *Fourth and Final Report of the Royal Commission on National Insurance: Membership, Finance and Administration*, Government Printer for the State of Victoria, Melbourne, 1927.

30   "Public Health. Royal Commission's Report", *The Australian Worker*, 23 December 1935.

31   Roe, *Nine Australian Progressives*, p. 140.

32   Geoffrey Sawer, *Australian Federal Politics and Law 1901–1929*, Melbourne University Press, Melbourne, 1956, p. 216; Cheryl Saunders, "Owen Dixon: Evidence to the Royal Commission on the Constitution, 1927–29", *Melbourne University Law Review*, Vol. 15, December 1986, pp. 553-74.

33   Sawer, *Australian Federal Politics and Law*, p. 217.

34   Ron Gilbert, *The Australian Loan Council in Federal Fiscal adjustments 1890–1965*, Australian National University Pres, Canberra, 1975.

35   Lee, *Stanley Melbourne Bruce*, p. 36.

36   Saunders, "Owen Dixon", p. 555.

37   Ibid., p. 567.

38   "W.A. and Federation. The Royal Commission. A Tariff Scandal; Navigation Act Effect", *The Mercury* (Hobart), 26 March 1925.

39   "Federal Royal Commission", *The Western Mail* (Ceduna), 24 August 1928.

40   Phillip Ayres, *Owen Dixon*, The Miegunyah Press, Carlton, 2007, p. 52.

41   "Royal Commission on the Constitution", *The Naracoorte Herald* (South Australia), 12 August 1927.

42   "Federal Constitution–Royal Commission's Report", *Narrandera Argus and Riverina Advertiser*, 24 September 1929; *Report of Proceedings and Minutes of Evidence. Royal Commission on the Constitution of the Commonwealth*, Government Printer, Canberra, 1928.

43   Sir Robert Garran, *Prosper the Commonwealth*, Angus & Robertson, Sydney, 1958, p. 207.

44   "Royal Commission on the Constitution. Some Varying Views by Witnesses", *Sunday Times* (Perth), 27 November 1927.

45   *Report of the Royal Commission on the Constitution: Together with Appendices and Index*, Commonwealth Government Printer, Canberra, 1929, p. 240.

46   "Federal Constitution–Royal Commission's Report", *Narrandera Argus and Riverina Advertiser*, 24 September 1929.

47   *Report of the Royal Commission on the Constitution: Together with Appendices and Index*, Government Printer, Canberra, 1929, pp. 256-6.

48   Sawer, *Australian Federal Politics and Law*, p. 326.

49   Saunders, "Owen Dixon", p. 573.

50   "Sugar Purchases", *The Argus*, 29 September 1923.

51   Royal Commission in Connection with Sugar Purchases by the Common-

wealth through Mr W E Davies in September and October 1920 – appointed in August 1923.

52 "Sugar Inquiry. Royal Commission Report", *The Daily Telegraph* (Sydney), 11 October 1923.

53 "Edward Granville Theodore (1884-1950)", in John Ritchie (ed.), *Australian Dictionary of Biography, Volume 12*, Melbourne University Press, Carlton, 1990, p. 199; *Report of the Royal Commission Appointed to Inquire into Statements in the Press in Regard to Offers Alleged to Have Been Made to Resign Seats in the Federal Parliament*, Government Printer, Canberra, 1928.

54 Fred Alexander, "A Royal Commission and its Sequel", *The Sunday Times* (Perth), 21 October 1928.

55 Diane Kirby, "The Sailor is a Human Being: Labour Market Regulation and the Australian Navigation Act 1912", Diane Kirby (ed.), *Past Law, Present Histories*, ANU E Press, 2012.

56 Francis West, *Hubert Murray: The Australian Pro-Consul*, Oxford University Press, Melbourne 1968, pp. 187-9.

57 "Navigation Royal Commission", *The Register* (Adelaide), 12 October 1923.

58 "Navigation Act. Conflict of Opinion. Royal Commission's Three Reports", *Daily Commercial News and Shipping List* (Sydney), 27 August 1924.

59 Ibid.

60 *Report by Royal Commission on the Navigation Act*, Government Printer, Melbourne 1924 and *Second Report of the Royal Commission on the Navigation Act (New Guinea and Papua)*, Government Printer, Melbourne, 1925.

61 Fred Alexander, "A Royal Commission and its Sequel", *The Sunday Times* (Perth), 21 October 1928.

62 Lee, *Stanley Melbourne Bruce*, p. 83.

63 Ibid., p. 83.

64 "Coal Industry. Personnel of Commission", *Goulburn Evening Penny Post*, 8 May 1929.

65 "Coal Industry. Commission's Decisions. Recommendations Reviewed", *The Argus*, 10 April 1930.

66 Ibid.

67 "End of Coal Commission", *Sydney Morning Herald*, 20 December 1929.

68 "Coal Commission. Board with Wide Powers Suggested", *The Age*, 1 April 1930.

69 Ibid.

70 "Coal Dispute. Control of the Industry. Owners Disagree with the Commission", *The West Australian*, 2 April 1930.

71 This was the Commissioner or Board of Inquiry appointed to Inquire into and Report upon the Coal Mining Industry, appointed in 1945 under the National Securities (Inquiries) Regulations which gave it similar powers as a royal commission.

72 Malcolm Ellis, *A Saga of Coal*, Angus & Robertson, Sydney, 1969, pp. 198-203.

73 "Picture Industry: Royal Commission Wanted", *Daily Standard* (Brisbane), 7 August 1926.

74 Ibid.

75 'Motion Pictures. Royal Commission. Distributors' Suggestion", *Sydney Morning Herald*, 16 March 1927.

76 "Motion Picture. Industry. Report of Royal Commission. Establishment of

Empire Quota Urged", The *Telegraph* (Brisbane), 25 April 1928.

77 Ibid.

78 "Motion Picture Inquiry. Sir V. Wilson's Evidence", *Barrier Miner* (Broken Hill), 9 June 1927.

79 Lee, *Stanley Melbourne Bruce*, pp. 86-8.

80 "Federal Commissions. Mr. Bruce 'Unrepentant'", *The Telegraph* (Brisbane), 29 January 1929.

81 David Lee, *The Second Rush: Mining and the Transformation of Australia*, Connor Court, Redland Bay, 2016, Chapter One.

82 List refers to name of inquiry, its chair and date of appointment.

3

Australian tax inquiries: Forms, processes and impacts

Paul Tilley

Introduction

A country's tax system has a "quasi-constitutional character"[1] in that it establishes in a community how the burden of funding government services is shared and substantially remains in force over long periods. Major tax reform exercises should therefore be few and far between. On occasions, though, a government needs to fundamentally rethink aspects of its tax structure that have become flawed or outdated. Given the significance of those occasions a formal review is typically warranted.

Tax reform attempts across Australia's federal history, at Commonwealth and State levels, have used various review methods, including public inquiries[2], with mixed results. This chapter uses a survey of Australia's tax reviews to assess the reasons for that and address the question of when having a public tax inquiry is worth it. It draws on six more detailed papers this author has published with the Tax and Transfer Policy Institute (TTPI) of the Crawford School of Public Policy, Australian National University on Australia's main tax reform exercises.[3]

Tax policy making

Most tax policy changes occur without a formal review process. In the typical course of events, issues are identified by stakeholders or within government, policy options are developed internally, a government decision is made, a consultation process is run by Treasury and draft legislation is prepared for parliament. At times, however, tax changes of sufficient magnitude are being contemplated that a more substantive process is called for and given the general unpopularity of taxes that process needs to be seen to be fair and open. A range of review types are then available to governments, from more extensive internal processes to external public inquiries.

Public inquiries offer the possibility of having complex and sensitive issues considered holistically, and away from the hothouse of government, but they do entail significant costs, take time and have their own risks.[4] Major tax changes involve an effective reconsideration of a community's tax burden shares, with potential winners and losers, and these will be transparent in a public inquiry.

As well as these tax share equity issues, a tax system inevitably imposes economic costs. By changing relative prices, taxes distort market outcomes, creating economic inefficiencies. There are also substantial tax administrative and compliance costs. The magnitude of these economic costs will also be relevant to whether a public inquiry is warranted.

Together these issues underpin the standard tax policy criteria of equity, efficiency, and simplicity. While other issues are also relevant, these three criteria are the standard starting point for any credible tax review.

Public tax inquiries

This chapter categorises Australia's tax reviews as generally taking one of two forms. Foundational reviews have been used to establish the tax reform case, even if that has not led to immediate implementation. Determinative reviews have been used to implement tax reforms where the policy case has been previously established and the political and budget opportunity presents for implementation.

Assessing the impact of a tax review, therefore, goes beyond whether actual tax reform immediately follows. Five criteria are listed to assess Australia's tax reviews:

1. The *terms-of-reference and panel* indicate the government's ambition – an open, searching inquiry as opposed to a narrow remit if particular recommendations are expected.

2. The extent of *gathering of evidence and calling of witnesses* indicate the panel's reliance on external experts as opposed to its own expertise/ predetermined views.

3. *Timeliness and relevance* indicate likely influence – a quick, focused review for immediate implementation, but a more open one as a platform for subsequent reform exercises.

4. The *approach to analysis of issues* indicates the rigour of the public finance framework and its framing against standard tax policy criteria.

5. The *quality of tax policy outcomes*, in the short or long term, remains the ultimate test of a reform exercise, although this is dependent on government actions.

In this context, tax reform efforts in Australia can be viewed in three main phases (as set out in the author's TTPI papers).

- The first phase covers the early decades of federation with overlapping taxes the subject of two Commonwealth royal commissions, leading to the 1942 Commonwealth takeover of income tax.
- The second phase covers the post-war period and the 1975 Asprey Review's tax blueprint, leading to the major tax reforms of 1985 and 1998.

- The third phase covers the 21st century featuring the 2009 Henry Review and several state government reviews which, for the most part, have not resulted in major tax reforms.

Early federation reviews and the 1942 income tax unification[5]

In the early decades of Australia's federation, tax policy was driven by the need to establish robust revenue bases and settle the relative taxing responsibilities of Commonwealth and state governments. The Constitution gave the Commonwealth exclusive access to customs and excise duties, but with other taxes open to both levels of government they soon found themselves competing. These overlaps became most significant with income tax and efforts to resolve this were a focus of early Commonwealth-State finance negotiations and tax reviews.

Royal Commission on Taxation 1920-23

With the Commonwealth introducing income tax in 1915 to help finance Australia's First World War involvement, the overlap with state income taxes was a problem for taxpayers. A series of Commonwealth-state conferences was unable to achieve greater uniformity in policy or administration, so in 1920 the Hughes Nationalist Government appointed a royal commission[6] chaired by prominent business leader Warren Kerr, who had also chaired the Commonwealth War Savings Council, to consider these overlapping tax issues. As Australia's first major tax review, the *Royal Commission on Taxation* was given a broad remit to consider the equitable distribution of the tax burden and the harmonisation of Commonwealth and State taxes. Its members were drawn from commercial, farming and labour interests.[7]

The Commission held 118 public sittings, examined 191 witnesses and produced five reports over three years, finishing in 1923. It argued that only a full delimitation of spheres of taxation would afford Australian taxpayers their sovereign right to a minimum of inconvenience and cost in paying their taxes. The Commission recommended that income tax be raised exclusively by the Commonwealth and that land tax, probate duties and entertainment taxes be raised exclusively by the States.

By the time of the Royal Commission's final report in 1923, however, the political environment had changed substantially. Stanley Bruce, previously Treasurer in the Hughes Administration had become prime minister following the 1922 federal elections, and the Nationalist Party had entered a coalition with the emerging federal Country Party under Dr Earle Page. The new Bruce-Page Nationalist-Country Party Government's negotiations with the States were now focussed on streamlining tax administration arrangements and the Commission's recommendations were not actioned.

Overall, while the 1923 *Royal Commission on Taxation* had been given a broad terms-of-reference and had conducted a high quality and thorough review, its lack of timeliness and relevance to the moving political debate detracted from its short-term effectiveness.

Royal Commission on Taxation 1932-34

Following the fruitless political negotiations on tax overlaps around the 1923 *Royal Commission on Taxation*, Commonwealth–State financial relations more broadly were addressed in the *Financial Agreement Act 1928*. With the overlapping tax issues unresolved, though, in 1932 the newly elected Lyons United Australia Party established another royal commission[8] chaired by ex-NSW Supreme Court judge David Ferguson.[9] Its remit was to consider the simplification and standardisation of Commonwealth and state taxes, with specific reference to unifying income tax provisions. The Commission held public sittings, examined 136 witnesses and produced four reports over two years.

The Royal Commission's analysis was cognisant of the ongoing political debates in the federation, with the Commonwealth and state governments still negotiating their respective roles. Rather than delimiting income tax to one level of government, it recommended a compromise whereby separate income tax acts would be maintained but with a uniform set of core provisions defining those elements of the tax base that could be agreed on, allowing for jurisdictional variations on other aspects and on tax rates.

This Commission reported in 1934 to the same government that had commissioned it, enabling more impetus for change. The Commission's members then worked with Commonwealth-State conferences to develop the common provisions, with agreement reached in time for the Commonwealth's *Income Tax Assessment Act 1936* and equivalent state legislation. This was a significant step towards uniformity of income taxes in Australia, but differences remained and over time ongoing changes across jurisdictions eroded the uniformity.

Overall, this Commission was given a more specific terms-of-reference and produced a high-quality report that built on the work of the previous Commission. Its greater timeliness and relevance to the current political debate made it more influential in the short term.

1942 income tax unification

Financing Australia's involvement in the Second World War again required large revenue increases and the Commonwealth raised both personal and company income tax rates. It also asked the States to suspend their income taxes to allow it unfettered access to that tax base, but they refused.

With war expenditures escalating, in 1942 the new Curtin Labor Government appointed the *Committee on Uniform Taxation*[10], chaired by economics professor Richard Mills, to specifically review the

Commonwealth being the sole income tax authority. While this was an external committee, its members were known supporters of a uniform income tax. With the policy case for income tax unification established in the previous inquiries, five weeks later the Committee's short report recommended that for the duration of the war, and one year after, the Commonwealth be the sole collector of income tax, with compensation paid to the States.

The Commonwealth then acted unilaterally with a legislative package that forced the States out of income tax – Commonwealth tax was prioritised over state tax and compensating grants were paid to the States conditional on them vacating their income taxes. Constitutional challenges by the States were unsuccessful. The Chifley Labor Government (1945-49) did not return income tax to the States after the war, with the expanding welfare state necessitating continued substantial revenues.

Overall, the 1942 *Committee on Uniform Taxation* built on the tax policy arguments established in the earlier inquiries to provide the Commonwealth with the report it was looking for. Its terms-of-reference were framed to elicit precise recommendations on income tax unification and the panel members' views were known. Unification of income tax at the Commonwealth level was a major tax reform but left the ongoing issue of substantial vertical fiscal imbalance in the Australian Federation.

Summary 1901-1949

The 1942 *Committee on Uniform Taxation* worked for the circumstances of the time. The tax policy arguments for income tax unification had been well established in the earlier two royal commissions and the Labor Government (led by Prime Minister Chifley following John Curtin's death in 1945) was now lining up a political solution. As is often the case, governments and bureaucracies need to be prepared with the policy case for when reform implementation opportunities present. A crisis, even a war, can provide the opportunity for reform. In this case, the royal commissions had established the foundational case for income tax unification, and a new government needing war finance provided the determinative opportunity.

Asprey Review tax blueprint and reforms of the 1980s and 1990s

In the post-war period in Australia through the 'golden years' of the 1950s and 1960s there was not an imperative to tackle basic economic reform. As such, underlying structural problems in the economy, including the tax system, went largely unactioned. Stagflationary conditions in the 1970s, though, exposed these problems and a major economic reform program was called for. Tax reform would be a major part of that.

Post-war tax reviews and the Asprey Blueprint[11]

With a limited constituency for reform, any tax inquiries in the 1950s and 1960s were partial and focused on compliance costs.[12] By the 1970s, though, with inflation pushing taxpayers onto higher tax rates Australia's flawed income tax base was exposed to attack and dissatisfaction with the tax system was acute. Tax avoidance and evasion flourished by those who could manipulate the form of their income, while wage and salary earners had little opportunity to do so. There was a strong case for reform but a lack of consensus on what that entailed.

In April 1972 the McMahon Coalition Government announced the *Taxation Review Committee*, chaired by NSW Supreme Court judge, Kenneth Asprey, with several other members.[13] The Whitlam Government, elected later that year in December, confirmed its continuation and extended its reporting date. The Asprey Review received over 600 submissions, and commissioned several studies and background papers. It sought to provide an integrated blueprint for the Australian tax system rather than recommendations for further piecemeal changes.

Using efficiency, fairness and simplicity as its 'big three' criteria the inquiry identified major flaws in the Australian tax system and laid out a comprehensive reform program. It favoured a relatively simple tax system, with a socially acceptable level of fairness, underpinning a proposed tax mix switch from personal income tax to a broad-based consumption tax.

To address gaps in the personal income tax base the Asprey Review recommended introduction of a capital gains tax (CGT) and reforms to the taxation of fringe benefits. Australia's existing 'classical' company income tax system double-taxed dividends and its replacement by a dividend imputation system was recommended. As part of the proposed income/consumption tax mix switch, replacement of Australia's narrow-based wholesale sales tax (WST) with a broad-based value added tax (VAT) was recommended.

The Asprey Review's full report was delivered in January 1975,[14] the final tumultuous year of the Whitlam Government. While aspects of the Asprey Review informed simplification of the personal income tax rate scale in the 1974 and 1975 budgets, there was no formal government response to its recommendations.

Overall, the Asprey Review was given a broad terms-of-reference and used its public inquiry status and timeframe to consult extensively. While it did not result in substantial tax reform in the short term it applied a strong public finance framework to produce a high-quality report and lay out a comprehensive blueprint for reform of the Commonwealth tax system.

1985 reform of the Australian tax system[15]

After the tumult of the Whitlam Government (1972-75), the Fraser Coalition Government (1975-83) saw consolidation with less reform.[16] The Asprey Report remained largely unactioned. The 1983 election of the Hawke Labor Government with Paul Keating as Treasurer, however, set in train a series of economic reforms.

Following a first term dominated by establishment of the Prices and Incomes Accord and floating the dollar, the Hawke Government's second term was dominated by tax reform. During the 1984 election campaign Hawke committed to holding a summit to seek consensus on a tax reform package. The *Reform of the Australian Tax System* (RATS) report, prepared in the first half 1985, set out the Hawke Government's preferred package – Option C encompassing close to the full Asprey blueprint. RATS was prepared within government, largely by a Treasury team led by Ted Evans and David Morgan, with an interdepartmental taskforce convened to oversight it.

RATS argued for structural broadening of the income and consumption tax bases to finance reductions in tax rates, in addition to a shift in the tax mix from personal income tax to indirect consumption tax. Consistent with the Asprey blueprint, personal income tax base broadening included a CGT, a fringe benefits tax (FBT) and measures to counter tax shelters. Consumption tax base broadening involved a switch from the WST to a broad-based consumption tax. With company tax, replacement of the classical system with a dividend imputation system was favoured, while with foreign source income, a foreign tax credit system (FTCS) was proposed.

At the July 1985 National Tax Summit support could not be established for the full Option C package. The consumption tax proposal was opposed by welfare groups and state premiers, and the income tax base-broadening measures were opposed by business groups. A 'fallback' option composed of the income tax reforms did, nonetheless, survive, that is a CGT, FBT, FTCS and dividend imputation – not a bad fallback!

Overall, the RATS package, even without the consumption tax, constituted a major reform of the Australian tax system. The package was prepared within government but then tested at the tax summit. The RATS paper was put together in less than six months with limited additional public consultations, drawing substantially on the Asprey blueprint. While on the face of it the tax summit was disappointing in being unable to achieve a consensus, without the consumption tax proposal the rest of the package may have had less chance of ultimate success.

2000: A new tax system[17]

Consumption tax reform remained unfinished business from the Asprey blueprint. In his *Fightback!* package John Hewson as Opposition leader promised to introduce a goods and services tax (GST), but this failed following the Coalition's defeat at the 1993 election. Consequently, in the run up to the 1996 federal election John Howard as Opposition leader said "never, ever" for a GST. In government, however, recognising the need for both tax and Commonwealth-State finance reform Howard and Treasurer, Peter Costello, sought to reopen that issue.

In 1997 the Howard Government announced a tax review, including consideration of a broad-based consumption tax and Commonwealth-state finances. The review was again to be internal to government with the work being done mainly by a Treasury-staffed taskforce headed by Ken Henry. The actual policy development was run through cabinet real-time, with the first use of powerpoint and spreadsheet presentations in the cabinet room.

In contrast to stakeholders' adversarial approach at the 1985 tax summit, welfare and business groups initially formed an alliance, accepting the need for tax reform including consideration of a GST, subject to improving the tax system's overall progressivity. The States were also more supportive with the potential for Commonwealth-State finance reform.

The review's focal point was reform of Australia's ramshackle indirect tax system, at both Commonwealth and State levels. The solution was for the Commonwealth to use its constitutional power to introduce a 10 per cent GST[18] to replace its WST and a raft of the States' inefficient transaction taxes, with all the GST revenue going to the States. The package also included a rationalisation of family assistance payments and personal income tax cuts.

The Howard Government took this *A New Tax System* (ANTS) package to the 1998 election and was returned, but only narrowly. Negotiating the legislation through the Senate, however, required the agreement of the Australian Democrats which necessitated, in addition to health and education, the exclusion of basic food from the GST base. The amended GST then took effect from 1 July 2000.

Overall, the ANTS package was a major consumption tax reform that complemented the RATS income tax reform and went a substantial way to completing the Asprey blueprint. It also constituted a significant reform of state taxes and Commonwealth–State financial relations. Preparation of the package was again done largely within government, with the 1998 election providing the political platform for public debate.

The ANTS review was unable to deal adequately with business tax issues and a separate public *Review of Business Taxation*, chaired by businessman John Ralph and supported by a Treasury-based secretariat, was commissioned. Unlike ANTS and its GST considerations, the optimal business tax system was less clear, so the Ralph Inquiry was more foundational in nature. Comprehensive reforms of the taxation of business investments and business entities were recommended. The Howard Government response to the inquiry included implementing some changes, such as a reduction in the company tax rate, but it did not ultimately implement the central recommendations on business investments and business entities.

Summary 1950-2000

With the income tax and consumption tax base broadening achieved in RATS and ANTS, the Asprey blueprint had been substantially implemented. While each of the tax reform outcomes was compromised by practical and political realities, they constituted major achievements and collectively amounted to a significant tax reform that would underpin more robust and efficient government revenues in the years ahead.

These three tax reviews can be seen as a group. The Asprey Review, a public inquiry, was the foundational review that established a blueprint for the Australian tax system, while RATS and ANTS were the internal determinative reviews that sought to implement that blueprint. It is arguable whether RATS and ANTS would have proceeded in the same way without Asprey – by the 1980s there was a growing consensus internationally of the need for and nature of tax reform – but the Asprey Review helped cement that consensus in Australia and so stands as our most significant foundational tax review. The extent of the RATS and ANTS reforms likewise make them, together with the 1942 income tax unification, Australia's most significant determinative tax reviews.

21ˢᵗ Century tax reform

The year 2001 marked the centenary of the Australian Federation and the new century promised fresh opportunities as the emerging resources boom drove economic growth and revenues. The 2008 global financial crisis (GFC), however, interrupted that momentum, and a fraught political situation further obviated economic reform opportunities. The more recent COVID-19 crisis then drove Australia into recession with the focus moving to macroeconomic stabilisation, pushing budgets deeper into deficit. The 21ˢᵗ century in Australia has, consequently, not featured significant tax reform.

Australia's future tax system[19]

The newly elected Rudd Labor Government, in 2007, convened the *Australia 2020 Summit* to generate ideas for the nation's future. One of those ideas was to use the strong fiscal position generated by the resources boom to 'buy' some more tax reform. The Rudd Government consequently announced a 'root and branch' review of the Australian tax system, but with changes to the GST ruled out.

The *Australia's Future Tax System* (AFTS) review panel was a hybrid of internal and external members, chaired by Ken Henry as Secretary of Treasury but with others drawn mainly from outside government.[20] The review's purpose was somewhat unclear. It was asked to consider the tax structure Australia needed for the 21st century but coming less than a decade after completion of the RATS/ANTS reform cycle there was a question of whether there was a sufficient 'burning bridge'. Nonetheless, the review made a good start receiving over 1500 submissions, meeting over 130 stakeholders and generating background and consultation papers.

Then there was a change of plan. The GFC came to a head in September 2008 and governments went into crisis-management mode. In Australia, three major fiscal stimulus packages and aggressive monetary policy easing helped avoid a major recession but the prospect of significant budget surpluses to 'buy' some tax reform had disappeared. The implications for the AFTS review were profound and the review panel had to reconsider its approach. Major tax reform in the short term was no longer realistic, so the review needed to be more conceptual, addressing long-term directions for the tax system.

The AFTS report outlined a comprehensive reform agenda for the Australian tax system. It proposed a simplified personal income tax system with a two-step rate scale. It proposed more progressive taxation of superannuation and, controversially, maintaining the superannuation guarantee rate at 9 per cent. It proposed a lowering of the company tax rate to 25 per cent, in conjunction with improvements to the taxation of Australia's non-renewable resources, in particular replacing state royalties with a resource rent tax.

By the time the AFTS report, with its 138 recommendations, was finalised in late 2009 the political environment had changed substantially, with the Rudd Government now struggling. The initial government response addressed just three recommendations, featuring a 40 per cent Resource Super Profits Tax (RSPT) and a cut in the company tax rate to only 28 per cent. The mining industry ran an aggressive anti-RSPT advertising campaign and as political events played out Julia Gillard replaced Rudd as prime minister and implemented a modified Minerals Resource Rent Tax. It raised little revenue and was subsequently repealed by the subsequent Abbott Coalition Government that came to office in 2013.

Overall, AFTS is a difficult tax reform exercise to assess because of the confusing context of its commissioning, progress and implementation. While substantial reforms were not implemented in the short term, it did provide an in-depth analysis of the Australian tax and transfer system and identified directions for reform in a foundational report that can be drawn on by future, more determinative reviews. Around a third of its recommendations have since been actioned, including regarding state tax reforms.

The one other attempted Commonwealth tax review this century was a tax white paper process commissioned by the Abbott Government in 2014. There was no terms-of-reference and no panel with the process conducted internally in Treasury. A discussion paper was issued in early 2015 but with the government struggling politically and the budget position deteriorating the process simply petered out. A parallel federation white paper suffered a similar fate.

State and Territory tax reviews[21]

In Australia's federation the Commonwealth has the main revenue-raising instruments, but the States retain large expenditures responsibilities, with the consequent imbalance dealt with by intergovernmental grants. The States still raise around half of their own revenue, though, through various tax and non-tax sources, many of which suffer from poor design and have been eroded by interstate competition. The States' main taxes are payroll tax, stamp duties and land tax, plus property rates at the local government level. Each state and territory has conducted reviews of their tax system at times and here I will survey a sample of those.

NSW governments have commissioned five significant tax reviews, three of which were public inquiries. The most recent of those, the *NSW Review of Federal Financial Relations,* established in 2019, was chaired by business leader David Thodey and reported in 2020.[22] It was asked to make recommendations on the State's tax system and its interaction with federal funding. The report argued that stamp duties on property conveyances were inefficient and inequitable, and its central recommendation was for their replacement with a reformed land tax. This recommendation has been agreed in principle by the government but not yet implemented at the time of writing.

Victorian governments have commissioned two significant tax reviews, both of which were public inquiries. The 1982-3 *Committee of Inquiry into Revenue Raising in Victoria* which was chaired by economist John Nieuwenhuysen and reported in 1983, was given a broad terms-of-reference to examine Victoria's revenue raising system.[23] It was the first public inquiry into the State's taxation system in Victoria's then 150 years of history. The Committee conducted an extensive public consultation process and recommended payroll tax simplifications, a broadening of the land tax base and replacement of stamp duties with a broad-based tax.[24] The immediate government response was limited but the report was used to support tax reforms to combat tax avoidance.

Western Australian governments have commissioned two significant tax reviews, both done within government but with an external reference group. The *State Tax Review* which was conducted by the Department of Treasury and Finance and reported in 2007 with the resources boom taking off, was asked to consider options for tax relief.[25] The report's highest priority tax reform was cutting stamp duty on property conveyances. The government response to the review abolished stamp duties on mortgages, hire of goods and non-real property transfers.

Tasmanian governments have commissioned one significant tax review. The 2010 *State Tax Review* was conducted by an across-party panel of parliamentarians chaired by Treasurer Lara Giddings.[26] The review assessed property stamp duties and insurance duties as relatively inefficient and land tax as relatively efficient. There was a discussion paper but no final report. With the State's finances deteriorating, there was no substantive government action on the review's findings.

Australian Capital Territory (ACT) governments have commissioned one significant tax review. The *ACT Taxation Review* was chaired by ex-Treasurer Ted Quinlan but with the ACT Under Treasurer on the panel.[27] Its 2012 report recommended the replacement of stamp duties on property conveyances and insurance with a broad-based land tax. The government response to the review was to implement a major tax reform package with a long-term plan to abolish insurance duties and replace stamp duties on property conveyance with restructured property rates.

South Australian governments have conducted one significant tax review, but it was fully internal to government. Northern Territory governments have also conducted one internal review.

Summary 2001-2021 and State Tax Reviews

So far in the 21st century in Australia significant tax reform has not been a major feature. While there have been some tax policy measures of note, such as State efforts to harmonise payroll tax and the replacement of fire services insurance levies with property-based taxes in some jurisdictions, mostly they have not emanated from formal tax reviews. The main exception is the ACT's transition from property conveyance duty to reformed property rates which followed a public inquiry.

The reasons for this lack of reform are, of course, complex. At the Commonwealth level especially, the political situation has been fraught, with governments generally operating with slim majorities. We have also experienced two major worldwide shocks, with the GFC and then the COVID-19 pandemic removing any fiscal room for revenue-negative tax reforms.

To be optimistic, there have been some high-quality tax review reports at both the Commonwealth and State levels which may yet operate as foundational reviews for future determinative processes.

Are tax public inquiries worth it?

This survey of tax reform exercises in Australia shows that public inquiries have played an important role in progressing needed tax reforms, although in modern times they have been used in combination with internal reviews. So, what lessons can we draw from history as to whether public tax inquiries might be worth it in the future?

Lessons from Australia's tax reform exercises

Looking back at Australia's three main phases of tax reform reveals changes in the role of public inquiries over time.

In the first tax reform phase during the early decades of federation, the main Commonwealth tax reviews were all public inquiries, consistent with the general approach at the time. Treasury was still developing as a policy agency[28] so governments needed to call on external expertise for substantive economic policy advice. The foundational royal commissions followed by the determinative *Committee on Uniform Taxation* was ultimately successful in achieving income tax unification.

In the second tax reform phase from the 1970s to 1990s, a combination of public inquiries and internal reviews was used. The Asprey public inquiry was the foundational review that established the tax reform blueprint, but internal reviews were also used for the more determinative processes of designing and implementing actual reforms. In these cases, the governments had well-formed ideas on what the reforms should be before these later reviews were commissioned (informed by Asprey).

In the third tax reform phase this century, the Commonwealth used an internal/external hybrid model for AFTS, initially conceiving it would serve as both a foundational and determinative review. The GFC changed that and AFTS was ultimately a more foundational review, with its hybrid model proving less suited for that purpose. With some decline in the policy advising capacities of the public service[29], though, public inquiries may have an important role going forward.

Overall, public tax inquiries were used to a greater extent earlier in the federation, with governments in modern times inclined to keep tax reviews more internal as the policy capacity of the public service, in this case Treasury, developed. History also shows that public inquiries have generally been used for forward-looking foundational reviews. Where governments have clear views of desired policy outcomes, internal determinative reviews provide greater control and lead more seamlessly into implementation.

Governments will be reluctant, however, to commission a tax review without the prospect of actual tax reform. As such, the genesis of a public tax inquiry will generally need to be both foundational and determinative – in the knowledge that the government commissioning it may ultimately not accept all of the review's recommendations, eg Ralph Inquiry and AFTS, or where the inquiry spans an election the inquiry may report to a different government, eg Asprey Review.

History also shows us that with the tax system establishing a community's sharing of the burden of funding government services, significant tax reform is contentious and typically requires substantial political capital and a strong budget position to accommodate a revenue negative package – two things that have been absent for most of this century and the latter of which is not in prospect.

Design of a public tax inquiry: Some suggestions

If a government does decide to commission a major public tax inquiry in the future there are some key design points it might like to consider.

The government's objective in commissioning the inquiry needs to be clear, particularly whether it is looking for wide-ranging or constrained advice, and the terms-of-reference should reflect that. A tax inquiry's terms-of-reference will also ideally include a revenue-neutral constraint, to ensure a focus on genuine tax reform issues, and the public finance criteria the panel is expected to operate within.

The inquiry panel will ideally contain sufficient tax expertise to explore issues in-depth and within a recognised policy framework. That said, panel members with strong pre-determined views may not think openly about issues and a strong chair, perhaps without specific expertise, is needed. Providing the panel with a good secretariat, including both Treasury and external members, is also important.

The timeframe for the inquiry needs to be long enough to enable the panel to consult widely and conduct in-depth examinations, but realistically also needs to fit within an electoral timetable. For a foundational tax inquiry, at least a year is needed, and 18 months is typical. For a determinative review a shorter timeframe, probably less than a year, will be more appropriate and will be ideally commissioning early in a government's term. The RATS review was commissioned early in the Hawke Government's second term while the Howard Government took the ANTS review to the 1998 election to manage the earlier political commitment to not introduce a GST.

Conclusion

Australia's experience with tax reviews shows that public inquiries can be an important option in the array of review types available to governments, supplementing the public bureaucracy as the usual source of policy advice. They will generally be most suited to foundational reviews where tax reform options are not obvious or the political or budget circumstances are not amenable to immediate reform. Assessing the impact of a taxation public inquiry though, needs to take a long-term view. Although an inquiry may at first seemed ignored, its influence may be considerably greater as its research and recommendations filter through to decision makers. Inquiry reports often become the starting point for discussion when an issue re-emerges on the policy agenda when circumstances make its tax reform recommendations more palatable or more urgent for implementation.

Public inquiries mentioned in this chapter[30]

Commonwealth

Royal Commission on Taxation (Kerr, 1920)

Royal Commission on Taxation (*Laws and Simplification and Standardisations of Taxation Laws*) (Ferguson, 1932)

Committee on Uniform Taxation (Mills, 1942)

Commonwealth Committee on Rates of Depreciation (Hulme, 1954)

Commonwealth Committee on Taxation (Ligertwood, 1959)

Taxation Review Committee (Asprey, 1972)

Review of Business Taxation (Ralph, 1998)

State

Committee of Inquiry into Revenue Raising in Victoria (Nieuwenhuysen, 1982)

ACT Taxation Review (Quinlan, 2011)

NSW Review of Federal Financial Relations (Thodey, 2019)

Notes

1   John Head, "Issues in Australian Tax Policy for the 1980s", in John Head, (ed), *Taxation Issues of the 1980s*, Australian Tax Research Foundation, Sydney, 1983, p. 1.

2   This chapter uses the term 'public inquiries' as defined in Scott Prasser and Helen Tracey, *Royal Commissions and Public Inquiries: Practice and Potential*, Connor Court Publishing, Ballarat, 2014, p. 37 which defined public inquiries as "temporary ad hoc bodies appointed by the executive to provide advice or to investigate some issue, with specific terms of reference and with members drawn from outside government and the bureaucracy" and the more general term 'review' to refer to tax reviews more broadly.

3   The six papers can be found at Tax and Transfer Policy Institute (TTPI) of the Crawford School of Public Policy, ANU, Working Papers https://taxpolicy.crawford.anu.edu.au/taxpolicy-publications/taxpolicy-working-papers

4   See Scott Prasser, *Royal Commissions and Public Inquiries in Australia*, 2nd ed, LexisNexis, Chatswood, 2021, pp. 140-49 for the roles inquiries are appointed to assist in policy development and see pp. 129-35 for risks in their appointment.

5   See Paul Tilley, "Early federation reviews and the 1942 income tax unification", *Tax and Transfer Policy Institute*, Working Paper 11/2020, September 2020.

6   *Royal Commission on Taxation* (1920-23) included William Kerr (Chair), John Garvan, John Jolly, John Farleigh, William Missingham, John Thomson, Stephen Mills and Maurice Duffy.

7   Douglas Copland, "Some Problems of Taxation in Australia", *The Economic Journal*, September 1924, p. 36.

8   David Ferguson, (Chair), *Royal Commission on Taxation*, (Laws and Simplification and Standardisation of Taxation Laws), 6 October 1932 – 28 November 1934.

9   The one other commissioner, Edwin Nixon, was a chartered accountant.

10   Committee on Uniform Taxation, Robert C. Mills, (Chair), J. H. Scullin, E. S. Spooner, *Report of the Committee on Uniform Taxation*, Commonwealth Government Printer, Canberra, 1942.

11   See Paul Tilley, "Post-war tax reviews and the Asprey Blueprint", *Tax and Transfer Policy Institute*, Working Paper 15/2020, November 2020.

12   The Spooner, Hulme and Ligertwood committees were established as public inquiries to provide advice on a range of technical tax law issues and simplification options. These were:
     - Commonwealth Committee on Taxation (Spooner – 1950) – for a time an ongoing advisory committee
     - Commonwealth Committee on Rates of Depreciation (Hulme – 1954)
     - Commonwealth Committee on Taxation (Ligertwood – 1959)

13   Other members included Sir Peter Lloyd, Professor Ross Parsons, Kenneth Wood and David Bensusan-Butt.

14   Kenneth Asprey, (Chair), Taxation Review Committee, *Full Report*, 31 January 1975, Government Printer of Australia, Canberra, 1975.

15   See Paul Tilley, "1985 reform of the Australian tax system", *Tax and Transfer Policy Institute*, Working Paper 7/2021, April 2021.

16   The Fraser Government did temporarily introduce indexation of the income tax rate scale, in response to the Whitlam Government's Mathews *Committee of Inquiry into Inflation and Taxation* that reported in 1975.

17   See Paul Tilley, "2000: A new tax system", *Tax and Transfer Policy Institute*, Working Paper 14/2021, July 2021.

18   A multi-stage Value Added Tax (VAT).

19   See, Paul Tilley, "Australia's future tax system", *Tax and Transfer Policy Institute*, Working Paper 17/2021, October 2021.

20   Ken Henry (Chair) – other members were: Jeff Harmer (Secretary, Department of Families, Housing, Community Services and Indigenous Affairs), John Piggott (Professor of Economics, UNSW), Heather Ridout (Australian Industry Group) and Greg Smith (former Treasury official).

21   See Paul Tilley, "State and territory tax reviews", *Tax and Transfer Policy Institute*, Working Paper 02/2022, February 2022.

22   David Thodey (Chair), Jane Halton, Bill English, John Anderson, Anne Twomey and John Freebairn, *NSW Review of Federal Financial Relations: Supporting the Road to Recovery*, August 2020.

23   John Nieuwenhuysen, (Chair), *Report of the Committee of Inquiry into Revenue Raising in Victoria*, F D Atkinson Government Printer, Melbourne, May 1983.

24   John Nieuwenhuysen, "Revenue Raising in Victoria", *Australian Journal of Public administration*, Vol XLIV, No 1, March 1985, pp. 29-33.

25   Western Australia Department of Treasury and Finance, *State Tax Review: Final Report*, May 2007.

26   Lara Giddings, Peter Gutwein, Tim Morris and Ruth Forrest, *State Tax Review: Discussion Paper*, December 2010.

27   Ted Quinlan, Megan Smithies and Alan Duncan, *ACT Taxation Review*, May 2012.

28   See Paul Tilley, *Changing Fortunes: A History of the Australian Treasury*, Melbourne University Press, Carlton, 2019, where I track how Treasury was initially an accounting and administrative agency, not developing a substantial

policy function until the post-Second World War period.

29 In *Changing Fortunes: A History of the Australian Treasury*, I trace this change for Treasury – see sections on *'Withering on the Vine'* (pp. 361-2) and *'A Lack of Trust'* (pp. 384-6).

30 List refers to name of inquiry, its chair and date of appointment.

Section 2: Inquiries in action: what they do and how they do it

Introduction:
Understanding inquiry processes

Scott Prasser

As highlighted in the Introduction one of the key features of a public inquiry is just that – they are public. However, that does have different meanings for different types of inquiries which is highlighted in the chapters in this section.

Some, like royal commissions have open hearings where witnesses give 'evidence' and can be cross-examined by inquiry members, or usually by senior counsel assisting and others legal representatives. These are very formal processes. Evidence is given under oath. Witnesses must respond to questions asked. Witnesses can be prosecuted for refusing to answer and for perjury, that is, lying under oath. Such inquiries look like courts of law, but they are not. What may be accepted as 'evidence' by a royal commission, is very different to what is admissible in a court of law where standards of evidence are much higher. In addition, royal commissions can procure files, demand information from government, business, other organisations, and individuals. In some cases, they can even request phone tapping. These processes reflect the topics that many royal commissions are asked to investigate – namely scandals, allegations of corruption and wrong-doing, or those concerning some calamitous event. Such processes are less the case with royal commissions examining some area of policy such as taxation or national insurance as has often been the case (see **Chapters 1-3**). The last full Commonwealth policy royal commission was the 1986 *Royal Commission of Inquiry into Costs and Efficiency of Grain Storage Handling and Transport*, chaired by an economist, rather than a current or former judge. Employing the royal commission instrument is dependent on several factors. It may be, in the case of some scandal, whether coercive powers of investigation are needed. Just as important, it can also be whether a government wants to signal the importance of an issue. The Australian Law Reform Commission recommended retention of the royal commission nomenclature and to reserve the most important inquiry powers for such bodies because it denoted the importance of the issue under review and sent clear signals to the public on this.[1] Predictably, when the public call for an inquiry into some issue, it is inevitably a call for a royal commission because of their perceived prestige, independence, and powers.

Other inquiries like the more common non-statutory policy advisory inquiries, use more informal processes. Most, until recently, had neither coercive investigatory powers nor were able to provide any legal protections to witnesses or inquiry members from defamation actions. Nor did they have powers to compel witnesses to attend, let alone to answer questions. Submissions were voluntarily given affected by the importance of the issue, the prestige of the government or sponsoring minister and perceptions that the inquiry is a serious one and a precursor to possible future government action. While there might be some public meetings these usually take the form of roundtables and workshops where discussion is free-ranging and in a more relaxed atmosphere than at a royal commission. Such processes explain why non-statutory inquiries tend to be more flexible in how they approach their task and are able to proceed more quickly than the traditional statutory based royal commissions.

Despite these differences in the way inquiries operate they do all share common traits. All are publicly announced and promoted. Their members are drawn mostly from outside government. All are expected to release their reports, though ultimately this is a decision for executive government. Delays sometimes occur in this regard. In some jurisdictions, there are now legislative requirements for governments to table inquiry reports in parliament within strict timeframes (see **Chapter 4**). There are few requirements in Australia, or in most other jurisdictions, for governments to have to formally respond to inquiry recommendations or for any time limit to make such a response.[2] The 2009 Commonwealth Australian Law Reform Commission review of the *Royal Commission Act 1902* rejected any suggestions that these requirements be introduced. Again, as with all matters concerning public inquiries from their appointment, membership, form, terms of reference and timeframes, it is the politics of the issue under review that determines how quickly a government responds to recommendations.

Lastly, it must be appreciated, that how an inquiry operates depends very much on its chair and members. Although the Commonwealth *Royal Commission Act 1902* and other State legislation prescribe public inquiry powers and tend to use the language of courts in relation to their processes, it is still dependent upon the inquiry chair to determine how each individual inquiry is conducted. Of course, as mentioned non-statutory inquiries, have more flexibility in how to run their particular investigation compared to royal commissions.

These issues are seen in the five chapters in this section which all cover very different aspects about public inquiries.

Chapter 4 by Anita Mackay brings us up to date with the new Victorian *Inquiries Act 2014* (Vic), which as mentioned earlier, was partly modelled on proposals in the Australian Law Reform Commission report and prompted by suggestions from the 2009 *Victorian Bushfires Royal Commission*. It inaugurated a three-tier inquiry system ranging from the most prestigious (royal commission) to boards of inquiry to formal inquiries. The chapter focuses on the first two forms of inquiry with six major inquiries – five royal commissions and one board of inquiry being assessed. That several of these inquiries had to operate under the pandemic which precluded face-to-face hearings relying instead of technology, was an added interesting dimension of this study. This had some impacts on how some witnesses came to view the whole inquiry process and may have potential long-term implications on how inquiries might operate in the future. Despite the formal powers of the *COVID-19 Hotel Quarantine Inquiry* it did not receive the co-operation from Victorian Government departments it needed to conduct the inquiry effectively. The impact of inquiries now working under the new legislation is thus given attention in this chapter. Overall, Mackay argues the legislation has now been thoroughly "road-tested" given the number of inquiries appointed, the issues covered and the circumstances in which they had to operate.

If Chapter 4 focusses on inquiry processes and important legislative developments, **Chapter 5** by Sue Regan examines how public inquiries interpret and use evidence not just in formulating their reports and recommendations, but in other more complex ways. This chapter gives special consideration to how, in two major Commonwealth social policy advisory inquiries, 'evidence' is identified, accepted, interpreted and interacts with the wider political system of which all inquiries are a part. The chapter concludes that given the increasing contestability of advice and evidence, public inquiries have a very important and continuing role in this increasingly complex world of developing policy. They perform functions not always possible by the more permanent public bureaucracy.

If you have wondered how effectively inquiries, especially of the royal commission type chaired by a current or former member of the judiciary, manage masses of information on complex technical issues, then Margaret Cook's **Chapter 6** on the 2012 *Queensland Flood Commission of Inquiry* (QFCI) makes for essential reading. The chapter examines the many challenges this inquiry encountered to sort out the technical issues involved in dam management and to resolve conflicting claims about responsibility. Certainly, such inquiries are often criticised for being too narrowly focussed, relying too much on public submissions or views expressed by particular witnesses in an adversarial setting where there is also considerable attendant media attention and hype. Cook argues that the QFCI came to the wrong conclusions and thus represented a "missed opportunity" to tackle the more important, longer term policy issues that lay at the heart of this particular Queensland disaster.

A very different inquiry, the *Independent Review of the Australian Public Service* (henceforth the Thodey Review) is examined by Paddy Gourley in **Chapter 7.** This was a non-statutory review of the Australian Public Service (APS) launched in 2018 and reported a year later. There have been numerous public inquiries into the Federal and State public services. They became especially prevalent during the 1970s and 1980s. The 1974 Commonwealth *Royal Commission into Australian Government Administration* (Coombs Review) is often seen as the 'gold standard' of these sorts of inquiries given its terms of reference, membership, submissions, research, processes and quality of its final report. With so many previous public service inquiries, Gourley was able to compare the more recent Thodey Review to these and comes to a critical assessment of both its final report, processes and the then Morrison Government's response to its recommendations.

Last in **Chapter 8** Andrea Wallace reviews the New South Wales *Independent Local Government Review Panel* (ILGRP). This was essentially an inquiry into local government amalgamation – a thorny policy and political issue at the best of times. Like so many other State government inquiries into this issue the ILGRP was not supposed to be an inquiry into amalgamation but that is exactly what it turned out to be. The author's conclusion is that, despite all the public consultation, interim reports, and statements to the contrary by the then premier and minister, here is a case where the result was known before the inquiry reported – the local government amalgamation. It was an inquiry appointed for politically expedient purposes of giving the New South Wales Coalition Government what it wanted – the rationale for local government amalgamation. It did little, however, to establish the grounds for amalgamation or even to assuage stakeholders that this was an appropriate decision.

Notes

1   Australian Law Reform Commission, *Making Inquiries – A New Statutory Framework*, Report 111, Commonwealth of Australia, Sydney, 2009, p. 107.

2   The *Commissions of Inquiry (Children in State Care and Children in APY Lands) Act 2004* SA, does require the responsible minister to provide regular reports to parliament in the recommendations of such inquiries.

4

Developments in Victoria since the commencement of the *Inquiries Act 2014*

Anita Mackay

Introduction and overview

When the Premier of Victoria introduced a Bill for a new Inquiries Act in Victoria in 2014, he described it as "Victoria's first dedicated legislation for royal commissions and other ad hoc executive inquiries" as well as the creation of "a flexible and effective modern legislative framework for the establishment and conduct of these inquiries".[1]

The *Inquiries Act 2014* (Vic) ('the Act') commenced in October 2014 and is the most up-to-date legislation governing the conduct of inquiries in Australia.[2] Other jurisdictions have long-standing legislation, with a number of Acts originally passed in the early 1900s eg *Royal Commission Act 1902* (Cth), *Royal Commissions Act 1917* (SA), and *Royal Commissions Act 1923* (NSW).

Since the commencement of the Act there have been four Victorian royal commissions and two boards of inquiry completed, and one further royal commission commenced in May 2021 (the *Yoo-rrook Justice Commission*). This is a significant number of major public inquiries in a seven-year period.

This chapter commences in part 1 with an overview of the Act. In part 2 it provides an overview of the inquiries conducted under its provisions that had been completed by the end of 2021. This is followed in part 3 by an exploration of key developments that are apparent after the first seven years of operation of the Act. The developments fall into three categories that relate to (a) the conduct of hearings (b) evidence gathering and (c) implementation of recommendations.

1. The Victorian legislative framework for inquiries

The Act was introduced in response to a recommendation by the 2009 *Victorian Bushfires Royal Commission* indicating that Victoria required updated inquiries legislation.[3] The Act makes provision for three tiers of inquiry: royal commissions, boards of inquiries and formal reviews. Different tiers of inquiry is what the Australian Law Reform Commission recommended be introduced at the Commonwealth level in 2009[4]; a recommendation that has not been implemented (nor responded) to by any government.[5]

The focus of this chapter is on first two tiers. The legislation provides a great degree of flexibility in the conduct of royal commissions and boards of inquiry. Both are required to operate with procedural fairness and within the confines of the terms of reference (for royal commissions these are contained in *Letters Patent* issued by the Governor (section 5(1) of the Act), and for a board of inquiry, they are contained in an order by the Governor-in-Council (section 53(1) of the Act)), but the Act provides that in both processes the commissioner or board "may inform itself an any matter as it sees fit" (section 14 of the Act for royal commissions and section 61 for boards of inquiries). Boards of inquiry do not have as extensive powers as royal commissions but do still have wide powers.[6]

Additional guidance on the operation of inquiries in Victoria stems from the *Guidelines for Appearing Before and Producing Documents to Victorian Inquiries* that were issue in December 2017.[7] The *Guidelines* give instruction to Victorian government officials when requested to provide documents (Part 3) and/or appear at a hearing (Part 4) of an inquiry being conducted under the Act (or a parliamentary committee inquiry, which is outside the scope of this chapter).

2. Overview of inquiries completed under the legislation

This part provides a brief overview of the four royal commissions and two boards of inquiry completed since the introduction of the Act in chronological order of reporting date.

The Board of Inquiry examination of the Hazelwood Mine Fire (located in the Latrobe valley) that occurred over 45 days in February to March 2014 was conducted in two parts, led by three Board members. The first part was completed prior to the commencement of the Act and reported in September 2014,[8] but when the inquiry was subsequently re-opened on 26 May 2015 the second stage of the inquiry was conducted as a Board of Inquiry under the Act. The second stage was completed on 31 August 2015 by the provision of a 4-volume report to Parliament.[9]

The *Royal Commission into Family Violence* (FVRC) was the first royal commission established under the new Act (*Letters Patent* were issued on 22 February 2015). It had three commissioners and was required to examine wide-ranging matters relating to family violence across Victoria, including: prevention strategies, systemic responses to family violence, better coordination between agencies (government and community) and how to evaluate strategies for stopping family violence.[10] The FVRC reported in March 2016 having heard from 220 witnesses and received over 1,000 submissions.[11]

The *Royal Commission into the Management of Police Informants* (PIRC) was established in December 2018 to be headed by a single commissioner. The focus of the PIRC was the impact on both individual cases and the criminal justice system more broadly of Victoria Police's use of a lawyer as an informant (Ms Nicola Gobbo). When providing a final report to the government in November 2020, Commissioner the Honourable Margaret McMurdo AC, described the work of the Royal Commission "as mammoth in scale and Janus-like in its need to look both the past and to the future",[12] noting that the PIRC had "identified 1,011 individuals with convictions or findings of guilt that may have been affected by the conduct of Ms Gobbo and Victoria Police".[13]

The Board of Inquiry's examination of Hotel Quarantine scandal (*COVID-19 Hotel Quarantine Inquiry*) reported a month later than the PIRC (21 December 2020) but had a much quicker process, having commenced with an Order by the Governor-in-Council issued on 2 July 2020. The inquiry was more contained, with a focus on the hotel quarantine infrastructure established in response to the Covid-19 pandemic. The Board of Inquiry commenced operations on 28-29 March 2020[14] and was led by the Honourable Jennifer Coate AO.

The *Royal Commission into Victoria's Mental Health System* (MHRC) commenced its two-year inquiry in February 2019 under the guidance of four commissioners and reported in February 2021. Significantly, the *Letters Patent* required the establishment of an "expert advisory committee" to the MHRC that included members with "lived experience", therefore the commissioners established an eight-member committee.[15] The report's 65 recommendations were directed at far-reaching reform of the way mental health is dealt with in Victoria, requiring "a complete transformation in the way mental health and wellbeing treatment, care and support will be provided in Victoria".[16]

The most recent royal commission to report – the *Royal Commission into the Casino Operator and Licence* (CORC) – was brief in duration (compared to most royal commissions[17]), having been established by *Letters Patent* in February 2021 and reporting in October 2021 (ie it was completed in 8 months). It was led by a single Commissioner:

The Honourable Ray Finkelstein AO QC. The CORC had much more contained terms of reference than the other royal commissions conducted under the Act. It was focused on the conduct of the casino operator (Crown Melbourne) and whether it should continue to hold a licence to operate.[18] It was conducted against the background of an inquiry into Crown Casino's operations in New South Wales (the Bergin Inquiry that reported in February 2021).[19]

It is immediately apparent from this brief overview that the Act has been relied upon to establish inquiries into diverse subject-matter and of varying durations (ranging from just under six months, to two years). There have also been both types of inquiries identified by Prasser[20]: "inquisitorial/investigatory"[21] and "policy advisory".[22] Four of the inquiries were inquisitorial/investigatory: both board of inquiries (Hazelwood and Quarantine), the PIRC and CORC; and two were policy advisory: the FVRC and MHRC.

3. Key developments

The six inquiries completed under the Act provide a good indication of how the Act works and the flexibility that it provides to those leading royal commissions and boards of inquiry. The rest of the chapter focuses on developments in the three areas of (a) the conduct of hearings (b) evidence gathering and (c) implementation of recommendations, which may be informative to other jurisdictions.

Conduct of hearings

A core feature of public inquiries is that they are provided with public resources to examine issues of importance to the community, therefore they gather information publicly and one of the primary mechanisms of doing so is public hearings. Hearings are an opportunity for the inquiry to gather evidence, establish facts, consider different versions of events and allow for procedural fairness. Public hearings facilitate the overarching aims of public inquiries to consult widely, maintain transparency and achieve an educative function.[23]

A major development in the conduct of hearings in 2020 and 2021 was the need to switch from in-person to virtual hearings due to extended periods of lockdown in Victoria. Virtual hearings were used by three royal commissions and one board of inquiry. The *Covid-19 Hotel Quarantine Inquiry* held all of their hearings virtually and the PIRC and CORC held a mixture of in-person and virtual hearings.

The changes to process necessitated by virtual hearings led those overseeing these three inquiries to issue practice directions about the conduct of virtual hearings: (*Practice Direction No. 4 – Conduct of Evidentiary Public Hearings in a Virtual Environment* (August 2020) (Board of inquiry) (BoIPD); *Practice Direction No 3 – Virtual Commission Hearings* (May 2020) (PIRCPD); and *Practice Direction 6 – Conduct of Public Hearings in a Virtual Environment* (May 2021) (CORCPD), respectively). Royal commissions may issue practice directions pursuant to section 16 of the Act and boards of inquiry pursuant to section 63.

The PIRCPD is the briefest of the three (2 pages compared to 5 pages for the BoIPD and CORCPD), and there is a lot of similarity between the BoIPD and COCRPD. The more detailed practice directions cover matters such as what online platform is being used and how to access the virtual hearing room, who is to be present in the hearing room, addressing the hearing and the correct etiquette when referring to those presiding ('the Board' and 'the Commissioner')[24] respectively and other matters of etiquette such as that Counsel is not required to wear robes. The two more detailed practice directions are likely to be a useful precedent should future inquiries in Victoria or elsewhere need to conduct virtual hearings.

The MHRC held some meetings online, but these were not 'hearings' as such and no practice direction was issued. The commissioners reported that there was not enough time to change the format of the final round of hearings scheduled for late April-2020 (ie early in the pandemic) and still meet their reporting deadline (October 2020[25]), but some other information gathering activities were held online, such as meetings and focus groups.[26] Those who were going to participate in focus groups relating to their lived experiences were instead "invited to share their personal story with the Commission via a one-on-one phone call with a Commission staff member, or via email or mail".[27]

The reports of the inquiries that held virtual hearings or other forms of online consultations did not make many observations on how this impacted the inquiry overall, with the CORC making no observations on this topic. The MHRC made some positive observations, including:

> … witnesses and Commissioners shared parts of their lives, meeting from their homes, which brought a personal flavour to the conversations. There were pictures hanging on walls, shelves of books and boardgames, and the sights and sounds of daily life continuing: children and pets in the background, ringing doorbells and cats walking in front of the camera.[28]

The report also provided some quotes from participants indicating they had had a positive experience, such as: "I actually preferred to be in my own home. It helped me feel that the power was more equal. And it was surprisingly comforting to have Angus [the cat] there with me".[29]

The *Covid-19 Hotel Quarantine Inquiry* observed that virtual hearings had allowed for increased access to public hearings that transcended national borders. The inquiry held 27 days of virtual hearings during which 63 witnesses appeared and the report notes that:

> … [t]he Inquiry had viewers from all over the world including Hong Kong, Canada, Malaysia and the Netherlands. Approximately 300,000 unique viewers tuned in to the hearings, via the live link on the Inquiry's website, over the course of all 27 hearing days.[30]

However, there are some potentially problematic aspects to the way virtual hearings were envisaged in terms of accessibility. The detailed practice directions on virtual hearings contained the following recommendations for participants (which includes witnesses required to give evidence) about the equipment they would need[31]:

> … a computer or tablet no smaller than an iPad (9.7"). Smartphones should not be used by Participants who will be addressing the Commission during the public hearings; ensure that they access the Virtual Hearing Room from a location that has a reasonable internet speed;

> wear a headset when attending the Virtual Hearing Room to improve audio quality and reduce any audio feedback (noting that mobile phone in-ear headphones do not generally provide reliable audio).[32]

Both inquiries only had an email address for participants experiencing technical difficulties,[33] which would not be of any use to a person whose internet access failed.

It may be the case that in practice both inquiries made provision for witnesses who could not meet these technical requirements, but the practice directions at least *on paper* demonstrate a lack of appreciation of unequal access to technology and "a potential problem of digital exclusion", which is a concern that has been raised about virtual court hearings.[34] They also overlook the challenges faced by people from disadvantaged groups in giving evidence in a virtual hearing environment; such as people who may require assistance communicating eg by an interpreter (again, a matter than has been raised in relation to virtual court hearings).[35]

Another observation about virtual court hearings that may well apply in virtual inquiry hearings is that there may be "a feeling of distance between participants" and those overseeing the proceedings (judge/commissioner/board member).[36] This may limit an inquiry's ability to provide a transitional space, or to achieve restorative justice; both of which have been argued to be possible with inquiries with in-person hearings (the *Royal Commission into Institutional Responses to Child Sexual Abuse* and the *Royal Commission into the Protection and Detention of Children in the Northern Territory*, respectively).[37]

Like many urgent changes necessitated by the pandemic, virtual inquiry hearings are a topic that requires further critical reflection before incorporation into standard practice. The value of virtual hearings to participants would be best assessed by qualitative research on their experiences, which should feed into the process of critical reflection.

Evidence gathering

Public inquiries are often responsible for investigating events that have occurred (eg natural disasters), establishing facts, analysing systemic problems and, in some cases, apportioning blame.[38] It is inherent in this truth-finding function of inquiries that a large volume of evidence will be gathered, with the type of evidence varying according to the subject-matter and terms of reference. For example, the FVRC received approximately 1,000 written submissions, held 25 days of public hearings during which 220 witnesses appeared, and also involved roundtables with experts and 44 community consultations around Victoria.[39]

The focus of this discussion will be on documentary evidence gathering. This is an endeavour places significant pressure on both the agencies providing the documents (particularly when timeframes are short) and the inquiry staff who need to sift through the documents and decide how they will inform witness examination during hearings, and other aspects of the inquiry and royal commission's operations.

There have been two inquiries under the Act where obtaining the necessary documents had a significant impact on the process, which reveal some challenges relating to the intersection between the Act and other Victorian legislation and guidelines. These are the PIRC and the *COVID-19 Hotel Quarantine Inquiry*.

The PIRC required significant numbers of documents from Victoria Police, given they were investigating the impact of a lawyer being engaged as a police informer over a long period of time. Of the 155,000 documents obtained by the PIRC, 84,000 documents were produced by Victoria Police (totalling over 740,000 pages).[40] The PIRC summarised the challenges associated with getting documents from Victoria Police as falling into the following categories:

- incorrect classification (not in accordance with the PIRC's document management protocol);
- delays;
- lost records;
- non-compliance with notices to produce;[41] and,
- claims of public interest immunity (PII).[42]

In relation to PII, the final report explained:

> the process for resolving PII claims hampered its ability to progress the inquiry in an effective, timely and transparent manner. It delayed the publication of hearing transcripts and exhibits on the Commission's website. It also prevented the Commission from promptly providing documents to potentially affected persons prior to Victoria Police conducting a review and redacting any material over which it claimed PII. At the time of finalising this report, the Commission was unable to assess and resolve many of Victoria Police's PII claims.[43]

The final report indicated that the protocol they developed was not sufficient for managing PII claims, indicating that "legislative guidance" is required,[44] and this led the PIRC to recommend an amendment to the Act to be made within 18 months to:

> a. remove the ability for a person to refuse to comply with a notice to give information to a royal commission on the basis that the

information is the subject of public interest immunity

b. insert a provision to make clear that it is not a reasonable excuse for a person to refuse or fail to comply with a requirement to give information (including answering a question) or produce a document or other thing to a royal commission on the basis that the information, document or other thing is the subject of public interest immunity

c. specify that any such information or document or other thing does not cease to be the subject of public interest immunity only because it is given or produced to a royal commission in accordance with a requirement under the Act.[45]

The Victorian Government has committed to the implementation of the 54 recommendations made by the PIRC directed to them,[46] and the most recent implementation progress report outlines (in response to this specific recommendation) that "[c]onsultation across government is underway and work is on track to introduce into Parliament amendments to the *Inquiries Act* by 31 May 2022, meeting the Commission's recommended timeframe".[47]

The *COVID-19 Hotel Quarantine Inquiry* was conducted in a restricted timeframe (less than 6 months from establishment to final reporting). This meant that delays in provision of documents by government agencies were particularly detrimental. The Board was in a situation where after all evidence had been collected, late provision of 494 documents by the Department of Health and Human Services (DHHS) and other agencies led to the need for further hearings and written submissions.[48]

The Board's Final Report goes into detail about the late provision of one document in particular that contradicted the evidence provided in a public hearing by the Chief Health Officer (Professor Sutton) in relation to a matter that was crucial to the Board's inquiry.[49] The document in question was an email chain informing Professor Sutton that private security was involved in hotel quarantine at a particular point in time, whereas in his evidence Professor Sutton indicated that his understanding was that private security was engaged later.[50] This point went directly to the Terms of Reference of the inquiry paragraph (2) "[c]ommunications between Victorian government agencies, hotel operators and Private Service Providers relating to COVID-19 Quarantine Containment".[51]

A particularly contentious point was that the Board's letter requesting documents from DHHS dated 19 July 2020 referred to "[t]he obligation on DHHS will therefore be akin to a party's discovery obligations in civil litigation as informed by s 26 of the *Civil Procedure Act 2010* (Vic)".[52] Section 26 of the *Civil Procedure Act* (Vic) refers to the provision of documents "which the person considers, or ought reasonably consider, are critical to the resolution of the dispute" (paragraph 26(1)(b)). DHHS defended their provision of documents on the basis that they only needed to provide "critical documents", which is 'not the same as "relevance"'.[53]

It is surprising that the Board's letter referred to this section that applies to litigation, given that the Board had a fact-finding function, rather than a dispute resolution function. This is especially the case given that the Board's terms of referencing indicate "It is anticipated that in conducting your inquiry, you will […] b. adopt informal and flexible procedures to ascertain the relevant facts as directly and effectively as possible". The reference to the *Civil Procedure Act* arguably increased the formality of the document gathering process.

As noted in Part 1, the Victorian Government issued *Guidelines* for production of documents by Victorian public servants to inquiries in December 2017. Despite the fact that two of the inquiries conducted under the Act had significant problems with the provision of documents to them by government agencies, neither report refers to lack of compliance with these *Guidelines* (or indeed makes any reference to the *Guidelines* at all).

Part of the reason the 2017 *Guidelines* were developed was in response to a Victorian parliamentary committee inquiry that had significant problems accessing documents (2015-16 Environment, Natural Resources and Regional Development Committee inquiry into the Country Fire Authority (CFA) Training College at Fiskville). The parliamentary committee that conducted that inquiry recommended that the 2002 *Guidelines* be updated.[54] The committee also recommended that the *Model Litigant Guidelines* that apply to government agencies involved in litigation be extended to government agencies and their legal representatives engaging with inquiries.[55] The Victorian Government rejected this latter recommendation.[56]

It is worth noting, therefore, that Counsel Assisting the *COVID-19 Hotel Quarantine Inquiry* submitted that the DHHS and its lawyers conduct had "fallen short of the standards set by the Model Litigant Guidelines".[57] The Board did not make such a finding because "in order to make such a serious finding, there would need to be a more detailed set of specific allegations as to why that finding should be reached and a more thorough exploration of those issues".[58] Therefore, the Board evidently did not agree with the government's assessment that the *Model Litigant Guidelines* did not apply in the inquiry context, and it is open to future boards and royal commissions to make such a finding.

The Act provides a high degree of flexibility for commissioners and boards to tailor evidence-gathering to the task at hand. However, practical application of the Act has revealed a lack of guidance surrounding claims of PII. This lack of guidance may be addressed by the implementation of the PIRC's recommendation in mid-2022. While it remains to be seen whether the Victorian Government will adopt the PIRC's wording when they amend the Act, legislative amendment will be an improvement on the current non-binding guidance contained in protocols issued by royal commissions and the Victorian Government's *Guidelines*.

Implementation of recommendations

One of the main measures of an inquiry's 'success' and effectiveness – particularly in the eyes of the public – is whether the recommendations are implemented. As Prasser highlights, "[s]uccessful implementation of recommendations is closely tied to an assessment that an inquiry was appointed for legitimate reasons to tackle an issue, while non-implementation is synonymous with an inquiry being established for politically expedient reasons of delay, obfuscation and inaction".[59]

A notable trend in completed inquiries under the Act is that the Victorian Government has a tendency to announce that they will implement all the recommendations made by such inquiries. This goes against the broader trend with inquiries in Australia, which are often criticised as a 'waste of time and resources' due to lack of implementation of recommendations, with this criticism coming "not just from jaded media commentators, but also even by some chairs of major public inquiries and interest groups frustrated with the lack of progress on an issue for which a public inquiry may have propounded some specific recommendations".[60] This criticism is sometimes based on a misapprehension that the inquiry has control over the implementation of the recommendations they make; whereas in fact the types of inquiries being analysed in this chapter cease to exist after the deliver a report to the government and their role is purely advisory.[61]

In Victoria such announcements are sometimes when the inquiry report is tabled in Parliament (the Act requires tabling to be within 30 days of receipt of the report (section 37 for royal commissions and section 77 for boards of inquiry), but there has also been one instance where the government has announced its intention at the time the inquiry is established, and another where the announcement was made shortly prior to the report being released.

The FVRC is an example of the Victorian Government announcing recommendations will be accepted at the time the royal commission was established.[62] The government announced that all recommendations of the MHRC would be implemented two weeks prior to the release of the report, with the Premier's media release stating: "The Andrews Labor Government will deliver on every single recommendation from the final report' and that $868.6 million would be allocated to implementation".[63] The CORC is an example of a royal commission where the announcement was made at the time the report was tabled in parliament.[64]

It is difficult to fathom how a government can commit to recommendations that have not yet been made, or that they have not had time to review closely. It places significant faith in the inquiry to make workable recommendations. In reality, as Prasser notes, inquiries "may not have got their assessment right, or their recommendations could be too costly, prescriptive, and thus non-implementable".[65] Therefore, committing upfront to implementation of recommendations may put elected government representatives and their departments, which are ultimately responsible for implementation once recommendations have been made, in an extremely difficult position by subverting their responsibility to make a broad assessment of "the wider public interest".[66]

A second notable feature of implementation of inquiry recommendations in Victoria is the use of a formal mechanism for monitoring implementation of recommendations. This was first implemented in response to a recommendation by the Bushfires Royal Commission (conducted prior to the commencement of the Act).

Initially the implementation of the recommendations contained in the two reports of the *Hazelwood Board of Inquiry* was being jointly monitored by the Inspector-General for Emergency Management ('IGEM') and the *Hazelwood Mine Fire Inquiry Implementation Monitor* (from October 2014 – January 2016) but from 1 February 2016 monitoring became the sole responsibility of the IGEM.[67] There have been some detailed implementation reports by IGEM. For example, the 2017 report was 160-pages long.[68]

An implementation monitor was also used for the FVRC[69], but a particularly notable feature of implementation of recommendations by the FVRC is that an entire department has been created to implement its recommendations: Family Violence Victoria.[70]

An individual is in charge of monitoring the implementation of the PIRC recommendations (Sir David Carruthers), with the government's *Response and Implementation Plan* detailing that he is charged with "oversee[ing] the implementation of recommendations and ensur[ing] accountability".[71] Specific legislation was passed that sets out the functions, powers and reporting requirements of the Implementation Monitor: *Police Informants Royal Commission Implementation Monitor Act 2021.* This includes requirements to prepare annual implementation reports that the Attorney-General is required to table in Parliament (see Part 3). It is envisaged that the monitor will be in place for at least 5 years, given that the legislation is to be reviewed 5 years after commencement (s 29).

The Victorian Government may be commended for its commitment to overcoming the perception that inquiries are often not good 'value' because of failure to implement recommendations. The formal infrastructure for monitoring implementation of recommendation is also praiseworthy because it puts in place an accountability mechanism and lack of progress towards implementation of recommendations (where relevant) will be highlighted, or in relevant cases justified. However, it would be advisable for time to be taken to review the details of the recommendations – particularly when they number in the hundreds – before publicly committing to implementation.

Conclusions

The up-to-date dedicated inquiries legislation in Victoria has certainly been put to the test by the six public inquiries completed in the first seven years of operation of the Act. It is not only the number of inquiries, but the diversity of both subject-matter and processes adopted that reveal the flexibility of the Act; with subject-matter ranging from family violence, mental health and the operation of a casino.

The flexibility of processes is shown in particular by those overseeing inquiries adapting to lockdowns by holding virtual hearings and consultations. Some areas for improvement have been identified, specifically in relation to the guidance provided by the Act surrounding gathering documentary evidence.

The Victorian Government has displayed a commitment to both implementing recommendations and monitoring their implementation on a long-term basis. The appointment of specific monitors, establishment of an entire department dedicated to implementation and enactment of specific legislation relating to monitoring implementation, all reduce the chances of public perception that inquiries are a 'waste of time and resources' and improve transparency in this area.

The developments in Victoria offer insights for other jurisdictions – particularly any that plan to modernise their legislation. The Act has been road-tested across a range of inquiries and has proven instrumental in the direction taken by inquiries in Victoria. The completed inquiries also demonstrate that the tiers of inquiry recommended by the Australian Law Reform Commission in 2009 work well. This is the model adopted in South Australia's draft *Inquiries Bill* (released for consultation in February 2021, but not yet passed).[72]

Public inquiries mentioned in this chapter[73]

Commonwealth inquiries

Royal Commission into Institutional Responses to Child Sexual Abuse (McClellan, 2013)

Royal Commission into the Protection and Detention of Children in the Northern Territory (White and Gooda, 2016)[74]

State inquiries

2009 Victorian Bushfires Royal Commission (Teague, 2009)

Hazelwood Mine Fire Inquiry (Teague, 2014)

Hazelwood Mine Fire Inquiry Report 2015/2016, (Report, August 2015)

Royal Commission into Family Violence (Neave, 2015)

Royal Commission into the Management of Police Informants (McMurdo, 2018)

Royal Commission into Victoria's Mental Health System (Armytage, 2019)

COVID-19 Hotel Quarantine Inquiry (Coate, 2020)

Royal Commission into the Casino Operator and Licence (Finkelstein, 2021)

You-rrook Jutice Commission (Bourke, 2021)

Notes

1   Denis Napthine, Premier, *Victorian Parliamentary Debates, Legislative Assembly*, 21 August 2014, p. 2923.

2   South Australia released a draft Inquiries Bill for consultation in early 2021 following a review of their inquiries Act, but this has not been passed (Amanda Vanstone, *Review of the Royal Commissions Act 1917 (SA): Report to the Attorney-General*, 2020.

3   Bernard Teague, (Chair), Victorian Bushfires Royal Commission, *Final Report*, Government Printer, Melbourne, July 2010, Recommendation 67. This rec-ommendation was supported by the first part of the *Hazelwood Mine Fire Board of Inquiry* that reported in September 2014 (Board of Inquiry, *Hazelwood Mine Fire Inquiry*, Report, 2014, Vol 1, p. 50); the second part of that inquiry was conducted after the passage of the Act and reported in August 2015.

4   Australian Law Reform Commission, *Making Inquiries: A New Statutory Frame-work*, Report No 111, Commonwealth of Australia, Sydney, 2009, Recommen-dation 5-1.

5   Scott Prasser, *Royal Commissions and Public Inquiries in Australia*, 2nd ed, Lexis-Nexis, Chatswood, 2021, p. 278.

6   For a comparison see, Anita Mackay and Jacob McCahon, "Comparing Com-missions, Inquests and Inquiries: Lessons from Processes Concerning Family Violence and Child Protection Victoria", *Monash University Law Review*, Vol 45, No 3, 2019, pp. 538-43.

7   The 2002 guidelines that preceded these were predominantly concerned with

parliamentary committee inquiries and only contained a brief reference to royal commissions at the end (see Department of Premier and Cabinet, *Guidelines for Appearing Before State Parliamentary Committees*, Victorian Government, October 2002, pp. 23-5), therefore detailed guidance for royal commissions is new from 2017.

8   Bernard Teague (Chair), Hazelwood Mine Fire Inquiry, *Report*, Victorian Government Printer, Melbourne, 2014.

9   *Hazelwood Mine Fire Inquiry Report*, 2015/2016, (Report 31 August, 2015).

10 Marcia Neave, (Chair), Royal Commission into Family Violence, *Report Vol 1*, Victorian Government Printer, Melbourne, March 2016, p. 1.

11 Anita Mackay and Jacob McCahon, "Comparing Commissions, Inquests and Inquiries: Lessons from Processes Concerning Family Violence and Child Protection Victoria", *Monash University Law Review*, Vol 45, No 3, 2019, p. 570.

12 Margaret McMurdo, (Chair), Royal Commission into the Management of Police Informants, *Final Report, Vol 1*, Victorian Government Printer, Melbourne, November 2020, p. 6.

13 Ibid., p. 7.

14 Jennifer Coate, (Chair), COVID-19 Hotel Quarantine Inquiry (Hotel Quarantine Inquiry), *Final Report, Vol I*, December 2020, p. 65; see also Ch 3.

15 Penny Armytage, (Chair), Royal Commission into Victoria's Mental Health System, (MHRC), *Final Report, Vol 5*, Victorian Government Printer, Melbourne, February 2021, pp. 326, 382, 407.

16 Ibid., p. 6.

17 The other Victorian royal commissions conducted since the Act commenced have ranged from 13 months to 2 years in duration.

18 Ray Finkelstein, (Chair), Royal Commission into the Casino Operator and Licence, (CORC), *Final Report, Vol 1*, Victorian Government Printer, Melbourne, 2021, p. 2.

19 Ibid., Appendix A, pp. 98-9.

20 Prasser, *Royal Commissions and Public Inquiries in Australia*, pp. 25-35.

21 That have the role of "investigating allegations or checking some suspected impropriety or maladministration of individuals and organisations in both government and the private sector. They may also be appointed to find the cause of a particular catastrophic event" (Ibid., p. 27).

22 These "seek to provide advice to government on a range of issues. They are not concerned with investigating allegations, improprieties or the causes of some disaster; instead, their aim is to inform, summarise and make suggestions to government on the possible solution to a particular policy problem" (Ibid., p. 33).

23 Scott Prasser and Helen Tracey, "What inquiries do and how they do it", in Scott Prasser and Helen Tracey, (eds), *Royal Commissions and Public Inquiries. Practice and Potential*, Connor Court Publishing, Ballarat, 2014, pp. 134-135.

24 See, *COVID-19 Hotel Quarantine Inquiry*, 'Practice Direction No. 4 – Conduct of Evidentiary Public Hearings in a Virtual Environment (August 2020)" para [23] and CORC, "Practice Direction 6 – Conduct of Public Hearings in a Virtual Environment (May 2021)" para [23].

25 The reporting date was changed to February 2021 by *Letters Patent* issued on 26 May 2020.

26 MHRC, (Final Report, Vol 5, February 2021) pp. 356-57.

27 Ibid., p. 357.

28 Ibid., p. 359.

29 Ibid.

30 COVID-19 Hotel Quarantine Inquiry, *Final Report, Vol II*, December 2020, p. 121.

31 COVID-19 Hotel Quarantine Inquiry, 'Practice Direction No. 4 – Conduct of Evidentiary Public Hearings in a Virtual Environment (August 2020)" para [6]; CORC, "Practice Direction 6 – Conduct of Public Hearings in a Virtual Environment (May 2021)" para [5].

32 COVID-19 Hotel Quarantine Inquiry, 'Practice Direction No. 4 – Conduct of Evidentiary Public Hearings in a Virtual Environment (August 2020)" para [9]; CORC, "Practice Direction 6 – Conduct of Public Hearings in a Virtual Environment (May 2021)" para [8].

33 COVID-19 Hotel Quarantine Inquiry, 'Practice Direction No. 4 – Conduct of Evidentiary Public Hearings in a Virtual Environment (August 2020)" para [29]; CORC, "Practice Direction 6 – Conduct of Public Hearings in a Virtual Environment (May 2021)" para [29].

34 Joe McIntyre, Anna Olijnyk and Kieran Pender, "Civil Courts and Covid-19: Challenges and Opportunities in Australia", *Alternative Law Journal*, Vol 45, No 3, September 2020, pp. 1-7.

35 Michael Legg and Anthony Song, "The Courts, The Remote Hearing and the Pandemic: From Action to Reflection," *UNSW Law Journal*, Vol 44, No 1, 2021, pp. 126-66.

36 McIntyre, Olijnyk and Pender, "Civil Courts and Covid-19: Challenges and Opportunities in Australia," p. 5.

37 See further, Michael Salter, "The transitional space of public inquiries: The case of the Australian Royal Commission into Institutional Responses to Child Sexual Abuse," *Australian and New Zealand Journal of Criminology*, Vol 5, No 2, 2020, pp. 213-30; Taylah Cramp and Anita Mackay, "Protecting Victims and Vulnerable Witnesses Participating in Royal Commissions: Lessons from the 2016–2017 Royal Commission into the Protection and Detention of Children in the Northern Territory", *Journal of Judicial Administration*, Vol 29, October 2019, p. 3.

38 Scott Prasser, "Royal Commissions in Australia: When Should Governments Appoint Them?", *Australian Journal of Public Administration*, Vol 65, No 3, September 2006, p.41.

39 Mackay and McCahon, "Comparing Commissions, Inquests and Inquiries", pp. 570-71.

40 PIRC, *Final Report, Vol IV*, November 2020, p. 136.

41 Ibid., p. 136; For more detail see pp. 136-38.

42 Ibid., p. 140.

43 Ibid.

44 Presumably the PIRC considered that the guidance contained in Part 3.3 and Appendix B of the Department of Premier and Cabinet's *Guidelines for Appearing Before and Producing Documents to Victorian Inquiries* (2017) were also insufficient, but this is an inference because the report does not refer to these *Guidelines*.

45   PIRC, *Final Report, Vol IV*, November 2020, Recommendation 91, p. 141.

46   Royal Commission into the Management of Police Informants – Victorian Government Response and annual reporting", (Web Page, 7 December 2021) <https://www.vic.gov.au/royal-commission-management-police-informants-victorian-government-response-and-implementation-plan>.

47   Royal Commission into the Management of Police Informants, *Annual Progress Report, 2020-21*, 30 November 2021, p. 18.

48   COVID-19 Hotel Quarantine Inquiry, *Final Report*, Vol II, 2020, pp. 124-25.

49   Ibid., pp. 125-7.

50   Ibid., p. 125.

51   Covid-19 Hotel Quarantine Inquiry, *Final Report*, Vol I, 2020, p. 52.

52   COVID-19 Hotel Quarantine Inquiry, (Further Submission 03- Department of Health and Human Services), 17 November 2020, para [11].

53   Ibid., para [12].

54   Environment, Natural Resources and Regional Development Committee, *Inquiry into the CFA Training College at Fiskville*, Final Report, May, 2016, Recommendation 3, p. 57.

55   Ibid., Recommendation 2, p. 56.

56   Victorian Government, *Victorian Government's Response to the Environment, Natural Resources and Regional Development Committee's Inquiry into the CFA Training College at Fiskville*, (24 November, 2016), p. 4; see further Anita Mackay and John Aliferis, "A Watershed in Committee Evidence Gathering: Victorian Parliament's Inquiry into the CFA Training College at Fiskville," *Australasian Parliamentary Review*, Vol 33, No 2, 2018.

57   Hotel Quarantine Inquiry, *Final Report*, vol II, December 2020) p. 127.

58   Ibid.

59   Prasser, *Royal Commissions and Public Inquiries in Australia*, p.185.

60   Ibid, pp. 4-5; see also pp. 187-91.

61   Ibid, p. 17.

62   Daniel Andrews, Premier of Victoria, "Premier Announces Royal Commission into Family Violence," Media Release, Victorian Government, 23 December 2014.

63   Premier of Victoria, *Date Set For Mental Health Royal Commission Final Report*, (Web Page, 18 February 2021), <https://www.premier.vic.gov.au/date-set-mental-health-royal-commission-final-report>.

64   Premier of Victoria, *Royal Commission: Sweeping Reforms Needed for Crown*, (Web Page, 26 October, 2021), <https://www.premier.vic.gov.au/royal-commission-sweeping-reforms-needed-crown>.

65   Prasser, *Royal Commissions and Public Inquiries in Australia*, p. 102.

66   Ibid., p. 198.

67   Inspector-General for Emergency Management, *Hazelwood Mine Fire Inquiry: Implementation of recommendations and affirmations*, (Annual Report, 2019) p. 14.

68   Inspector-General for Emergency Management, *Hazelwood Mine Fire Inquiry: Implementation of recommendations and affirmations*, (Annual Report, 2017).

69   Victorian Government, "The Family Violence Reform Implementation Monitor", (Web Page, 16 December, 2021) <https://www.fvrim.vic.gov.au/>.

70   Mackay and McCahon, "Comparing Commissions, Inquests and Inquiries", p. 573.

71   Victorian Government, "Royal Commission into the Management of Police Informants – Victorian Government Response and annual reporting", (Web Page, 7 December 2021) <https://www.vic.gov.au/royal-commission-management-police-informants-victorian-government-response-and-implementation-plan>.

72   Attorney-General for South Australia Media Release "Consultation Begins on Royal Commission Reforms", (Web Page, 12 February 2021) https://www.vickiechapman.com.au/consultation_begins_on_royal_commission_reforms

73   List refers to name of inquiry, its chair and date of appointment.

74   This royal commission was established jointly between the Commonwealth and Northern Territory governments.

5

The multiple uses of evidence in public inquiries

Sue Regan

Introduction

It is well known that public inquiries can involve extensive evidence-gathering processes.[1] However, less well understood is how evidence is interpreted and used in public inquiries. Indeed, much is assumed about how evidence is used, and these (often implicit) assumptions underpin conventional characterisations of public inquiries. So, portrayals of public inquiries as providing 'impartial advice'[2] suggest evidence is being used instrumentally to develop findings and recommendations. On the other hand, depictions of public inquiries as 'political puppets'[3] suggest that the use of evidence is largely symbolic and being employed selectively to support a predetermined policy position. These characterisations do little to shed light on the potential evidentiary complexity of public inquiries.

This chapter digs deeper into the role of evidence in public inquiries and explores the different ways in which evidence can be used. The analysis is based largely on empirical research into two Australian social policy inquiries. This research did not take a bird's eye view, but instead drew on how actors actively involved in each inquiry described using evidence in the inquiry process. In addition, in this chapter, references are made to other contemporary public inquiries that the author has been engaged with as a policy practitioner.[4] The chapter draws on the public inquiry literature alongside policy studies scholarship that is concerned with the relationship between evidence and public policy. The central question being explored is: how is evidence used during public inquiries and why is this important?

The 'evidence-based policy' movement has evolved over time with many scholars and practitioners now associating with 'evidence-*informed* policy' which claims a less deterministic role for evidence in policymaking. An evidence-informed policy approach recognises the complex social and political processes at play and that policy emerges from an interplay between evidence, political values, argument, norms and power.[5] In contemporary evidence-informed policy literature[6], the term 'evidence' has been conceptualised as a label that becomes attached to certain types of knowledge and ways of knowing. What gets labelled evidence in public inquiries matters because it reflects the information and knowledge that is being valued. How this evidence is then used has implications for the efficacy and legitimacy of a public inquiry and for the role that it might be playing in the wider policy ecosystem. Focusing attention on the use of evidence in public inquiries helps explain why they remain important, and perhaps even indispensable, vehicles in modern democracies.

It should be noted that this chapter conceptualises public inquiries not by central reference to the 'advisory body' (for example, the commissioners or reference group) but rather as a 'process of inquiry' which involves a range of activities occurring over time. Emphasising the inquiry process provides insight into the dynamism of public inquiries and how they interrelate with the wider ongoing policy process. It also brings into view a wider range of actors than is usually considered. So, in addition to the members of the advisory bodies, this chapter considers the perspectives of members of the official secretariat, other officials working within government (who were involved in the inquiry or subsequent decision making), and external actors who were actively engaged in the inquiry. This wider group of actors are particularly important in the context of this chapter because they undertake important evidence-related inquiry work.

Overall, this chapter reveals that evidence is used by these inquiry actors in a variety of ways as a public inquiry progresses. Drawing on empirical research, it shows how evidence was used to inform policy advice and inquiry recommendations, but also in other ways: to frame the policy problem; to promote public debate and build legitimacy; to bridge stakeholder interests; to publicly substantiate findings; and to support the subsequent policy reform and implementation process. Those involved in the inquiry process (referred to in this chapter as policy 'actors') seemed to make sense of using evidence in the context of the wider roles that the inquiry was playing in the policy process, thus highlighting the political nature of the relationship between evidence, its use, and the wider policy process. The chapter concludes by arguing that one of the most valuable characteristics of public inquiries is their ability to bring in, creatively deploy, and reconcile diverse meanings of evidence. Few policy arrangements have this capability. In the face of growing complexity and plurality of public policy[7], arrangements equipped to navigate diverse evidence – such as public inquiries - are perhaps needed more than ever.

The diversity of public inquiries and implications for evidence

As discussed elsewhere in this book, public inquiries are diverse in several ways, and this has implications for how evidence is understood and used. We know public inquiries have been deployed in relation to a vast range of policy issues and come in many forms: a single commissioner or a diverse multi-person taskforce; a highly formal royal commission with statutory backing and authority or an informal reference group. To make sense of this diversity, various ways of categorising public inquiries have been suggested, for example by their organisational or institutional form or the powers they have at their disposal. One common classification of inquiries is based on their core function[8]: *inquisitorial* inquiries which investigate allegations or catastrophic events, and *policy advisory* inquiries which advise governments in relation to specific policy problems. In Australia, inquisitorial inquiries are mostly set up under statute[9], whereas policy advisory inquiries tend not to have a statutory basis and are established at the discretion of a government minister or prime minister.

As with most classifications, there is no hard and fast line between these two types of inquiry. Inquisitorial inquiries usually provide policy recommendations; and policy advisory inquiries can seek to establish the facts or 'truth' of a particular policy problem. However, the main aim of policy advisory inquiries is to provide advice to government on a particular policy problem and they tend to adopt a more informal style than inquisitorial inquiries. For example, they tend not to engage in formal public hearings nor have legislative power to summon witnesses.[10] The advisory bodies of policy advisory inquiries typically have multiple members and are appointed for their relevant expertise. As such, the advisory bodies usually include people from a wide range of backgrounds including academia, government, interest groups, and private professionals. This contrasts with inquisitorial inquiries which are frequently set up as a single member (the 'commissioner'), who is typically an eminent lawyer, or a small number of commissioners.

The different foci and institutional form of policy advisory and inquisitorial inquiries are likely to have implications for how evidence is understood and used. For example, inquisitorial public inquiries often rely on a legal approach[11] to the production and evaluation of evidence and prize expert submissions. The broader composition of the advisory bodies of policy advisory inquiries and the more informal nature of their evidence gathering processes has implications for what counts as evidence and how it might be used. In this chapter, my empirical research is primarily inquiries which are policy advisory in nature, but references are made to inquisitorial inquiries where evidence is being used along similar lines.

Two examples of Australian policy advisory inquiries

The case-studies explored here are two contemporary Australian public inquiries, policy advisory in character, and from the social policy domain: the *Ministerial Taskforce on Child Support* (2004-05) and the *Reference Group on Welfare Reform* (1999-2000). The inquiries are referred to subsequently as the *Child Support Inquiry* and the *Welfare Reform Inquiry* and are part of a long history of social policy inquiries in Australia.[12] Both cases involved highly complex and contested social policy issues, yet the inquiries were able to reach agreement as to the recommended policy advice and the final reports were widely supported.[13] They took place during the extended prime ministership of John Howard (1996-2007) and his Coalition (Liberal–National) governments. During this time, the social policy agenda was being shaped by conservative norms and values and neo-liberal economic policy dominated. Another significant contextual factor during this period was Prime Minister John Howard's advocacy of a "social coalition" approach to public policy.[14] This involved trying to harness the resources of government, individuals, the business community, and voluntary organisations in tackling policy problems. One manifestation of this was the use of public inquiries by the government, a common occurrence throughout this time.[15]

Some brief background on each inquiry is warranted.

The *Child Support Inquiry* was established by the then Prime Minister, John Howard, and its focus was the Child Support scheme, with a particular emphasis on advising on the Child Support formula. Child Support is the payment that non-resident parents (usually fathers) make following parental separation to the costs of raising their children. The inquiry involved a Taskforce (of people with expertise in social and economic policy, family law, family policy, and research), a Reference Group (of people drawn from advocacy groups and professionals with experience in issues relating parenting after separation, counselling and relationship mediation) and a secretariat (formed in the Department of Family and Community Services, drawing in staff from across the department.) Professor Patrick Parkinson, an academic lawyer at the University of Sydney, chaired the Taskforce and Reference Group with David Stanton AM FASS (a former senior public servant and former Director of the Australian Institute of Family Studies) as deputy chair.

The *Welfare Reform Inquiry* was established by Senator Jocelyn Newman, the Australian Federal Minister for Family and Community Services at the time. The inquiry's purpose was to provide policy advice on income support and associated services that would prevent and reduce 'welfare dependency' among people of working age. The Reference Group was chaired by Patrick McClure, then Chief Executive of Mission Australia, and other members of the group were drawn from academia, the private sector, the voluntary sector and from within government. In addition to the Reference Group, a Welfare Review Team was established within the Australian Department of Family and Community Services, which operated as the inquiry secretariat.

These inquiries are of particular interest from an evidence perspective. It has been suggested[16] that the *Child Support Inquiry* was an exemplar of 'evidence-based policy', with extensive research being undertaken by the Ministerial Taskforce, and with several reports[17] existing of how this evidence had informed the inquiry's recommendations and subsequent policy reform. The *Welfare Reform Inquiry* was a different type of endeavour from an evidence perspective with the main stated purpose[18] being to engage the community in a discussion about the direction of welfare reform, suggesting that inquiry actors might view evidence differently.

The breadth and diversity of 'evidence' itself

Before turning to the focus of this chapter (how evidence gets used in public inquiries), it is important to acknowledge the breadth of knowledge-gathering activities undertaken in these inquiries and the diversity of what actors counted as 'evidence'. In the *Welfare Reform Inquiry*, various consultation exercises to garner public input and research-related activities were undertaken. This included: focus groups with income support recipients; a call for public submissions; a questionnaire; a customised website; stakeholder meetings; and the publication of an interim report to generate further public input. There was little new research undertaken during the inquiry, but actors did refer to: analysing administrative data of trends in welfare receipt; assessing labour market trends; literature reviews of international research and practice; and some high-level modelling of tax/transfer interactions. Regarding the *Child Support Inquiry*, multiple research activities were undertaken, and public input was received from various sources. This included: analysis of administrative data to evaluate the current child support formula; three studies into the "costs of children"; a new survey of community attitudes; a literature review covering international research and practice; and the development of a micro-simulation model. Public submissions from the immediately preceding parliamentary inquiry[19] were available, overseas experts were consulted, and the chair of the Taskforce undertook a visit to the United States (US) to garner knowledge about alternative child support systems. The child support system had been reviewed on many previous occasions[20] and this material was also available to the new inquiry. In summary, both inquiries had access to an extensive range of information and knowledge.

That evidence is drawn from diverse sources is of course not uncommon. Much of the policy studies literature highlights the multidimensionality of knowledge that can become evidence. For example, Brian Head's work[21] proposes 'three lenses' of evidence-based policy and suggests these derive from three bodies of knowledge: political knowhow; scientific and technical analysis; and practical and professional field experience. Similarly, Ray Pawson and colleagues[22], in their work exploring evidence use in social care, theorise five foundations of evidence: organisational knowledge; practitioner knowledge; user knowledge; research knowledge; and policy community knowledge. Indeed, one of the early United Kingdom (UK) Cabinet Office documents[23] promoting evidence-based policy in the late 1990s advocated that evidence should be based on information from several sources, including expert knowledge, research and statistics, stakeholder consultation, and evaluation of previous policies.

A further layer of complexity needs to be highlighted. It cannot be assumed that there is shared understanding of what actors consider to be 'evidence' in a policy process such as public inquiry. As Wesselink and colleagues[24] have shown, evidence is socially constructed by actors engaging in policy work. In the research into the Child Support and Welfare Reform inquiries, actors placed different meanings on 'evidence'. Many actors considered the evidence to be the research gathered or created during the inquiry; others referred to the input from public consultations. Some took a broad and multifaceted view of evidence; others saw evidence in narrow terms and were interested primarily in what they saw as the 'facts'. This full evidentiary complexity should be noted. So, when actors referred to using evidence in different ways in the Child Support and Welfare Reform inquiries, they frequently had different interpretations of 'evidence' and of what knowledge and information was being used.

The multiple uses of evidence in public inquiries

The extent to which evidence is used instrumentally to inform the development of policy advice has received much attention from scholars and practitioners and is the focus of the evidence-based policy movement. However, there has been growing awareness that evidence is used in other ways and these other uses might be important facets of policy processes. Research into the Child Support and Welfare Reform inquiries revealed that evidence was being used in multiple ways and that these 'uses' changed over the course of the inquiry. This research suggests six interrelated uses of evidence:

1) to inform policy design and inquiry recommendations;
2) to frame the policy problem;
3) to promote public debate and build legitimacy;
4) to bridge stakeholder interests;
5) to publicly substantiate findings; and,
6) to support the subsequent policy reform process.

1. *Using evidence to inform policy design and advice*

In both inquiries, evidence was used to inform policy options and ultimately the inquiry's recommendations and policy advice to government. In the *Welfare Reform Inquiry*, many actors referred to evidence which revealed the extent of welfare dependency and how this had turned their attention to designing a system which encouraged active participation. This was then reflected in the core recommendations of the *Welfare Reform Inquiry* for a "Participation Support System".[25] Other actors discussed evidence of how the tax and transfer systems interacted and how this had shaped recommendations for a simplified payment system. In the *Child Support Inquiry*, many actors described how evidence was used in designing the new child support formula and in associated recommendations. The intention to base advice on evidence was explicit in the terms of reference and that this approach had been followed was highlighted throughout the final report.[26] How the evidence informed the Taskforce's advice and subsequent decision-making has been the subject of written commentary by several members of the Taskforce.[27]

Public inquiry reports typically set out how evidence was used to inform recommendations. A recent example in Australia is the *Royal Commission into Aged Care Quality and Safety* established in October 2018, and which reported in March 2021. The Commission undertook extensive evidence-gathering processes, with Volume 5 of the Final

Report setting this out in detail and which referred to submissions, hearings, Community Forums, service provider visits, international research, plus internal and commissioned research. In the Foreword to the Final Report[28], one of the Commissioners, Lynelle Briggs AO highlights explicitly that the recommendations have been informed by the evidence: "In developing these reforms, I have drawn on the evidence, information and research findings available to me…" Interestingly, the Commissioners were not in full agreement over the inquiry conclusions and indeed the Chair, the Hon Gaetano T Pagone QC, reflects on this and refers to differing interpretations of evidence and how "we have differently seen and evaluated the vast amount of material we have considered and the accounts we have heard".[29]

2   *Using evidence to define and frame the problem*

A second way in which evidence can be used in a public inquiry is in defining and framing the problem under scrutiny. In the *Welfare Reform Inquiry*, several actors pointed to evidence that illustrated the extent of 'welfare dependency' and how this had informed the terms of reference of the inquiry. Some government officials discussed how, in the lead-up to the inquiry being established, there was greater awareness within the department of how long some people were staying on welfare payments; this having been revealed through new analytical capability that could track individuals through the income support system. This evidence was cited by the Minister in the speech announcing the inquiry, and which framed the problem as one of 'welfare dependency'. Similarly, in the *Child Support Inquiry*, several actors reported how evidence was used to describe and frame the policy problem. Some actors talked about the problem being technical in nature and emphasised the research data on the 'costs of children'. However, other actors described how the problem was one of 'fairness' and about balancing the interests of mothers and fathers, and they invoked the views of the public and interest groups in discussing this.

A key part of any public inquiry process is an investigation of the policy problem, allegation or event, and evidence plays an important role here. A contemporary example is the Australian *Royal Commission into Violence, Abuse, Neglect and Exploitation of People with Disability* which was established in April 2019. The Commission's terms of reference and its first Progress Report framed the problem as an abuse of the human rights of people with disability. The Commission has centred the voices of people with disability in its work, collecting evidence through a wide range of hearings, forums and opportunities designed to be accessible to the diverse range of people with disability. This evidence has been released and promoted throughout the inquiry, publicly reinforcing the framing of the problem as an ongoing abuse of human rights.

As Mintrom and colleagues[30] have highlighted, policy problems such as aged care or responses to disasters are typically highly complex. So how a problem is framed and the lens through which a royal commission (or other form of public inquiry) portrays the problem are important elements of the process, and evidence plays an important role within this. It should be noted that the process of problem definition and framing is inherently political, given it involves actors contesting different meanings[31], with evidence often sought to justify a particular framing or to validate a set of assumptions.

3   *Using evidence to promote public debate and build legitimacy*

Evidence, alongside preliminary findings, are often made public throughout an inquiry to promote public debate and build legitimacy for the inquiry recommendations. This can be through a variety of means such as issues papers, proactive media commentary, and interim reports. In the *Welfare Reform Inquiry*, members of the official secretariat referred to the evidence set out in the Interim Report and how it served as an important vehicle to generate further public debate and community engagement in the inquiry process. Members of the Reference Group also highlighted the role that the evidence played in enhancing the legitimacy of the inquiry findings and in building public support for the process of welfare reform. Whilst the *Child Support Inquiry* was not a particularly public process (given there was no formal public consultation or interim report), it was still the case that the final report, together with its supporting evidence documentation, was published. This meant the evidence was open to scrutiny following the inquiry and informed the ensuing public debate.

Using evidence to generate public debate and to demonstrate the rigour of an inquiry process is a common inquiry tactic, often enacted through the publication of interim reports. In December 2013, Patrick McClure was asked to lead a further inquiry into Australia's Welfare System.[32] Again, during the inquiry process, an interim report was published containing a preliminary evidence base and seeking public input and feedback. The aforementioned *Disability Royal Commission* has been deploying a similar strategy, with (to date) four progress reports, an interim report and several 'Issues Papers' having been published, all describing the emerging evidence and published to enhance public engagement, build legitimacy, and fulfil a stated commitment to transparency.

4   *Using evidence to bridge stakeholder interests*

A further way evidence can be used in public inquiries is to bridge stakeholder interests. This use of evidence supports an important role of public inquiries as sites to debate, contest, and reconcile diverse interests.[33] For example, in Whitford and Boadle's study[34] of Australia's *Rural Reconstruction Commission* (1943–46), analysis of transcripts of oral evidence and inquiry correspondence revealed the role that the inquiry played in negotiating between different stakeholders and across jurisdictional boundaries throughout the inquiry process. In a similar vein, Degeling and colleagues[35] provide a participant account of the *Drug Evaluation Review* in Australia and highlight the negotiation and bargaining between stakeholders that the inquiry facilitated.

In the *Child Support Inquiry*, many actors referred to the interplay between the Taskforce (policy and technical experts) and the Reference

Group (interest groups and practitioners). Actors recounted how members of the Taskforce met regularly with the Reference Group, and members of the Reference Group recalled being presented with extensive research, data, and modelling during the inquiry. During interviews, several actors referred to the extent of division and acrimony between the two main interest groups (representing mothers and fathers respectively) on the Reference Group. The development of the evidence base, and the engagement of the Reference Group in its consideration, was seen by some actors as a way of bridging the different perspectives through getting all involved. In this sense, evidence was distanced from specific interests, and used as a tool to bridge different points of view. In a similar fashion, actors in the *Welfare Reform Inquiry*, reported using evidence to bridge stakeholder views. Here, the main opposing interest groups were the community welfare sector and the government itself. The government officials pointed to the evidence of 'welfare dependency' being important in discussions with the community members of the Reference Group and the wider community sector. Conversely, actors from the community sector pointed to how they brought in other evidence to illustrate the broader structural nature of the problem and to persuade government officials of the need to look at a wider scope of solutions (for example, beyond 'mutual obligation').

Another contemporary example of an inquiry using evidence to reconcile diverse stakeholder views is the UK *Pensions Commission* established by the Labour Government in 2004. The *Pensions Commission* undertook careful evaluation of the existing pension system. This involved extensive modelling and drawing on the advice of experts, particularly on the macroeconomic implications of continuing with current policy settings. This evidence was published in their first report[36] which painted a stark picture of why reform was needed. This report and its "killer facts"[37] became a key tool in successfully negotiating with the various diverse stakeholders, which included the UK Government (principally the Department of Work and Pensions and the Treasury), the Trades Union Congress and the Confederation of British Industry, as well as the pensions industry bodies, the pensions firms, and UK citizens. The recommendations of the Pensions Commission received broad support and were introduced through the Pensions Acts of 2007 and 2008.

1   *Using evidence to justify findings publicly*

Once an inquiry report is published, evidence is often invoked to justify the findings and recommendations. Public inquiries are perhaps distinct in this regard from ongoing policy processes where evidence used to inform decisions is often not made public. In the *Welfare Reform Inquiry*, actors pointed to how evidence garnered from the public consultations was used throughout the final report in support of the recommendations and the "balanced approach" to welfare reform that was proposed. Other actors referred to the evidence of reforms occurring in other countries, and how this was used to provide backing for the Participation Support System that was advocated by the Reference Group. In the *Child Support Inquiry*, several actors described using the evidence to substantiate the Taskforce's findings and recommendations. Actors reported that the evidence was used in this way during the press conference and other media activities to launch the final report and to brief backbenchers and opposition members of parliament.

Invoking evidence from an inquiry to justify findings and recommendations is common practice. A high profile example in Australia is the *Royal Commission into National Natural Disaster Arrangements* which followed the Black Summer (the extreme 2019-20 Australian bushfire season). The Commission used evidence gathered from over 1700 submissions to justify publicly the need for a "national approach", a clearer role for the Federal Government, greater cooperation and co-ordination, and a set of institutional reforms to support this.[38]

2   *Using evidence to support policy development and implementation*

Finally, evidence is used after a public inquiry has reported and 'wrapped up' to support the process of further policy development and implementation. During this stage, evidence is reused or reframed to support implementation. In relation to the *Welfare Reform Inquiry*, some government officials suggested that the 'McClure Report'[39] became a source of evidence used in brokering agreement across government over what reforms should be implemented. Actors from the *Child Support Inquiry* similarly described how evidence created during the inquiry was used to further develop the reform proposals. A specific example is how the modelling developed by the Taskforce was first used to inform the advice in the inquiry report but then used within government to develop the recommendations further. Actors recounted how the micro-simulation model developed by members of the Taskforce was adapted and subsequently used within government. Furthermore, some actors reported how the final report and supporting evidence was instrumental in the implementation process itself. One government official described the evidence generated during the inquiry and the final report as 'evidence touchstones' in taking the policy reforms forward.

That evidence is used to support subsequent policy development and implementation can be seen in other inquiries. The Australian *Royal Commission into Institutional Responses to Child Sexual Abuse* reported in December 2017 following a four-year investigation and its final report continues to guide ongoing reform. A National Strategy to Prevent and Respond to Child Sexual Abuse[40] was a key recommendation of the Royal Commission. Now published, the National Strategy refers explicitly to the Royal Commission and the evidence collected during 8000 private sessions and more than 1000 written accounts.

The enduring nature of evidence from a public inquiry can be significant. It can be argued that in Australia, the hallmark evidence base for taxation policy reform is still the *Australia's Future Tax*

System Review (aka the Henry Tax Review, after its chair Ken Henry) which was completed over a decade ago. In debates about poverty in Australia, evidence from the *Commission of Inquiry into Poverty in Australia* (aka the Henderson Poverty Inquiry, after its chair Professor Ronald F Henderson) which was established in 1972, fifty years ago, still resonates. That evidence created during public inquiries can be so enduring is a valuable trait, perhaps enhanced by the 'publicness' of public inquiries. It is harder to ignore or forget evidence when it is firmly in the public domain.

Implications for the role of public inquiries

Public inquiries have complex evidentiary traits. The sources of evidence brought into public inquiries are typically diverse ranging from research knowledge to various forms of public input. What is interpreted as evidence by the various actors involved in public inquiries is diverse, with different meanings being placed on evidence, because of individual predilections for particular types of knowledge and reflecting context. Then the primary focus of this chapter has revealed that evidence has diverse uses in a public inquiry: informing the findings and recommendations, but also supporting the public dimensions of the inquiry (promoting public debate, enhancing public legitimacy, justifying publicly why a position was reached) as well as being an evidence touchstone in the often-protracted process of subsequent policy development and implementation. These different uses of evidence should not be seen as necessarily in tension. In his seminal discussion of policy analysis as a process of argumentation, Majone[41] distinguishes between the process of discovery (through which conclusions are reached) and the process of 'justification' (through which conclusions are justified) and he argues that it makes sense and indeed is entirely 'rational' to use different forms of knowledge and argument for these different purposes.

Putting a spotlight on evidence reveals the dynamism of public inquiries and how they evolve and unfold over time. At the beginning of an inquiry, we can see evidence being used to frame the problem under investigation. As the inquiry progresses, evidence is used to promote public debate and enhance the legitimacy of the inquiry process. Throughout, evidence is being used to build understanding, develop options and determine recommendations. Once the final report is published, evidence is used to justify the findings and to support subsequent policy reform. Tracking the use of evidence reveals the unfolding process of an inquiry and how it is interacting with and influencing the wider policy process. Grant Hoole[42] makes a related point in suggesting that "the 'point' of an inquiry is not so much the formulation of concrete policy proposals (at least not exclusively), rather, it is the intrinsic value of the process itself". In her research into public inquiries, Sheriff reflects on their contribution to public policy and similarly argues "…it is not so much *what* policy is formulated, but *how* it is formulated that takes precedence".[43]

How evidence is used in public inquiries also points to how public inquiries are inherently political. A public inquiry process typically involves reconciling diverse evidence, interests and values. How evidence is used to frame a particular problem demonstrates this point well. The framing of the problem during the *Welfare Reform Inquiry* as being largely one of 'welfare dependency' or 'welfare reliance' was not uncontentious nor unanimous. Several actors in the *Welfare Reform Inquiry* were keen to reframe the problem as structural and relating to social exclusion and used evidence to support this view. The chair of the inquiry reported bringing two researchers from Mission Australia into the inquiry to ensure this perspective on the problem was included. Evidence which demonstrated wider structural problems was included in the interim and final reports alongside evidence seeking to demonstrate welfare dependence. As Patrick McClure has discussed[44], he saw his role as being to navigate the political terrain, reconcile "conflicting paradigms" and broker a consensus.

Fundamentally, the rich and dynamic evidentiary characteristics of public inquiries bring great value to the policy process and these qualities would appear rare amongst ongoing institutions or processes of government. Two traits are suggested here as being pivotal to the evidentiary potential of inquiries – their openness and independence. Through their open nature (their 'publicness'), public inquiries enable diverse sources and interpretations of evidence to be brought in, aired and debated. This can enable an inquiry to be a genuinely 'hybrid' form of policy arrangement which brings in both research evidence and public input, and so tempers the rationality of old school 'evidence-based policymaking' but also ensures scientific and research expertise complements participatory approaches. The independent (or quasi-independent) nature of public inquiries allows evidence to be considered one step removed from the heat of everyday politics, although this chapter does reveal that politics (and how this influences the use of evidence) is never far away. However, some independence or 'separation' would seem to allow evidence to be considered and debated at a distance from the ongoing business (and busyness) of government. This combination of 'publicness' and a degree of independence enables public inquiries to bring in diverse sources and meanings of evidence and to use evidence in multiple ways to support the progression of the inquiry.

Conclusions

This chapter reveals a nuanced and dynamic account of the evidentiary practices of public inquiries, which challenges conventional characterisations of public inquiries as either 'political puppets' deploying evidence symbolically or 'impartial advisers' using evidence objectively and unsullied by politics. Instead, the alternative account offered provides insights into the diversity of 'evidence', the multiple ways in which evidence is used, and how public inquiries operate as important settings for evidence deliberation and reconciliation.

With these qualities, the relevance of public inquiries is likely to remain. This might be all the more so given modern processes of public policy are becoming more complex and plural: more complex through increased involvement of market and civil society actors (often working across sectors and jurisdictions[45]) and more plural through enhanced opportunities for public input and political expression.[46] This growing complexity and plurality of public policy continues to broaden ideas about the value of different kinds of 'evidence', policy knowledge, and ways of knowing. These trends have thereby renewed interest in policy arrangements that are equipped to gather and consider diverse forms of evidence in the policy process - such as public inquiries.

Indeed, the need for policy settings equipped to navigate diverse evidence has become arguably more pressing in our so-called 'post-truth' era of politics in which ideology and emotions are considered to take precedence over evidence and reasoned debate. This has prompted much public commentary and academic reflection over the potential devaluing of evidence and expertise in public policy.[47] Yet this chapter has revealed that public inquiries facilitate the inclusion and use of a diversity of evidence and expertise. In this context, public inquiries may be needed more than ever.

Public inquiries mentioned in chapter[48]

Commonwealth inquiries

Commission of Inquiry into Poverty in Australia (Henderson, 1972)
Review of the Future of Drug Evaluation in Australia (Baume, 1991)
Reference Group on Welfare Reform (also called Welfare Reference Group) (McClure, 1999)
Ministerial Taskforce on Child Support (Parkinson, 2004)
Australia's Future Tax System Review (Henry, 2008)
Reference Group on Welfare Reform (Review of Australia's Welfare System) (McClure, 2013)

New directions in royal commissions and public inquiries

Royal Commission into Institutional Responses to Child Sexual Abuse (McClellan, 2013)

Royal Commission into Aged Care Quality and Safety (Briggs and Pagone, 2018)

Royal Commission into National Natural Disaster Arrangements (Binskin, 2020)[49]

International inquiries

The (United Kingdom) Pensions Commission (Turner, 2004)

Notes

1   Scott Prasser, *Royal Commissions and Public Inquiries in Australia*, 2nd ed, Lexis-Nexis, Chatswood, 2021, pp. 141-45.
2   Ibid., pp. 20-1.
3   Martin Bulmer, *The Uses of Social Research: Social Investigation in Public Policy Making*, Allen and Unwin, London, 1982.
4   This includes as Deputy CEO and Policy Director of Volunteering Australia, as a secondee to the Australian Department of Social Services, and as a Civil Servant and Special Adviser at the United Kingdom, Department of Work and Pensions.
5   Giandomenico Majone, *Evidence, Argument, and Persuasion in the Policy Process*, Yale University Press, Yale, 1989.
6   For example, see Annette Boaz, Huw Davies, Alex Fraser, and Sandra Nutley, "What works now? An Introduction," in Annette Boaz, Huw Davies, Annette Fraser and Sandra Nutley, (eds), *What Works Now? Evidence-Informed Policy and Practice*, Policy Press, Bristol, 2019, pp. 1-15.
7   For example, see Ian Bache, Ian Bartle, and Matthew Flinders, "Multi-level governance", in Christopher Ansell and Jacob Torfing, (eds), *Handbook on Theories of Governance*, Edward Elgar Publishing, Cheltenham, 2016, pp. 486-498.
8   Prasser, *Royal Commissions and Public Inquiries in Australia*, pp. 25-27.
9   The *Royal Commission Act 1902* (Cth) or the *Public Service Act 1922* (Cth).
10   Prasser, *Royal Commissions and Public Inquiries in Australia*, pp. 33-4.
11   See Alec Fraser and Huw Davies, "Systematic approaches to generating evidence", in Boaz, Davies, Fraser and Nutley, *What Works Now?* pp. 197-224.
12   Sue Regan, *Australia's Welfare System: A Review of Reviews 1941-2013*, HC Coombs Policy Forum, Crawford School of Public Policy, ANU, Canberra, 2014.
13   Sue Regan and David Stanton, "The Henderson Poverty Inquiry in Context", in Peter Saunders, (ed.), *Revisiting Henderson: Poverty, Social Security and Basic Income*, Melbourne University Press, Carlton, 2019, pp. 47-66.
14   David Hazlehurst, *Networks and policy making: From theory to practice in Australian social policy*, Discussion Paper No 83, Australian National University, Canberra, 2001.
15   Prasser, *Royal Commissions and Public Inquiries in Australia*, pp.66-8.
16   David Stanton, "The Ministerial Taskforce on Child Support", Speech to Institute of Public Administration Australia (ACT Division) Conference on

Public Inquiries and Royal Commissions: Issues and Trends, Canberra, Australia, 22 September 2005.

17 For example, see Anne Harding, and Richard Percival, "Australian child support reforms: A case study of the use of microsimulation modelling in the policy development process", *Australian Journal of Public Administration*, Vol 66, No 4, December 2007, pp. 422-37.

18 Patrick McClure, (Chair), Reference Group on Welfare Reform, *Final Report, Participation support for a more equitable Society*, Department of Family and Community Services, Commonwealth of Australia, Canberra, 2000.

19 House of Representatives Standing Committee on Family and Community Affairs, *Every Picture Tells a Story: Final Report of the Inquiry into Child Custody Arrangements in the Event of Family Separation*, Commonwealth Parliament, Canberra, 2003.

20 Meredith Edwards, "The Child Support Scheme: What innovative collaboration can achieve", in Joannah Luetjens, Michael Mintrom and Paul t'Hart, (eds), *Successful Public Policy. Lessons from Australia and New Zealand*, ANU Press. Canberra, 2019, pp. 139-83.

21 Brian Head, "Three lenses of evidence-based policy", *Australian Journal of Public Administration*, Vol 67, No 1, March 2008, pp. 1-11.

22 Ray Pawson, Annette Boaz, Lesley Grayson, Andrew Long, and Colin Barnes, *Types and quality of knowledge in social care*, Social Care Institute for Excellence, London, 2003.

23 United Kingdom Cabinet Office, *Professional Policy Making for the Twenty First Century*, Cabinet Office, London, 1999.

24 Anna Wesselink, Hal Colebatch, and Warren Pearce, "Evidence and Policy: Discourses, Meanings and Practices", *Policy Sciences*, Vol 47, No 4, 2014, pp. 339-44.

25 McClure, (Chair), Reference Group on Welfare Reform, *Final Report*.

26 Patrick Parkinson, (Chair), Ministerial Taskforce on Child Support, *Report, In the best interests of children: Reforming the Child Support Scheme*, Department of Family and Community Services, Commonwealth of Australia, Canberra, 2005.

27 For example, see Bruce Smyth, "Modernising the child support scheme: Some reflections", *Family Matters*, Vol 71, 2005, pp. 58-61.

28 Lynelle Briggs and Tony Pagone, (Chairs), Royal Commission into Aged Care Quality and Safety, *Final Report: Care, Dignity and Respect Volume 1 Summary and recommendations*, Commonwealth Government, Canberra, 2021, p. 23. https://agedcare.royalcommission.gov.au/publications/final-report

29 Ibid., p. 2.

30 Michael Mintrom, Deirdre O'Neill and Ruby O'Connor, "Royal Commissions and Policy Influence", *Australian Journal of Public Administration*, Vol 80, No 1, March 2021, pp. 80-96.

31 Martin Rein and Donald Schön, *Frame Reflection: Toward the Resolution of Intractable Policy Controversies*, Basic Books, New York, 1994.

32 Patrick McClure, (Chair) Reference Group on Welfare Reform, *Final Report*, Commonwealth of Australia, Canberra, 2015.

33 For example, see Robert Frederick Ingram Smith and Patrick Weller, (eds), *Public Service Inquiries in Australia*, University of Queensland Press, St. Lucia, 1978.

34 Troy Whitford and Don Boadle, "Australia's Rural Reconstruction Commission, 1943, 46: A Reassessment", *Australian Journal of Politics and History*, Vol 54, No 4, 2008, pp. 525-45.

35 Pieter Degeling, Peter Baume, and Ken Jones, "Staging an official inquiry for policy change: The Case of the Drug Evaluation Review in Australia", *Policy and Politics*, Vol 21, No 4, 1993, pp. 259-73.

36 Adair Turner, (Chair), Pensions Commission, *First Report, Challenges and Choices*, Vol 1, The Stationery Office, London, 2004.

37 Adair Turner referred to the contents of this report and its "killer facts" at the Institute for Government Policy Reunion on the Pensions Commission, 9 December 2010; details available at: http://www.instituteforgovernment.org. uk/our-events/77/policy-reunion-pensions-commission

38 Mark Binskin, (Chair), Royal Commission into National Natural Disaster Arrangements, *Final Report*, Commonwealth of Australia, Canberra, 2020

39 Patrick McClure, (Chair), *Participation support for a more equitable Society: Final Report of the Reference Group on Welfare Reform*, Reference Group on Welfare Reform (Australia), Department of Family and Community Services. Commonwealth of Australia, Canberra, 2000.

40 National Office for Child Safety, Department of the Prime Minister and Cabinet, National Strategy to Prevent and Respond to Child Sexual Abuse 2021-2030, of Australia, Canberra, 2021.

41 Majone, *Evidence, Argument, and Persuasion in the Policy Process.*

42 Grant Hoole, "Commissions of inquiry in Canada", in Scott Prasser and Helen Tracey, (eds), *Royal Commissions and Public Inquiries: Practice and Potential*, Connor Court Publishing, Ballarat, 2014, pp. 331-55.

43 Peta Sheriff, "State theory, social science, and governmental commissions", *American Behavioral Scientist*, Vol 26, No 5, 1983, p. 673.

44 Patrick McClure, "Hearts and heads: The challenge of welfare reform", in Tom Frame, (ed), *The Desire for Change, 2004-2007: The Howard Government, Volume IV*, UNSW Press, Sydney, 2021, p. 180.

45 See for example, Bache, Bartle, and Flinders, "Multi-level governance", pp. 486-98.

46 Selan Ercan, Carolyn Hendriks, and John Dryzek, "Public deliberation in an era of communicative plenty", *Policy and Politics*, Vol 47, No 1, 2019, pp. 19-36.

47 "Whatever happened to evidence-based policymaking?" *The Mandarin*, 30 November 2018. Available at https://www.themandarin.com.au/102083-whatever-happened-to-evidence-based-policymaking /(Accessed 30 June 2019)

48 List refers to name of inquiry, its chair and date of appointment.

49 This royal commission was established jointly between the Commonwealth and all States and Territories.

6

Drowning in data: The Queensland Floods Commission of Inquiry

Margaret Cook

Introduction

Four days after floods devastated much of Queensland in 2011, the State Government called the *Queensland Floods Commission of Inquiry* (QFCI). While the initial brief was broad, aimed at improving future flood outcomes, the focus soon narrowed to a forensic examination of complex hydrologic and meteorological data that required detailed technical knowledge. At the QFCI the data was variously interpreted and explained by experts, the public, and the legal fraternity. This chapter considers how the Commission gathered and used the evidence and the influence of the media on public inquiries.

Background to the appointment of the inquiry

By mid-January 2011 more than 78 per cent of Queensland had been flooded, 35 people had died (with a further three missing) and 29,000 premises were inundated as the damage reached in excess of $5 billion.[1] The Locker Valley was devastated, and central Brisbane lay under water, submerged by 4.46 metres of floodwater as recorded at the city gauge.

In the face of the flood devastation and public debate, on 17

January 2011 the Queensland Government, established the QFCI. In announcing the inquiry, Premier Anna Bligh declared "this is not a criticism of what we have done. It will identify what we did well and what we can do better".[2] Bligh vowed that "no question will be left unexamined".[3] Premier Bligh's stated intent was to "help honour those who had lost their lives, by learning the lessons of the event" and which would "inform our response in the future".[4] Advocates felt the inquiry would provide answers, its recommendations might increase the city's preparedness and reduce risk, improving future flood outcomes. The editor of *The Australian* expressed a popular aspiration: "we need an inquiry not to lay blame but to recommend new ways to protect life and property".[5] The engineers who managed the dual purpose water supply and flood mitigation dam, Wivenhoe Dam, 80 kilometres upstream from Brisbane, welcomed the opportunity to offer their account of events, to clear their besmirched reputations.[6] In his opening remarks to the QFCI, Peter Callaghan SC, as Counsel assisting the QFCI, suggested that as the lessons of 1974 flood had been lost, the Commission afforded an opportunity to learn from the 2011 floods so they could be "recorded for the future". He hoped Queenslanders would not be "condemned to the fate of those who cannot remember the past, nor left vulnerable at the hands of those who might choose to forget it".[7] But did the Commission achieve these outcomes?

While the terms of reference were broad, aimed at improving future flood outcomes, I argue that the intent of the inquiry was redirected from the outset, shaped by a legal system designed to find guilt rather than determining better processes and strategies in the future or preventative measures. The focus soon narrowed to a forensic examination of complex hydrologic and meteorological data that required detailed technical knowledge. The inquiry dragged on over months of proceedings that were mired in hydrological and meteorological data variously interpreted and explained by experts, cross-examined by the legal fraternity, and assessed by three government-appointed commissioners. The public commentary ran in parallel with, and was shaped by, the media. The inquiry allowed the government to portray itself as pro-active, responding to the will of the people to investigate the flood, but with much of the hard work left to those charged with implementing its recommendations, the inquiry did little to improve Brisbane's flood responses or reduce the hazard. Instead, aided by elements in the media, the QFCI did harm by perpetuating a myth that Wivenhoe Dam could flood proof Brisbane, if only it was operated correctly in the future.

This chapter will provide a background to the QFCI, its historical precedent, establishment, proceedings, and outcomes. It will critically analyse the efficacy of an inquiry as a means of assessing what happened in a disaster or as a tool of disaster prevention (as implied by Premier Anna Bligh) by examination of the 2011 flood case study. Finally, it will suggest alternative approaches that may have answered the questions and delivered better outcomes.

Establishing a commission of inquiry

The QFCI was established under the Queensland *Commissions of Inquiry Act 1950* (Qld) on 17 January 2011. The brief was to examine the preparation, planning and response by three tiers of government, early warning and forecasting, dam operations (release strategies), performance of insurance companies, and local area planning/construction in flood prone areas. The inquiry was headed by Commissioner and sitting Supreme Court judge Catherine Holmes and two Deputy Commissioners – Jim O'Sullivan (former Police Commissioner) and Phil Cummins (engineer). An interim report was presented on 11 August 2011 that largely focused on the operational and planning requirements to be better prepared for the 2011-12 storm and cyclone season. The final report, presented on 16 March 2012, made 177 recommendations, 119 dealt with floodplain management and planning and building controls, while 41 dealt with dam management issues.[8]

The Bligh Government's establishment of an inquiry followed a long history of reviews of disasters, often regarded as an appropriate way to investigate catastrophic events such as floods or bushfires.[9] According to the 2009 Australian Law Reform Commission they are designed to establish accountability and responsibility and provide knowledge on the event, "catharsis or reconciliation" and restore public confidence.[10] As Prasser suggests, most inquisitorial inquiries are ad hoc, advisory bodies with extensive coercive powers of investigation. The appointment of a judge, he notes, elevates the status of the inquiry, as judges are respected, independent and separate from the political process.[11]

Inquiries after disasters are common. Wettenhall, who has studied bushfires, argues governments have little choice but to do so, otherwise looking derelict in their duty. As there were multiple deaths during the 2011 floods (including 23 in the Lockyer Valley), a coronial inquiry was mandatory, the question for the government remained what other type of inquiry should be conducted.[12] Royal commissions have been held for the 1939, 1949, 2009 and 2020 bushfires in Victoria. By contrast, when Brisbane experienced a flood in 1974, larger than the 2011 floods, no inquiry was held. Although many in the community called for an inquiry, Premier Bjelke-Petersen refused to hold one. The 2011 QFCI would be Queensland's first major flood inquiry.

In a study of inquiries, Boin and colleagues devised a typology of inquiries prompted by disasters.[13] One type identifies public officials and agencies as responsible and the ensuing debate becomes a morality play focussed on "questions of responsibility and guilt".[14] Another may focus on learning from mistakes and systemic improvement.[15] The latter, the professed aim of the QFCI, can be threatened if the inquiry and media coverage become combative and adversarial, with a focus on blame. This, I argue, is what happened in the QFCI as the emphasis was shifted (at least in media and public eye) to an assessment of blame.

Part of the Bligh Government's motivation in establishing the inquiry was to give the public a voice, a chance to air its opinions, grievances, and grief – the opportunity to be heard. As Mackay and Mccahon explain, giving people an "avenue to be heard" is an important motivation for the establishment of an inquiry, sometimes an "explicit objective".[16] In disaster inquiries, this is considered cathartic, part of the process of healing. As Bernard Teague, Chairman of the 2009 *Victorian Bushfires Royal Commission* wrote in his summary, their "work could, and should, contribute to individual and community healing".[17] The "priority was to listen to people directly affected by the fires" and to secure the memories.[18]

The QFCI sat for 68 days over 13 months, received more than 700 written submissions, 345 people gave evidence and 6133 pages of transcripts of evidence were produced.[19] Public meetings were held in Grantham and Murphys Creek and in 16 other flood-affected places across Queensland. To ensure openness and accessibility to the general public, the QFCI created a website and email to accept information. Livestreaming of the public hearings was provided on the website as were the daily transcripts within 24 hours. As the QFCI noted, this proved popular with 60,000 visits and nearly 280,000 page views between September 2011 and February 2012. The Interim and Final reports were made available on the website.[20] Although meetings with the flood affected communities were not open to the media nor livestreamed, following a precedent set by the *Victorian Bushfire Royal Commission*, formal hearings were, the transcripts made public, and the media given as much access as possible.[21] There is an underlying assumption under the *Commissions of Inquiry Act 1950* that the commission will be held in public and while there was no compulsion to do so, the report and evidence was made publicly available.[22] Commissioner Holmes hoped this transparency would maintain public confidence.[23]

The QFCI's interim report was issued in August 2011 with 175 recommendations concentrated on short term issues. It found the engineers had been "diligent and competent" and "acted in good faith throughout the flood event".[24] Like the 2003 Victorian bushfire inquiry's interim report, this suggested actions that should be taken before the next summer when floods are more likely. As such, it steered away from blame, conforming more to the systemic reform model of inquiries suggested by Boin and colleagues.[25] A final report would address longer term issues including floodplain management, emergency responses and insurance. Journalist Hedley Thomas rejected the interim report findings and in January 2012 claimed in *The Australian* that the flood engineers had not correctly implemented the W1 to W4 strategies and hence breached the manual, citing "unearthed emails" by the engineers as his proof of a cover-up.[26] As a direct consequence of these allegations and claims by Thomas that the engineers had misled the inquiry, additional documents were sought.[27] The QFCI re-opened for ten days, placing the flood engineers firmly in the spotlight to determine if they had lied to the Inquiry, falsified documents and not complied with the manual. The media shaped the narrative. As the *Brisbane Times* stated – the inquiry will "investigate allegations that the four engineers who controlled Wivenhoe Dam botched the water releases, caused unnecessary flooding and misled the QFCI over what water release strategies they were working under".[28] The media context was set as the inquiry moved well towards the second model with its focus on blame.[29]

A premier who establishes an inquiry to "identify what we did well and what we can do better"[30] sets a high bar. As Knowles writes, "learning" from errors and disasters is "central to the epistemologies of science and engineering" but it is also a "political act". The government needs to take control and place "technical experts in positions of power over the process of sense-making and blame laying".[31] Knowles agrees that the "stakes are high", if the experts cannot determine cause and means of prevention, then it creates communal anxiety about the hazard and future risk. Political legitimacy after a disaster rests on restoring order and faith in the government's ability to prevent recurrences.[32] Experts are used to "soothe public fears and restore faith in experts". The announcement of the QFCI was deemed by the media as "politically astute".[33]

Investigations that reveal negligence erode public confidence and expose the government to fault, particularly when the experts are State employees. Knowles argues, where this occurs, experts can be pitted against expert, to shift blame. Prasser has noted that royal commissions and public inquiries can also serve as "blame minimisers", after the fact damage control that can divert attention away from governments and ministers and the inquiry's independence gives the necessary imprimatur of credibility.[34] The Queensland Opposition seized on this idea, with Jeff Seeney, Leader of the Opposition, politicising the report to suggest that the government was seeking to "shift responsibility to everyone except themselves".[35]

At the opening of the QFCI Peter Callaghan SC presented the inquiry as a learning opportunity. But Knowles regards this is as disingenuous as mistakes may have been made and there is culpability in question. Inquiries seeking the truth, he argues, need to accept that the problem and the solutions may be vast.[36] I concur with his thinking and that in the case of Brisbane's floods the culpability is societal and systemic; both the causation and solutions are vast. Despite his opening, Callaghan quickly diverted the inquiry towards his key issues focused on the Brisbane River: the wisdom of maintaining Full Supply Level in Wivenhoe Dam, the dam operation, compliance with the Manual and the impact of dam releases – issues almost solely concentrated on water management. The Bligh Government justified this narrow approach arguing that the interim report must focus on short-term problems including flood warnings and dam management in case of another flood. Longer term problems of land use and insurance that are a root cause of flood hazards, would be addressed later.

From the outset, this redirected the inquiry away from a search for answers to an adversarial environment, more focused on fault. The four operational flood engineers became key witnesses at the QFCI as their actions came under intense scrutiny. When the inquiry was announced, they were preparing an event report, required by the Manual within six weeks of flood. This report, the dam operations manual and documents generated during the floods became evidence. A concentration on procedural adherence and blame detracted from the Commission's potential to expose systemic problems in pursuit of flood resilience.[37]

A shift towards an adversarial environment and questioning shapes the narrative and the outcomes. In writing on the *2009 Victorian Bushfires Royal Commission*, Holmes expresses a similar criticism, arguing that the "adversarial and provocative style polarised views and exacerbated tensions" and had a dominant influence on the media reporting.[38] He maintains that the human default is to assume it is someone else's responsibility, often government or, in particular, public servants who manage the crisis. This allows avoidance of individual responsibility, for example, not evacuating with flood warnings or building a house in a flood zone. It does not address issues of government versus individual choices, public education, and individual resilience and mitigation strategies.[39]

It is human nature to blame uncontrollable events on human intervention and to seek "certainty over uncertainty" according to Ashkanasy, engineer and psychologist.[40] The QFCI acknowledged this human tendency:

> Contemporary society does not countenance a fatalistic approach to such inevitabilities, even if their occurrence is unpredictable. There is an expectation that government will act to protect its citizens from disaster, and that all available science should be applied so that the nature and extent of the risk is known, and appropriate action taken to ameliorate it.[41]

But looking for someone to blame undermines the value of an inquiry. A focus on specific crisis managers, who most likely will never be in the same position ever again, erodes the opportunity to look at broader, systemic issues. An alternative approach, as suggested by Ebern and Dovers would, as Premier Anna Bligh stated, "identify what we did well and what we can do better" and would recognise the wider cultural environment and human choices to improved future outcomes in future.[42] But, Wettenhall argues, "there is little chance" that in an adversarial "inquiry dominated by lawyers" experts can do this and the result is "that it will distract political leadership from taking sensible remedial steps" and retard organisational learning.[43] Tellingly, Eburn and Dovers note that despite more than 50 post-disaster inquiries in Australia over the past 75 years, they have not led to useful learning.[44] This questions the efficacy of inquiries for analysing disasters.

An expert inquiry?

Are commissions of inquiry (or royal commissions) able to deal adequately with the expert testimony presented? All inquiries are dependent on the material presented — inaccuracies and biases withstanding — and from that they will draw their findings and recommendations. But they need to deal with complex, technical evidence and may lack the skills "collect, analyse and evaluate scientific data", according to Prasser in his assessment of inquiries and royal commissions.[45] This can make them susceptible to error, misunderstandings and fallacies. Maslen and Hayes raise the critical question: "who should have the power to judge the actions of experts in the wake of disasters?"[46] In a 1988 article, Baker posed the question, "are scientists special?" He argues that "all inquiries are dependent on expert testimony" and many with legal training are adept at processing detailed evidence. The critical factor, he believes, is that their advice must be listened to.[47] However, the engineers and hydrologists appearing before the QFCI felt they were not heard, and were left frustrated by its process. To them the inquiry was a technical debate based on hydrological and hydraulic data and modelling. Yet they found themselves hamstrung by an instruction not to use tables and diagrams, their tools of trade, instead having to reduce all data to words to be understood by all involved in the Inquiry. Lawyers are wordsmiths, engineers are technocrats – a cultural clash.[48] Linguistic issues plagued the QFCI.

Law academic Hugh Selby maintains that the appropriate specialists are those with expertise in disasters or emergencies as they know "what questions to pursue" and they should be given the authority to compel people to answer questions but away from public glare and media scrutiny, free of the risk of their answers being used against them in "criminal, disciplinary or civil proceedings". But a coronial or public inquiry, he argues, "puts a confusing inquisitorial gloss over an adversary process".[49] Disasters are unpredictable, and the expert must understand all the complexities and report accordingly. Engineers (and others) believed a flood investigation was needed with questions raised about rainfall predictions (accuracy and application), dam operation (water release strategies and timings, observation of rules) and what should be done better next time. Not in a culpable sense but as a genuine attempt to find out what went wrong to develop strategies and policies to minimise future floods. The QFCI did employ technical experts as advisors, but the process was rushed and some expertise (for example ecologists or land use managers) was not obtained.[50] Floodplain manager Mark Babister, one expert appointed by the Commission, was only given four weeks to produce his report without the benefit of a comprehensive flood study that was estimated to take three years to complete.[51]

Participants maintain that more expertise was required from practicing hydrologists with on the ground experience. One problem facing inquiries is the level of expertise required and the limited pool on which to draw for expert opinion. The number of experts in flood risk modelling, mapping and floodplain management in Australia is small,[52] and with many employed, at the time or previously by the State, in SunWater and Seqwater (the organisations responsible for dam operation) or in their preceding government departments, the pool was further reduced. With the Inquiry established, Seqwater's hydrological data were embargoed, and government departments silenced. While Commonwealth-employed meteorologists and hydrologists could address the media about the science, State employees could not. This issue became most apparent with the dismissal of Deputy Commissioner and engineer Phil Cummins, a recognised international expert on dams. He was stood down through a media challenge of conflict of interest as a company he had contracted to work for after the QFCI had been engaged by Seqwater to review the Wivenhoe and North Pine Dam operation manual.[53] Although Justice Holmes declared "the media story is wrong", Cummins took no further part in the QFCI to avoid a "possible perception of a conflict of interest".[54] Justice Catherine Holmes told the media "it was 'just simpler' not to have Mr Cummins involved". She added, "that won't present me with any particular difficulty, because the decisions I have to make are essentially about credibility, and they are not ones in which I can be helped by technical advice".[55] Emphasis had shifted to "credibility" rather than fact finding and lessons for the future. Cummins' departure, while commended in the media, was criticised by the engineering profession as many felt this left the commissioners devoid of the necessary expertise to understand the issues at hand, matters they say were essentially technical.

The Wivenhoe and Somerset Dam operating manual, the application of W1 to W4 strategies, and the language used during the flood to describe and record flood management decisions was forensically scrutinised at the QFCI. This terminology W1 to W4 codified objectives and strategies but was not routinely used in flood operations, with engineers focused on data, water releases and consequences, not the nomenclature of their actions. The flood engineers testified the terms W1 to W4 were "seldom referred to by engineers, who rarely called them by their technical names". Robert Ayre explained that "strategy labels were generally attributed after the event as part of the reporting process".[56] They felt slighted by accusations that that they did not follow manuals. As Stephen Goh, Engineers Australia (Queensland) President, explained, professional engineers rely on extensive training and experience and "when making decisions in time of crisis [they] do not just blindly follow manuals".[57] Nor do floods, each one differing from designed flood scenarios. Blind adherence to a manual "may deliver a detrimental outcome".[58] There is a gap between written guidelines and practice, in this case the Manual and dam management, as well as "expert practice and lay expectations".[59] But this sits uncomfortably with an increasingly risk-averse society that wants assurances and absolutes and misunderstands how experts operate.[60] Engineers maintained the correct strategies were employed, while Callaghan SC accused them of fixing the report, writing "fiction".[61] Journalists wrote of a manufactured cover-up to hide the implementation of the wrong strategies.[62]

The role of the media

Imposed gags on experts left journalists reliant on limited information to fill the news vacuum. Newspapers re-circulated the same information, the dam engineers were named and criticised, denied the right of reply. For some journalists, the silence became the story as it suggested a cover up or conspiracy. Some suggested it was a "good tactic" to prevent public servants from talking publicly.[63] Hedley Thomas at *The Australian* unrelentingly pursued his story, citing sources who expressed views consistent with his theory. Retired engineers, not gagged by conditions of employment, were quoted. Self-professed – or media labelled – experts, some hiding behind anonymity, came forward. Into the knowledge void came chemical engineer Michael O'Brien, described by *The Australian* as a dam expert, who became the quoted expert despite his lack of expertise in this field. He condemned the dam management, later conceding (although unreported in the media) that his analysis had been based on the "very limited" public information, notably from BoM.[64] A 24-hour media cycle leaves little opportunity for analysis or fact checking, or retraction of inaccuracies, which allowed these opinions to grow in authority.[65] The use of spuriously labelled "experts" fanned unfounded media speculation and misinformation as Thomas cited an economics professor, farmers and a lawyer to challenge hydrologists.

Many had opinions on the causes of the flood and the QFCI received more than 700 written submissions from experts and non-experts alike.[66] These were not fact checked by the QFCI, experts, the media, or the public. As Justice Holmes stated "It would have been quite impracticable for the commission to take all the evidence given on oath and check it for inconsistency against the mountain of documents received. Time did simply not allow that".[67] If considered by the QFCI, these unvalidated submissions most likely shaped the findings and recommendations.

It is the role of the media to critique public policy, ask difficult questions and frame political issues. However, media portrayals can be "politically motivated and presented back to communities for specific social or political purposes".[68] Or they can undermine confidence in an inquiry but casting doubt on expert opinions and evidence presented as was the case in the QFCI. Journalist Hedley Thomas wrote "experts get it wrong, self-interested parties lie, and the media's role in challenging the spin, and highlighting wrongdoing, is a vital as ever". As he acknowledged in *The Australian*, his findings were based on documents provided by farmer John Craigie, chemical engineer Michael O'Brien and modelling by independent engineers who "calculated almost all of the flooding could have been avoided".[69]

O'Brien, promulgated the view of "an avoidable disaster", exonerating the dam and claiming "prudent operation would have prevented most of the flooding", a theme that grew in the media and among the wider public.[70] This highlights the need to consider the role of the media, experts, and the community in public inquiries.

Just as lawyers may have struggled to understand the hydrological complexities, so too did journalists and the public. A survey of Brisbane residents after the 2011 flood found that flood-affected people did not understand the role of dams (as flood mitigation not prevention), nor did they understand the risk. This was acknowledged by the QFCI.[71] Maslen and Hayes are definitive: "neither lawyers nor the media are in a position to assess the quality of expert engineering judgements".[72] All can "legitimately raise questions about expert decisions but have no direct claim to the assigning of blame".[73] Scholars have also raised the issue of scientific literacy among journalists acknowledging that accurate reporting relies on journalists having the skills to comprehend the science, "recognise scientific legitimacy and appropriately represent scientific claims".[74] Even those who did possess the necessary skills to comprehend the complex hydrology and hydrography presented to the QFCI, had the further challenge of translating complex science into popularly accessible news accounts for the general reader.[75]

Dissenting viewpoints were covered by the media, reflecting the division in public opinion. In a study of 2011 media, Bohensky and Leitch identified 28 articles where the role and management of Wivenhoe Dam before and during the flood was a key narrative (28 articles) and a further 29 articles by January 2012, where the discourse "focused on the flood inquiry proceedings and the adequacy and implementation of the Wivenhoe Dam manual in the evidence, expertise and decision-making processes concerning the water release from the dam".[76] Some journalists argued that the dam managers should be praised, with Premier Bligh and Lord Mayor Campbell Newman offering the defence that the unprecedented rain left few alternatives.[77] However, championed by Thomas, the opposite view prevailed – the flood was largely the product of water released from the dam, either too early or too late.[78] With each iteration the belief became more entrenched. The flood became framed as the "great avoidable catastrophe", caused by dam mismanagement.[79] Thomas claimed the community "increasingly" viewed Wivenhoe Dam "as the chief culprit behind the Brisbane flood".[80] This view gained credibility when the Insurance Council of Australia-funded report stated the dam created the flood peak, causing a "dam release flood".[81] Questioning the dependence on the dam hinted at government culpability or poor land use management. Rather than challenge faith in engineering to control floods, the public debate shifted to blaming individuals.

The assessment

The QFCI offered a forum to investigate Queensland's real flood problems and collaboratively seek solutions. As McGowan argues, unlike the *Victorian Bushfires Royal Commission* that advocated "shared responsibility" including that of individuals, the QFCI focussed on prescriptive regulation rather than a nationally accepted "resilience-based approach" of building individual and community resilience. This was a "missed opportunity", to influence public policy debate towards mitigation and adaptation.[82] Krasovitsky agrees that information sharing and developing trust and collegial relationships was more likely to provide the necessary lessons, than an adversarial inquiry.[83] There is a need for knowledge sharing, without pitting expert against the other. A more collaborative (rather than combative approach) could be considered where stakeholders are heard before an independent inquiry panel, supported by specialist panels with skills and experience to interpret the technical information presented. This, Eburn and Dovers argue, would create inclusive processes of collecting knowledge that will enhance learning outcomes.[84] Geoffrey

Davies, who conducted the *Queensland Public Hospitals Commission of Inquiry* in 2005, disagrees, as he argues that informal evidence, "free of the risks of perjury and cross-examination" potentially compromises the reliability of evidence. It may, he says, allow those involved to shift or absolve themselves of blame.[85] I suggest that should the evidence suggest misconduct, that is the role for the courts or Crime and Misconduct Commission (CMC). The search for knowledge and determining fault should be treated as two separate processes.

Some form of flood inquiry was necessary, justified alone by the magnitude and loss of life. Calling a commission of inquiry provided generous resources, the opportunity to call witnesses and receive extensive testimony and evidence under oath. However, despite its separation from state, public servants (past and present) were gagged, which limited its information gathering potential, a recognised benefit of a public inquiry.[86] As a legal process, it quickly became adversarial and pitted expert against expert shifting the focus to blame rather than knowledge acquisition and reduced the possibility of the development of a deep understanding of the science and analysis of the hazard that a more collaborative process may have achieved. A public inquiry provided the community with the opportunity to be heard and informed as the proceedings were made accessible. However, unlike an internal departmental inquiry, the QFCI was unduly influenced by the media. Overall, these faults impeded the QFCI's stated objective to learn lessons to inform the future.

The QFCI undermined public confidence in experts and left engineers feeling professionally slighted. The selected and selective key issues, media debate and use of technical experts had certainly shaped the outcome. Deputy Commissioner, Phil Cummins was critical of the QFCI as he and Deputy Commissioner Jim Sullivan had little input into the final report.[87] Cummins asserted the Inquiry had been "a very political process", limited greatly by the terms of reference, despite the claim by Deputy Premier, Andrew Fraser, that the inquiry was about the "truth" and never about politics.[88] Discrediting the Government's "non-political" claim, Premier Bligh delayed both State and local council elections, until the release of the final QFCI report. The final report was released on 16 March 2012, eight days before the Queensland State election on 24 March 2012 and five weeks before the local government polls on 28 April 2012. Despite a temporary boost in popularity during the flood, with a Galaxy poll recording an increase from 25 to 60 percent,[89] Bligh's unpopular government suffered a landslide defeat in March 2012.

Many southeast Queensland residents considered the report costly and thought it did not resolve matters. It did little to "put their minds at rest", left unable to determine who was at fault.[90] Dissatisfied with the outcome, thousands signed up for a class action against the government entities that operated the dam. What society wanted was for science and government to remove the risk altogether, an unattainable goal.

Interstate newspapers expressed what many Queenslanders were unwilling to hear. "The drama has proven once again that forces of nature in Australia respect little, if any, human intervention", deduced the *Sydney Morning Herald* editor.[91] *The Australian* journalist, Stephen Lunn, described the Brisbane River in flood as "an untameable torrent", explaining:

> ... as the deadly Queensland floods once again so shockingly show, thousands of years of human ingenuity and endeavour, of trial and error, and in more recent times of great technological advancement still sees us unable to bend nature to our will.[92]

Premier Bligh reminded Queenslanders that "dams do not stop floods", they can only mitigate and minimise the impact, a fact many refused to accept.[93]

The QFCI did little to discourage the myth of flood immunity by fuelling the media debate and public perception that framed the flood as a bureaucratic error. In the minds of many within the community, the Inquiry affirmed what they wanted to believe – the dams and managers had caused the flood. Engineer, Trevor Grigg recognised the inherent risk of blaming the bureaucrat, arguing it reinforced a dangerous view that "if only we get the operation of the dam right, we won't have any flooding of this river".[94] Allocating fault to dam mismanagement may help reassure public confidence in governments,[95] but it buttressed the delusion of control over nature and the myth that a river can be controlled with technology could be upheld. It reduced the likelihood of changing floodplain management practices and legislation and the implementation of adaptative behaviours to accommodate future floods. Lessons for the future were not learned. Instead, the QFCI and public debate reaffirmed a faith in dams, if only they were operated differently, when the real problem facing Southeast Queensland is that many of us continue to live on a floodplain.

Public inquiries mentioned in this chapter[96]

Queensland Public Hospitals Commission of Inquiry (Davies, 2005)

Victorian Bushfires Royal Commission (Teague, 2009)

Queensland Floods Commission of Inquiry (Holmes, 2011)

Notes

1   Catherine Holmes, (Chair), Queensland Floods Commission of Inquiry, *Interim Report*, Queensland Government, Brisbane, August 2011, p. 20.
2   State Disaster Management Group Minutes, 17 January 2011, p. 8 in Anna Bligh Submission to QFCI, 6 February 2012.
3   "Question Time", *Courier-Mail*, 18 January 2011.
4   Megan Neil and AAP Reporters, "Inquiry to seek answers on Qld floods", *Sydney Morning Herald*, 17 January 2011.
5   "Editorial, "Queenslanders stood strong during disaster", *The Australian*, 15–16 January 2011.
6   Terry Malone (flood engineer) in discussion with author, 14 February 2017; Geoffrey Heatherwick (former BoM hydrologist) in discussion with author, 21 August 2015.

7   Transcript of Proceedings, QFCI.
8   QFCI, *Final Report,* March 2012, pp. 12-29.
9   Scott Prasser and Helen Tracey, "An inquiry by any other name . . . types of public inquiry", in Scott Prasser and Helen Tracey, (eds), *Royal Commissions and Public Inquiries: Practice and Potential,* Connor Court Publishing, Ballarat, 2014, p. 41.
10 Australian Government Australian Law Reform Commission, *Making Inquiries Report: A New Statutory Requirement,* Report 111, Commonwealth Government, Sydney, October 2009, p. 57.
11 Scott Prasser, "Royal Commissions in Australia: When Should Governments Appoint Them?", *Australian Journal of Public Administration,* Vol 65, No 3, September 2006, pp. 28-47.
12 Roger Wettenhall, "Inquiring into Disasters: Contrasting styles and forms", in Prasser and Tracey, *Royal Commissions and Public Inquiries,* p. 97.
13 Arjen Boin, Paul 'T Hart, Eric Stern and Bengt Sunderlius, *The Politics of Crisis Management: Public Leadership Under Pressure,* Cambridge University Press, Cambridge, 2005, p. 5.
14 Ibid., p. 5.
15 Ibid., p. 102.
16 Anita Mackay and Jacob Mccahon, "Comparing Commission, Inquests and Inquiries: Lessons from Processes Concerning Family Violence and Child Protection in Victoria", *Monash University Law Review,* Vol 45, No 3, 2019, pp. 531-588, p. 534.
17 Bernard Teague, (Chair), 2009 Victorian Bushfires Royal Commission, *Final Report Summary,* Victorian Government Printer, Melbourne, 2010, p. 1.
18 Ibid., p. vii.
19 QFCI, *Final Report,* p. 35.
20 Ibid.
21 Victorian Bushfires Royal Commission, p. 396.
22 Geoffrey Davies, "Some reflections on commissions of inquiry" in Prasser and Tracey, *Royal Commissions and Public Inquiries,* p. 45.
23 Catherine Holmes, Opening Hearing, QFCI, 2011, p. 4.
24 QFCI, *Interim Report,* 2011, p. 62.
25 Wettenhall, "Inquiring into Disasters", p. 99.
26 Hedley Thomas, "What the floods inquiry didn't hear: Wivenhoe 'breached the manual'", *The Australian,* 23 January 2012, p. 1; Hedley Thomas, "Missed again: unearthed emails point to Wivenhoe breach", *The Australian,* 24 January 2011, p. 1.
27 Maria Hatzakis, "Qld floods inquiry resumes hearings", *ABC News,* 2 February 2012, Thomas and his sources took credit for the QFCI re-opening in Hedley Thomas, "The Flood Uncovered," *The Weekend Australian,* 17 March 2012.8.
28 QFCI, *Final Report,* p. 438; Nathan Paull, "Flood Inquiry won't hurt government: Fraser," *The Age,* 5 February 2012, accessed November 13, 2017.
29 Boin, 'T Hart, Stern and Sunderlius, *The Politics of Crisis Management,* p. 5.
30 State Disaster Management Group Minutes, 17 January 2011, p. 8 in Anna Bligh Submission to QFCI, 6 February 2012.
31 Scott Gabriel Knowles, "Learning from Disaster?: The History of Technology and the Future of Disaster Research", *Technology and Culture,* Vol 55, No 4, October 2014, pp. 773-84, and p. 781.
32 Ibid., p. 782.
33 "Judicial Inquiry is the right move", *The Australian,* 17 January 2011.
34 Scott Prasser, "The Queensland Health Royal Commissions", *The Australian*

Journal of Public Administration, Vol 69, No 1, March 2010, pp. 79-97, p. 81.

35 Jeff Seeney, MP, Queensland Parliamentary Debates, *Hansard*, 2 August 2011, p. 2225.

36 Knowles, "Learning from Disaster?", p. 783.

37 Maslen and Hayes concur. Sarah Maslen and Jan Hayes, "Experts under the Microscope: The Wivenhoe Dam Case", *Environmental Systems and Decisions Journal*, Vol 34, 2014, p. 184.

38 Allan Holmes, "A Reflection on the Bushfire Royal Commission - Blame, Accountability, and Responsibility", *Australian Journal of Public Administration*, Vol 69, No 4, December 2010, pp. 387-91, p. 387.

39 Ibid., pp. 388-89.

40 Tom Reilly, "Don't blame dam operator, says designer", *Sydney Morning Herald*, 21 February 2011; Neal Ashkanasy, "Stop playing the flood blame-game", *Courier-Mail*, 10 May 2011.

41 QFCI, *Final Report*, p. 38.

42 State Disaster Management Group Minutes, 17 January 2011, p. 8. In Anna Bligh Submission to QFCI, 6 February 2012; Michael Eburn and Steve Dovers, "Learning Lessons from Disasters: Alternatives to Royal Commissions and Other Quasi-Judicial Inquiries", *Australian Journal of Public Administration*, Vol. 74, No 4, December 2015, p. 501.

43 Wettenhall, "Crisis and Natural Disasters", p. 258.

44 Eburn and Dovers, "Learning Lessons from Disasters", p. 505.

45 Dominique Hogan-Doran, "Lessons for Government from Recent Royal Commissions and Public Inquiries", Paper presented to Law Society of New South Wales, Government Solicitors' Conference 2019, 3 September 2019, para 50, p. 17.

46 Maslen and Hayes, "Experts under the Microscope", p. 184.

47 Richard Baker, "Assessing Complex Technical Issues: Public Inquiries or "Commissions?", *Political Quarterly*, Vol 59, No 2, April-June 1988, pp. 178-189, p. 180.

48 This account is expanded in Margaret Cook, *A River with a City Problem: A History of Brisbane Floods*, University of Queensland Press, Brisbane, 2019, pp. 179-83.

49 Hugh Selby cited in Roger Wettenhall, "Crisis and Natural Disasters: A Review of Two Schools of Study Drawing on Australian Wildfire Experience", *Public Organization Review*, Vol 9, Issue 3, 2009, pp. 247-61, p. 257.

50 Caroline Wenger, Karen Hussey and Jamie Pittock, "Living with Floods: Key lessons from Australia and Aboard", National Climate Change Adaptation Research Facility, 2013, p. 11.

51 QFCI, *Final Report*, pp. 41-2.

52 Jim McGowan, "A Missed Opportunity to Promote Community resilience? –The Queensland Floods Commission of Inquiry", *Australian Journal of Public Administration*, Vol 71, No 3, September, 2012, pp. 353-63, and p. 361.

53 Mark Solomons, "Flood commissioner Phil Cummins must quit to save inquiry, says Ipswich councillor Paul Tully", *Courier-Mail*, 4 February 2012.

54 "Flood inquiry addresses conflict of interest claims", *ABC News*, 5 February 2012; Matthew Cranston, "Flood inquiry lambastes newspaper", *Australian Financial Review*, 6 February 2012; QFCI, *Final Report*, p. 35.

55 "Queensland floods commission of inquiry extended further", *Courier-Mail*, 10 February 2012.

56 Robert Ayre, Seventh Statement to QFCI, 1 February 2012, point 28.

57 Maslen and Hayes, "Experts under the Microscope", p. 188.

58 Engineers Australia, "Comments on Queensland Flood Commission of In-

quiry Final Report", July 2012, p. 11.

59　Maslen and Hayes, "Experts under the Microscope", p. 185.

60　Ibid., p. 84.

61　QFCI, Transcripts, 3 February 2012, p. 5204.

62　Jared Owens, "Wivenhoe Dam report 'a fiction'", *The Australian*, 3 February 2012; Michael Madigan, *'We've been duped,"* *Courier-Mail*, 3 February 2012; Hedley Thomas, "Strategy to unravel cover-up claims," *The Australian*, 3 February 2012.

63　Marlene Krasovitsky, "Putting the 'Public' back into Inquiries: Assessing the success of Public Inquiries in Australia", PhD Thesis, Department of Government and International Relations, Faculty of Arts and Social Sciences, University of Sydney, 2019, p. 133.

64　Michael O'Brien, "Brisbane Flooding January 2011: An Avoidable Disaster", Submission to QFCI, 20 March 2011, p. 4.

65　Cook, *A River with a City Problem*, p. 179.

66　QFCI, *Final Report*, p. 33.

67　Ibid., p. 29.

68　Wendy Madsen and Cathy O'Mullan, "Responding to disaster: Applying the lens of social memory", *Australian Journal of Communication*, Vol 40, No 1, April 2013, pp. 57-70, and p. 67.

69　Hedley Thomas, "The flood uncovered", *The Australian*, 17 March, 2012.

70　Hedley Thomas, "Engineers bores a hole in dam untruths", *Weekend Australian*, 19-20 March 2011.

71　QFCI, *Final Report*, p. 39.

72　Maslen and Hayes, "Experts under the Microscope", p. 184.

73　Ibid., p. 185.

74　Susanna Priest, "Critical Science Literacy: What Citizens and Journalists Need to Know to Make Sense of Science", *Bulletin of Science, Technology and Society*, Vol 33, No 5-6, 2013, p. 141.

75　Janice L. Krieger and Cindy Gallois, "Translating Science: Using the Science of Language to Explicate the Language of Science", *Journal of Language and Social Psychology*, Vol 36, Issue 1, 2017, pp. 3-13.

76　Erin L. Bohensky and Anne M. Leitch, "Framing the flood: a media analysis of themes of resilience in the 2011 Brisbane flood", *Regional Environmental Change*, Vol 14, 2014, pp. 475-488, p. 483.

77　Mark Solomons, "Dam saves city but punishes farmer," *Courier-Mail*, 18 January 2011; Rory Callinan, "Engineers cut flow gushing from dam", *The Australian*, 13 January 2011.

78　Hedley Thomas, "Bligh's tough people owed a tough inquiry", *The Australian*, 14 January 2011; Michel Raymond, "January 2011 Brisbane River Floods and Examination by Media of the Dam Operations," ANCOLD, 2011.; Hedley Thomas, "The Great Avoidable Flood: an inquiry's challenge", *The Australian*, 22-23 January 2011; Hedley Thomas, "Releases too little, too late," *The Australian*, 21 February 2011.

79　Hedley Thomas, "The Great Avoidable Flood", *The Australian*, 22-3 January 2011.

80　Hedley Thomas, "Engineers bores a hole in dam untruths," in *Weekend Australian*, 19-20 March 2011.

81　Insurance Council of Australia. "Flooding in the Brisbane River Catchment, January 2011", ICA Hydrology Panel: Sydney, Australia, 20 February 2011.

82　McGowan, "A Missed Opportunity to Promote Community resilience? –The Queensland Floods Commission of Inquiry", p. 355.

83　Krasovitsky, "Putting the 'Public' back into Inquiries", p. 138.

84   Michael Eburn and Steve Dovers, "Reviewing high-risk and high-consequence decisions: finding a safter way", *Australian Journal of Emergency Management*, Vol 32, No 4, October 2117, p. 27; Eburn and Dovers, "Learning Lessons from Disasters", p. 504.

85   Davies, "Some reflections on commissions of inquiry" pp. 47-9.

86   Scott Prasser and Helen Tracey, "Preface" in Prasser and Tracey, *Royal Commissions and Public Inquiries: Practice and Potential*, p. viii.

87   Mark Solomons and Tuck Thompson, "Queensland Government Drags the chain on implementing flood inquiry's main points", *Courier-Mail*, 8 January 2013.

88   Sarah Vogler and Mark Solomons, "Seeney defends lag in recovery", *Courier-Mail*, 9 January 2013.

89   Iskhandar Razak, "Bligh's popularity soars in wake of disasters: Queensland Premier Anna Bligh has staged a major turnaround in the latest opinion poll", ABC News NT (ABC1 Darwin).

90   *Courier-Mail*, 17 March 2012; p. 132; Krasovitsky, "Putting the 'Public' back into Inquiries", p. 133.

91   Editorial, *Sydney Morning Herald*, 14 January 2011.

92   Stephen Lunn, "The Untamable Torrent", *The Australian*, 15-16 January 2011.

93   Ibid.

94   Sophie Cousins, "Wivenhoe releases could've prevented floods? Nonsense, say experts", *Crikey*, 16 February 2011.

95   Eburn and Dovers, "Reviewing high-risk and high-consequence decisions", p. 27.

96   List refers to name of inquiry, its chair and date of appointment.

7

The 2018-19 Thodey Review of the Australian Public Service

Paddy Gourley

Introduction

On 4 May 2018 the Prime Minister, Malcolm Turnbull, and the Minister for the Public Service, Kelly O'Dwyer, announced a review of the Australian Public Service (APS) – to be the *Independent Review of the Australian Public Service* (henceforth the Thodey Review). They said that "Many of the fundamentals of Australia's public sector reflect the outcomes of a royal commission held back in the 1970s. It is therefore timely to examine the capability, culture and operating model of the APS...".[1] It probably does not matter that many, and possibly most, of the fundamentals of Australia's public sector do not reflect the "outcomes" of the 1974 Coombs *Royal Commission into Australian Government Administration* (henceforth Coombs Commission) and many of the weaknesses in Commonwealth administration are because they do not.[2] However, that may be, the Turnbull-O'Dwyer observation falls short of explaining why the Thodey Review came to be. But first a warning: this chapter contains material some readers might find distressing.

Genesis

In 2017, Industry and Science Australia (ISA), a statutory advisory body within the Industry, Science, Energy and Resources portfolio which says it is composed of "entrepreneurs, investors, researchers and educators", published a report titled *Australia 2030: Prosperity through Innovation*. Without saying how, that report asserted that "The structure of the Australian Government public service reflects the needs of governments in the 1980s, not the 2000s".[3] From this unsubstantiated foundation the ISA report went on to say that "The APS should aim for transformative … reform to deliver in a new digital economy" and that "Government should consider reviewing the APS to ensure it is ready to lead the transformation [of the economy] out to 2030 and beyond".[4] It is odd that the ISA, ostensibly with scientific sensibilities at its heart, should be so careless about evidence when it comes to public administration; perhaps it would be better to stick to its knitting.

Anyway, the ISA cudgels, however rootless they may have been, were grasped by the then Secretary of the Department of Industry, Science, Energy and Resources, Dr Heather Smith, an ex-officio member of the Industry and Science Australia Board. As a member of a panel, along with Mr David Thodey in March 2018, she delivered a keynote address at the launch of an Institute of Public Administration Australia (IPAA) program called *Doing Policy Differently*.[5] Dr Smith claimed that the APS "is neither structurally configured, nor culturally aligned, to help government navigate" the policy challenges in front of it. She went on to say that "If the government agrees to the Innovation and Science Australia 2030 report recommendation to review the APS, it would be the first root and branch look at the APS since the mid-1970s to examine whether we are fit for purpose".[6] While Dr Smith might be surprised to be told that there have been several "root and branch" reviews of the APS since the mid-1970s, her advocacy of the ISA recommendation pushed the notion of a review into congenial territory, she being the partner of the then Secretary of the Department of the Prime Minister and Cabinet, Dr Martin Parkinson, who was in a second to none position to get the Turnbull Government to set one up.

Terms of reference

The terms of reference said the Review's purpose was to "ensure that the APS was fit for purpose for the coming decades" and that it would "identify an ambitious program of transformational reforms...". On particulars, the Review was asked to examine "the culture, capability and operating model of the APS" and the "suitability of the APS's architecture and governing legislation" and how "it monitors and measures performance, and how it ensures the transparent and most effective use of taxpayers' money in delivering outcomes".[7]

So, the remit was broad and abstruse. That can be an advantage although the character of the final report leaves scope for a range of judgments as to just how advantageous in this case. Certainly, the remit contrasted with the Coombs Commission of the 1970s whose terms of reference were detailed and specific. Moreover, the Thodey Review was not asked to look at the role of ministers and their relations with departments, devolution and the role of central management, workplace relations and related policies, machinery of government policy and practice, the use of consultants and labour hire and contractors.

The Thodey Review was also confined to the public service proper, as it were, that is those organisations whose staff are employed under the *Public Service Act* comprising about 60 per cent of Commonwealth civilian employees.

Membership of the Review

Mr David Thodey, Dr Smith's fellow panelist from the IPAA function in March 2018, was appointed chair of the Review. He was a former CEO of Telstra and at the time chair of the board of the CSIRO. The other review members were:

- Ms Maile Carnegie, a senior executive of the ANZ Bank and

another member of the board of the ISA.

- Professor Glyn Davis the CEO of the Paul Ramsay Foundation and a former Vice Chancellor of the University of Melbourne.
- Dr Gordon de Brouwer, formerly Secretary of the Commonwealth Department of the Environment and Energy and an honorary/adjunct professor at the ANU and the University of Canberra.
- Ms Belinda Hutchison, a company director including with Telstra and Chancellor of the University of Sydney.
- Ms Alison Watkins, then the Managing Director of Coca-Cola Amatil and a non-executive director of the Centre for Independent Studies.

The Review was given the aid of a "reference group" comprised of the Hon Mike Baird a former Liberal Premier of New South Wales, Her Excellency Janice Charette a former Secretary to the Cabinet in Canada, the Hon Helen Coonan a former Liberal Federal Minister and director of the gaming company Crown Limited; Mr Bill English a former National Party New Zealand Prime Minister; Mr Peter Hughes the New Zealand Public Service Commissioner; Lord Gus O'Donnell and former UK Cabinet Secretary; Mr Peter Ong Boon Kwee; former head of the Civil Service in Singapore, Dr David Morgan, a former CEO of Westpac Bank and before that a senior officer in the Commonwealth Department of the Treasury; and the Hon Stephen Smith, a former Federal Labor Minister and chair of the board of a cyber security company.

So, four of the members of the Thodey Review from the private sector did not appear to have significant knowledge or experience of Commonwealth public administration. Dr de Brouwer did, and Dr Davis had some claims in public administration more generally. Consistent with the relevance and background of the members of the Thodey Review, in a speech in November 2018, the head of the Review's Secretariat said "I am certainly not steeped in public service reform".[8]

To test the balance of the Review's representation and expertise, it might be asked if a major private sector company, say NewsCorp, seeking to review its operations would bring in a group of six people that included four from the public service, one with a university background and one of its alumni? By way of counterpoint, the reference group contained people with a great deal of knowledge and working experience in public administration including that from other countries with similar government systems to Australia. The Review had two formal meetings with the reference group and the extent to which advantage was taken of its expertise is moot.

Finally, despite the rhetoric in the Review's terms of reference about "improving citizens experience of government" and "providing enriching work for its employees",[9] neither the Review nor Reference groups benefitted from representation from a body advocating on behalf of those reliant on government services or one from staff or a union.

Methodology

In the announcement of the Thodey Review and in all the documentation associated with it, much is made of its independence. It was branded as the "Independent Review of the Australian Public Service".[10] Except to the extent members of the Review and Reference groups brought their own minds to their tasks, the Review was not independent.

The panel was supported by a secretariat, headed by an officer at the deputy secretary level, and located in the Department of the Prime Minister and Cabinet, an agency that should have been a prime object of investigation. And it was to report to the Prime Minister through the Secretary of the Department of the Prime Minister and Cabinet who in that role was to be supported by the Public Service Commissioner whose agency also should have been subject of close investigation. That is to say, the organisation of the work for the Thodey Review, all of whose members had important day jobs, was able to be significantly guided by the Prime Minister's Department and the Public Service Commissioner, if in ways that remain opaque. By way of analogy, it was as if the Hayne Royal Commission on financial institutions[11] had relied on staff from one of the banks to conduct investigations and prepare drafts for the Commissioner rather than rely on the services of independent counsel. While the Coombs Commission had some public servants seconded to it, its secretariat was complemented by academics and others, all of whom worked directly to the Commission which was not contained within any department or agency. To be clear – the Thodey Review was not independent in any of the ordinary senses that adjective is used to characterise public inquiries and that appears to have affected its methods, not always helpfully.

Reflecting its quasi-inside nature, the Review did not ask public service departments and agencies to make submissions.[12] Despite urging their staff to put in submissions, few Secretaries of departments or agency heads did so. In particular, there were no public submissions from the Secretary of the Department of the Prime Minister and Cabinet or the Public Service Commissioner. Like the Duke of Plaza Toro, they presumably contented themselves with fighting their battles from behind and influencing the course of events from positions on the inside rails, a less exciting prospect.

By way of contrast, the Public Service Board provided the Coombs Commission with seven substantial volumes of background information, two large submissions on over-arching topics and 24 memorandum on specific matters such as the appointment of departmental secretaries, machinery of government, staff planning and the rights and obligations of public servants – more than 1000 pages of close packed documentation replete with many recommendations. All this documentation was open to the public and the Board was subject to many hours of public sessions on it before the Coombs Commission, as were other government agencies who made submissions. All government agencies were kept at arms-length from the Coombs Commission, and none had any part in the preparation of its report.

The Thodey Review issued a general invitation for submissions but initially allowed fewer than five weeks to them to be lodged. That caused sufficient push back for the deadline to be extended by six weeks.

Mr Thodey also wrote to 160 community groups, peak bodies and "business leaders" asking for their views.

While 755 submissions were received, their value was not reflected in their numbers. Of the first 200 submissions received:

- More than 50 per cent were anonymous.
- More than 70 per cent were of 300 words or fewer.
- About 80 per cent covered only a couple of issues or a single one.
- Around 20 per cent were from public servants.
- There were a couple from academics and one from a union, the Commonwealth Public Service Union (CPSU).
- Fewer than 10 per cent addressed the terms of reference in substantive ways.

This picture likely changed somewhat with later submissions although perhaps not significantly.

The few submissions eventually received by the cut-off date from departments and agencies were underwhelming although those from the Department of Home Affairs, the Human Rights Commission, the Institute of Aboriginal and Torres Strait Islander Studies and the Australian Tax Office were impressive, as were a couple from unions, including the CPSU. The failure of the vast majority of government agencies to make public submissions was not just a failure of intellectual fortitude. It was a failure to be willing to promote public discussion and to have ideas tested in open debate.

It might have been hoped that the Institute of Public Administration Australia would take up the slack. It did not. Its submission was slick and disappointing. It made a reasonable fist of explaining what it would like the public service to be, but it made almost no practical suggestions as to how its noble hopes might be achieved.

In all, only a relatively small number of submissions were substantial and addressed a wide range of issues.

While the Thodey Review held no open hearings, workshops were conducted around the country usually attended by one of the reviewers. Some 771 people signed up for the workshops with most attendees self-nominating it would seem. They provided opportunities for staff in particular, to have a say. There was not a great deal of information available about the procedures of the workshops although photographs of them in session suggest butcher's paper, large post it notes and white boards were given a thorough work out. The Review also arranged what it called "roundtables" which were attended by 122 people, no doubt selected worthies, with useful things to offer.

The Review made a general request for comments on line and listed topics on which they would especially like to be addressed including such things as "emerging challenges", "policy priorities", "delivering services", "a new professions model" and so on.

There is something to be said for workshops and roundtables although getting a group of people in a room and asking them to let fly with whatever they want to get off their chests has inherent analytical limitations. Indeed, workshops and roundtables are no substitutes for the hard slog of defining problems, carefully gathering and sifting evidence, sorting out the best solutions and backing them with cogent rationales.

The Review sought to make up any analytical deficit by commissioning six research papers through the Australian and New Zealand School of Government (ANZSOG). These covered such topics as evaluation, relations between ministers and the public service, the integrity "framework", working with other "jurisdictions" and the like. These papers were generally sound, and no doubt helped the Review to settle its views even if they were not produced until the Review as in its final stages.

The Boston Consulting Group was engaged to prepare a document titled *Scenarios for 2030*. It was delivered late in 2018. It need not give pause for comment other than to say that it was yet another testament to the hazards of long-term crystal ball gazing.

Still, to benchmark the volume of research material available to the Thodey Review, it can be safely said that it represented but a small fraction of that done for the Coombs Royal Commission in the 1970s.

Throughout its life the members of the Thodey Review made speeches and comments about what they were up to. This was all admirable although not without risk. For example, in a podcast a Review Panel member said that an inquiry he was associated with (identified as the 1982-3 Reid *Review of Commonwealth Administration*) resulted in "no change whatsoever". In fact, almost all recommendations of the Reid Report[13] were acted on.[14]

Finally, the Review maintained a website through which it communicated and solicited views.

Precursor to the final report

In March 2019, the Review issued a document titled *Priorities for Change* as a basis for further consultation. It would have been useful if something like it could have been provided closer to its beginning than its end but no matter the document attracted a good deal of comment and a further 30 submissions. According to the Review, the three main strands of commentary urged clear and specific recommendations, the need to bolster public service capability and the importance of a proper balance between standardising the way the service works while giving organisations the flexibility to meet their differing responsibilities.

In a speech at the time, the Review Chair, Mr Thodey, said that *Priorities for Change* document aimed to set out "the transitional shifts we believe will transition the public service to be fit for purpose in the decades to come".[15] (It is unlikely that any review of a public service anywhere in the world has more used the words "fit for purpose" than the Thodey one).

Mr Thodey said that the "organising principle" for the views it was putting forward was "a trusted APS, united in serving all Australians". While the Review attached much weight to this, can anyone seriously believe it is of much utility, especially as it neglects to indicate that the public service is primarily there to serve governments and do the things they want done for the citizenry at large. Moreover, such obscure aspirations are about states of being – being trusted, being united, being whatever. It is a form of organisational narcissism where looking good comes before doing good. The cart is before the horse.

The public service will be trusted and will look good when it performs tasks given to it by governments and the parliament effectively, efficiently and properly. Yet even if aspirations were to be formed around doing, how helpful could this be to staff on the front line of customs work, naval stores or a social security counter, still less to boffins fiddling with high policy? Could this great variety of officials often or even every now and again think about their work as building trust in the APS and "serving all Australians"? Surely an officer in army logistics, for example, would be better off thinking about getting the baked beans and ammunition to soldiers on the front line than trying to think of her work as "serving all Australians".

In an attempt to be helpful, the Review's document, said the public service needs "an operating model that dynamically responds to new and shifting priorities, with a culture and shared ways of working that allows teams to come together to tackle priorities for government and the Australian people." Unfortunately, the document is so thoroughly suffused with such rhetoric that it confuses meaning and shrouds intent.

The Review organised its *Priorities for Change* document around four broad objectives:

- Strengthen the culture governance and leadership model.
- Build a flexible APS operating model.
- Invest in APS capability and talent development.
- Develop stronger internal and external partnerships.[16]

These are objectives that could be applied to just about any organisation. That is to say, the Review decided to be one primarily focused on general management and subordinated questions of public administration and thus in many parts lost its way.

And while fretting about the quality of policy analysis in the public service, the review panel did not practice what it preached. Thus, against various topics it set out dot points on "context" and hopped directly into what it called "the transformation opportunity" with virtually no policy analysis in the usually accepted meaning of that term in between.

For example, it asserted that the Secretaries Board is "the APS's principal service-wide governance body".[17] It is not. The Cabinet is, an elementary point in the Review's analytical shyness allowed it to overlook this important issue. It then proceeded to hope that the Secretaries Board could be given decision making powers so it could be "driving cross-portfolio policy and delivery outcomes".[18] Put it this way, would the prime minister and other relevant ministers be happy for the Secretaries Board to be "driving cross-portfolio policy" in the area of foreign affairs and defence or anything else? The irony of the Review's promotion of the Secretaries Board turned out to be the Board's role in advising the government to knock off many of the Review's most important recommendations. That is to say, far from being the instrument of progress the Secretaries Board has been regressive, something the Review should have been able to anticipate if it considered the inexorable dynamics of the Board's machinations.

Another example: the *Priorities for Change* document rightly emphasised the importance of community "confidence in the appointment, performance management and termination of departmental secretaries".[19] Yet apart from saying there should be a "codified process" using "selection criteria", that process was not elaborated save for the observation that the Review was thinking about an advisory panel of the Secretary of the Prime Minister's Department, the Public Service Commissioner and "a ministerial nominee". The Review did not seem to appreciate that a "ministerial nominee" would all too frequently bring along the name of the person the Minister would like in a job, leaving the advisory panel with the simple task of crafting an accommodating recommendation. The Review's thinking on this matter is imperceptive and it did not consider serious problems associated with fixed period appointments for Secretaries and other matters related to their tenure that are critical to community confidence in the system.

A final example: The Review said that "a move towards common pay and conditions across the service"[20] was needed. This suggestion was not supported, however, by any analysis of the working of the existing remuneration policy, how that might be changed or any consideration of possible institutional consequences of which there are many. When asked what this could mean, Mr Thodey said "It's trying to move towards an environment that would have greater transparency and more common terms because one of the problems...is there's so many of them out there".[21]

The treatment of the Secretaries Board, departmental secretary appointments and "common pay and conditions"[22] in the *Priorities* document was typical of the treatment of just about all other matters it raised. That is, many of the thoughts and suggestions it contained were opaque and imprecise, were not supported by analysis and rationale and were clouded in the difficult verbiage of modern management cliché. It was better than nothing as a means of advancing consultation and getting further suggestions, but it should have been much better. Nevertheless, several commentators, presumably disturbed by the *Priorities* vacuums, including former Public Service Commissioners Helen Williams and Andrew Podger, stepped in and contributed in ways that seem to have helped sharpen up some of the Thodey Review's recommendations in its final Report.

Talking with the "APS200"

In April 2019, members of the Review panel met with the APS200, a collection of heads and deputy heads of departments and agencies to, according to its website, "talk about change and the future of our service". Presumably the *Priorities* document was on the table. It is difficult to know what this meeting might have produced and the report of the event on the Review's website doesn't give much away.

The Secretary of the Department of the Prime Minister and Cabinet said, "To me it's really simple…I want [public servants] to be bound together by the one idea that we are the APS and we work for Australia".

Another departmental Secretary, Kerri Hartland[23] said, "we have the opportunity to stop being the bouncer and instead be the DJ" and that "we are able to use this review to hold a mirror up to ourselves".

A departmental deputy secretary said, "What I found interesting was the level of energy in the room and I guess how engaged and willing people are to think about what the future of the APS should look like."

If these are representative of the highlights of the session with the APS, they suggest once again a concentration on what things should look like but with less concern about specific actions to get there to burnish appearances; without that the room can ooze with energy but progress will be awkward.

Words from the Prime Minister

As the Thodey Review was finalising its report in May 2019 and after that year's election, Prime Minister Morrison gathered heads of departments for what was seen as a 'pep talk'. He said that he "deeply respects...the role of the public service in delivering on the agenda of the government." He also said he wanted "frank and fearless advice" but added that he depended on the public service being "professionally responsible for the delivery of services".[24] Some saw these remarks as playing down policy advising although they were ambiguous enough to avoid that construction.

Then in August 2019 the Prime Minister made speech setting out his intentions for the public service as a whole. Now he invoked what he said his rugby coach called "the bacon and egg principle, the chicken is involved but the pig is absolutely committed to the task".[25] While the relevance of this "principle" was not entirely clear, Morrison set out half a dozen "guideposts" to give a greater understanding of "how the APS can better support the Government...and our nation".[26] These were:

1. Ministers should respect the public service's "policy advice and implementation skills" and once policy is settled "expect them to get on and deliver it".[27]

2. "It's about implementation" and public servants "are the implementers".[28]

3. "Look at the scoreboard", that is to say set targets and evaluate.[29]

4. "Look beyond the bubble" and have a "laser like focus on serving quiet Australians" with noisy ones taking second place perhaps.[30]

5. Drawing on another "rugby league legend", "read the play and stay ahead of the game".[31]

6. "Honour the code", which the Prime Minister explains as "it's all about governance and integrity" and that he's all for "an APS that is apolitical, merit-based and committed to the highest standards of integrity".[32]

It is difficult to know how helpful this folksy advice was to the Review or the public service in general.

The Thodey Report: What it said

The Review members signed off on their report on 20 September 2019. They said it "looked at key actions that must be taken to ensure the APS is fit for purpose to serve all Australians now and in the decades ahead" adding that implementation of its recommendations "needs to commence with strong leadership and direction by the Government and the Secretaries Board", a hope that was soon to run into rough weather.[33]

Badging its views under the "aspiration" for a "Trusted APS, united in serving all Australians", the Review organised its report and recommendations under eight headings – "deliver better outcomes", "transform for the future", "unite to succeed", "partner for greater impact", "embrace data and digital", "invest in people", "build a dynamic and responsive organisation" and "empower leaders to make a difference".[34]

In 2018, Thodey said "if we end up with a list of fifty recommendations, we will have failed." The Review managed to avoid this unusual criterion for success (or failure); it made a mere 40 with a few sub-recommendations. It is not possible here to go through all of these though a small selection can be taken to indicate their character and worth:

- While sensibly recommending principles for machinery of government changes and decisions about the outsourcing of functions, the Review refrained from making suggestions about what those principles should be.

- After making a largely unevidenced claim that the public service "is failing to recruit people with diverse skill sets", "a targeted program to recruit external mid-career and senior professionals" to be "modelled on graduate recruitment" was commended. However, the report does not say how this would work and how it might fit with the current promotion system that allows all and sundry to apply for all vacancies above the base level as they arise and compete openly for them on merit.

- Arguing for the value of diversity in staffing, the report recommends that the Secretaries Board set a "2030 diversity goal" although it made no suggestions about how such goals might be met nor did it show any awareness of experience with legislated equal employment opportunity plans in the 1980s.

- Sensible suggestions were made about building up staff capability and improving research and analysis to assist with policy advice. But these suggestions were confined to the supply side and nothing was said about encouraging ministers and governments to demand greater policy support from the public service. Relatedly, no practical suggestions were made about the widespread use of consultants and contractors to undertake tasks usually performed by public servants and the effect of such habits on capability and merit staffing.

- On the appointment and tenure of Secretaries, the Review said that the Secretary of the Department of the Prime Minister and

Cabinet should have "joint responsibility" with the Public Service Commissioner for advising the Prime Minister on appointments and two lines below says the Public Service Commissioner should "advise the Prime Minister on Secretary appointments" (in agreement with the PM&C Secretary). It then says that the Commissioner should advise on terminations "in consultation with the PM&C Secretary". These recommendations blur responsibilities and imply a mismatch between appointment and termination powers.

- On implementation, the Review gave no indication it had studied the successful implementation of the Coombs and Reid reviews. Their lessons seem ignored and a claim that the Coombs Commission proposals "were addressed over a 30 year period" is not true.

These criticisms may seem trivial. However, they are typical of great swags of the report and its recommendations reflecting inadequacies of analysis leading to inexactitude and imprecision and an inability to provide practical mechanical suggestions for change in too many instances.

Government's response to the Report

On 19 December 2019, the Morrison Government released the Thodey Report and set out its response to its 40 or so recommendations.[35] Fifteen were agreed, 20 agreed in part, three not agreed while two were noted. That is not a bad numeric strike rate although a few qualifying observations are warranted.

Of those agreed, some were proverbial and could only be rejected out of spite rather than reason. For example, who could not agree with a recommendation to "establish dynamic portfolio clusters to deliver government outcomes"? Similarly, others like bringing back "capability reviews" of departments and agencies were sensible.

Some recommendations in the "agreed in part" or "disagreed" categories deserved to be there. For example, the thought that experience in two or more "portfolios" be a mandatory requirement for entry to the Senior Executive Service was silly and deserved to be binned. As did the recommendation that the Public Service Act be amended to make the Secretaries Board the "principal decision making forum ... for the APS" with its decisions "binding" and "taking primacy over individual Secretary decisions". This reflects a stunted appreciation of the ways in which the machinery of government works.[36]

More seriously, in rejecting recommendations to drop arbitrary staff ceilings and their inflexibilities, moving to common pay scales and other conditions of employment and improving procedures for advising on Secretary appointments the Government abandoned much of the structural muscle in the Thodey wish list. Interestingly, the Government was pleased to say that these rejections came at the urging of the Secretaries Board, the agent Thodey saw as leading the charge into the sunny uplands of a better and brighter future.

More words from the Prime Minister

In announcing the Government's response to the Thodey Report, Prime Minister Morrison set out his "expectations for the APS in six guideposts"[37] presumably displacing those largely based on rugby league "principles" he enunciated in August. The new "guideposts" were:

- clear roles and priorities
- better services
- getting delivery right
- connecting the APS to all Australians
- adapting to change and,
- reinforcing integrity[38]

In a way these are variations on his August themes although not markedly more helpful. Still the Prime Minister added that taking on the Thodey Report was "part of our commitment to build the APS's capability and workforce to better support Australians, grow our economy and create jobs, and keep Australians safe".[39]

Implementation

The Review's report included a brief appendix setting out what it saw as the essentials for successful implementation of its recommendations.

It emphasised the need for investment and suggested around $100m as a start. The Morrison Government offered $15m.

On the mechanics, Thodey recommended the appointment of a "transformation leader" who would develop a "transformation program in close consultation and agreement by the Secretaries Board".[40] These officials would work to the Prime Minister and the Public Service Minister.

If the Review had studied the successful implementation of the recommendations of the Coombs and Reid reports, and there is no evidence that it did, it would have been made aware that the critical element in implementation is for ministers to take the lead and gain political commitment. With that, both funding and the prospects of priority for legislation can be more assured. The Fraser Government had a Cabinet Committee direct implementation of the Coombs Report. The Hawke Government had the Minister for Finance, who was the Public Service Minister, take direct charge of dealing with outstanding Coombs recommendations together with those of the Reid Report. Consequently, government action on both of these reports was comprehensive and thorough and the vast majority of their sensible recommendations were implemented.

The Thodey Report has had no such luck and its over-hyped claims about ensuring "the APS is fit for purpose for the coming decades" now appear largely as pipe dreams.

In April 2022 the Department of the Prime Minister and Cabinet was asked if it could provide an indication of the state of play on the Thodey recommendations accepted by the Morrison Government simply indicating those that had been implemented in whole or in part and those that had not been implemented. Consistent with the Department's unwillingness to provide information to former Senator Rex Patrick on the operation of the so-called "National Cabinet" for which it was castigated by the Judge in the Administrative Appeals Tribunal, the Department declined to provide any information on implementation of the Thodey recommendations accepted by the Morison Government. How this fits with the Thodey notions of a "trusted APS, united in serving all Australians" is not obvious.

Wrap up

The motivation for the Thodey Review remains unclear.

It was saddled by imprecise terms of reference, and it was not independent.

Its members were predominantly from the private sector and had no obvious background and experience for the task.

Its methodology was fumbling and inept. It neither encouraged contributions from departments and agencies and it got very little from them if the public record is anything to go by.

It held no public hearings in which evidence and suggestions could be tested.

It worked off a thin research base.

It wrapped such documentation as it produced, including its final report, in a mesmerising mix of management mumbo jumbo.

It was commissioned by the Turnbull Government and reported to its successor the Morrison Government.

It is hard not to think of the Thodey Review as a missed opportunity for which Mr Thodey and his fellow reviewers, together with relevant Secretaries of the Department of the Prime Minister and Cabinet and the Public Service Commissioner can take the bulk of the credit. There are important lessons to be learned here and they should not be wasted.

Public inquiries mentioned in this chapter[41]

Royal Commission into Australian Government Administration (Coombs, 1974)
Review of Commonwealth Administration (Reid, 1982)
Independent Review of the Australian Public Service (Thodey, 2018)

Notes

1 Malcolm Turnbull, PM and Kelly O'Dwyer, Minister, "Review of the Australian Public Service", *Media Release,* 4 May 2018.

2 For an outline of Commonwealth reviews of the public service, see Paddy Gourley, "Inquiring into government administration", in Scott Prasser and Helen Tracey, (eds), *Royal Commissions and Public Inquiries: Practice and Potential,* Connor Court Publishing, Ballarat, 2014, pp. 204-23.

3 Industry and Science Australia, *Australian 2030: Prosperity through Innovation,* Australian Government, Canberra, 2017, p. 57.

4 Ibid.

5 This address is in the possession of the author.

6 Dr Heather Smith, Address, IPAA Seminar, *Doing Policy Differently: Challenges and Insights,* Canberra, 22 March 2018.

7 See David Thodey, (Chair), *Our Public Service Our Future – Report of the Independent Review of the Australian Public Service,* Commonwealth of Australia, Department of Prime Minister and Cabinet, Canberra, 2019, pp. 13-14 (henceforth, Thodey Report).

8 See transcript of speech on Review's website.

9 Thodey Report, p. 14.

10 Ibid., p. 13.

11 *Royal Commission into Misconduct in the Banking, Superannuation and Financial Services Industry* was appointed in December 2017 and reported in February 2019 and

was chaired by former High Court Justice Kenneth Hayne.

12   For details about the process see Thodey Review, *Report*, pp. 352-63.

13   John Reid, Chairman of James Hardies Industries was appointed by the Fraser Government in September 1982 to chair the *Review of Commonwealth Administration*. It reported in January 1983 just a few months before the Fraser Government lost office at the March elections.

14   See JR Nethercote, "Public Service Reform: Its Course and Nature", in Alexander Kouzmin, JR Nethercote and Roger Wettenhall, (eds), *Australian Commonwealth Administration*, CCAE, Canberra, 1983, pp. 32-3.

15   David Thodey, Address Institute of Public Administration Australia (ACT Division), *Priorities for Change*, 19 March 2019 - available of the Review's website, https://www.apsreview.gov.au/

16   Thodey Review, *Priorities for Change*, Commonwealth of Australia, Department of Prime Minister and Cabinet, Canberra, March 2019, p. 15.

17   Ibid., p. 27.

18   Ibid.

19   Ibid., p 29.

20   Ibid., p 35.

21   see Thodey Review website under heading "Media Questions on Review Priorities", containing an article by Stephen Easton, *The Mandarin*, 21 March 2019.

22   Thodey Review, *Priorities for Change*, p. 35.

23   In 2017 Ms Harland was made Secretary of the Commonwealth Department of Employment, Skills, Small and Family Business

24   Scott Morrison, PM, Public Sector Informant, *The Canberra Times*, 4 June 2019, p. 6.

25   Scott Morrison, PM, "Prime Minister's Address to the Australian Public Service", 19 August 2019, in *IPAA Speeches 2019*, Institute of Public Demonstration Australia, ACT Division, Canberra, 2019, p. 42.

26   Ibid., p. 39.

27   Ibid., p. 41.

28   Ibid., p. 42.

29   Ibid., p. 44.

30   Ibid., p. 46.

31   Ibid., p. 46.

32   Ibid., p. 48 and see Public Sector Informant, *The Canberra Times*, 3 September 2019, p 6.

33   Thodey Review, *Final Report*, p. 8.

34   Ibid., p. 10.

35   *Delivering for Australian - A world class Australian Public Service: The Government's APS reform agenda*, Commonwealth of Australia, Canberra, 2019.

36   Ibid.

37   Scott Morrison, PM, "Foreword", in Ibid., pp. 4-5.

38   Ibid.

39   Ibid., p. 5.

40   Thodey Review, *Final Report*, Chapter 2, pp. 56-80.

41   List refers to name of inquiry, its chair and date of appointment.

8

Fit for the Future: Public inquiries and NSW local government

Andrea Wallace

Introduction

In 2016, after nearly four years of deliberation and a 'consultative' public inquiry, the New South Wales (NSW) Coalition Government embarked upon its *Fit for the Future* policy. This policy was focused on improving the financial state of NSW local government councils through a program of forced council amalgamations.

The *Independent Local Government Review Panel* (ILGRP) was appointed by the NSW Government in April 2012 to provide independent policy advice and governance options for NSW local government. The ILGRP is a public inquiry as it was temporary, composed of members from outside of government, obliged to conduct open processes of investigation, collect evidence and report its findings publicly, and was independent to its appointing government.[1] As an investigative policy inquiry, the ILGRP was deemed responsible for identifying alternative governance models, researching and developing alternative structural models for NSW local government, which included identifying the barriers and incentives to encouraging voluntary council amalgamations or boundary adjustments. The ILGRP possessed no powers as it was formed to provide policy options, make recommendations to government and was narrowly focused on local government reform.

As a case study of a public inquiry, the formation of the ILGRP, and adoption by the NSW Government of a number of its recommendations, is an interesting, and perhaps unique example of how a new government, elected on a promise of no-forced council amalgamations, appointed a public inquiry to provide policy advice on how to reform and improve NSW local government, adopted the public inquiry recommendations, and created significant financial and political upheaval in NSW. This case study of the ILGRP may also illuminate why implementing public inquiry recommendations without conducting rigorous due-diligence may cause more problems than it set out to solve.

This chapter focuses on the policy inquiry conducted by the ILGRP between 2012-14 in NSW, which recommended the wholesale forced amalgamation of a number of NSW councils and informed the NSW Government's disastrous *Fit for the Future* structural reform policy program.

The paradox of Australian local government

Every State and Territory in Australia has its own system of local government. All local government systems in the Australian federation face the same challenges, regardless of jurisdiction. Australian local government has no constitutional recognition, and exists at the behest of its State government, which has extensive powers over it, including to forcibly amalgamate councils if it so chooses. Local government, as the handmaiden of its ruling State government, is limited in its ability to raise its own revenue and is an unequal governance partner.

Australian councils operate and exist within a paradox. Councils, as the third-tier of the Australian trinity of government, are democratic institutions with democratically-elected councillors representing the community it serves. Conversely, councils are obliged to operate like a corporate entity. The Bains Report of 1978[2] influenced the way councils operate and saw the increased integration of corporate management practices into council administration and operation, such as how resources were allocated, and changing from a Town Clerk system to an all-powerful General Manager. This economic and political paradox, expectations of a democratic institution operating like a corporate entity, is the political and economic environment in which much of the world's local government systems endeavour to operate, and it is this paradox that has been the impetus for structural reform programmes of councils world-wide.

The functions of local government and the role it fulfils above and beyond the trope of 'roads, rates and rubbish' are integral to a community's quality of life, however these functions are costly when councils operate both as a democratic institution and as a corporate entity. Public policy advice and reform, throughout much of the world and increasingly over the last few decades, has focused on structural reform through forced council amalgamations in an effort to transform local government into a more economic, efficient and financially self-reliant level of government. Proponents of structural reform believe that a bigger council is more cost efficient and is more able to capture economies of scale and scope. The notion that a bigger council is cheaper to operate has, repeatedly, underpinned the narrative of structural reform programs in Australia.

Local government is a significant part of Australia's economy; in 2018-19 it employed approximately ten percent of Australia's public service, collected $18.9 billion in rates, and its total expenditure was $38.8 billion.[3] It is one of Australia's largest employers, and especially so in regional, rural, and remote Australia. Local government provides a significant amount of community and state infrastructure and owns a considerable number of assets. In addition, local government is the government of 'last resort' in non-metropolitan areas and provides services to its community because it is the only form of government with on the ground services and staff in that location. Councils, however, are constrained in their ability to raise revenue: rate-pegging is common throughout Australia and many non-metropolitan areas have a low population base from which to raise revenue. This has resulted in a council system that is reliant upon State revenue and grants and combined with the cost-shifting of services and functions from State to local government, many Australian councils possess a significant infrastructure backlog and operating deficits.

Why was this public inquiry appointed?

There are a multitude of reasons why governments appoint public inquiries. At face value the reasons for a public inquiry may include its appointment for fact-finding and research services in the absence of more suitable in-house research units. Promoting public consultation and input into significant policy change, or providing independent, expert advice on a complex policy issue are also both legitimate reasons for the appointment of a public inquiry. Alternatively, the appointment of a public inquiry can be politically expedient; if government has already decided on a course of action, it seeks to have that legitimised through the public inquiry mechanism and can thus ensure government is perceived to be acting in a rational manner and in the public interest, and therefore minimise any criticism and opposition.

In early 2011 a new Liberal-National Coalition was voted into power in NSW. Led by Premier Barry O'Farrell, they branded their election campaign with the slogan "Real Change for NSW" to signify its departure from its Labor predecessors which had been in office for 16 years. Included in the Coalition's election campaign for "Real Change for NSW" was their explicit policy promise of "no more forced council amalgamations".[4] However, the new Coalition Government was also determined that its plans for economic growth would not happen without local government reform.[5] The local government sector in NSW, at this stage comprised of 152 general purpose councils, agreed to partake in a special local government conference on 17 and 18 August 2011 at Dubbo, NSW to discuss the future of NSW local government.

The conference, *Destination 2036*, was organised and facilitated by Elton Consulting under instruction from the NSW Government, in partnership with the Local Government and Shires Association of NSW (LGSA) and the NSW branch of the Local Government Managers Australia (LGMA NSW). It was the largest conference of its type ever held in NSW for local government. *Destination 2036* was attended by elected and executive representatives from every NSW council. Seminars held considered NSW's future development and growth, and also expanded upon anticipated future council challenges. Over two days, conference participants attended forums, workshops and raised questions about NSW local government.

Immediately after the conference, Don Page, then Minister for Local Government, a National Party member, announced the formation of an Implementation Steering Committee (ISC) to refine the outcomes of the conference into a plan of action. The ISC, comprised of presidents of the Local Government Association of NSW, The Shires Association of NSW, LGMA NSW, and the Chief Executive of the Division of Local Government, was Chaired by the Department of Premier and Cabinet. Conference proceedings were refined into an Action Plan. Members of the ISC met frequently and included representation from the Australian Centre of Excellence for Local Government (ACELG), a research centre based at the University of Technology Sydney (UTS).

The *Action Plan: Destination 2036* (2012) was presented to NSW local government, nearly one year after the aforementioned conference, and following extensive consultation and collaboration between ISC members. Minister Page was careful to reiterate that the *Action Plan* was not an answer to, nor was it a plan of action designed to implement

solutions to problems raised by conference participants at Dubbo but
written to elicit further dialogue into areas where further research
and consultation, beyond the remit of the ISC, was required.[6] The
document outlined the ISC's 'vision' and was presented to councils
and stakeholders as "Stronger Communities through Partnerships".
Attention was directed toward local government's ability to provide
efficient and effective services to their communities; the quality of
council governance; financial sustainability; and strengthening local
government's relationships with other tiers of government, business,
and community stakeholders.[7] The most appropriate council structure
was also considered in the report.

Appropriate council structure, defined by the ISC as "a number
of different structural models for local government"[8] was raised.
Participants at the Dubbo conference had questioned what appropriate
council models and structures were and had very clearly stated that the
usual 'one-size-fits-all' policy approach to local government employed
by previous State governments was not adequate for the heterogenous
mix of NSW councils.[9] Structural reform through forced municipal
merger was not a concern at this stage, after all, the Coalition had
promised to implement its policy of no forced municipal mergers and
Minister Page emphatically emphasised how this remained Coalition
policy. Voluntary boundary changes, however, were raised as being
a means to achieve the ISC vision of strong communities through
partnerships but would not be the first policy employed because
"boundary alteration or amalgamation is complex and costly".[10] It
was made explicit that despite conference outcomes, new options for
NSW councils were required, and further expert research and public
consultation was required.

In April 2012 the Coalition Government, as part of its commitment
to further research and consultation into the state of NSW councils
and in partnership with LGNSW, announced the establishment of a
public inquiry into the sector with the appointment of the *Independent*

Local Government Review Panel (ILGRP).

The publicly stated reasons for the formation of the ILGRP, from both the NSW Government and the ILGRP itself, was that a public policy inquiry, led by experts, was the most rational and informative process of researching future policy options for the State's local government sector. As an independent body operating outside of its appointing government, the ILGRP would be unconstrained by government sympathies or agendas, thus the ILGRP would be the ideal vehicle to provide expert, independent, and evidence-based policy advice to the government. The external membership of its members, the combined experience of the group, and the research capabilities of the appointed ILGRP would better reflect the importance of the local government sector to the NSW economy.[11]

Membership of the inquiry

The ILGRP was formed in April 2012 and consisted of three members drawn from outside of its appointing government. All members were considered experts in the field of local government and had experienced council consolidations throughout their careers. The Chairman of the ILGRP was Professor Graham Sansom, and the other two members were Glenn Inglis, and Jude Munro.

Graham Sansom, at the time of his appointment as Chairman of the ILGRP, was also employed as Professor of Local Government at the Australian Centre of Excellence for Local Government (ACELG), at the University of Technology Sydney (UTS), a federally-funded 'think-tank' consortium established in 2009. The ACELG was originally proposed in the Commonwealth's *National Skills Shortage Strategy* in 2007, and officially announced in 2008 by then Prime Minister Kevin Rudd. Rudd, during his speech announcing the formation of the ACELG, made clear his concerns regarding the financial planning and asset management capabilities of the Australian local government sector. Prior to Sansom's appointment as an ACELG professor, he had been the CEO of the Australian Local Government Association (ALGA), and employed as a general manager of various Australian local government councils.

The second member of the ILGRP, Jude Munro, was a former general manager of several Australian councils, including CEO of the Brisbane City Council until 2010. Glenn Inglis, the third member, had previously been employed as General Manager of the Tamworth Regional Council and was an occasional academic of local government at Charles Sturt University in NSW.

Membership of the ILGRP was thus comprised of one current academic and two former local government general managers. All had shared the 'lived experience' of having consulted for local government: either directly to, or via the ACELG, and all had guided an individual council or council stakeholders through a structural reform programme of forced municipal mergers.

The public inquiry process

The ILGRP was requested by its appointing government to present several different policy recommendations for NSW local government within a timeframe of 18 months. Its terms of reference focused on investigating and identifying options for local government governance models, structural arrangements and boundary changes in NSW, and considered five key themes for NSW local government:

1   Ability to support the current and future needs of local communities
2   Ability to deliver services and infrastructure efficiently, effectively and in a timely manner.
3   The financial sustainability of each local government area.
4   Ability for local representation and decision making.
5   Barriers and incentives to encourage voluntary boundary changes.[12]

Open consultation is an important and key feature of the public inquiry process. The ability to solicit public opinion on the matter at hand and availability of information and evidence used to by the inquiry to support its final recommendations is considered a significant strength of the public inquiry mechanism. However, open processes, including public consultation, did not form any part of the ILGRP's terms of reference. The need to consult widely with stakeholders and the wider community; ensure recommendations were suited to different types of councils; and to consider the Liberal-National's 2011 election policy of no forced amalgamations, were further points the ILGRP were to be mindful of whilst conducting its inquiry. However, these considerations were not part of its explicitly stated terms of reference.[13] Instead, the ILGRP stated its intention to consult widely with the community and its stakeholders in an open and transparent fashion, and because no limits had been placed on how the ILGRP would address its terms of reference, it would make recommendations to government based on evidence gathered and superior supporting research.[14] From its outset, the ILGRP thwarted good policy outcomes by way of its flawed processes and structures.

Empowered with "sufficient resources"[15] with which to conduct its core business of presenting policy options to the NSW Government, the ILGRP began its task of investigating local government policy and structural options from Australia and abroad.

During its duration of 19 months the ILGRP released three interim reports approximately six months apart. Each report outlined the problems NSW councils faced, such as the adverse financial circumstances the sector operated under; and how NSW councils were unable to raise sufficient own-source operating revenue; or how councils were unable to attract or retain adequate numbers of skilled staff to enhance the sector's capacity or capabilities.

Public consultation tours and hearings, both with NSW communities and councils, were held by the ILGRP across the State after the release of each report. Hearings and public consultation meetings held by the ILGRP were often inadequately advertised and raised the ire of affected communities who were not fully informed of when, or where their consultation meeting with the ILGRP would be held. Jude Munro stated that the ILGRP operated with limited funds and was therefore unable to provide extensive advertising for the consultation meetings,[16] directly contradicting Sansom's claim that the ILGRP had sufficient resources at its disposal, and no limits had been placed on how it addressed its terms of reference.

The ILGRP released three public reports. Each report included supporting research conducted by the ACELG, Sansom's employer. For example, research conducted by the ACELG in 2011, such as *Consolidation in Local Government: A Fresh Look*[17] was used to support the majority of the ILGRP proposals and recommendations. Other recommendations made by the ILGRP, such as proposing the NSW local government sector increase its debt level through borrowing, was also supported by ACELG research conducted just slightly ahead of the ILGRP recommendation.

Other research used by the ILGRP was a result of the inquiry outsourcing research to former members of the ACELG, or consultants constrained by extraordinarily narrow terms of reference. It is widely known, for example, that consolidating two or more councils into one operational unit is costly and fraught with problems, however the ILGRP tasked Jeff Tate Consulting to produce a report reviewing the merger outcomes of five NSW councils merged in 2004. Tate's report[18] was used to support the ILGRP's recommendations of wholesale state-wide mergers, even though it used a cherry-picked sample to support the ILGRP's narrative. Tate's report neglected to capture details or data beyond the perspectives of a few especially selected council managers. The financial implications of compulsory council consolidations were not considered by Tate's report at all.

What did each interim report say?

During its tenure as a public inquiry mechanism, all three of the ILGRP's publications outlined its perception of the extant problems facing councils, and proposed recommendations to remedy these problems. These problems facing NSW councils were framed and presented by the ILGRP within an economic narrative. It was conveyed bluntly as "NSW simply cannot sustain 152 councils".[19]

The Inquiry's first report, *The Case for Sustainable Change*[20] was publicly released in November 2012 and established the ILGRP's narrative: that several aspects of NSW local government, including its relationship with the State government, were most in need of change. For example, The ILGRP noted that councils should better develop their strategic capacity to deal with anticipated future challenges such as demographic shifts, fiscal responsibility, asset management and infrastructure backlogs. The enhanced role of mayors was mentioned also, and supported by ACELG research, and that council structures and boundary changes were necessary if the local government sector were to evolve into a mature, and competent third-tier of government.

The second interim, *Future Directions for NSW Local Government*[21] was released in April 2013, six months after the first report. This report echoed the narrative portrayed in the first report: that NSW local government was in a dire state and required "new directions to transform the culture, structures and operations"[22] to improve its capacity to further the State Government's objectives of making NSW number one. This report, however, focused on wide-spread structural reform for councils through the policy tool of forced council amalgamations, and invoked the Barnett Committee Report released in 1973.[23] The ILGRP recommended extensive amalgamation options to "strengthen regional centres" and to remedy the financial problems faced by many of the State's councils, extraordinarily similar to recommendations made by the Barnett Committee. All councils in NSW were subject to a structural, or boundary change recommendation: municipal merger was the preferred option for 105 out of 152 NSW councils. The ILGRP expected that mergers would be finalised by 2016, and if a council had managed to evade any structural or boundary change, its fate would be reviewed in 2020.[24]

The ILGRP's final report, *Revitalising Local Government* was released October 2013[25] and summarised recommendations made in its earlier reports. It presented 65 recommendations for the Government to consider but softened its previous recommendations of merging 105 out of 152 NSW councils to that of 'incentivising' voluntary amalgamations and reconstituting the NSW Boundaries Commission to allow it to independently review municipal merger proposals without undertaking the usual process of Ministerial intervention.

Despite being asked to consider the Coalition's election promise of "no forced council amalgamations" the ILGRP recommended the wholesale merger of NSW councils.

Impact and implementation

Implementation is the most difficult part of any public inquiry process and the one most criticised either for the lack of subsequent government action, or in other cases for being the wrong ones. The ILGRP, like all public inquiries can only make recommendations. It is up to the government of the day to decide what to accept, reject and how to implement those recommendations it may support. Because policy is a political process, government decisions on these matters reflect the politics involved in the issue. Government alone must manage the politics.[26] Real or perceived policy change can result in political repercussions for any government, whether directly related to the recommendations being implemented, or simply from increased scrutiny over the actions and conduct of its members. The ILGRP, once its final recommendations of council consolidations and reconstituting the NSW Boundaries Commission were presented to the NSW Government, disbanded in late 2013. The public inquiry process, whilst primarily utilised to solve policy problems, can create further problems. Public anger and backlash to the ILGRP's publicly released recommendations, alongside NSW Government's refusal to publicly release crucial supporting documentation justifying the merger policy, such as the secretive KPMG report outlining how the mergers would realise NSW approximately $2 billion, created a political failure. The then unfolding political problems facing the NSW Government at this time, although unrelated to the inquiry, had placed the activities of its leaders into the spotlight, and had revealed the questionable behaviour of Premier O'Farrell.[27] So, this meant that prior to decisions concerning the adoption of the ILGRP's recommendations, the Premier and Deputy Premier who had been responsible for appointing the inquiry, were stood down, and the Minister for Local Government, Don Page, was moved to another portfolio. Such a change, like a change in government, can have a significant impact on the fate of public inquiry reports as they have essentially lost their sponsor.

Nevertheless, in September 2014 the Government now under new Premier Mike Baird[28] adopted the ILGRP's recommendations in its *Fit for the Future* policy package. Implementation of the *Fit for the Future* policy package was both contentious and controversial. In May 2015 the Legislative Council initiated a parliamentary inquiry, *General Purpose Standing Committee Number 6*. Led by Christian Democrat Paul Green and supported by both the Greens and the Shooters parties, this upper house parliamentary inquiry focused on the processes leading to, and the implementation of the *Fit for the Future* amalgamation policy. The majority of submissions presented to this inquiry refuted the notion of cost saving through amalgamation claims that underpinned the *Fit for the Future* policy. Submissions presented by two former members of the ILGRP, however, did not. Sansom's submission contradicted the actions of the ILGRP; for example, Sansom denied making explicit recommendations to the NSW Government[29] even though the

ILGRP's final report contained 65 explicit recommendations, and he claimed that the NSW Government and public had misinterpreted the ILGRP's proposals. Amalgamation, claimed Sansom, was not the ILGRP's prime focus.

The Parliamentary Committee's final report was publicly released in October 2015. Its findings queried whether *Fit for the Future* was the best way to achieve structural local government reform and made several recommendations including that the Premier and the Government withdraw their statements that 70 per cent of Sydney councils, and 56 per cent of regional councils were "unfit", and to offer voluntary merger incentives to all NSW councils.

Finally, the NSW Government formally announced its forced council amalgamation program on 19 December 2015. Five months later, on 12 May 2016, 19 newly merged councils were proclaimed.

Conclusion

This chapter has outlined the formation, processes and implementation of the recommendations made by the ILGRP, a public policy inquiry established by the NSW Government in 2012. The majority of its recommendations firmly focused on council consolidation and were adopted by NSW Government as part of its *Fit for the Future* policy reform package. Secondly, despite other options for providing policy advice available for NSW Government, the government chose to use an external public inquiry. Thirdly, the ILGRP's recommendations to the NSW Government demonstrate why, despite protestations to the contrary, NSW local government is in a far more parlous financial state than what existed before the ILGRP.

The significance of this particular public inquiry for local government is two-fold. Firstly, State government, in both NSW and elsewhere in Australia, continues to regard local government as its handmaiden, and something that can be changed or restructured at will to reflect a changing State government agenda or when some window of opportunity presents itself. Secondly, partnerships between State and local government are not possible if ill-considered policy recommendations ignoring extant research are implemented. The ILGRP, the focus of the present chapter, ignored the financial implications of forced council amalgamations, and this ignorance of the financial costs associated with forced municipal mergers has resulted in several NSW councils, such as the Central Coast Council, verging on the brink of bankruptcy, or other councils later undergoing an expensive de-amalgamation review. The significance of this public inquiry for NSW's democratic processes is also significant because the ILGRP was a politically expedient policy inquiry. Public inquiries should be open, transparent and receptive to public opinion because these are its main strengths. The ILGRP, however, ignored both public sentiment about forced council mergers, the evidence about their costs and neglected to engage effectively with those communities who were most impacted by its recommendations.

Independence, perceived or real, in the agenda, processes and recommendation of a public inquiry is important because it maintains trust in its appointing government. The ILGRP recommended a course of action contrary to its appointing government's explicitly stated policy stance, however as a politically expedient policy inquiry, the ILGRP could be considered to have reflected the implicit agenda of its appointing government.

Public inquiries and the processes they employ, should inspire trust in democratic government mechanisms. Policy decisions, when made poorly, can create an enormous amount of mistrust in government, but good policy processes through an effective open public inquiry process can assist in gaining support for important policies, even if they may initially be unpopular.

Public inquiries mentioned in this chapter[30]

New South Wales Committee of Inquiry into Local Government Areas and Administration (Barnett, 1973)

Independent Local Government Review Panel (Sansom, 2012)

Notes

1   See Scott Prasser, "Royal Commissions in Australia: When Should Governments Appoint Them", *Australian Journal of Public Administration*, Vol 65, No 3, September 2006, p. 31, for definition of a public inquiry.

2   Malcolm Bains, (Chair), *Report to the Minister for Local Government into Local Authority Management in New South Wales*, NSW Government Printer, Sydney,1978.

3   Australian Local Government Association, *Key Facts and Figures*, 2022, Accessed: https://alga.com.au/facts-and-figures/

4   Julia Kurtz. 3AD, "Toole: It's a Promise." *Oberon Review*, 9 March 2011.

5   *Sydney Morning Herald*, "A Bold and Welcome Stance on Council Mergers", 24 October 2014..

6   Destination 2036 (D2036), *Destination 2036: Action Plan*. Elton Consulting, Sydney, 2012, p. 6.

7   Ibid., p. 7.

8   Ibid., p. 15.

9   Ibid., p. 30.

10 Ibid., p. 31.

11 New South Wales Government, *NSW 2021: A Plan to make NSW Number One*, Government of New South Wales, Sydney, 2011.

12 Graham Sansom, (Chair), Independent Local Government Review Panel, (ILGRP), *Better Stronger Local Government: The Case for Change*, Government of New South Wales, Sydney, 2012, p. 5.

13 Ibid.

14 Ibid.

15 ILGRP, *Revitalising Local Government.*, 2013, p. 10.

16 "Forum Poorly Planned", *St. George and Sutherland Shire Leader*, 30 May 2013.

17 Australian Centre of Excellence for Local Government. (ACELG), *Consolidation in Local Government: A Fresh Look*, Australian Centre of Excellence for Local Government, Sydney, 2011.

18 Jeff Tate Consulting Pt. Ltd., *Assessing processes and outcomes of the 2004 Local Government boundary changes in NSW*, 2013, McLaren Vale, South Australia.

19 ILGRP, *Revitalising Local Government*, p. 72.

20 ILGRP, *Better Stronger Local Government: The Case for Change*, 2012.

21 ILGRP, *Future Directions for NSW Local Government- Twenty Essential Steps*, 2013.

22 Ibid., p. 4.

23 Cedric J. Barnett,(Chair), New South Wales Committee of Inquiry into Local Government Areas and Administration, *Final Report*, Department of Local Government, NSW, Sydney, 1973.

24 ILGRP, *Future Directions for NSW Local Government- Twenty Essential Steps*, 2013,

pp. 61-2.

25   ILGRP, *Revitalising Local Government,* 2013.

26   For discussion of this issue see Scott Prasser, *Royal Commissions and Public Inquiries in Australia,* 2nd ed, LexisNexis, Chatswood, 2021, pp. 183-208.

27   "Barry O'Farrell's resignation an error of tragi-comedic proportions", *Canberra Times,* 16 April 2014.

28   Mike Baird had been Minister for Infrastructure, but the unexpected resignation of Barry O'Farrell as premier in 2014 resulted in Baird taking on that role. He held the position until he retired in 2017.

29   Graeme Sansom, (Chair), *Inquiry into Local Government in New South Wales, Submission No 132* Legislative Council Inquiry into Local Government in New South Wales 8 July 2015

30   List refers to name of inquiry, its chair and date of appointment.

Section 3: Impacts of inquiries

Introduction: Is impact important?

Scott Prasser

Introduction: Is impact important and how do we know?

As highlighted in the Introduction there is great dissatisfaction with the implementation and impact of public inquiry reports. This is not a new complaint. It is as old as public inquiries themselves. Someone, at sometime, believes an inquiry's recommendations have not been implemented, or only partially, or possibly wrongly. Of course, it is sometimes forgotten that public inquiries in Westminster systems, are appointed by executive government, for executive government. Public inquiries do not exist as a separate entity in the political system with powers of implementation. They are temporary bodies that disband once their report is submitted. They and their members usually have no ongoing formal role unless executive government wishes it.

Complaints about the impact of public inquiries come from many sources. Stakeholders and more particularly, those who agitated for a particular inquiry to be established, are often disappointed that the inquiry report did not give what was expected or wanted. This was the case with *Royal Commission into Agent Orange*[1] (1984). Other complainants include those who have chaired an inquiry – they sometimes feel either their report was ignored or deliberately misinterpreted. Occasionally, chairs, appropriately or not, go public with their frustrations or concerns about how a government is responding to their report (see **Chapter 11**). The media are eager to highlight what recommendations have been accepted by government, but perhaps not progressed. The media also often expects and even demands, without any critical analysis of the quality, practicality or costs, the full acceptance and implementation of all the recommendations.

The reason why inquiry implementation and impact are so stressed is that for many it is the most important signal as to whether an inquiry was established for legitimate reasons to address a problem or whether it was only appointed for politically expedient reasons to show concern, and to buy time. As a result, given certain political circumstances like an impending election, governments often promise to accept all recommendations – even before the report has landed. Anita Mackay highlighted this earlier in **Chapter 4** concerning the Victorian Andrews Government in relation to the *Royal Commission into Victoria's Mental Health System*.

It is also important to distinguish between acceptance of an inquiry's recommendations and their actual implementation and whether these have any impact on the issue under review. Recommendations may be readily accepted by a government, but little action may follow. Implementation must be more than just acceptance of recommendations or of good intentions to do so. For instance, have extra needed resources been allocated or not? Numerous committees may have been formed to oversee the recommendations, but what exactly have they done? Have existing administrative practices or personnel that may have been part of the problem that was investigated by an inquiry been changed? It is also essential to identify what exactly is being accepted by the government – lots of technical recommendations may be accepted which looks impressive, but will it lead to the more wide-ranging reforms that are needed? There is also the issue of whether any urgency is being given to the implementation of recommendations. If the government's response is slow, delayed by resource constraints, interdepartmental territorial boundary disputes, or other competing priorities, then needed changes may not happen in time before a similar crisis causes the same problems to reoccur.[2] Patrick McClure who chaired the 2001 *Welfare Reference Group* (see

Chapter 5) has commented that although there had been a high level of endorsement to his report's recommendations by the Howard Government implementation was "disappointingly slow" and caused the recommendations "to lose momentum".[3]

Then there is the issue of measuring impact. Writing in the 1930s American political scientist HF Gosnell's conclusion that "it is enormously difficult to trace the influence of a given royal commission"[4] remains pertinent today for the same reasons as it was then. It is often difficult to disentangle the recommendations of a royal commission being implemented from other developments and changes happening at the same time. Also, some inquiry recommendations may take a long time to have an effect. As discussed in **Chapter 3** concerning taxation inquiries, the *Asprey Tax Review* proposed a goods and service tax in 1975, but it was not until 1999 that it became law. The related issues is that any assessment of impact must be framed as to whether an inquiry's recommendations led to better public policy.

In addressing these issues Alastair Stark in **Chapter 9** focuses on measuring inquiry success and proposes four criteria in gauging this programmatic; political; process; and the durability of recommendations across time. These are complementary. An inquiry needs to produce recommendations that address the problems (programmatic), but which are also politically acceptable. Legitimacy, as well as the quality of an inquiry's recommendations will always be enhanced if it is supported by a good process in terms of properly structured meetings, collection of evidence, and reports that reflect or show careful deliberation of the evidence received or researched. Other public policy practitioners have also long preached the importance of process.[5] Last there is the durability of the recommendations. Do they stand the test of time as well as changing governments? Overall, Stark is more positive about the successful impact of public inquiries than others, but warns that there needs to be a consistent framework to measure their success or otherwise.

Marlene Krasovitsky in **Chapter 10** in asking whether inquiries are worth it responds by suggesting an additional framework of analysis. This goes beyond assessing inquiry impact just from the viewpoint the executive government, but more from the perspective of society as a whole. After all, many inquiry reports are on issues of considerable social importance. Public inquiries, it is argued, are not just tools of government, but also tools of society, because they express a significant dimension of the social contract, and the reciprocal acceptance of obligations between citizens and their governments. Public inquiries are appointed to respond to crises, scandals, or failed policies that violate public expectations of these reciprocal obligations. Krasovitsky suggests three lenses to assess inquiry success – whether the inquiry responds to a crisis and restores legitimacy; whether it gives voice to those most adversely affected; and whether it provides an opportunity for policy change and real improvement in the underlying issues that caused problems to develop. These lenses are applied to three major royal commissions as a means of evaluating their worth and in so doing this Chapter provides a new and much wider perspective in assessing the impact of inquiries than previously.

On a different tack, Robert Carling in **Chapter 11** in his assessment of the 2021 *Royal Commission into Aged Care Quality and Safety*, questions whether its recommendations were appropriate involving as they did large increases in Commonwealth expenditure, given the growth in social spending since 2002. Carling highlights how the sensitive nature of the issue being investigated, the timing of the report on the eve of the federal budget, combined with interest group and media pressure meant the hard-pressed Morrison Government had little alternative but to increase aged-care funding regardless of wider budget consequences. Even so, this increased funding was deemed too low by one of the former commissioners who subsequently publicly attacked the Morrison Government. This raises an altogether different issue about the appropriate post-inquiry behaviour of former commissioners as to whether they should actively promote their report or just leave it for the government to decide.

Chapter 12 by Dominic Elliott on the impact of major UK inquiries into child abuse provides an international perspective on this issue and asks whether governments can learn and remember from single one-off inquiries? Although the chapter focusses on horrific cases of child abuse the issues raised are like those raised about disaster inquiries whereby lessons are often not fully remembered, and policies not changed so that similar problems reoccur. Elliott warns that too much might be expected of single, ad hoc inquiries in having lasting impacts on particular problems given the realities of modern organisational life with the operation of multi-agency involvement in addressing complex social issues. In addition, frequent government departmental restructurings, high turnover of senior and on-the-ground personnel, and changing professional practices do not help.

Following on, John Phillimore and Peter Wilkins in **Chapter 13** tackle an issue that deserves attention given the increasing complexity of the issues royal commissions are being asked to resolve. Phillimore and Wilkins acknowledge the strengths of the public inquiry instrument, like royal commissions, to probe deeply, to uncover corruption, and to allocate responsibility. However, they question whether such bodies, dominated as they are by current or former judges and characterised by legalistic and formal processes, are the appropriate mechanisms to make wide-ranging policy recommendations. Such issues were also raised in the preceding **Chapter 11**, in several earlier chapters and by others who have studied the role of inquiries.[6]

Notes

1. *Royal Commission into the Use and Effects of Chemical Agents on Australian Personnel in Vietnam*, rejected a link between Agent Orange and disease among Australian defence staff resulting in a severe backlash from veterans and criticisms from the Hawke Government.

2. Graham Dwyer, "Learning to learn from bushfires: perspectives from

Victorian emergency management practitioners", *Australian Journal of Public Administration*, Vol 80, No 3, September, 2021, pp. 602-612; Heath Whiley, *Post-Disaster Royal Commissions: Lesson-Learning and the Implementation of Recommendations*, PhD Thesis, Schools of Social Sciences, University of Tasmania, 2017.

3   Patrick McClure, "Hearts and Heads: The Challenge of Welfare Reform", in Tom Frame, (ed), *The Desire for Change, 2004-2007, The Howard Government, Vol IV*, UNSW Press, Sydney, 2021, p. 177-93

4   Harold F Gosnell, "British Royal Commissions of Inquiry", *Political Science Quarterly*, Vol 49, 1934, p. 112.

5   Peter Bridgman and Glyn Davis, *The Australian Policy Handbook*, 2nd ed, Allen and Unwin, Sydney, 1998, p. 27.

6   Michael Eburn and Stephen Dover, "Learning Lessons from Disasters: Alternatives to Royal Commissions and other Quasi-Judicial Inquiries", *Australian Journal of Public Administration*, Vol 74, No 4, December, 2015, pp. 175-82

9

Measuring public inquiry success

Alastair Stark

Introduction

The title of this edited collection invites us to reflect on the value of the public inquiry in the modern polity. Are inquiries a help or a hindrance today when it comes to the challenges of contemporary governance? The truth is that those of us who have studied inquiries for some time still struggle to answer that question. This is partly because of the impossibility of making a definitive and generalisable call about the worth of every inquiry. However, it is also in part a consequence of the fact that we are still unsure about how we ought to go about systematically evaluating single inquiries. This chapter responds to this issue by asking a more modest, but still significantly challenging, question than the one that headlines this book; namely, how can we know when a single public inquiry is a success? In answer, a framework for the evaluation of inquiry success is presented here in the hope that it might improve the way in which we evaluate them. Only once that step has been taken can we genuinely move closer to addressing the larger question of whether these institutions are still relevant in the twenty-first century.

The single biggest issue when it comes to properly evaluating an inquiry is the fact that they have the potential to perform many different functions simultaneously. Inquiries are regularly used by ministers and bureaucratic elites, for example, to perform *political* functions. In this regard they are often defined as 'agenda management' mechanisms, which can ensure that hot political issues get cooled or, conversely, that cool issues get enflamed.[1] Inquiries can also be used to produce *policy learning* outcomes, which can subsequently drive meaningful reform and change.[2] This function is often turned towards when policy issues appear to be 'wicked', cyclical or so profoundly shocking that an exceptional policy response is required. However, inquiries can also deliver important *symbolic outputs* that are necessary in the wake of large-scale trauma or institutional failures which de-legitimise the status quo.[3] This is not an exhaustive list by any means. Inquiries can do much more, but the crucial point is that their outputs are multi-dimensional in nature and any evaluation must reflect that. Answering the question of whether an inquiry is a success therefore requires an evaluative framework that is also multi-dimensional and underpinned by an understanding of the many things that an inquiry can produce. This is what this chapter attempts to deliver.

This endeavour is aided by the fact that the study of success is a growing concern in the policy sciences where one can find a small strand of thinkers who have been steadily developing multi-dimensional frameworks, which seek to evaluate policy across several measures. These frameworks can be re-purposed and re-applied effectively to evaluate the multi-dimensional character of the public inquiry. To show how this can be done, the chapter sets out a fourfold framework for evaluating policy success[4], which examines policy, politics and process across time, and then adapts it to the study of the public inquiry. The chapter concludes by discussing the elephant in this particular room, which is the inescapable fact that all institutional evaluations of this nature are coloured by their subjective nature.

Thinking about success

Before laying out the framework that will be developed, a brief precis of the success literature is required as context. Initially, analysts that thought about policy success were content to evaluate it across two criteria, which they labelled 'programmatic' and 'political'.[5] In the former the focus is calibrated on the extent to which a policy addresses the social issues that it is intended to and in the latter attention is given to the ways in which that policy gets represented in the political arena. This distinction between how a policy performs objectively and how it is perceived to perform is the first value to be gained from using the success literature because it directs attention to the asymmetries that can exist between those evaluations. This was well articulated in one early study of policy success in Europe:

> Programmatic success or failure is one thing, the *political* legitimacy of programmatic decisions quite another. The programmatic and political levels need not correlate. Policy and politics in this respect resemble the private firm in which the logic guiding the production division is quite different from the logic of the sales division. ... Thus, successful indicators at the programmatic level may easily be followed by indicators proving high controversy, even 'scandals', and obvious political failure. Or vice versa: something which is definitely a programmatic failure may never attract the attention of the media, the population or important political actors.[6]

Building on this important distinction, Allan McConnell[7] added a third component for the evaluation of success, which relates to process. The accompanying argument that was presented with this new component was that the process through which a political or programmatic output is pursued can produce successful outcomes, and that these can be distinct from the other categories. Thus, for example, an executive enjoying a slim electoral majority might accrue benefits from successfully navigating a piece of legislation through a hostile parliament regardless of whether the legislation is effective or not. Similarly, governments often turn to specific ways of designing policy because they know that there are benefits associated with using them. Perhaps, for example, they wish to show a sensitivity to the lived experience of a specific community and therefore employ a participatory process so that they might co-design a policy with them. Regardless of the detail, the important point is that it is the process itself that produces a benefit, and this is distinct from the programmatic or political output that will subsequently be generated. What this means is that we might see successes in terms of process but failures in programmatic or political assessments. For example, our co-designed policy might still be a spectacular failure in terms of its programmatic impact.

What we can now say is that an evaluation of a policy success can be conducted in terms of programmatic, political or process measurements. However, most recently a fourth piece of the jigsaw has been added to the evaluation puzzle through the addition of a category relating to time. More specifically, it has been argued that policy success must be *durable*. This category has a few components to it.[8] For example, we might choose to look at the cause-effect relationship that underpins a policy and evaluate whether it still holds. In simple terms this means examining whether the theory behind a policy still has the capacity to deliver the objective. It may be, for example, that new technologies overtake older ones, that new forms of evidence bring unintended consequences to light or that notions of appropriateness change in ways which indict historical actions. In each case, the means-end proposition in a policy gets criticised and then replaced. Moreover, policy instruments can also be degraded or forgotten over time as new priorities take over, resource allocation and energy dwindle and the rationale for action wanes.[9] Bringing all of this together leads us to the claim of success scholars that:

> A policy is a complete success to the extent that (a) it demonstrably creates widely valued social outcomes; through

(b) design, decision making, and delivery processes that enhance both its problem-solving capacity and its political legitimacy; c) sustains this performance for a considerable period of time, even in the face of changing circumstances.[10]

As we shall see below, this definition of success and the metrics that are deployed to evaluate its existence can be adapted to produce a comprehensive framework for evaluating public inquiries. However, some work still must be done to re-purpose the framework's categories away from public policies and towards public inquiries. That work requires us to synthesise the framework with existing inquiry literature. We turn to that task below.

Public inquiry success

In the sections below we take the four criteria for assessing success that have been suggested by Paul 't Hart and Mallory Compton and we discuss them in relation to the literature on public inquiries. The purpose is to show how a success framework can be easily re-purposed and applied to the study of a public inquiry in ways which will produce novel findings.

Programmatic success

A programmatic evaluation requires several steps. The first is an evaluation of the 'public value proposition' and 'theory of change' that sits behind a policy. This means examining its objective and the ideas that sit behind it and whether it represents a solution to a recognised problem. The second element involves an examination of whether the policy achieves its intended outcome, and a third evaluation considers what costs and benefits it has created so that intended and unintended outcomes can be uncovered. It is not difficult to adapt these elements to the evaluation of an inquiry. This is because, at a general level, an inquiry's recommendations are policy proposals, underpinned by ideas and theories about change, which seek to encourage policy outcomes. What this means is that a programmatic inquiry analysis would focus upon: 1) the quality of the policy lessons that have been produced; 2) the extent to which those lessons were implemented, and; 3) the outcomes that were produced through implemented policies.

Step one would therefore be centred around determining whether the inquiry produced recommendations that had a capacity to address the problems that caused it to be convened in the first place. In methodological terms, the easiest way to make this assessment is to engage directly with would-be implementers and apposite experts and simply ask: was this an inquiry that produced valid lessons that, if implemented, could address the problem? On one extreme, it is relatively easy to find those inquiries which would encourage a negative response to this question. These will typically be those that were created for reasons other than lesson-learning. For example, it is difficult to argue that the *Royal Commission into Trade Union Governance and Corruption* (2014) was convened to lesson-learn and prompt policy change within Australia's unions. The party-political effects it produced, its combative approach to evidence-taking, its focus on criminal prosecutions and, most importantly, the fact that its recommendations tended to promote pre-existing Coalition policy all meant that its recommendations have not been perceived as genuine attempts at programmatic reform. This can be contrasted against more review-like inquiries, such as the *Equine Influenza Inquiry*, which delivered a series of policy-focused recommendations about the minutia of horse importation in Australia, which we were much more favourably received within the respective policy community.

Step two involves asking whether an inquiry's recommendations got implemented. However, assessing inquiry implementation is incredibly difficult. The first reason for this relates to the willingness of executives to publicly accept recommendations when they have little interest in actioning them. In this regard, governments often report recommendations as accepted or implemented when little has occurred, reframe recommendations in ways which make them less threatening or burdensome, and 'offload' recommendations to other agencies beyond central government.[11] Indeed, these machinations have been a feature of almost every royal commission convened in Australia since the turn of the century. However, would-be evaluators need not despair because analysing these machinations is actually instructive as it delivers an appreciation of the willingness of a government to champion an inquiry's recommendations.

The second reason why analyses of implementation are difficult relates to the challenges involved in tracking specific types of recommendations through complex public sector contexts. However, inquiries are often defined through flagship or big-ticket recommendations that attract attention. For example, the *Royal Commission into the Building and Construction Industry* (2001) recommended the creation of an Australian Building and Construction Commission to regulate that industry, the *Victorian Bushfires Royal Commission* (2009) recommended an extensive overhaul of powerline cabling and, further abroad, *The Independent Commission to Investigate the Introduction and Spread of Severe Acute Respiratory Syndrome (The SARS Commission)* in Ontario recommended the creation of a new public health agency to address pandemic responses. Recommendations of this nature tend to be large in scale, formal-institutional in nature and they often attract public commentary. Therefore, even if every recommendation cannot be tracked to a conclusion, assessment of these easy-to-observe recommendations can deliver a broad assessment of the extent of implementation. Care must be taken here, however, not to conflate implementation rates with policy change outcomes. The implementation of one recommendation out of a hundred might produce game-changing policy effects while a hundred recommendations may only facilitate superficial change. There is therefore a need to perform an analysis of outcomes when it comes to ascertaining programmatic success. This is the third step in evaluating programmatic success.

This step can be assisted by studies that have examined the policy learning outcomes produced by inquiries as these have created typologies which classify outcomes in terms of the policy change that they create.[12] These types of outcome can exist over a range of different scales. For example, some types provide an indication of the scale of a reform outcome. So-called 'instrumental learning' can be compared in this regard against 'social learning'. In the former, the production or revision of small-scale policy tools with associated effects will be an outcome of inquiry implementation. An excellent example here comes from the Pitt Review which examined the United Kingdom (UK) summer floods of 2007. Rather than propose large-scale structural changes to government, its authors instead presented recommendations that suggested the need for many small instrumental adjustments in relation to flood forecasting, warning and response. These small instrumental changes ultimately added up to large-scale reform outcomes.[13] Social learning relates to more seismic changes which affect state-society relations on a more holistic level as the state 'puzzles' its way through changing sociological dynamics. An excellent example of this type of inquiry outcome comes from Canada where the *Mackenzie Valley Pipeline Inquiry* changed the nature of state-society relations by encouraging large-scale debate about the nature of indigenous people's sovereignty.[14] That inquiry started life as an investigation about the viability of an oil pipe but ended as an inquiry which redrew the relationships between indigenous communities and the state. Other differences in policy learning types relate to the focus of recommendations. So called single loop lessons for example can be distinguished from double loop lessons on the basis that the latter focuses on assumptions, values, and cultural norms and leads to value orientated change in public policy while the former concentrates on more observable and ostensible issues of a formal kind. A single loop lesson, for example, might tell us that a fire service needs specific types of equipment to properly fight a bushfire while a double loop lesson might stress how they need an organisational culture which allows them to collaborate with a variety of different agencies at the scene of a disaster. Thus, the *Victorian Bushfires Royal Commission* managed to create a double loop lesson by reforming the so-called 'stay or go' policy in a way which privileged life before property.[15] Once this value was changed, a range of more specific single loop reforms around warning and evacuation were also produced because of that inquiry's recommendations.[16] These kinds of distinction reflect other types, such as that which distinguishes between formal-institutional outcomes and cognitive learning outcomes. For example, an inquiry may propel the creation of a new agency for regulatory purposes (a formal-institutional outcome), but it may also encourage a network of policy actors to understand and learn about each other to enhance policy coordination (a shared cognitive outcome). After the SARS epidemic, for example, the Ontario SARS Commission recommended the creation of Public Health Ontario to lead on disease control policy and, at the same time, encouraged the siloes that separated emergency management and public health to be bridged through better collaboration. Finally, policy learning outcomes can be measured in terms of an individual (the minister better appreciates an issue) or a collective (the ministry learns as an organisation).

Regardless of the specifics, these types allow us to ascertain the nature and extent of a policy outcome following an inquiry and they can be matched to the expectations found in an inquiry report as a measurement of programmatic success.

Political success

When examining political success, the focus is on *legitimacy* and whether a policy has the capacity to generate support or criticism amongst the political classes. More specifically, three questions are used here.[17] First, does the policy attract a broad and deep coalition of support? Second, does association with the policy enhance the political capital of policymakers? And third, does association with the policy enhance the organisational reputation of the apposite agencies associated with it? Once again, these questions are easily adaptable to an evaluation of inquiries, and this adaptive exercise is well supported by a wealth of pre-existing inquiry literature that focuses on the politics surrounding these institutions.

We can begin an evaluation on these grounds by asking whether an inquiry has attracted a broad coalition of support. A simple definition of 'broad coalition' would cover *party politics* in which we might expect, at the very least, bipartisan support for an inquiry as an initial measure of success, *policy communities* in which we might expect the key stakeholders to be supportive and, more broadly, *social support* which would be reflected in positive media coverage and public opinion evaluations. With this baseline, an assessment can begin by analysing the reactions of actors in these spheres to the decision to convene an inquiry in the first instance. In some cases, the convening of an inquiry will be expected, and support will be broad but typically tacit in nature. Few question the convening of an inquiry after large-scale natural disasters for example. In policy areas in which political positions are entrenched, however, the establishment of an inquiry can create a furore. For example, The *Royal Commission into National Natural Disaster Arrangements* after the extreme bushfires of 2019-20 was received with little criticism while the *Royal Commission into Trade Union Governance and Corruption* was dogged by accusations of partisanship from the moment it was convened. Other inquiries are often criticised when they are appointed because of the perception that they are 'tall grass' into which an issue demanding quick action will be punted and forgotten about.[18] Thus, those wishing a quick decision about the legitimacy of the Iraq War felt frustrated by the years of evidence taking that led *The Iraq Inquiry* to its eventual conclusion in England[19] while in Scotland's capital *The Edinburgh Tram Inquiry* into the cost overruns of that city's tram project has become an amusing anecdote for the people of Edinburgh. Convened for the purpose of quickly determining what had gone wrong with a large tram project that was to connect the capital to its airport, the inquiry has been running for seven years but is yet to publish its first report, leaving Edinburgh's citizen to reflect on which is faster: those building the tramline or those investigating it.[20] Often, however, inquiries which are specifically designed to investigate government wrongdoing on a large-scale basis receive broad support from the watching public on the basis that their independence and willingness to speak truth to power are democratic virtues. However, after they have been convened the decisions that an inquiry makes will also affect levels of support. As decisions are made about the terms of reference, the appointment of a chair, and the manner of evidence-taking, legitimacy can be affected. And of course, coalitions of support will be hugely influenced by the quality of the final reports that are produced. The spectacular fall-out between the two chairs who led the *Royal Commission into Aged Care Quality and Safety* (2018), for example, shows how political support for an inquiry can be undermined when personalities and professional backgrounds clash within an inquiry.[21]

The question of whether association with an inquiry enhances political capital and organisational reputation can be addressed with relation to the mass of literature that examines the politics of public inquiries. A great deal of this research tells us that inquiries are agenda management tools that can be used by executives or bureaucrats to reduce threats, enhance credibility and generally ensure that that outcomes are going to work in their favour.[22] Thus, inquiries are said to be 'placebos' that can be convened to give the appearance of action without any firm commitment.[23] An example of political success from this view would be an instance in which a minister receives political capital for establishing an inquiry but subsequently avoids reform once it has reported. Other researchers have shown how inquiries can be steered or stage managed in a way that produces pre-ordained outcomes which appear, from the outside, to have been produced through an independent mechanism.[24] An example of success here might mean an actor or an organisation using an inquiry to enhance the legitimacy of a controversial decision that might otherwise be questioned or undermined.

However, an inquiry need not be used in a Machiavellian manner for it to be considered a political success. Simply accepting the recommendations of an inquiry that is generally seen in a positive light, for example, can produce some short-term good will for any minister and as a consequence, they often make a good show of accepting reports, especially when they are willing to implement their recommendations. Over and above the daily trials and tribulations of party politics, however, sits a view that suggests that inquiries can generate positive sentiments by producing democratic goods. In this regard, they can act as the crucibles for public debate on important topics and the future directions that institutions ought to take (for example, the 2015 South Australian *Nuclear Fuel Cycle Royal Commission*) or alternatively champion the causes of disenfranchised groups who are often marginalised by state structures and dominant institutions (for example, the 2013 *Royal Commission into Institutional Responses to Child Sexual Abuse*). Examples of this sort provide support for an argument that a successful inquiry will draw legitimacy when it is seen as a valuable mechanism that supports the pluralism of a democratic political system.[25] Association with such inquiries, either as sponsor or implementing agency, can therefore enhance reputation, leading to the claim that it has been a political success.

Process success

Public inquiries can work through the analysis of an issue, develop recommendations, but then be completely ignored by government. However, even these inquiries can still produce effects. These are created by the way in which an inquiry goes about its business rather than the outputs and outcomes it does or does not propel. A process evaluation is therefore important (and novel) precisely because it draws us towards a study of those effects which can exist even if an inquiry's recommendations are shelved.

The focus here is therefore directly calibrated towards the effects that are created via evidence-taking and report writing procedures rather than what comes after reports are published. This focus needs to be maintained quite strictly if a process evaluation is to take place as it allows us to sidestep a debate in the success literature which centres on the fact that process effects can also be political or programmatic in nature, thus, so the argument goes, rendering the process evaluation redundant.[26] This debate need not detain an evaluator interested in inquiries, however. By focusing very squarely on inquiry process and ignoring the effects created after reports have been published in their analysis, an inquiry researcher will inevitably produce a process-orientated evaluation that is distinct.

When thinking about the criteria for evaluating evidence-taking and report writing, we can once again be guided by the success literature, which suggests that it is useful to direct attention towards whether "robust deliberation" and "thoughtful consideration" have been involved in the policy process and whether stakeholders experience the making of policy as "just and fair".[27] Taking this into consideration, what might we examine and expect in terms of an analysis of inquiry process? Once again, inquiry literature can help us answer this question.

The most obvious avenue for consideration relates to a strand of research which explores the ways in which inquiries produce 'symbolic outputs'. These are in effect social-psychological benefits which are produced through the act of evidence-taking and report writing. Amongst other things, feelings of reassurance and cathartic tension-release can be produced when inquiries get to work and positive sentiment can be generated around processes that deliver representation and accountability to affected communities.[28] For example, when it comes to reassurance the act of public questioning, the quasi-courtroom staging and rituals used by judges and lawyers, and the production of certain findings about uncertain events can all play an important role in assuring communities that the failures that led to the inquiry will not be repeated.[29] These forms of ritual, and the reassurance they produce, are recognised as one outcome that was produced via the procedures of the *9/11 Commission* in the United States while others have argued that the simplified narratives presented by the *Cullen Inquiry* (into the 1988 Piper Alpha disaster)[30] and the 1993 *Allitt Inquiry* (into the murder of children in UK hospitals)[31] were both aimed at re-legitimising elements of the status quo. Moreover, giving those who have been affected by those failures an opportunity to tell their story can deliver a cathartic outlet that relieves pressure in a political system. Ultimately, this points towards the fact that inquiry processes can provide forms of representation that foster feelings of acknowledgement and inclusion. Correlated around all these outputs is a central concern with accountability, which can be explanatory (what went wrong?), amendatory (how do we fix this?) or sacrificial (who is getting blamed?). Once again, simply playing out an accountability process through a public and independent mechanism can be a process that produces social-psychological outcomes which allows closure of an issue and subsequent movement to a new future.[32] In all of these instances the symbolic output produced through the process emerges because, to use the language of the success literature, the process that inquiries work through presents an image of a mechanism that is 'just and fair' and working in the public interest.

A final point worth considering here in relation to process outcomes relates to the criteria of 'robust deliberation' and 'thoughtful consideration'. When thinking about this in relation to policy we can reflect on the ways in which a good process of policy formulation brings stakeholders together and allows them to understand each other, invites in forms of public participation so that lived experience can be understood and, ultimately, considers evidence in a more rational (and correspondingly less political) manner. These can all be applied to the study of an inquiry as they too can bring actors together and connect them into debates and discussions. Inquiries can encourage disparate groups to build consensual positions around policy and they can deliver evidence and impetus to stakeholders who can use both to forward their own agendas. Thus, even if not implemented by government, the work of an inquiry can still produce effects amongst policy communities who can utilise it for their own ends.

Durable success

The final category in our evaluation of inquiry success is perhaps the most meaningful because it introduces *time* into the equation. The reason that time is important stems from the fact that the issues that inquiries are created to focus on are often long running and re-occurring. Consequently, 'new' inquiries and 'innovative' solutions are often repetitions of the past. One can spend some time in the Australian context, for example, tracking through a legion of public inquiries that have investigated bushfires and whether one examines the Stretton Commission of 1939 or the *Victorian Bushfires Royal Commission* of 2009 the issues remain broadly comparable and, while technologies change, many of the proposed solutions share a great deal of similarity.

The conclusion that some draw from these historical themes is that inquiries are an insufficient means of learning and prompting reform and a significant reason why we seen the failures of the past returning. However, introducing time into an evaluation alongside the other criteria discussed above challenges this assumption. This is because we often see re-occurring issues despite the existence of inquiries which score very well on the programmatic front. This means that learning has taken place, recommendations have been implemented and substantive reforms occurred after an inquiry, yet similar problems in the future reoccur. One explanation for this tells us that good learnings and effective reforms are being forgotten because of institutional amnesia.[33] There are many ways in which this forgetting occurs. Governments are voted out, bureaucracies turn over and get reformed, new policy priorities emerge continuously and public sectors are no longer effective at record-keeping or recalling history. This all means that good inquiry recommendations, even if they are institutionalised into policy, may not last. Thus, one indicator of a successful inquiry ought to be whether its programmatic outcomes have proved to be durable. This indicator is most important in relation to those inquiries which focus on crises and disasters because their lessons may not be relevant until the next one arrives and in the interim their lessons can be forgotten and lost, thus leading to the accusation that we are not learning effectively.

As discussed above, durable successes are those in which the value proposition, performance and support for a policy all maintain across time. There is no reason why these criteria cannot also be directly applied to the policies that are implemented after an inquiry. However, this only speaks to half the story vis-à-vis durability because memory is not just about 'hard' institutional legacies but also about stories, narratives and memorialisation.[34] These are important because if no one can remember the reasons why they do the things they do then reforms will not last. Therefore, assessing durability is not just about whether inquiry driven policies last but also about whether social and cultural memory recalls the inquiry and the story that it told. This second dimension represents an even harder test than the first. Who can remember the collapse of HIH and the narrative that the *HIH Royal Commission* (2001) that investigated it told? Will the lessons generated by the *Royal Commission into the Home Insulation Program* (2013) exist in another decade? Perhaps there is some hope here as certain inquiries do manage to stand the test of time as touchstones that are often returned to in public debate. Names such as Fitzgerald, Coombs and Cole, for example, all resonate with connotations about corruption, the need for good public administration and the fundamental importance of accountability. In those cases, the combination of long-term institutionalised policy reforms alongside forms of socio-cultural memory that recall the reasons why those policies are important, can ensure that inquiries become durable successes.

Conclusion

Hanging over all types of evaluation is the issue of subjectivity. Indeed, the tension between 'objective' and 'constructed' forms of measurement is a well discussed issue in the success literature.[35] The need for brevity here does not permit a full discussion of this issue but, thankfully, we can encapsulate it easily by stating the heart of the issue: namely, that two evaluators can use the framework presented above to examine the same inquiry and come to different conclusions.

Moreover, within and across the four categories presented above we can observe differences in the degree to which they encourage objective forms of analysis. On the one hand, evaluating durability seems clear cut. Inquiry propelled reforms and memorialising stories will either exist or not and an objective analysis can establish that. On the other hand, political success takes us into territory in which beauty really is in the eye of the beholder. This is similar to a process evaluation in which social-psychological outcomes, which, for example, re-legitimise the status quo might be seen by some as a good thing because of the stability they create while others will see those outcomes in a problematic light because of a perceived need to create change. To muddy the water further, a policy learning assessment will have elements of subjective and objective evaluation. Examining the frequency of implemented recommendations, for example, is much more objective than ascertaining the value of an inquiry recommendation or its outcome.

However, the crucial point is that it is not necessarily the job of the evaluator to overcome this issue. It can be accepted as can the fact that the analyses that this framework produces can still be beneficial. It is certainly the case that if the framework presented here is used by different researchers, they may not always concur with each other's conclusions, but they will have used similar metrics which at least allows them to have that debate in the first instance. In other words, if we genuinely want to come to conclusions about the value of inquiries, then we need to first understand that comparisons require a shared evaluative grammar. Thinking about program, politics and process across time can deliver that in a way that allows the debate about public inquiries to begin in earnest.

Public inquiries mentioned in this chapter[36]

Australian – Commonwealth

HIH Royal Commission (Owen, 2001)

Royal Commission into the Building and Construction Industry (Cole, 2001)

Equine Influenza Inquiry (Callinan, 2007)

Royal Commission into the Home Insulation Program (Hanger, 2013)

Royal Commission into Institutional Responses to Child Sexual Abuse (McClellan, 2013)[37]

Royal Commission into Trade Union Governance and Corruption (Heydon, 2014)

Australian – State

Royal Commission to Inquire into the Causes of and Measures Taken to Prevent the Bush Fires of January 1939 (Stretton, 1939)[38]

Commission of Inquiry into Possible Illegal Activities and Associated Police Misconduct (Fitzgerald, 1987)

2009 Victorian Bushfires Royal Commission (Teague, 2009)

Nuclear Fuel Cycle Royal Commission (Scarce, 2015)

Canadian

Independent Commission to Investigate the Introduction and Spread of Severe Acute Respiratory Syndrome (Campbell 2006)

Mackenzie Valley Pipeline Inquiry (Berger, 1977)

United Kingdom

The Public Inquiry into The Piper Alpha Disaster (Cullen, 1990)

The Allitt Inquiry: Independent Inquiry Relating to Deaths and Injuries on the Children's Ward at Grantham and Kesteven General Hospital During the Period February to April 1991 (Clothier, 1994)

The Pitt Review: Lessons learned from the 2007 floods (Pitt, 2008)

The Iraq Inquiry (Chilcott, 2016)

The Edinburgh Tram Inquiry (Hardie, ongoing)

Notes

1   Alastair Stark, "Left on the shelf: Explaining the failure of public inquiry recommendations," *Public Administration*, Vol 98, No 3, September 2020, pp. 609-24.

2   Alastair Stark, *Public Inquiries, Policy Learning and the Threat of Future Crises*, Oxford University Press, Oxford, 2018, pp. 81-104.

3   Adam Ashforth, "Reckoning Schemes of Legitimation: On Commissions of Inquiry as Power/Knowledge Forms," *Journal of Historical Sociology*, Vol 3, No 1, March 1990, pp. 1-22.

4   Mallory E. Compton and Paul 't Hart, (eds), *Great Policy Successes*, Oxford University Press, Oxford, 2019, p. 6.

5   Mark Bovens, Paul 't Hart and B.G Peters, (eds), *Success and Failure in Public Governance*, Edward-Elgar, Cheltenham, 2001, pp. 20-21.

6   Erik Albæk, "Managing Crisis: HIV and the blood supply", in Mark Bovens, Paul 't Hart and B.G Peters, (eds), *Success and Failure in Public Governance*, p. 466.

7   Allan McConnell, *Understanding Policy Success: Rethinking Public Policy*, Palgrave, Basingstoke, 2010, pp. 63-4.

8   Compton and 't Hart, *Great Policy Successes*, pp. 5-6

9   Alastair Stark, "Explaining Institutional Amnesia in Government", *Governance*, Vol 32, No 1, January 2019, pp. 143-58.

10   Compton and 't Hart, *Great Policy Successes*, p. 5.

11   Prudence R. Brown and Alastair Stark, "Policy inaction meets policy learning: four moments of non-implementation," *Policy Sciences*, Vol. 55, January 2022, pp.47-63.

12   Stark, *Public Inquiries, Policy Learning and the Threat of Future Crises*, p. 27.

13   Ibid.

14   Frances Abele, "The Lasting Impact of the Berger Inquiry into the Construction of a Pipeline in the Mackenzie Valley" in Gregory J. Inwood and Carolyn M. Johns, (eds), *Commissions of Inquiry and Policy Change: A Comparative Analysis*, Toronto University Press, Toronto, 2014, pp. 88-113.

15   Stark, *Public Inquiries, Policy Learning and the Threat of Future Crises*, pp. 101-02.

16   Ibid.

17   Compton and 't Hart, *Great Policy Successes*, pp. 5-6.

18   For one example of many, Simon Jenkins, "Public inquiries are institutionally corrupt, we should just give the money to victims", *The Guardian*, 18 June 2021.

19   James Ellison, "Why the Chilcot Inquiry has taken so long – and why we should wait to judge it", *The Conversation*, 28 August 2015.

20   Ian Swanson, "Why is Edinburgh's wait for tram inquiry report now longer than for Chilcot verdict on Iraq?" *The Edinburgh Evening News*, 22 November 2021.

21   Anne Connolly, "Aged care royal commission public split in the final days shows how controversial change will be", *ABC News*, 23 October 2020.

22   Patrik Marier, "Public inquiries" in Marleen Brans, Iris Geva-May, Michael Howlett, (eds), *Routledge handbook of comparative policy analysis*, Routledge, Abingdon, pp. 169-80.

23   Allan McConnell, "The use of placebo policies to escape from policy traps", *Journal of European Public Policy*, Vol 27, No 7, 2020, p. 964.

24   Harold Acland, "Research as Stage Management: The Case of the Plowdon Committee" in Martin Bulmer, (ed), *Social Research and Royal Commissions*, Allen and Unwin, London, 1980, pp. 19-34.

25   Catherine Althaus "Legitimation and Agenda Setting: Development and the Environment in Australia and Canada's North" in Patrick Weller, (ed), *Royal Commissions and the Making of Public Policy*, Macmillan, Melbourne, 1994, pp. 186-97.

26   Mark Bovens, "A comment on Marsh and McConnell: Towards a Framework for Establishing Policy Success", *Public Administration*, Vol 88, No 2, June 2010, pp. 584-85.

27   Compton and 't Hart, *Great Policy Successes*, pp. 5-6.

28   Bryan Schwartz, "Public Inquiries", *Canadian Public Administration*, Vol 40, No 1, March 1997, pp. 72-85.

29   Charles Parker and Sander Dekker, "September 11 and the post-crisis investigation: exploring the role and impact of the 9/11 Commission" in Arjen Boin, Allan McConnell and Paul 't Hart, (eds), *Governing after crisis: The Politics of Investigation, Accountability and Learning*, Cambridge University Press, Cambridge, pp. 255-82.

30   Andrew Brown, "Making Sense of Inquiry Sensemaking", *Journal of Management Studies*, Vol 37, No 1, January 2000, pp. 45-75.

31   Andrew Brown, "Authoritative Sensemaking in a Public Inquiry Report", *Organization Studies*, Vol 25, No. 1, pp. 95-112.

32   Stark, *Public Inquiries, Policy Learning and the Threat of Future Crises*, p. 164.

33   Stark, *Governance*, pp. 143-58.

34   Ibid.

35   McConnell, *Understanding Policy Success*, pp. 30-9.

36   List refers to name of inquiry, its chair and date of appointment.

37   This royal commission was established jointly between the Commonwealth and all States and Territories.

38   This royal commission has a considerably longer formal title.

10

Impacts: Are inquiries worth it?

Marlene Krasovitsky

Introduction

I was in a taxi on my way to Sydney University for my last session with my supervisor before handing in my PhD. The taxi driver asked what I was studying and I told him I was doing a PhD. He asked about what? I said it's about royal commissions.

He asked, are they successful? Do they make any difference? I asked how he knew the subject of my thesis. He said, well, isn't that the obvious question?

Feeling slightly chastened, and notwithstanding that it took me some years to get to that 'obvious' question, I then started responding by saying that "it depends", "not all royal commissions are the same", "it depends on the terms of reference", "it depends on who's perspective you take"… and so on.

Clearly not happy with my equivocal answer, the taxi driver asked again, "but are they worth it? Does anything change? Do they get the bad guys? Because they sure do cost a lot!" All I could say was, we don't know….and you're right, we should.

This is my contribution to that question.

Social contract and the significance of public inquiries

Public inquiries are powerful institutions established by governments to address some of the most distressing, disturbing, and controversial issues and events of public policy and society. Public inquiries occupy a special, often revered, place in many societies. They are mechanisms by which many societies around the world aim to discover the truth, redress wrongs, restore the public's confidence, and give voice to the most disempowered and aggrieved members of society. Public inquiries are the "the highest form of inquiry on matters of substantial public importance".[1] Governments frame these inquiries as trusted, wise, impartial investigators or advisers.

Public inquiries are an important tool of government. With their wide-ranging powers, they have investigated, reported and made recommendations on natural disasters, allegations of corruption, and systemic policy and practice failures.

However, public inquiries are also a powerful instrument of society. The uproar, the outrage, the public interest and the importance of the matters public inquiries are established to investigate are difficult to overstate. Calls for a public inquiry are a potent expression of society's concern over a matter, and a yearning for a means to cut through 'politics' so that it can be dealt with impartially and independently.

This is not to underplay the inherent political, and highly contested, nature of some inquiries. However, even if some inquiries can be characterised as "election stunts"[2], or as a "witchhunt"[3], a public inquiry promises to discover truth, dispassionately investigate and get to the heart of a matter which has fundamentally and egregiously violated the community's expectations.

As such, public inquiries express a significant dimension of the social contract between state and citizens; the agreement between state and citizens to cooperate for reciprocal social and economic benefit. When such mutual obligations or expectations are breached there are consequences. The breach requires repair and remedy. For an individual, such consequences may be prosecution in a court of law and possibly imprisonment. For society, it may be the establishment of a public inquiry to investigate the breach and advise government on response and repair.

It is acknowledged that social contract "is a strongly evocative phrase"[4] and is highly contested. Yet "for more than two centuries, it has stood as a symbol of a political order founded on agreement among rational individuals who are equal participants in the political process".[5]

Weale argues that the:

> ... social contract is a representation of the implicit logic in the normative order of a society, [that is] that the political legitimacy that any social order requires has to be built upon substantial agreement about the social bases of authority... Individuals have to accept certain collective practices and norms if their individual interests are to be secured...In this sense the basic institutions of a society may be regarded as the product of a social contract... Pressure to renegotiate the social contract suggests that dominant institutions are not serving the general interest to a sufficient degree.[6]

It is argued therefore that social contract theory is a valuable and pertinent construct to apply to our thinking of public inquiries.

Public inquiries are a revered part of the social contract. They provide a special place to right wrongs; "[t]hey will always be considered a vital instrument for discovering the truth, for good governance, for improving accountability".[7] They "play an important and indispensable role in checking up on the leaders, in making them responsive to the longer-term interests of a free society".[8]

The following examples in **Table 1** further demonstrate the connection between the breach of the social contract and the public inquiry they triggered.

Table 1: Breach of social contract and the public inquiry response

Breach	Public inquiry response
Trusted officials allegedly act corruptly and breach Australia's international sanctions obligations and gain from holding positions of power.[9]	The Inquiry into certain Australian companies in relation to the UN Oil for Food Programme, 2005
Parents who are well known to the statutory child protection department continue to neglect their seven year old child and she dies alone and in squalor because the department failed to act.[10]	Special Commission of Inquiry into Child Protection in NSW, 2007
Family, friends and neighbours die in floods because they were unaware of the proximity and intensity of danger, or because help failed to arrive.[11]	Queensland Flood Commission of Inquiry, 2011
Trusted clergy abuse and betray children and are subsequently protected by their institution.[12]	Royal Commission into Institutional Responses to Child Sexual Abuse, 2013
A news program broadcasts children being brutalised and tortured in juvenile detention centres.[13]	Royal Commission into the Protection and Detention of Children in the Northern Territory, 2016
On the back of many previous reviews of aged care, a news program presents a view into the lives of those living in residential aged care facilities highlighting instances of poor care within the aged care system.[14]	Royal Commission into Aged Care Quality and Safety, 2018

These triggers were breaches of the social contract, of the shared understandings and expectations we have, as citizens, of our institutions. As citizens we experienced a "crisis of confidence in the integrity of public life or about other matters of vital public importance".[15] Such breaches contravene our expectations of a 'good society'. Citizens build pressure for an independent and powerful body to investigate, right wrongs and strengthen our society and systems so such things are properly and impartially investigated and can never happen again.

Keating's landmark Redfern Speech[16] captured the essential link between wrongdoings, a royal commission, and the need for repair. The report of the *Royal Commission into Aboriginal Deaths in Custody* (RCADIC) showed "with devastating clarity that the past lives on in inequality, racism and injustice" and that this was "a fundamental test of our social goals and our national will". Notwithstanding the controversy that continues to surround this royal commission, Keating believed that the RCADIC and its report is part of our national story, it belongs to us all.

Former Prime Minister Gillard also underlined this link when, referring to the final report of the *Royal Commission into Institutional Responses to Child Sexual Abuse*, she stated; "[i]t really belongs to the nation this Royal Commission and so everything that it has found belongs to the nation, and has to be received by it".[17]

Government is not the only stakeholder in the impact and outcomes of a public inquiry. Writing in the context of the *Royal Commission into the Protection and Detention of Children in the Northern Territory* (reported November 2017), Deslandes reinforces this point, "As public inquiries with far-reaching powers that report to the nation's highest authority, royal commissions do important moral work in Australia. They represent an attempt to reckon with systemic failures in leadership. As an exercise of moral authority they say something forceful about what is right...Indeed the term 'commission' itself refers in some way to the delegation of trusted authority".[18]

This is not to suggest that all citizens are equally as interested or invested in every public inquiry that is established. Nor is it to assert that citizens are one homogenous group, all looking for the same outcome, or assessing success in the same way. As Benington states, "the public sphere is heavily contested territory".[19] It is, of course, true that some public inquiries are more relevant and important to some individuals, interest groups and sectors of the community than others. For instance, while there may be broad community outrage at child deaths and failed child protection systems, there may be a narrower community of interest in a *Royal Commission into the Home Insulation Program*.[20] While there may be broad community concern about banking practices there may be narrower interest in a public inquiry such as the 1986 *Commonwealth Royal Commission into the Costs and Efficiency of Grain Storage Handling and Transport*.[21] However, every public inquiry will have a community of interest other than government. Within this community, people and organisations will undoubtedly have different interests. These varied perspectives on success will always be relevant and are pertinent to questions of success, impact or worth.

However, despite their importance, the significant matters they investigate, the expectations and trust citizens vest in them, and the wide powers delegated to them, we have not yet adequately addressed the question of how successful public inquiries are, nor how success might be assessed. Given the ubiquity and cost of these inquiries, and the significance of the matters they investigate, this must be a pressing question.

A promising but nascent approach may be assessing impact. Prasser and Tracey suggest that an "appropriate measure of the impact of a public inquiry is a judgment about the value of the policy changes it recommends, assessed in terms of the public interest or common good...followed by a second more meaningful question...is the outcome of the inquiry better public policy? ...The soundness of an inquiry's findings rather than their actual implementation is therefore what should be measured".[22]

This two-step process is also echoed by Banks.[23] This is a promising approach but is yet to be reflected in the literature. This chapter expands on the centrality of the notion of the 'public interest or common good' in assessing the success of a public inquiry.

This chapter poses the question, "are they worth it?" The idea of 'worth' is associated with value and has many dimensions: costs and benefits; quality and risk. In the context of public inquiries this chapter will not attempt to divide cost by benefit, weigh up quality of recommendations or risks of implementation, or monetise the value flowing to citizens. It will however focus on success to explore whether public inquiries are 'worth it'.

A word on 'success'

There are many lenses of success. At its most elemental, success can be defined simply – did the public inquiry fulfil the duties assigned to it.[24] Given the diversity of purposes, structures, powers and political environments within which they operate this idiosyncratic, particularised assessment of success is relatively straightforward.

It is a truism to say that success means different things to different people at different times.[25] Subjectively, and as a relational term, success depends in great measure on who you are, where you sit, and your interest or investment in the area under scrutiny by a public inquiry. Success is also relative to intention, that is, what was the intention of the inquiry or proposed reform?[26]

Success can also be assessed on a comparative basis – was the inquiry successful as compared with what would have been achieved through a judicial process, a parliamentary inquiry, regular democratic or policy processes? Significantly, success is also multi-dimensional, so success may be partial.

Assessing success therefore emerges as a complex, nuanced task. Critically, success is always a judgement which is deeply contextual, probably temporal[27] and usually asymmetric between programmatic, policy and political success.[28]

A proxy often used in the literature is effectiveness, that is, the degree to which something is successful in producing a desired result. But what is the desired result of an inquiry? Sometimes the answer to this questions is less than explicit, and as Sulitzeanu-Kenan, observes, is "typically covert, and – in the unlikely event that …[it is] articulated by office holders – unreliable".[29]

What is clear however, is that effectiveness does not equal success. Effectiveness is important but insufficient. Effectiveness pertains to a particular public inquiry and does not provide any explanatory power across public inquiries. Effectiveness goes to questions of the extent to which a public inquiry met its terms of reference; was inclusive; the number and type of submissions it received; the breadth of its hearings; the quality and scope of its research or investigatory efforts; whether it came within budget; met its reporting deadlines; the quality of its report and recommendations. Effectiveness, however, sheds limited light on the success of the institution of public inquiries.

What does the literature say about success of public inquiries?

There is not an extensive empirical or theoretical literature on public inquiries. Prasser[30] argues, in fact, that public inquiries are a largely ignored area of study.

There is literature on the uses, functions and operations of public inquiries, the political context, how commissions are established, terms of reference, processes, reports and recommendations. However, questions pertaining to the success of public inquiries are typically eschewed with a cursory, explanatory note that, the role of public inquiries is only to make recommendations to government. It is the responsibility of government to accept or reject recommendations, to choose the mechanisms and timing of implementation, and to meet funding obligations. It is therefore unfair or misplaced to assess the success of a public inquiry by virtue of the extent to which its recommendations were accepted and have led to positive outcomes.

Most discussions of success, therefore, pertain to a particular inquiry and revert to its internal workings, namely, its processes of consultation and deliberation, whether it came within budget and met its reporting deadlines. However, internal perspectives are not enough. Inquiries happen in a societal context and the external environment matters. For instance, the media can play a powerful role in shaping expectations about an inquiry; its processes, its outcomes and the public interest it serves.

Given society's expectations of public inquiries, particularised, individualistic assessments fall short of recognising the significance of these powerful institutions for citizens and society.

Questions of success, impact or 'worth' are broader than any one public inquiry. They are pertinent to assessing the success of the institution of public inquiries itself, not on the outcomes or perspectives of a particular public inquiry.

Critically, where they do exist, most perspectives on success contemplate success from the point of view of government. This is necessary but insufficient. There is scant deliberation on the extent to which public inquiries have 'served the public interest'. This omission significantly underplays the importance of these powerful bodies for citizens and does not acknowledge citizens' expectations of repair and remedy of the social contract.

Assessing success – developing an analytical framework

In an attempt to build an analytical framework to assess success, three recurring, although often untested, propositions of success were identified from a synthesis of public administration, political science, crisis and public policy literatures. These propositions assert that an assessment of the success of a public inquiry should examine the ways in which it:

1. *Responds to crisis and restores legitimacy*

Public inquiries are often, but not exclusively, established in response to a crisis of some sort. Crisis disrupts legitimacy. Legitimacy is essential for the maintenance of any system of political rule.[31] Legitimacy is conferred, and as such, citizen perspectives are at the heart of considerations of legitimacy. Our institutions require the trust and confidence of citizens to maintain their legitimacy.[32] Restoration of legitimacy is a critical task for executive government.[33] The establishment of a public inquiry is a powerful tool which can be used by governments to restore legitimacy.

2. *Gives voice*

Public inquiries are not 'faceless' bureaucratic systems. They are intended to be open, transparent, public processes. A public inquiry is almost a promise of participation. Prasser argues that it is "precisely their 'publicness' that gives public inquiries a particular standing and legitimacy"[34] to investigate and advise on a range of issues. He argues that public inquiries satisfy other requirements of the policy process and political system such as promoting participation, providing forums for debate and putting issues on the agenda.[35]

3. *Provides the opportunity for policy change and improved outcomes*
Kingdon's[36] work identifies separate 'streams' flowing through agenda setting and decision-making structures, that is, problems, politics and policies, each of which has its own life. Sometimes two or three streams connect, often they do not. Public inquiries can be "some of the times 'when the three streams are joined in a 'single package,' "[37] and a policy window is opened. This "dramatically enhances the odds that a subject will become firmly fixed on a decision agenda".[38] It might be argued that the mere establishment of a public inquiry (providing a policy window) is demonstration that the three streams have come together, at least providing the possibility for policy change.

These three recurring propositions formed the basis of an analytical framework to assess success. The framework was applied to three illustrative case studies to test the extent to whether these propositions could be used to assess success.

The three case studies

Three in-depth case studies of public inquiries in Australia were undertaken to test the assertions in the literature about what a successful public inquiry looks like.[39]

Using Prasser's[40] classification system, one of each 'type' of public inquiries was chosen.

The case studies examined were:

1. The federal *Inquiry into certain Australian companies in relation to the UN Oil of Food Programme*, (the Cole Inquiry)[41] formed in 2005 – an example of an inquisitorial public inquiry;
2. The *Queensland Child Protection Commission of Inquiry* (QCPCI)[42] appointed in 2012 – an example of a policy advisory public inquiry;
3. The *Queensland Floods Commission of Inquiry* (QFCI)[43] established in 2011– an example of a hybrid public inquiry.

The following section includes a brief outline of each public inquiry and a summary of the outcome of the analysis.

Case Study 1: The Inquiry into certain Australian companies in relation to the UN Oil of Food Programme, 2005 - an example of an inquisitorial inquiry

The inquiry

The Oil for Food Programme was authorised through United Nations Security Council Resolution 661. Trade with Iraq could only legitimately and legally occur under United Nations (UN) supervision. The Australian Wheat Board (AWB) Limited was a statutory marketing authority. It was the monopoly single wheat desk for Australia's wheat exports and held approximately 70 per cent of Australia's bulk wheat export market.[44]

There had been concerns about the conduct of the AWB for some time, however, these were consistently dismissed as rumours, and 'the way business is done' in the Middle East.

After the invasion of Iraq in 2003, the Oil for Food Programme ended. At that time documents came to light providing evidence of 'kickbacks' to President Saddam Hussein and his regime. In 2004, the UN established the Volcker Inquiry which found that the AWB had been the "single biggest contributor of kickbacks to the Iraqi government".[45] Rumour was now established as fact. The Australian Government was compelled to respond. On 31 October 2005 Prime Minister Howard announced that an independent inquiry would be established to determine whether there was any breach of law by the Australian companies referred to in the Volcker Report. The inquiry was established under the *Royal Commissions Act 1902* with coercive powers of investigation. This was an unusual act for the Howard Government which was typically reluctant to appoint royal commission-type inquiries.[46]

Wheat is one of Australia's biggest export industries. Australia was involved militarily in the war in Iraq. The 'wheat for weapons' scandal is still described as "the greatest international trade scandal in Australian history, a terrific stain on our good name".[47]

Assessment

The analysis using the three propositions of success drawn from the literature produced an ambivalent result. In relation to the first proposition of success, the Cole Inquiry responded to the 'crisis' of the Volcker Report's confirmation of the AWB's corrupt practices, but it did not restore the legitimacy of government. It was also not successful in depoliticising the scandal. The Inquiry was, however, very successful in shielding government elites and the public service from blame. With respect to the second proposition of success, giving voice, the Cole Inquiry revealed the AWB's corrupt practices and transformed them from being 'non-issues' to serious allegations requiring investigation. The rumours were given voice. Apart from calling witnesses, however, the Cole Inquiry did not give voice to those more broadly impacted by the practices of the AWB. Regarding the third proposition of success, providing the opportunity for policy change and improved outcomes, the scandal itself and the practices uncovered by the Cole Inquiry were a clear indicator that Australia's wheat marketing arrangements needed to change. These changes and policy reforms came about through regular, robust democratic parliamentary processes in which many people actively participated on all sides. Specific policy changes attributable to the Cole Inquiry are those that related to increasing Australia's accountability for upholding United Nations sanctions and legal professional privilege vis-a-vis public inquiries.

Case study 2: The Queensland Child Protection Commission of Inquiry 2012 – an example of policy advisory public inquiry

The inquiry

There have been multiple reviews and inquiries into child protection in Australia. Most often these are convened after a horrific child death or scandal which is perceived, or framed, as demonstrating catastrophic failure of the child protection system. The *Queensland Child Protection Commission of Inquiry* (QCPCI) was not. It was established to fulfil an election commitment by the Liberal National Party (LNP) government. The QCPCI was the third child protection inquiry held in Queensland in thirteen years[48] and was appointed under the *Commissions of Inquiry Act 1950* (Qld).

The task of the QCPCI was comprehensive: to review the whole system, not just the operation of the child protection agency; to look back at what previous inquiries had achieved, and to map a way forward.

Child protection is a recurring issue of concern to the community, whether because of gross systemic failings, shocking child deaths, underfunding, lack of appropriate services or coordination. Child protection is not a marginal or peripheral issue affecting a small proportion of our community. In 2019-2020, one in 32 children in Australia received child protection services.[49] However, child protection systems are regularly described as unsustainable and overloaded.

Assessment

The analysis using the three propositions drawn from the literature yields an equivocal assessment of success. In relation to the first proposition, responding to crisis and restoring legitimacy, there was no identified 'crisis' or 'focussing event' to which to respond. However, child protection was framed as a potent election strategy to differentiate the opposition from the long standing, incumbent government. The QCPCI served to buoy the legitimacy of the new LNP government by being framed as a definitive, systemic look into an unsustainable and overburdened child protection system. The new LNP government was able to undermine the legitimacy of the previous Labor government which was portrayed as not adequately responding to its own previous inquiries into the system.

With respect to the second proposition, giving voice, the conclusion is again ambiguous. The QCPCI gave voice using similar mechanisms as all other child protection inquiries held around this time, namely, submissions, hearings, publication of transcripts on websites.[50] There is evidence that enduring changes have been made to broaden policy networks and actors, possibly in keeping with government's broader public administration reform agendas.

However, there is limited evidence that the voices of children and families directly impacted by the system were heard. Children and families were typically represented by peak advocacy, service and religious organisations. The extent to which these proxies are appropriate and truly representative is unknown. There is also no evidence of support, capacity building or feedback mechanisms for participants. Given that those who are part of child protection systems can be the most marginalised, vulnerable members of the community and that there is a risk of harm from participating in such inquiries,[51] this is a significant omission.

In relation to the third proposition of success, providing the opportunity for policy change and improved outcomes, while there has been much activity and various policy changes, to date there is no compelling evidence of better outcomes for children and families.[52]

Case Study 3: The Queensland Floods Commission of Inquiry 2011 - an example of a hybrid public Inquiry

The inquiry

Queensland has extensive experience dealing with natural disasters however, the floods in Brisbane and South East Queensland in 2010-2011, followed by the Category 5 Cyclone Yasi, caused immense damage. Thirty-three people died and around 80 per cent of the state was declared a disaster zone; over 2.5 million people were affected, many thousands of homes and businesses were flooded. The Queensland economy was 'smashed'[53] – roads, railways, crops, coal exports and the tourism industry were all devastated.

The ferocity and impact of the weather events, the lives and properties lost and unrelenting questions about the management of the floods, particularly the operation of the flood mitigation dams, led to the establishment of this public inquiry. The inquiry was appointed under the *Commissions of Inquiry Act 1950* (Qld).

Assessment

The analysis using the three propositions of success drawn from the literature once again yielded an ambivalent result. With respect to the first proposition of success, responding to crisis and restoring legitimacy, the inquiry was a swift and humane response to the crisis and the devastation of the Queensland floods. The inquiry was part of a suite of measures to respond to, learn, and recover from the floods. However, the Bligh Labor Government struggled to restore its legitimacy in the face of the Opposition's successful framing of the management of the floods, and the QFCI, as symptomatic of a government that was 'out of touch' and had been in power too long. The QFCI promised to establish whether any more could have been done to avert the tragic loss of life and property: from flood preparation and land use; to the adequacy of forecasts and early warning systems; and the operation of dams. For many, however, it failed to do just that. Further, the credibility of the inquiry was seriously undermined by the independent investigations conducted by *The Australian* which found shortcomings in certain evidence.[54] This was further eroded by the subsequent Crime and Misconduct Commission findings which found that the flood engineers had no case to answer.[55]

In relation to the second proposition of success, giving voice, the inquiry worked hard to encourage members of the public to participate, and many people had their say.[56] However, some argued that the legalistic way in which the QFCI was conducted was a barrier to participation.

With respect to the third proposition of success, providing the opportunity for policy change and improved outcomes, there was some policy change because of the inquiry and the inclusion of new policy voices in institutional settings. Critically, however, the inquiry and subsequent efforts by government failed to consistently or effectively engage local councils which are central to response and recovery coordination.(see also **Chapter 6** for further assessment of this inquiry).

In summary, the analytical framework enabled a nuanced dissection of various aspects of each public inquiry. However, the assessment of success of each case study produced an ambiguous result.

Overview of case studies

The key finding of the analyses of the three illustrative case studies is that the propositions for success drawn from the public administration and political science literature were found to be incomplete. They miss an essential perspective – the significance of public inquiries to citizens and the role public inquiries play in rebuilding the breach of the social contract after it has been broken.

However, each case study analysis revealed several 'proxies' which shed light on how citizens viewed the deliberations and outcomes of the public inquiry. These proxies include media commentary, legal action, parliamentary processes, and in one instance, a subsequent inquiry.

Citizen perspectives on success

The 'proxies' for citizen responses to the inquiry were then applied to each case study. This yielded a much sharper assessment of success.

From a citizen's point of view, the Cole Inquiry cannot be assessed as successful in repairing the breach of the social contract represented by the AWB scandal. The Cole Inquiry failed not only to depoliticise the AWB scandal but also failed to reassure citizens of the competence or legitimacy of their government. The Cole Inquiry was roundly viewed as a whitewash and, arguably, the inquiry process itself significantly delayed any subsequent legal action or prosecutions against AWB executives. A class action was commenced and eventually settled.[57] Commissioner Cole acknowledged the "daily commentary" and "intense political debate and widespread media coverage"[58] about his inquiry. However, he interpreted his commission unequivocally as serving government, not the public interest.[59]

The fact that the QCPCI was established to fulfil an election commitment is testament to the importance of child protection to citizens. This commitment to address a matter of significant public concern was a way for an opposition to differentiate itself from an incumbent government which had 'failed' to fix the child protection system and keep children safe from harm. However, given how ubiquitous child protection inquiries are, it is arguable that multiple child protection inquiries have consistently failed to meet citizens' expectations of functional and responsive child protection systems.

Concerning the QFCI, it failed to find anyone responsible for the devastation and loss of life. A class action representing thousands of people was commenced. Many citizens were left fearful and anxious about how their government would respond to future natural disaster events. Because of ongoing community anxieties, devastating losses and unanswered questions, a successive government instituted a subsequent inquiry (the Grantham Floods Commission of Inquiry 2015) "because the community deserve and require further closure. ..They [still] want the truth to prevail".[60]

These analyses highlighting citizens' views offer a powerful lens on success.

The case study analyses, therefore, suggest that criteria of a different order are required to assess success of public inquiries more holistically and to incorporate the perspectives of citizens.

Toward a theory of a 'successful public inquiry'

The case study analyses confirm that the propositions of success drawn from public administration and political science literatures focus on the perspective of the state and highlights the significant omission of citizen perspectives.

Each public inquiry examined is clearly different. Each was established for different reasons, to investigate matters of grave public importance in different ways. Fundamentally, however, they all have something in common. Drawing on the positioning of public inquiries as expressing a significant dimension of the social contract between government and citizens demonstrates that the overarching, unifying purpose of public inquiries is to rebuild the social contract after breach.

Within this unifying purpose, three enduring functions of public inquiries are identified: to respond, to hear and to prevent. These functions hold across the variety of issues public inquiries interrogate, the conditions under which they are established and the various forms they take. These reframed functions bring the breach of societal expectations, restoring trust and the public good into the centre of the challenge of assessing the success of public inquiries.

These three functions necessitate a reframing of the propositions for success and provide the backbone for an overarching analytical framework against which success, or otherwise, may be assessed, as outlined below in **Table 2.**

Table 2: Revised analytical framework to assess the success of public inquiries

Enduring functions of public inquiries	Current propositions of success drawn from the examined literature	Reframed propositions of success
To respond	The ways in which the public inquiry responds to crisis and restored legitimacy.	The ways in which the public inquiry is trusted to make sense of the events or the violation of the public's expectations.
To hear	The ways in which the public inquiry gives voice.	The ways in which people were heard.
To prevent	The ways in which the public inquiry provides the opportunity for policy change and improved outcomes.	The ways in which the public inquiry rights wrongs and changes policies, processes or outcomes for the better.

Public inquiries are not just about governments – concluding comments

Public inquiries express a significant dimension of the social contract between the state and citizens, the reciprocal acceptance of obligations. The overarching purpose of a public inquiry is to rebuild the social contract after it has been breached by way of a crisis, a scandal, problematic policy, or when inadequacies have been revealed and can no longer be tolerated.

The Cole Inquiry was triggered by the allegedly corrupt and unethical actions of AWB executives which could no longer be denied, and accusations that government and its agencies had turned a 'blind eye' to these practices. The QCPCI was a powerful acknowledgement that the child protection system was failing children and families. The QFCI was triggered by perceptions of an inadequate response to, and possible exacerbation of disastrous flooding.

Public inquiries are a powerful means for society to express their concerns and their expectation of repair and remedy. Given their significance to society, the importance of the matters they investigate, and their significant cost to the public purse, theoretically informed, evidence-based assessments of the success of public inquiries is a justifiable aspiration. Further, if as Prasser and Tracey[61] argue, public inquiries are to continue to be a powerful tool available to government, there is value in pursuing this question. Learnings from such assessments may also serve to inform the future conduct of public inquiries to maximise the extent to which they do perform their important functions and repair the breach of the social contract.

An analytical framework to assess the success of public inquiries incorporating the perspectives of citizens has been developed to contribute to this task. It began with the propositions for success drawn from public administration and political science literature which properly go to questions of politics, public administration and management.

However, relying solely on these perspectives sheds limited light on the extent to which the inquiries were able to repair these breaches, from the perspective of citizens. They rely on the perspective of government: the ways in which the legitimacy of government was restored; the ways in which government (through the independent inquiry) gave voice; the ways in which government policy, processes and outcomes were improved.

These perspectives are necessary, but insufficient. An assessment of success must include the perspectives of citizens and address the extent to which the public inquiry rebuilds the social contract, repairs the breach of public trust and the violation of expectations. By extension, it therefore must include a consideration of the ways in which the public inquiry is trusted to make sense of the events, people are heard, wrongs are corrected, and policies, processes or outcomes will change for the better. If a public inquiry does not do these important things it has fallen short of success.

Ben-Josef Hirsch, MacKenzie and Sesay[62] and Brahm[63] offer insights which may be pertinent to this task. In summary, an approach to assessing the success of a public inquiry would:

- be part of the initial design and construction of the public inquiry;
- not be conducted by anyone who is part of, or a participant in, the public inquiry;
- include a multi-method approach to minimise biases;
- be multi-layered assessing success for the individual, families, community, society and institutions;
- occur over relevant time periods, that is, short, medium and long term;
- include an analysis of the extent to which the outcomes could have been achieved in the absence of a public inquiry.

From a public policy perspective, Stark and Yates[64] frame public inquiries as procedural tools. Some inquiries can be framed as 'catalytic procedural tools' in that they "take control away from policymakers, punctuate equilibria and transform policy agendas".[65] Stark and Yates argue that "[f]rom a design point of view, this demands that those who convene and run public inquiries conceive their efforts as one part of a larger and longer reform effort which they can influence (but not control) prospectively, and that they strategize accordingly".[66] Stark and Yates offer three arenas in which an inquiry can strengthen its effectiveness as a procedural tool, namely, in the:

- 'inquiry room': This is "the collage of knowledge creating actors, procedures and relationships that combine to build inquiry recommendations";
- 'actioning environment': The agencies and sectors which determine the extent to which an inquiry's outcomes are accepted and actioned;
- 'institutionalising environment': the extent to which "lessons [...] fall prey to forms of institutional amnesia and get forgotten or, alternatively, get hard-wired into organisations and frameworks in ways that can ensure their survival".[67]

These principles and insights are offered as a starting point to design ways in which to incorporate citizen perspectives into the conduct and assessment of success of public inquiries.

It is entirely possible that assessments of success using this more holistic perspective will also yield equivocal results and reveal the "asymmetries" identified by Bovens, 't Hart and Peters.[68] Success "is not all or nothing"[69] it is a judgement. However, to make this judgement, citizen perspectives are critical - and are currently missing.

Even if public inquiries are cast as 'witch-hunts', initiated for highly politicised reasons, or appear to be genuine attempts by government to investigate and resolve vexed public policy issues or events, public inquiries are serious, weighty instruments of society, not just government. This chapter recasts the wide variety of purposes, forms and types of public inquiries into one unifying purpose - to rebuild the social contract. The three essential functions they fulfil are identified as: to respond; to hear; to prevent.

Citizen perspectives provides a powerful means by which to assess the ways in which a public inquiry has been successful in repairing the breach of the social contract. This is an important task because, if for no other reason, then "when they succeed, they start to build a shared narrative that may make repair possible for those who most need it".[70]

Public inquiries mentioned in this chapter[71]

Australian - Commonwealth

Royal Commission of Inquiry into the Costs and Efficiency of Grain Storage Handling and Transport (McColl, 1986)[72]

Royal Commission to Inquire into Aboriginal Deaths in Custody (Muirhead/Johnson, 1987)[73]

The Inquiry into certain Australian companies in relation to the UN Oil for Food Programme (Cole, 2005)

Royal Commission into Institutional Responses to Child Sexual Abuse (McClellan, 2013)[74]

Royal Commission into the Protection and Detention of Children in the Northern

Territory (White and Gooda, 2016)[75]

Royal Commission into Aged Care Quality and Safety (Briggs and Pagone, 2018)

State inquiries
Special *Commission of Inquiry into Child Protection Services in NSW* (Wood, 2007)
Queensland Flood Commission of Inquiry (Holmes, 2011)
Queensland Child Protection Commission of Inquiry (Carmody, 2012)
Royal Commission into the Home Insulation Program (Hanger, 2013)
Grantham Floods Commission of Inquiry (Sofronoff, 2015)

Notes

1   Australian Law Reform Commission, *Making Inquiries: A New Statutory Framework*, Report 111, Commonwealth of Australia, Sydney, 2009, p. 31.
2   Australian Council of Trade Unions 2014, "Abbott Royal Commission announcement a red hot political stunt", 31 October, viewed 9 December 2017, https://www.actu.org.au/actu-media/archives/2014/abbott-royal-commission-announcement-a-red-hot-political-stunt
3   Eoin Blackwell, "Union labels inquiry a witch-hunt", AAP, April 9, 2014, viewed 9 December, 2017, http://www.news.com.au/national/breaking-news/union-inquiry-to-begin-insydney/newsstory/635f3478ecd2990cb-51fbc5d6c18cab7
4   Laurent Dobuzinskis, *The European Legacy*, Vol 5, No 5, 2000, p. 688.
5   Ibid.
6   Albert Weale *Democratic Justice and the Social Contract*, Oxford University Press, Oxford, 2013, pp. 22-23.
7   Christian Kerr, 'Royal commissions and the press-seagulls at the lawyers' picnic'", in Scott Prasser and Helen Tracey, (eds), *Royal Commissions and Public Inquiries: Practice and Potential*, Connor Court Publishing, Ballarat, 2014, p. 293.
8   Richard N. Spann, *Public Administration in Australia*, New South Wales Government Printer, Sydney, 1967, p. 10.
9   *The Economist*, 'Wheat Scandal', https://www.economist.com/node/5452325, 26 January 2006, viewed 5 May 2015
10 The death of Shellay Ward, see http://www.abc.net.au/news/2007-11-09/docs-warned-repeatedly-about-starved-girls-family/721224, 9 November, 2007, viewed 15 July 2012
11 Lorraine Murray, https://www.britannica.com/event/Australia-floods-of-2010-2011, (undated), viewed 6 May 2015
12 Katie Wright, Shurlee Swain and Kathleen McPhillips, "The Australian Royal Commission into Institutional Responses to Child Sexual Abuse", *Child Abuse and Neglect*, Vol 74, December 2017, pp. 1-9.
13 Neda Vanovac, http://www.abc.net.au/news/2017-11-17/nt-royal-commission-calls-closure-of-don-dale-systemic-changes/9160460, 17 November 2017, viewed 18 January 2018

14 The ABC's Four Corners program's two-part 'Who Cares?', which aired on 17 September 2018 and 24 September 2018, (the following day Prime Minister Scott Morrison announced the Royal Commission into Aged Care Quality and Safety) https://www.aph.gov.au/About_Parliament/Parliamentary_Departments/Parliamentary_Library/pubs/rp/rp1920/Quick_Guides/RoyalCommissionAgedCare

15 Cyril Salmon, "Tribunals of Inquiry", Lionel Cohen Lecture (Fourteenth Series) delivered at the Faculty of Law, Hebrew University of Jerusalem, 28 December 1966, *Israel Law Review*, Vol 313, 1967, p. 313 viewed 3 April 2016, , review/article/tribunals-of-inquiry/56B-8515604D08674A68A6A7A2A9981A7

16 Paul Keating, "Redfern Speech", Year for the World's Indigenous People, Redfern Park, Sydney, 10 December, 1992, https://antar.org.au/sites/default/files/paul_keating_speech_transcript.pdf

17 Julia Gillard, "Gillard wants strong embrace of abuse recommendations", 14 December 2017, viewed 15 December 2017, https://www.msn.com/en-au/video/lifestyle/gillard-wants-strong-embrace-of-abuse-recommendations/vp-BBGImFc

18 Ann Deslandes 2016, "Responsibility for royal commissions' effectiveness lies with us", https://www.eurekastreet.com.au/article/responsibility-for-royal-commissions--effectiveness-lies-with-us

19 John Benington, "Creating the Public in Order to Create Public Value", *International Journal of Public Administration*, Vol 32, 2009, p. 235.

20 Ian Hangar, (Chair), Royal Commission into the Home Insulation Program, *Report*, Commonwealth of Australia, Canberra, 2014.

21 Jim McColl, (Chair), Royal Commission of Inquiry into Costs and Efficiency of Grain Storage, Handling and Transport, *Report*, Australian Government Publishing Service, Canberra, 1988, viewed 15 July 2018, www.parliament.wa.gov.au/intranet/libpages.nsf/WebFiles/Royal+Commission+into+grain+storage+vol+1/$FILE/Grain+storage+v+1.pdf

22 Scott Prasser and Helen Tracey, "What is there to show for it? Assessing inquiry effectiveness" in Prasser and Tracey, *Royal Commissions and Public Inquiries: Practice and Potential*, p 227

23 Gary Banks, "Public Inquiries, Public Policy and the Public Interest", *Inaugural Peter Karmel Lecture in Public Policy*, The Academy of Social Sciences in Australia in conjunction with ANZSOG, 3 July 2012, Shine Dome, Canberra, p. 7.

24 Eric Brahm, "Uncovering the Truth: Examining Truth Commission Success and Impact", *International Studies Perspectives*, Vol 8, 2007, p. 17.

25 Mark Bovens, and Paul 't Hart, *Understanding Policy Fiascos*, Transaction Publishers, New Brunswick, 1996.

26 Stephen Harrison, as cited in Mark Bovens, Paul 't Hart and B. Guy Peters, *Success and Failure in Public Governance*, Edward Elgar, Cheltenham, 2001, p. 277.

27 Bovens, 't Hart and Peters, *Success and Failure in Public Governance*, p. 10.

28 Allan McConnell *Understanding Policy Success. Rethinking Public Policy*, Palgrave Macmillan, Basinstroke, 2010.

29 Raanan Sulitzeanu-Kenan, "Reflections in the Shadow of Blame: When do Politicians Appoint Commissions of Inquiry?", *British Journal of Political*

Science, Vol 40, No 3, July 2010, p. 632.

30   Scott Prasser, *Royal Commissions and Public Inquiries in Australia*, LexisNexis Butterworths, Chatswood, 2006.

31   Andrew Heywood, *Political Theory: An Introduction*, 3rd ed., Palgrave Macmillan, Basingstoke, 2004, p. 147.

32   Ryan Parks, *Rhetorical Strategies of Legitimation: The 9/11 Commission's Public Inquiry Process*, PhD thesis, University of St Andrews, 2011, p. 1, viewed 18 January 2018, https://research-repository.st-andrews.ac.uk/bitstream/handle/10023/2470/RyanParksPhDThesis.pdf;sequence=6

33   Arjen Boin and Marc Otten, "Beyond the Crisis Window for Reform: Some Ramifications for Implementation", *Journal of Contingencies and Crisis Management*, Vol 4, No 3, 1996, p. 151.

34   Scott Prasser, *A Study of Commonwealth Public Inquiries*, PhD thesis, School of Politics and Public Policy, Griffith University, 2003, viewed 13 May 2011, p.i, https://www120.secure.griffith.edu.au/rch/file/86b4d151-0d7c-e839-01d8-800d9d7afa3a/1/02Whole.pdf

35   Ibid., p. 308.

36   John Kingdon, *Agendas, Alternatives, and Public Policies*, 2nd ed, Longman, New York, 1995, p. 85.

37   Ibid., pp. 201-02.

38   Ibid., p. 202.

39   Marlene Krasovitsky, *Putting the Public Back into Inquiries: Assessing the Success of Public Inquiries in Australia*, PhD Thesis, Department of Government and International Relations, University of Sydney, 2019.

40   Scott Prasser, *A Study of Commonwealth Public Inquiries*, pp. 85-91.

41   Terence Cole, (Chair), Inquiry into Certain Australian companies in Relation to the UN Oil for Food Program, *Report, Volumes 1-4*, Commonwealth of Australia, Canberra, 2006, viewed 3 October 2012, http://apo.org.au/system/files/3765/apo-nid3765-81446.pdf

42   Tim Carmody, (Chair), Queensland Child Protection Commission of Inquiry: Taking Responsibility: A Roadmap for Queensland Child Protection, *Final Report*, Queensland Government, Brisbane, June, 2013 viewed 2 March 2015, https://www.cabinet.qld.gov.au/documents/2013/dec/response%20cpcoi/Attachments/report%202.pdf

43   Catherine Holmes (Chair), Queensland Floods Commission of Inquiry, *Final Report*, March 2012, viewed 2 July 2016, http://www.floodcommission.qld.gov.au/__data/assets/pdf_file/0007/11698/QFCI-Final-Report-March-2012.pdf

44   Sasha Grebe, "Rebuilding a Damaged Corporate Reputation: How the Australian Wheat Board Overcame the Damage of the UN 'Oil for Food' Scandal to Successfully Reintegrate into the Australian Wheat Marketing Regulatory Regime", *Corporate Reputation Review*, Vol 16, No 2, 2013, p. 119.

45   Linda Botterill and Anne McNaughton, "Laying the Foundations for the Wheat Scandal: UN Sanctions, Private Actors and the Cole Inquiry", *Australian Journal of Political Science*, Vol 43, No 4, 2008, p. 586.

46   Scott Prasser, "Royal Commissions in Australia: When should Governments Appoint Them?", *Australian Journal of Public Administration*, Vol 66, No 3, September 2006, p. 29. During its eleven years in office the Howard Government only appointed four royal commissions including the Cole Inquiry.

47 Caroline Overington, "Wheat for weapons scandal fails to cook ex-AWB boss's goose", *The Australian*, 16 December 2016 viewed 20 December 2016, http://www.theaustralian.com.au/opinion/columnists/wheat-for-weapons-scandal-fails-to-cook-exawb-bosss-goose/news-story/03ec4f2b-7f4e8018a997387c9dc54e47

48 The other two inquiries were the *Commission of Inquiry into Abuse of Children in Queensland Institutions 1999* (the Forde Inquiry) and the Crime and Misconduct Commission of Inquiry *Protecting our Children: An Inquiry into the Abuse of Children in Foster Care*, 2004.

49 Australian Institute of Health and Welfare, *Child protection Australia 2019-20*, Child welfare series No 74, Commonwealth of Australia, Canberra, 2021 https://www.aihw.gov.au/reports/child-protection/child-protection-australia-2019-20/summary

50 Krasovitsky, *Putting the Public back into Public Inquiries*, Appendix 5.

51 Brahm, "Uncovering the Truth", p. 20.

52 See for example Australian Institute of Health and Welfare, Child protection Australia 2019-20 https://www.aihw.gov.au/reports/australias-welfare/child-protection and Productivity Commission, *Report on Government Services 2022*, 16 Child protection services, Commonwealth of Australia, Canberra, 2022 https://www.pc.gov.au/research/ongoing/report-on-government-services/2022/community-services/child-protection

53 Andrew Fraser MP, State Budget 2011-2012, Budget Speech, Budget Paper No. 1, Appropriation Bill 2011 (Second Reading Speech, 14 June 201), Queensland Government, viewed 12 June 2015, https://s3.treasury.qld.gov.au/files/bp1-2011-12.pdf

54 See Hedley Thomas 2011, "Operator of dam "invented" rain data", *The Australian*, 26 March, viewed 23 August 2015, Factiva database, Hedley Thomas 2012, 'What the floods inquiry didn't hear: Wivenhoe 'breached the manual'-Exclusive, 23 January, viewed 23 August 2015, Factiva database.

55 https://www.ccc.qld.gov.au/news/cmc-finalises-examination-wivenhoe-dam-engineers-conduct

56 See Catherine Holmes, (Chair), Queensland Floods Commission of Inquiry, *Final Report*, Queensland Government, Brisbane, Queensland Government, Brisbane, March 2012, see 1.3 'The Commission's work', pp. 33-35.

57 See Senate Legal and Constitutional Affairs References Committee, Work undertaken by the Australian Federal Police's Oil for Food Taskforce, The Senate, Commonwealth Parliament, Canberra, March 2015, para 4,26, p. 37.

58 Cole, *Report*, Vol 1, p. 170.

59 Ibid., p. 165, p. 169, pp. 176-77.

60 Anastasia Palaszczuk, Premier, *Queensland Parliamentary Debates*, 5 May, 2015, p. 279, viewed 23 September 2017, http://www.parliament.qld.gov.au/documents/hansard/2015/2015_05_05_WEEKLY.pdf,. Also, https://statements.qld.gov.au/statements/76379.

61 Prasser and Tracey, *Royal Commissions and Public Inquiries*, p. 393.

62 Michal, Ben-Joseh Hirsch, Megan MacKenzie, and Mohamed Sesay, "Measuring the impacts of truth and reconciliation commissions: Placing the global 'success' of TRCs in local perspective", *Cooperation and Conflict*, Vol 47, No 3, 2012, pp. 386-403.

63 Brahm, "Uncovering the Truth", pp. 24-9.

64   Alastair Stark and Sophie Yates, "Public inquiries as procedural policy tools", *Policy and Society*, Vol 40, Issue 3, 2021, pp. 345-61.
65   Ibid, p. 345.
66   Ibid, p. 346.
67   Ibid, pp. 352-58.
68   Bovens, 't Hart and Guy Peters, *Success and Failure in Public Governance.*
69   McConnell, *Understanding Policy Success*, p. 55.
70   Jill Stauffer, *Ethical Loneliness: The Injustice of Not Being Heard*, Columbia University Press, New York, 2015, p. 49.
71   List refers to name of inquiry, its chair and date of appointment.
72   Established jointly with the Commonwealth, NSW, Victorian, Queensland, Western Australian and South Australian governments.
73   Established jointly with the Commonwealth and all States and Territories.
74   Established jointly with the Commonwealth and all States and Territories.
75   Established jointly between the Commonwealth and Northern Territory governments.

11

The fiscal implications of public inquiries

Robert Carling

Introduction

One of the features of governments' use of external inquiries in recent years has been their strong influence on social policy development in areas such as education, health, disability support, childcare and aged care. At the same time, there has been rapid growth in public social spending in these program areas.

This chapter explores the place of public inquiries in the complex and inherently political process of government budgeting. The topic is not the cost of the inquiries themselves – although that can be substantial – but the fiscal cost of the expenditure programs that are the subject of inquiries.

External inquiries can make a valuable contribution to policy development, but at the same time can detract from the flexibility governments need in making public policy choices within a broad framework of fiscal discipline.

Inquiries are not responsible for the policy choices governments make, but they have contributed to the strong pressures on governments in the modern world to continuously expand and enhance social benefits at a substantial fiscal cost, which creates pressure for higher taxation and/or deficit spending.

While it is governments that create public inquiries, it is the same governments that need to consider whether their fiscal flexibility is being unduly compromised by the proliferation of external inquiries focusing on matters of public policy. They also need to consider whether the balance needs to shift back towards policy development inside the core of government.

The chapter begins with a description of the broad fiscal setting that has evolved over recent decades and then discusses the benefits and disadvantages of external public inquiries in more detail.

Fiscal setting

Government spending has grown strongly since the turn of the century and inquiries have been active in several of the areas of most rapid expenditure growth.

The growth of expenditure has been concentrated in what can be broadly described as social spending: health, education (especially primary and secondary), and social security and welfare (a catch-all that includes pensions, unemployment benefits, aged care, childcare, and disability pensions and care).

The following table **(Table 1)** illustrates the growth in these expenses since 2002-03. The selection of five-year intervals highlights trends and avoids the distortions resulting from inflated expenses on health and social security and welfare in 2019-20 – 2021-22 because of the coronavirus pandemic. The table therefore provides a better picture of the underlying trend.

Table 1: Commonwealth social spending, 2002-03 to 2022-23

			$ billion			
	Health	School education	Social security & welfare	Total social	Other expenses	All expenses
2002-03	29.4	6.0	71.3	106.7	94.7	201.4
2007-08	44.4	9.2	97.8	151.4	128.9	280.3
2012-13	61.3	12.4	131.9	205.6	177.8	383.4
2017-18	76.0	18.3	157.7	252.1	209.4	461.5
2022-23	109.7	28.0	228.8	366.5	284.4	650.9

Table 2: Total government social spending as percentage

	All expenses	Total social spending	Other
2002-03	25.1	13.3	11.8
2007-08	23.8	12.9	10.9
2012-13	25.0	13.4	11.6
2017-18	25.0	13.6	11.3
2022-23	26.2	14.8	11.4

Source: Commonwealth Budget Papers, Budget Paper No. 1, Statement 6 (Expenses and Net Capital Investment), 2022-23 and prior years.

The table (**Table 1**) only includes Commonwealth budget expenses, although the same trends are apparent in state budgets to the extent that state governments have expenditure responsibilities in these fields. However, there is a degree of double counting here because some of the growth in Commonwealth spending has been driven by the growth in grants to the states to finance their spending, particularly on schools and public hospitals, the operation of which is entirely a state government responsibility.

As can be seen from **Table 2** total Commonwealth expenses in the identified social spending areas have risen from around 13% of GDP to 15% projected for 2022-23, while all other Commonwealth expenses have been flat.

In the 20 years covered in the above table, the Commonwealth budget began in surplus but has been continuously in deficit since 2008-09.[1] Net debt has risen from $33 billion in 2002-03 to a projected $572 billion 20 years later and $767 billion in 2025-26. The coronavirus pandemic has been a factor, but accounts for less than half the increase.

Independent inquiries in areas of social spending

Royal commissions and independent inquiries have been active in the functions of government covered by social spending. These include the following:

School Education

Review of Funding for Schooling, 2011 (colloquially known as Gonski 1.0)

Review to Achieve Education Excellence in Australian Schools, Through Growth to Achievement, 2018 (Gonski 2.0)

Education and Training Workforce: Schools Workforce, 2012 (Productivity Commission)

Child Care

Education and Training Workforce: Early Childhood Development, 2011 (Productivity Commission)

Childcare and Early Childhood Learning, 2015 (Productivity Commission)

Aged Care

Caring for Older Australians, 2011 (Productivity Commission)

House of Representatives Standing Committee on Health, Aged Care and Sport, Report of Inquiry into Quality of Care in Residential Aged Care Facilities in Australia, 2018

Royal Commission into Aged Care Quality and Safety, 2021

Health

Performance of Public and Private Hospital Systems, 2009 (Productivity Commission)

Mental Health, 2020 (Productivity Commission)

A Healthier Future for all Australians, 2009 (National Health and Hospitals Reform Commission)

Disability Care

Disability Care and Support, 2011 (Productivity Commission)

Joint Standing Committee on the National Disability Insurance Scheme: General issues around implementation and performance of the NDIS, 2019

Royal Commission into Violence, Abuse, Neglect and Exploitation of People with Disability (to report 2023)

This list includes several Productivity Commission reports. It is unclear to what extent the Productivity Commission should be considered independent of government. Although it is an agency of the Commonwealth, it is more independent than departments and research bureaux. It can, and has made, recommendations that cause political discomfort to governments. For these reasons, the Productivity Commission is included here, while recognising that it is different from royal commissions and other special purpose inquiries led by appointees from outside government.

There have also been numerous relevant parliamentary committee inquiries. While these are not necessarily independent of the executive government, they are often at a distance from government because they include non-government members and, in some cases, may have been established against the wishes of the executive government. However, they are clearly the most political form of inquiry.

Benefits of independent public inquiries

If we compare independent public inquiries with investigation and policy development within government, several benefits of the independent public inquiry form are apparent.

Inquiries draw in knowledge and expertise from a wider range of sources than government departments on their own. Indeed, it has been observed that analytical and policy development capabilities within government departments have decayed.[2] For this reason, inquiries are a partial substitute for functions that used to be performed by departments.

Then there is the reality that departments work under the constant pressure of day-to-day events and demands from their political masters, whereas inquiries have the luxury of being able to focus on a single topic without distraction and are usually given generous resources and time to do it.

Inquiries may also be better at keeping interest groups and lobbyists at arm's length. Their analysis is more likely to be free of the 'spin' and political distortion that governments apply. And inquiries are likely to have more public credibility and trust.

The power of investigation and cross examination that royal commissions have can also put them at an advantage depending on the nature of the inquiry being undertaken.

While independent public inquiries offer these benefits, they are more relevant to some types of inquiry work than others. For example, independence, credibility and investigative powers are especially important in the case of inquiries into alleged wrong-doing, abuse of power or systemic failure.

However, the advantages of public inquiries into purely policy or program issues are less clear-cut. Indeed, if the use of public inquiries to facilitate policy development has flourished as departments' capabilities of this type have diminished, there is a question as to why departments can no longer do what they once did, and whether those capabilities can be rebuilt.

Policy development within government using the green paper/white paper model has been successful in the past. One example of it was the tax system review (A New Tax System) initiated by the Howard Government in 1997. The work was done within Treasury drawing on outside expertise as required, leading to a White Paper proposal by the government. This was a success, but there have been few similar exercises since.

To the extent departments lack the full range of expertise to develop policy, they can draw on outside experts as consultants. This is an approach that keeps the policy development process inside government and short of contracting the whole task out to independent public inquiries but is not without problems of its own.

The disadvantages of public inquiries

In an era of unrelenting pressures for increased public spending in many spheres, inquiries weaken governments' resistance to those pressures.

Inquiries are, by their very nature, focused on single issues and are not concerned with broader issues such as management of the overall level of government spending, taxation, deficits and debt.

This is not a criticism of inquiries, as it is for the elected government to juggle the competing demands on the public purse and determine overall budget aggregates. Equally, however, inquiries can make the fiscal management task of government more difficult. Inquiries never suggest reductions in government spending and typically recommend increases. 'Gold plating' is often the order of the day. Inquiries typically take an incremental approach, favouring increased spending rather than reallocating the current level of spending in a particular area.

The purpose of inquiries is often to enhance or expand service delivery by government, but the inquiries usually see such improvements as requiring increased financial allocations by government rather than reallocations or increased efficiency in the use of existing resources.

Governments can, of course, simply reject inquiry recommendations in part or whole. However, this is difficult when the government itself has appointed an inquiry and the public regards the report as the outcome of an independent review by experts and therefore as producing the 'right' answers. It is also made politically difficult when oppositions and pressure groups use inquiry reports to increase pressure on the government. Often governments come under pressure to adopt inquiry recommendations whatever they are and sometimes even before they are received and known.

Indeed, pressure groups know the value of pressuring governments to hold inquiries into their topics of interest, especially a royal commission. Securing a public inquiry is winning half the battle towards securing more government spending.

Timing is an important variable in fiscal management. New spending programs should not be adopted until they can be fitted in to an overall budget envelope consistent with a disciplined approach to fiscal policy. Inquiry reports, however, create community expectations of immediate action by government regardless of budget circumstances. Even if a government accepts the broad thrust of an inquiry report, the timing of its response should be a variable.

Governments must be aware of the ways in which inquiries can complicate the task of balancing competing interests. Menzies viewed some inquiries as being fundamentally incompatible with responsible government and as a way for politicians to avoid the value judgements and balancing acts that only elected officials can undertake. Menzies also believed that inquiries could come to exercise a coercive influence upon government.[3]

Menzies made those observations many years ago, yet governments have resorted to inquiries increasingly. Sometimes they do so with the full intention of increasing spending on the matter under review and see the inquiry as helping to define the spending program. However, even in these situations and with tight terms of reference matters can easily get out of control and balloon beyond anything government might have contemplated.

None of this is to suggest that inquiry reports always lack merit – far from it. Rather, the point is that the good is packaged with the marginal, the questionable and the downright bad. These distinctions tend to be overlooked in the public reaction to inquiry reports. Moreover, the broad fiscal perspective within which any public policy issue must be set tends to be completely lost as governments come under pressure to do whatever inquiries recommend.

Case study: Royal Commission into Aged Care Quality and Safety

The Royal Commission into Aged Care is part of the story of how aged care has become one of the key sources of financial pressure on the federal budget along with the NDIS, childcare and defence and will become even more so in the years ahead.

The royal commission was established primarily in response to reports of abuse and neglect of residents of aged care facilities. This is reflected in the terms of reference, which identify substandard care, mistreatment, abuse and systemic failures as matters of concern. In this regard, the aged care inquiry can be viewed as an appropriate use of the inquisitorial royal commission type of public inquiry to investigate systemic wrong-doing and institutional failure and to explore remedies and make recommendations.

However, the terms of reference were also much broader, referring for example to "what the Australian Government, aged care industry, families and the wider community can do to strengthen the system of aged care services to ensure that the services provided are of high quality and safe." The commissioners were also required and authorised to inquire into "any matter reasonably incidental to a matter referred to in (other) paragraphs or that the commissioners believe is reasonably relevant to the inquiry."

It is therefore clear that the government intended the royal commission to be wide-ranging and not confined to matters of mistreatment, abuse and systemic failure. This broad interpretation of its task is reflected in the Commission's final report. It was an inquiry of both the inquisitorial and policy development kind.

The final report was released in early March 2021, just as the 2021-22 Commonwealth budget was being prepared. Although the commission did not (and could not) put a price tag on its recommendations, they were clearly far-reaching and expensive to the taxpayer if implemented in anything like full measure.

The immediate media, political and public response was to accept that the commission had exposed major shortcomings in aged care and that a great deal more money would need to be spent, and quickly, although the increased spending was not confined to addressing abuse and neglect. Various media reports put the incremental annual cost of the commission's recommendations at a conservative estimate of

$7.6-8.7 billion but potentially as much as $15.5 billion.[4] This was on top of the already approximate doubling of Commonwealth expenses on aged care in the eight years from 2012-13 to 2020-21.

The very existence of the report put pressure on the government to make provision for additional aged care expenditure in the 2021-22 budget, which was already under the strain of vastly increased expenditure and debt associated with the coronavirus pandemic. In the event, the government budgeted an extra $1.6 billion in 2021-22, rising to an extra $5 billion in 2024-25. Coming on top of an already rising base level of spending, this would bring to 38% the cumulative increase in total aged care spending in the four years to 2024-25. The 2021-22 budget measures were, however, widely seen as just a first instalment of responses to the royal commission report.

Since the May 2022 election, the new Labor government has budgeted for incremental aged care spending reaching $1.3 billion a year in 2025-26 and further increases are likely to result from aged care sector wage increases awarded by the Fair Work Commission.

In the political atmosphere surrounding the final report, the government would have been excoriated had it decided not to increase aged care spending in the 2021-22 budget or had it announced that it would take the time to review the royal commission's recommendations and make any financial provisions it deemed necessary in future budgets.

The Commission's report was used by pressure groups to agitate for more government spending, and in an extraordinary intervention even one of the commissioners was quoted as saying that the government's response to the Commission's report in the 2021-22 budget was inadequate.[5] Royal commissioners' jobs should end with the submission of their reports. It is not for them to then take on an advocacy role on the subject matter of their reports, which is what appears to have happened in this case. A royal commissioner became a public advocate of her own report.

Notably absent from public discussion in the report's aftermath was any recognition of the extent to which spending on aged care had already risen, or whether that money could be spent differently and more beneficially, before consideration was given to spending more.

Rather, the public's attention was quickly focused on the possibilities for increasing taxation to pay for increased aged care spending. In fact, the royal commission helped point public attention in this direction by including a discussion of two different funding models in its report.

One commissioner leaned towards a hypothecated income tax levy (either flat, like the Medicare levy, or at graduated rates) for aged care. The other commissioner favoured a non-hypothecated but 'earmarked' personal income tax levy of 1% to be known as the "aged care improvement levy".

This difference of opinion between the two commissioners had the effect of lessening the impact of this part of the report. However, they left no doubt that they thought the government should increase taxation to pay for their recommendations for aged care. Although the terms of reference did not invite the commission to report on funding, the catch-all wording of the terms of reference left the door open to this.

Even so, it seems strange that a royal commission into aged care would opine on taxation policy. It seems to have been lost on the commissioners that an increase in personal income tax – whether labelled a hypothecated or earmarked levy or whatever – was at odds with the clear policy of the government of the day.

Wittingly or not, the *Royal Commission into Aged Care* acted in the spirit of interest groups, which have taken to advocating special levies to finance their causes. Not satisfied with pressuring governments to spend more for the benefit of those they represent, pressure groups want dedicated revenue sources in the belief that this makes the spending 'funded' and protected from any future budget 'razor gang' reviews.

In the event, after briefly appearing to be open to the general idea of a levy, the Morrison Government dismissed it. Following the change of government in May 2022, the idea remains on the record – with the aura of a royal commission blessing – for this or a future government under budget pressure to act upon.

Conclusion

The growth of social spending has been a key factor in the weakening of the Australian government's underlying fiscal position over the past 15 years and in prospect for the foreseeable future. It would be an over-simplification to blame this on the numerous public inquiries in the social policy domain or to suggest that the government should abandon the use of such inquiries. They usually have something positive to contribute.

At the same time, however, independent public inquiries can add to the complexity of the broad policy-making and fiscal management function of government. Inquiry reports tend to reinforce interest groups in imposing absolute and immediate demands that can be difficult to balance against the many competing demands for public funding. Matters of balance, proportionality and timing are part of the broad perspective that governments must have if they are to adhere to principles of fiscal responsibility. But it is this broad perspective that tends to be lost when inquiries, by their very nature, focus on single issues.

The challenge for governments is to ensure that public policy issues are viewed within this broad perspective without foregoing the positive contribution external inquiries can make to the policy development process. This is partly a matter of how terms of reference for inquiries are written, but it is also the case that governments have become too willing to contract out policy development to external inquiries and need to ensure that more of this work is done within departments, drawing on outside expertise to fill capability gaps.

The case for independent public inquiries is strongest where wrong-doing and systemic failure need to be investigated.

Public inquiries mentioned in this chapter[6]

Royal Commission into Aged Care Quality and Safety (Briggs and Pagone, 2018)
Royal Commission into Violence, Abuse, Neglect and Exploitation of People with Disability (Sackville, 2019 and expected to report in 2023)
Review of Funding for Schooling, 2011 (Gonski, 2010)
Review to Achieve Education Excellence in Australian Schools, Through Growth to Achievement, (Gonski, 2017)

Notes

1 The deficit was small enough in 2018-19 to be described as a balanced budget, but with the onset of the coronavirus pandemic the budget has been heavily in deficit and is expected to remain in deficit for the foreseeable future.
2 For example, Gary Banks, "Making public policy in the public interest – the role of public inquiries", Chapter 7 in Scott Prasser and Helen Tracey, (eds), *Royal Commissions and Public Inquiries – Practice and Potential,* Connor Court Publishing, Ballarat, 2014, pp. 112-32.
3 Scott Prasser, "Public Inquiries in Australia: An Overview", *Australian Journal of Public Administration,* Vol XLIV, No 1, 1985, pp. 5-8.
4 For example, Elias Visontay, "Cost of Australia's aged care system to soar to $36 bn a year if cheapest royal commission reforms adopted", *The Guardian,* Australian edition, 3 March 2021. https://www.theguardian.com/australia-news/2021/mar/03/australias-aged-care-system-could-require-extra-9bn-per-year-to-adopt-royal-commission-reforms
5 Lynelle Briggs speaking at the Aged and Community Services Australia National Online Summit, 19 May 2021. www.Australianageingagenda.com.au/executive/budget-measures-insufficient-to-fix-aged-care-says-briggs
6 List refers to name of inquiry, its chair and date of appointment.

12

Protecting children at risk:
The limitations of public inquiries in organisational learning from child deaths

Dominic Elliott

Introduction

We may forgive failures of foresight but how often do we repeat our mistakes, despite the benefits of hindsight? Public Inquiries play a vital role in developing new insights, a first step in the process of learning from failures. This chapter explores the role of public inquiries as mechanisms for learning from crisis or extreme events. When an event is of a certain magnitude or of significant public concern, an investigation is commissioned. Within the United Kingdom (UK), only a government minister may instigate a public inquiry, viewed as an independent process which collects evidence with the intention of identifying lessons and making recommendations. The unspoken expectation is that we learn from the investigation and, in theory at least, use the insights gained to reduce the risk of recurrence. A limitation of public inquiries, however, is that whilst they may conclude with recommendations these often fail to feed into new practices; lessons identified are not necessarily lessons learned.

In this chapter there is a clear distinction between policy learning, which create new bodies, rules, regulations and guidelines and, organisational learning where these translate into new beliefs, norms and behaviours. In a seminal work, Turner argued that a "cultural readjustment" would, typically, follow a public inquiry. Turner optimistically posited that:

> Recommendations following public inquiries are seen as part of a process of cultural readjustment after a disaster, allowing the ill-structured problem which led to the failure to be absorbed into the culture in a well-structured form.[1]

Drawing upon Gouldner's work,[2] Elliott and Smith[3] argued that there is limited evidence that "cultural adjustment" follows on from public inquiries. New laws and regulations might be introduced but, without proper enforcement or without changing the mindsets of organisations a mock bureaucracy often emerges, one in which neither the regulators nor regulated alter established behaviours. This has led to some authors labelling inquiry reports as little more than "fantasy documents".[4] There may be little appetite on the part of the organisations and public bodies associated with an inquiry's findings to act. For example, despite there were eight public inquiries concerning football stadium disasters in the UK over a 60-year period. Elliott and Smith highlighted the limited cultural or behavioural change. What emerged was a "mock bureaucracy," in which rules and regulations were ignored by football clubs combined with the poverty of enforcement by the regulatory bodies involved. Failures to adapt may also reflect the complexity of the context in which recommendations are developed. Many extreme events will involve a wide range of state and private agencies each with their own norms and cultures. Within the football industry this included football clubs, police, fire services, local government, new regulatory bodies and stadia designers. In the field of child protection social services, child protection workers, housing officials, teachers, nursery nurses, medics and accident and emergency ideally work together in a multi-agency collaboration to support children at risk. Few public inquiries, however, provide a full consideration of how to secure the implementation of findings. The appointment of professionals with expertise in change management might provide rich insights in closing the gap between lessons identified and their translation into new perspectives, processes, practices and behaviours across the multiagency network that combines to protect children at risk.[5]

This chapter focuses upon child protection within the United Kingdom and explores the impact of Lord Laming's *Victoria Climbié Inquiry* (2003) with its recommendations for a new policy framework. The context for this chapter is that the same pattern of failures across various agencies concerned with child protection have recurred many times. The primary aim of this chapter is to explore the impact of public inquiries as an effective mechanism for learning within child protection services. Effectiveness may be measured in a variety of ways, in the validity of its findings, in its recommendations but most importantly, in the opportunity to shape policies, new practices and new behaviours which together may limit the likelihood of a recurrence of such failures.

Public inquiries in policy development

Public inquiries are a vital tool in UK Government's repertoire of responses to extreme events or complex issues where significant public concern exists. At the heart of the inquiry is a wide-ranging investigation, shaped by the agreed terms of reference. Inquiries have considered a range of events and issues within the UK. In March 2022, the UK Government announced its draft terms of reference for a public inquiry relating to the Covid-19 Pandemic.[6] The initial scope of the inquiry included, preparedness, the public health response, the response in the health and care sector and the UK's economic response. The appointed chair, Baroness Hallett, a retired Court of Appeal Judge. Most inquiry chairs in the UK, unlike in Australia, (see Chapter 1)[7] are recruited from the ranks of the judiciary. They may consider one-off events, such as the Covid-19 Inquiry or the Chilcot Inquiry, launched in 2009 explored the UK's role and government decision making in the Iraq War. Repeated patterns of failure such as rail accidents during the latter part of the 20th Century or the failures of child protection services over the last 20 years may also be investigated.

Starr provided a brief history of UK public inquiries and from royal commissions to committee and parliamentary inquiries.[8] There is further updated discussion of developments in the UK in Chapter 15 of this volume. Seeking greater consistency, legislation enacting the *Inquiries Act 2005* (UK) has shaped the form and style of most inquiries since. From a government perspective the primary purpose is to "prevent recurrence".[9] Other motives may exist such as a political agenda. Bias may arise in the setting of the terms of reference or in the determination of the scope for an inquiry, potentially shaped by the political interest of government or, from the professional expertise of the inquiry chair and principal investigators.[10] Beck[11] argued that risks may be viewed narrowly and assessed technically with little thought given to the organisational cultures of multi-agencies whose practices may have contributed to the failure. Inquiries may be used as a smokescreen, a delaying tactic in the hope that by the time an inquiry has reported any initial furore and upset has died down.[12] Other criticisms include the focus of inquiries upon failures with little consideration of cases of higher reliability organisations.[13] Despite the potential for inquiries to be flawed, they have had significant impact. For example, the two Taylor public inquiry reports (1989, 1990) concerning football stadium disasters resulted in significant improvements to crowd safety.

Learning from crisis

Starr suggested there were four broad questions to frame an inquiry:[14]

- What happened?
- Why did it happen?
- Who is to blame?
- What can be done to prevent a recurrence?

Of forty-six inquiries commissioned within the UK between 1990-2017, 40 were chaired by people predominantly from judicial backgrounds. Most inquiries are now convened using the *Inquiries Act 2005*, which provides a uniform set of powers and rules for how an inquiry operates. However, the length of inquiries can pose a challenge, with high staff turnover. In the case of the *Independent Inquiry Child Sexual Abuse*, initially established in 2014 under the *Inquiries Act 2005*, had four inquiry chairs were appointed over four years. There had been objections arising from the perceived closeness of the first two chairs to individuals and establishment institutions which would be investigated. A third chair struggled in moving from New Zealand.[15] By the end of 2017, the inquiry had its fourth chair, an academic in the field of social work, who has continued to lead this review into 2022. It is unusual in that it has investigated a series of failures, each separate but linked in that they concern child protection. The various contexts included religious organisations and settings, allegations of child abuse linked to Westminster and in custodial settings.

Lessons and learning

Two areas of research are especially pertinent to this field of enquiry, organisational learning and policy learning, respectively. Within the policy literature there is a regular misperception that learning is the same as identifying lessons where "enacted legislation and regulations' indicate policy change and . . . that some sort of learning had occurred".[16] Policy learning also explores how advocacy coalitions may shape policy development. Organisational learning from crises studies includes consideration of lessons learned but is concerned with how these might translate into new practices and behaviours. There has been a particular emphasis upon understanding the forces that may facilitate or hinder learning within a single organisation or, more typically within complex multi-agency networks.[17]

Toft and Reynolds, distinguished between "passive" and "active" learning, referring to "identifying lessons" and "acting upon them," respectively.[18] Reflecting the narrowing of scholarly enquiry, research often deals with either knowledge acquisition, or transfer, or assimilation, and rarely upon the three combined as an interconnected process. A fragmented piecemeal conceptualization of organisational learning from crisis is the result, with the absence of a holistic view.[19] Another limitation is the potential lack of fit between lessons from the past and the likely demands of future events; given the idiosyncratic nature of even superficially similar crisis events, it is unlikely that a blueprint for one will be entirely suitable for another.

As noted above, lessons identified may not translate into new and appropriate practices. Different patterns of regulation may also differ in their effectiveness in promoting sustained change, as may a variety of field configuring mechanisms such as conferences and standards that shape and institutionalise behaviour.[20] A second potential weakness is that the lessons identified may not be the right ones. Advocacy coalitions may opportunistically pursue policy change by influencing agendas to address their own purposes. The knowledge base of the leading investigators may shape how the collection and interpretation of evidence is conducted. Some professions may be more 'privileged' than others in terms of the perceived authority they have.[21]

Rigidities in beliefs also play a key role in the effectiveness of learning. Within a context of multiple agencies, organisations and professions resistance to change often emerges. The interpretation of new rules, practices and policies will differ between the various agencies and professions associated with child protection. The established norms and values of organisations and professions will shape the absorption of new rules and recommended practices into new ways of doing.[22] For example, the recent arrangements for managing fans in the FIFA European Cup Final in Paris (2022), contested between Liverpool and Real Madrid, illustrated, the persistence of negative attitudes towards spectators who were primarily viewed as potential hooligans rather than paying customers. Deeply held beliefs had played a vital role in the deaths of British football fans during the latter half of the last century and it was as if any lessons identified from this period had been forgotten.[23] Another overlooked issue is that public inquiries focus upon past events, resulting in the potential tension between institutionalising new practices developed in a past context and retaining the potential for adaptation

Policy learning suggests a top-down view of learning, often linked to notions of standards of 'best practice'.[24] Alternatively, organisational learning suggests a bottom-up approach triggered by fresh ideas, resulting from intuition or from the stimulus of lessons identified from an inquiry process. This may trigger a spur for collective interpretation of the lessons identified and consideration of how these may flow into new ways of doing, new practices, norms and policies, for example. From an institutionalist perspective in which there is a synchronous interchange between three layers of macro (policy), meso (institutional), and micro (organisational) levels in learning during, after, and before an extreme event. Knowledge may be fashioned within each level concurrently. Recognition of this interplay allows for drawing together the fragmented literature dealing with organisational learning from extreme events, one typically focused upon only one of the levels, such as macro level public policy,[25] or micro level organisation and individual learning.[26] Little attention has been directed towards the processes of institutionalization and the diffusion of norms across a multi-agency context.

The role of artifacts, such as policies, professional conferences, regulations and guidance notes as institutionalising forces has received limited attention.[27] The contribution of an institutional theory approach to learning through public inquiries is surprisingly sparse. Central to institutional theory is the organisational field, which includes any constituent exerting a coercive, mimetic, or normative influence.[28] The field provides a nexus where prescriptions meet emergent practice. As the fragmented and contested nature of fields is increasingly recognised[29] the role of artifacts such as policies and conferences receives greater attention.[30] Drawing from Greenwood, Oliver, Sahlin, and Suddaby,[31] the legitimacy of new standards may be secured because they are seen to embody "taken-for-granted" or "explicitly identified" norms and values created through collaborative development involving field members. At a micro level, institutional theory increasingly acknowledges the influence of an organisation's meaning systems in shaping new practice adoption.[32] In summary, an institutional perspective provides a basis for considering trans-organisational structures within which artifacts play a vital, field-shaping role. Institutional theory recognises that practice may be diffused in the pursuit of legitimacy rather than as a rational process and that what is termed 'best practice' may only be 'best' within a particular context. New procedures, guidelines, and rules may not only provide a measure of the efficacy and legitimacy of the review process, but they may also constrain future behaviours.

Context

Over the last 70 years there have been approximately eighty-five public inquiries concerned with child protection in the United Kingdom. A burning issue during the first quarter of the 21st Century has concerned failures in child protection with UK child deaths by assault, averaging sixty-eight per year between 2015-2019.[33] Laming's 2003 *Victoria Climbié Inquiry*, concerned failures of public services to prevent the neglect, abuse and death of a young girl Victoria Climbie in 2000. Seven years later, the death of Baby Peter Connolly occurred, in a home only one hundred metres from the site of Victoria's death. What was notable was that not only was there was a recurrence of multiple agencies failing to intervene or share data and act to protect a vulnerable child but that many of the key personnel associated with Victoria's death were also involved with Peter. Lord Laming's Inquiry, investigating the circumstances of Victoria's abuse and death had resulted in a new policy regime. Lessons had been identified through a series of 108 recommendations, but these had not flowed into new behaviours or new collaborative working. Seven years on, and four years after the well-regarded Laming Report was published in 2003, how could the same agencies with many of the same people involved in Victoria's case fail to protect Peter?

In these two cases, the professional interventions provided were woefully insufficient, despite the strong suspicions from various public services that Victoria and Peter were being systematically abused by their carers. These agencies included Brent Social Services, Haringey Social Services, Tottenham Child and Family Centre, medics at the Central Middlesex Hospital and at the North Middlesex Hospital at the Metropolitan police. In Victoria's case there were at least sixty-seven interactions between Victoria, her carers and multiple agencies. As the Laming Report concluded:

> Had this tragedy of Victoria Climbié been because one doctor, one social worker, one police officer, had failed to see one telling sign indicating deliberate harm, frankly there is no system in the world that can prevent that; any one of us can make mistakes ... However, when you get the whole system engaged, when the second day this child was in the country she was referred under the Children Act as a child in need, and the very day that she died the case was being closed as no further action was needed, that was the day she was in the third hospital when her life could not be saved, I am strongly of the view that nothing more was known

about Victoria Climbié at the end of the process than was not in the first referral on the second day she was in this country. Never once was an assessment of need made; never once, whether by the hospital, social services or the police service. What happened to this little girl was shocking in the extreme.[34]

Laming's inquiry concluded that previous public inquiries had provided an adequate legislative framework and sought to focus upon bridging the gap between policy and practice. In this spirit, although Laming's recommendations focused upon accountability, law and regulation with a strong emphasis upon extending legislation and regulatory or oversight bodies it also took account of a technical-rational managerialist approach. Here there was greater emphasis to determining lines of responsibility to senior executives as well as recommendations for practice, decision making processes and a range of tools to enhance child safety.[35] Compared to legalistic approaches, practice-based research is more granular especially, when they consider differing processes, practices and cultures within the multiple agencies tasked with protecting children. Where a legalistic approach dominates it is less likely that full consideration will be given to practice.[36] This is a significant gap in the literature relating to the implementation of public inquiry findings.

Baby Peter

This account is taken from the first Serious Case Review (SCR) of Peter, completed in February 2009. A Serious Case Review (SCR) of Peter's death was convened by the Haringey Local Safeguarding Children Board in March 2009. It provided a more granular view of practice than any public inquiry. It contrasts with the public inquiries where the final balance of big picture versus a more granular perspective favours the former over the latter. In cases where a child is seriously harmed or dies from abuse or neglect, a Serious Case Review is conducted to identify how the various agencies and professionals can improve how they work to safeguard children at risk. As in the case of Victoria, Peter was seen by a range of different agencies. On 1 March 2006, the day of his birth, a health visitor undertook a new birth visit and identified that there was a cause for concern of Peter. In mid-September, Peter was examined by a family doctor for nappy rash and noted Peter's mother's complaint that Peter bruised easily and that mother was worried that she might be accused of hurting him. The SCR notes the lack of experienced social workers who lacked the confidence to challenge Peter's carers and failed to intervene. Peter Connolly, for example, spent two hours with his mother and a social worker at home with his face covered in jam and chocolate. There was no attempt to clean his face which may have revealed the bruises and cuts beneath and this reflects a professional training may not prepare effectively social workers or give them the confidence to challenge manipulative and deceitful carers. The SCR identified the need for "Authoritative Child Protection Practice," reflecting that child abusers often lie, and mislead professionals. Descriptions of Peter's mother identified a dominating and forceful personality which may have intimidated professionals, even more so when she brought legal representation to support her.

In early December Peter was referred by the family doctor to a hospital given his injuries and bruising. A strategy meeting of child protection social workers and police met a week later and decided that he could not return home. The consultant paediatrician who had examined Peter did not attend the strategy meeting but provided a detailed letter indicating that there was a high probability of non-accidental injury. Reflecting the potential messiness of multi-agency working when a child protection conference was organised on 23 December, the family doctor was not invited, the consultant paediatrician had other commitments, a doctor from the Child Development Centre gave apologies. Only one police officer, a child protection social worker and a legal representative attended. The legal officer argued that the threshold for care proceedings had been met, but this did not prompt the authorising authority, namely the Children and Young People's Service, to initiate care proceedings.

On 26 January 2007, Peter returned home, and his family moved elsewhere with a change of social worker. On 5 March a school nurse contacted social services to say that she had observed Peter's mother slapping another of her children. This report of a public slapping of one of Peter's siblings, witnessed by a school nurse, was taken less seriously than if it had been evidence from a police officer or paediatrician might have been given. There are hierarchies across with some professions judged as more reliable. There were further visits to accident and emergency for Peter, but there was no reference to non-accidental injuries, despite swellings to Peter's head, unsteadiness on his feet and multiple bruises and scratches. The police were informed but elected not to investigate jointly with social services.

On 8 June 2007, a review child protection conference was held, with a small number of agencies in attendance. It concluded that the injuries were, probably, not accidental. A legal planning meeting on 23 July concluded that the case did not merit the threshold for care proceedings. On 1 August Peter admitted into hospital with visible bruises and significant weight loss, which the doctor ascribed to possible viral infection. In August the police informed Peter's mother that they would take no legal proceedings against her. On 3 August Peter was readmitted to hospital and was pronounced dead at 12.19 pm

There was no public inquiry following the death of Peter. Laming[37] opined that all that was required was to implement the recommendations to ensure that every agency develops "good practice". The following year his frustrations were evident, in his view that the legislation was more than adequate and that the various agencies should "JUST DO IT".[38] There is a lack of realism having such high expectations of the abilities of poorly resourced, multi-agency working. This will unlikely be effective without the necessary levels of collaboration, shared understandings, recognition of professional competences and respect. Change takes time, clear two-way communications energy, resource and mutual respect.

The SCR (2009) highlighted interagency communication as an area of concern. The examples of medics missing case meetings is one example of the limited interagency communications. Another example related to a new initiative, called the "Mellow Parenting" programme which supported parents with relationship problems with their children. Peter's mother attended the sessions regularly, but he was rarely present, and his absence was not communicated to the child protection team, probably because the focus was upon the mother rather than the "invisible child." A family friend who cared for Peter while the police investigated allegations of abuse noted that the bruises from him head banging and headbutting were not behaviours she observed under her care. These minute details, so easily missed, went below the radar and yet were crucial information from which decisions and interventions might have been triggered.

Another area of concern related to the quality of support provided by social work line managers. Child protection work is both complex and potentially stressful. Case supervision and support of staff, by a line manager, should be able to occur without them becoming embroiled in a particular case. However, in this case the social workers charged with Peter's care experienced ad hoc and inconsistent support from line managers, with meetings persistently postponed. The conclusion to the SCR (2009) reported that the interventions were, lacking urgency and thoroughness, insufficiently challenging to the parent, Lacking action in response to reasonable inference, insufficiently focussed on the child's welfare and interventions based on too high a threshold with low expectations of outcomes[39] (SCR 2009: p24).

It might be argued, from an institutional perspective, that the Laming Report (2003a) was a macro level analysis and the SCR (2009) more concerned with micro or organisational matters. Both highlighted the importance of developing more effective interagency collaboration with ideas of developing a 'common language' for use across all agencies to avoid miscommunications, a requirement for interagency-training and each professional body demonstrating effective joint working within each professional group within their own national training programmes. Training plays a significant role in the findings such as equipping social workers to have the confidence to question the opinions in other agencies. In SCR (2009) police and paediatricians had a louder voice than other professions, reflecting long standing attitudes. Ensuring cover for absent professionals to ensure continuity of care was another recommendation, and changes to the Data Protection Act to ensure the ease of sharing information between professional groups as apt.

What is missing from the otherwise comprehensive Laming Report is the finer detail of individual professional bodies, each with their own priorities, cultures and norms, languages and hierarchies. It is at the level of micro-behaviours, whether it be reluctance to challenge an intimidating parent or medical consultant, or to demand clearer support from line managers that is missing. The shortage of resources, heavy workload, antiquated technology with each profession having systems designed for their use rather than agencies from social services, local government, police, schools and hospitals which would ideally all speak to one another, but do not. Although the 108 recommendations reflect useful insights, they do not deal with the messiness of people's lives or with organisational complexities. There is a risk that public inquiries make recommendations as if we operate with in an ideal world. A useful metaphor to think of as the mindset of such reports is that we enact lessons learned within a sterile, controllable laboratory, where all variables may be controlled which is not possible in the complex, messy context of child protection. Abusers cannot be trusted and are often manipulative, deceitful and dishonest.

It was evident that in the four years following publication of Laming's

(2003) Report that there had been few changes to practice and little evidence of more effective improvements in multiagency working. There is a level of complexity and nuance that may be difficult to capture. Drawing from Gillingham and Whittaker the decision environment for child protection matters is often complex and stressful. Social work, policing, nursing and teaching professionals will seek to establish working relationships with parents, carers and children while collaborating with professionals from other agencies. Each agency will possess its own norms, priorities, value. Some professions may have higher status and take primacy in child protection such as medics and police. Medics and the police have, potentially the strongest voice in making decisions. There may be threats of violence or intimidation from parents or carers. Within such a complex, dynamic decision environment cognitive depletion may occur[40] (Gillingham and Whittaker, 2022). A common feature, evident in the cases of both Victoria and Peter, is the "invisible child" whereby professionals focus their efforts upon the adult carers. Case notes may say little about the child at risk with a much stronger representation of the adult carer, seen as the key means of protecting a child. It is evident from reports concerning Victoria and Peter and a third study presented by Gillingham and Whittaker[41] that few practitioners stepped beyond the main living areas of the child's home, showing instead a lack of curiosity to explore further.

Although valuable artifacts, policies, regulations and guidance may not always fit the context in which professionals work. Judgement is required, but the penalty for misjudging may result in vilification down the line, by other professions or from the media. Not only may relevant knowledge cut across the policy, institutional and organisational levels but they will also cut across the various agencies with their already established ways of doing. A significant gap concerns the processes of institutionalization and the diffusion of norms across a multi-agency context. Public services within the UK have seen their resources stretched as they seek to do more with less making it less likely that collaborative working and joint training and working will occur. A challenge is to find a way in which the separate fields linked to each profession can extend to encourage joint working. In developing civil contingency preparedness fire, police and ambulance come together with local government and other agencies to train together through simulations or external exercises. Such exercises help develop a shared understanding and insight and respect for the knowhow of different agencies. This may be more difficult to arrange and organise within the context of child protection, however, it is not impossible. Only through shared artifacts, be they inductions, training sessions, simulations, secondments will there be a joined-up thinking and action to minimise failures in child protection.

Conclusions

The failures of multi-agency working in preventing the deaths of Victoria and Peter occurred between 15 and 20 years ago. At least fifty-eight children die each year from neglect and abuse at by the hands of their parents and carers. The recent death of 6-year-old Arthur Labinjo-Hughes, murdered through ongoing abuse by his stepmother with encouragement from his father is a stark reminder of the threats. Arthur's food was laced with salt, and he was forced to stand on a stair for hours on end. Concerned grandparents and other family members persistently reported concerns to the police and social services. There was the all too familiar pattern of the failure of multi agencies to work together, with insufficient coordination, the absence of data sharing and the reluctance of overstretched public services to intervene. There was little evidence of any authoritative child practice where professionals challenged the carers. Twenty years have passed since Victoria's death and Laming's Inquiry Report. The micro-behaviours of practices and behaviours outlined from an institutional field perspective are still work in progress.

An institutional perspective of learning through public inquiries draws together the macro, policy level with the meso and micro, organisational levels. First, it recognises the importance of a legal and regulatory framework. Second, it gives emphasis to a more granular understanding of the processes by which organisations and the professionals working within, make sense of the need to develop practice alongside new understandings and through doing so to create new norms, behaviours and practices. Laming's frustrations with the limited implementation of the recommendations of Laming[42] indicates a lack of understanding of how organisations and individuals learn, particularly within the context of multi-agency working. Put crudely, public inquiries are useful mechanisms for collecting and investigating evidence as a form of knowledge acquisition. In the case of the Laming Inquiry consideration be given to the creation of opportunities for professionals to engage in training and to consider ways of improving processes and practice. Laming's main emphasis, however, is upon recommendations for each agency with a more limited consideration of multi-agency working. Institutional fields evolve through interactions between actors which tend to produce and reproduce the norms, values, beliefs and practices that constitute the field.[43]

In the context of child protection, most agencies exist in 'semi-silos', with their own norms, prejudices, practices, values and beliefs. It may be argued that there is an institutional field each for the police, for medics, for social workers, respectively, with their different training, their own professional conferences, training programmes and strong norms. At this level knowledge is communicated and shared with each agency making sense of the "lessons learned" through processes of interpretation and integration with reference to their own professional norms, values, beliefs and practices. Knowledge may be assimilated through the cultural filter of each profession or agency. Recognition of a multi-agency institutional field is a vital step in supporting more effective multi-agency working, in this context aligned to child protection, building drawing together the various agencies to make sense as a collective rather than simply bringing their own, narrow professional disciplines to the fore.

Public inquiries have a key role in identifying lessons, but too often their focus is directed to the macro level of policy. There is a confusion between identifying lessons which may viewed as an endpoint. To ensure the effectiveness of organisational or multi-agency learning requires further steps, which may be best shape by the various agencies working to engage with change management experts to ensure that better practices emerge supported by adjusted norms and values to take account of the lessons learned. Without further efforts, inquiries may result in policy or regulatory change, but fails to influence the practice of the different agencies working with children at risk and their potential abusers. An institutional perspective gives insights into how this might be achieved and would benefit from further research.

Inquiry reports mentioned in this chapter[44]

Hillsborough Stadium Disaster Inquiry (Taylor, 1990)

The Victoria Climbié Inquiry (Laming, 2003)

Serious Case Review: Baby Peter (Jones, 2009)

Iraq Inquiry (Chilcot, 2009)

Independent Inquiry Child Sexual Abuse (Butler-Sloss/Woolf/Goddard/Jay, 2014)

The UK COVID-19 Inquiry (Hallett, 2021)

Notes

1   Barry Turner, "The Organisational and Interorganisational Development of Disasters", *Administrative Science Quarterly*, Vol 21, 1976, p. 379.
2   Alvin Gouldner, *Patterns in Industrial Bureaucracy*, Routledge and Kegan Paul, London, 1954.
3   Dominic Elliott, and Denis Smith, "Patterns of Regulatory Behaviour in the UK Football Industry", *Journal of Management Studies*, Vol 43, No 2, 2006, pp.

291-318

4   Lee Clarke, *Worst cases: Terror and catastrophe in the popular imagination*, Chicago University Press, Chicago, 2006.

5   Dominic Elliot, "The failure of organisational learning from crisis: A matter of life and death", *Journal of Contingencies and Crisis Management*, Vol 17, No 3, 2009, pp. 158-68.

6   Heather Hallett, Cabinet Office *COVID-19 Inquiry Terms of Reference* https://www.gov.uk/government/news/covid-19-inquiry-terms-of-reference, accessed April 10th 2022.

7   Although in Australia sitting members of the judiciary have been appointed to chair inquiries at both national and State levels this has becoming increasingly rare in recent times because of concerns that separation powers is being compromised – see Scott Prasser, *Royal Commissions and Public Inquiries in Australia*, LexisNexis, Chatswood, 2021, pp. 117-20.

8   Graeme Starr, "Public inquiries in the United Kingdom", in Scott Prasser and Helen Tracey, (eds), *Royal Commissions and Public Inquiries: Practice & Potential*, Connor Court Publishing, Ballarat, 2014, pp. 301-315.

9   Cowie, G (2022) Statutory public inquiries: the Inquiries Act 2005, accessed

10 Dominic Elliott, and Martina McGuinness, "Public Inquiries, Panacea or Placebo", *Journal of Contingencies and Crisis Management*, Vol 10, No 1, 2002, pp. 114-25.

11 Ulrich Beck, *Risk Society: Towards a New Modernity*, Sage, London, 1992.

12 Elliott and McGuinness, "Public Inquiries, Panacea or Placebo", pp. 114-25.

13 Charles Perrow, "Organizing to Reduce the Vulnerabilities of Complexity", *Journal of Crises and Contingencies Management*, Vol 7, No 3, pp. 150-155.

14 Starr, "Public Inquiries in the United Kingdom", pp. 307-08.

15 Peter Saunders, *"Victims' group insist on new abuse inquiry head" 2014 accessed at* https://www.bbc.co.uk/news/av/uk-29845110 accessed on May 1, 2022.

16 Thomas Birkland, *Lessons of disaster: Policy change after catastrophic events*, Georgetown University Press, Washington DC, 2006, p. 23.

17 Dominic Elliott, and Allan Macpherson, "Policy and practice: Recursive learning from crisis", *Group & Organisation Management*, Vol 35, No 5, 2010, pp. 572-605.

18 Brian Toft and Simon Reynolds, *Learning from Disasters; A Management Approach*, Palgrave Macmillan, London, 1997

19 Elliot, "The failure of organisational learning from crisis".

20 Joseph Lampel, and Alan D. Meyer, "Guest Editors Introduction, Field Configuring Events as Structuring Mechanisms", *Journal of Management Studies*, Vol 45, No 6, 2008, pp. 1025-35.

21 Thomas Birkland, *After disaster: Agenda setting, public policy, and focusing events*, Georgetown University Press, Washington, DC, 1997; Andrew Brown, and Matthew Jones, "Honourable members and dishonourable deeds: Sense making, impression management and legitimation in the arms to Iraq affair", *Human Relations*, Vol 53, 2000, pp. 655-89.

22 Mary Crossan, Roderick White, and Richard Ivey, "An organisational learning framework: From intuition to institution", *Academy of Management Review*, Vol 24, No 3, 1999, pp. 522-37.

23 David Conn, "Uefa apologises to Liverpool and Madrid fans over Champions League chaos", *The Guardian* accon 3 June 2022 at https://www.theguardian.com/football/2022/jun/03/uefa-apologises-to-fans-at-liverpool-v-real-madrid-champions-league-final

24 Michael Power, *The Audit Society: Rituals of Verification*, Oxford University Press, Oxford, 1997.

25 Birkland, "Lessons from disaster"; Arjen Boin, Paul t'Hart, and Allan McConnell, "Governing after crisis", in Boin, McConnell, and t'Hart, (eds), *Governing after Crisis. The Politics of Investigation, Accountability and Learning*, Cambridge University Press, Cambridge, 2008, pp. 3-32.

26 John. Carroll, Jenny Rudolph, and Sachi Hatakeneka, "Learning from Experience in High-Hazard Organisations", *Research in Organisational Behaviour*, Vol 24, 2002, pp. 87-137.

27 Power, *The Audit Society*.

28 Melissa Wooten and Andrew Hoffman, "Organisational Fields: Past, Present and Future" in R. Greenwood, C. Oliver, T. B. Lawrence, and R.E. Meyer, (eds), *The SAGE Handbook of Organisational Institutionalism*, 2nd ed, SAGE, London 2008.

29 Michael Lounsbury, "A tale of two cities: Competing logics and practice variation in the professionalizing of mutual funds", *Academy of Management Review*, Vol 50, 2007, pp. 289-307; Tammar Zilber, "Institutionalization as an interplay between actions, meanings, and actors", *Academy of Management Journal*, 45, 2002, pp. 234-54.

30 Lampel and Meyer, "Guest Editors Introduction".

31 Royston Greenwood, Christine Oliver, Kerstin Sahlin, and Roy Suddaby, (eds), "Introduction," *The Sage Handbook of Organisational Institutionalism*, Sage, London, 2008.

32 Thomas Lawrence, Roy Suddaby, and Bernard Leca, *Institutional work: Actors and agency in institutional studies of organisations*, Cambridge University Press, Cambridge, 2009.

33 NSPCC, *Statistics briefing: child deaths due to abuse or neglect*, 2021, accessed at https://learning.nspcc.org.uk/media/1652/statistics-briefing-child-deaths-abuse-neglect.pdf

34 *Laming Report, 2003* pp. 9-10.

35 *Laming Report*, 2003; Philip Gillingham, "Driving Child Protection Reform: Evidence or Ideology?" *Australian Social Work*, Vol 64, No 3, 2014, pp. 377-89.

36 Elliott, 'The failure of organisational learning from crisis", pp. 158-68.

37 Laming, *Interim Report*, 2008.

38 Laming, *Final Report*, 2009.

39 Serious Case Review: Baby Peter, 2009 p. 24.

40 Philip Gillingham, and Andrew Whittaker, "How Can Research and Theory Enhance Understanding of Professional Decision-Making in Reviews of Cases of Child Death and Serious Injury", *British Journal of Social Work* 2022, accessed at https://academic.oup.com/bjsw/advance-article/doi/10.1093/bjsw/bcac116/6609239?login=true

41 Ibid.

42 Laming, *Final Report*, 2009

43 Walter W. Powell, and Paul Di Maggio, "Introduction", in Powell and DiMaggio, (eds), *The New Institutionalism and Organisational Analysis*, University of Chicago Press, Chicago, 1991, pp. 1-38; Lawrence, Hardy & Phillips, 2002 Thomas Lawrence, Cynthia Hardy, and Nelson Phillips, "Institutional effects of inter-organisational collaboration: The emergence of proto-institutions", *Academy of Management Journal*, Vol 45, 2002, pp. 281-90.

44 List refers to name of inquiry, its chair and date of appointment.

13

Can – and should – royal commissions provide policy advice?

John Phillimore and Peter Wilkins

Introduction

Royal commissions are established for a variety of reasons. They may be initiated in the wake of natural disasters, suspected wrongdoing in public administration, or notable failures in government programs. But how well suited is the vehicle of a royal commission to developing policy? That is the question this chapter seeks to answer.

As Prasser and others have noted,[1] it is now quite rare for a dedicated policy-focused royal commission to be appointed, especially at the Commonwealth level.[2] Instead, almost all royal commissions are nowadays what is termed 'investigatory' or 'inquisitorial'. They aim to investigate facts or allocate responsibilities with respect to incidents, problems or failures. However, this does not mean that such royal commissions have no policy relevance. Clearly, they do. Indeed, "such royal commissions are also expected, and indeed often required by their terms of reference, to make policy recommendations so that similar problems do not reoccur".[3] Several recent royal commissions established by the Commonwealth Government have included the following explicit instruction in their *Letters Patent:*

> We direct you to make any recommendations arising out of your inquiry that you consider appropriate, including recommendations about any *policy*, legislative, administrative or structural reform.[4]
> [emphasis added]

This does not mean, however, that royal commissions are the only, or the most appropriate, vehicle for developing policy. As the recent absence of policy-dedicated royal commissions would suggest, governments have found many other avenues for developing policy. However, the unique authority and prestige of royal commissions mean that they may have disproportionate influence when they do weigh into a policy debate. As Kerr noted several years ago:

> The 'royal' in royal commission is hugely significant. Even if only subliminally, it elevates a public inquiry and awards it an entirely different degree of status in the eyes of both the media and the general public. It guarantees that the commission will be seen as more than just another committee or taskforce or whatever.[5]

As a consequence, governments will be under pressure to implement the recommendations arising from royal commissions, even if much of their focus is on identifying misbehaviour or neglect. Therefore, it is worth considering in more detail the strengths and weaknesses of royal commissions as policy analysis and advisory bodies, and at whether there might be better alternatives.

Strengths

We need to begin with a recognition that there is dissatisfaction with existing policy making processes. For example, the Institute of Public Administration Australia (IPAA) in 2012 argued that 'policy on the run' and 'policy by fiat' were rife within government and made for poor policy outcomes.[6]

The first approach of 'policy on the run', hints at the reactive basis of much policy making, which involves responding to crises and events as they arise, without due process or considering alternatives, or evidence about what works. The focus might instead be on partisan gain or on an attractive (or crisis-induced) 'announceable' for the media, without considering the full implications (or effectiveness) of the policy.

The second approach, 'policy by fiat', reflects a desire by governments to show decisiveness, but is often accompanied by a lack of consultation with stakeholders and a failure to secure or even seek consensus and support for policy decisions. This reduces the chances of successful implementation. Too often, IPAA argues, ministers decide first, and then justify their decisions. Often, their decisions are considered to be to be partisan, or to reflect certain interests (usually corporate) over others (eg consumers, or the taxpayer, or the environment). They often do not consider carefully enough the relative costs or benefits of the policy, or of how it will be implemented. This can then lead to delays, cost overruns, or poorly targeted or ineffective programs.

The IPAA argues there is a need for a better evidence base for policy making, and that a 'business case' approach should be demonstrated, so that policies can be proposed, discussed, and debated before being adopted. The ideal process is to have a Green Paper followed by a White Paper, with the former providing a range of alternatives and seeking feedback from the public and key stakeholders, while the latter outlines the final form that policy will take before legislation or new funding is adopted.

The IPAA approach accords with a preference amongst many policy academics and observers that good policy should, where possible, be evidence based (or at least evidence-informed),[7] and involve consultation with those most likely to be affected. Ideally, it should be discussed, debated, maybe even piloted or trialled, with feedback being sought to test its feasibility, desirability, and effectiveness, before a final decision is made.

Royal commissions, at least in principle, provide an antidote to what are often seen as the common failures of modern policymaking, such as short-termism, partisanship, reliance on selective evidence, and reacting to rather than anticipating events. By contrast, they offer the prospect of a more rational, evidence-based approach. Even the adversarial, inquisitorial, and investigative forms of royal commission inquiry have been able to adopt many "instrumental or problem-solving model[s] of research utilisation and policy development"[8] that are common to policy advisory inquiries and 'best practice' policy making. For example, royal commissions:

- Can obtain views from all stakeholders and participants, through both public submissions and the conduct of public hearings. Importantly, this now often includes engagement with citizens and consumers of government services, as well as 'street level bureaucrats', whose perspective is often ignored by government agencies or private think tanks.
- Usually have a significant amount of time to gather relevant evidence, use powers to demand access to documents and oral evidence, and to conduct and commission research to shed light on issues, and to then consider a range of policy alternatives. This contrasts strongly with the tendency identified by IPAA towards 'policy on the run'.
- Can test out their policy ideas through discussions with interested parties and through issuing an interim report. Such a report can be seen as akin to a Green Paper, with the final report being regarded as similar to a White Paper, with the important difference being that government is not necessarily bound to accept a royal commission's final report recommendations.

In addition to these important procedural strengths, royal commissions also possess the "qualities of independence, neutrality, transparency" that "make them attractive tools to government"[9], as well as normally being strongly supported by the public. As Prasser and Tracey argue, "by introducing substance and objective analysis to policy issues and having a clear focus on the national interest or public good, public inquiries play an important role in building confidence in public decision-making".[10]

A royal commission can be seen as providing a 'policy window', using the terminology of Kingdon,[11] through which reform can be initiated. In this model, such a window often follows a 'focusing event' – such as a natural disaster or public administration scandal – which then allows governments to break through the more familiar pattern of policy incrementalism or stasis. As a former counsel to a royal commission has noted, royal commissions can

> ... help open up difficult public policy issues requiring broad based public support: they have the potential to 'cut through' a confronting, complex problem, and better assist policy development.[12]

The publicity and authority afforded to a royal commission can help bring certain issues and policy possibilities to light that have previously languished. Public hearings and media reporting of these promote wider awareness and debate of the issues addressed. Recent royal commissions provide examples of giving attention to issues which have long been hidden from view (such as child abuse, exploitation of people with disabilities, aged care), put in the 'too hard basket' (nuclear energy), or 'captured' by certain interests (banking and finance). These often work best when they are not regarded as partisan issues on which the major parties have settled – and opposite – policy positions.

Whether the recommendations are then adopted and whether they succeed is another matter of course, which is discussed in other chapters in this volume. However, Mintrom and colleagues note that some royal commissions have taken these aspects quite seriously too, adopting particular communication and alliance-building techniques in order to build support for policy recommendations, and to try to ensure that they are implemented after the royal commission has concluded.[13]

Weaknesses of royal commissions

Despite the many potential and actual advantages that royal commissions are able to bring to bear on policy development, there are also several weaknesses and criticisms that can be directed at them.

One is a simple matter of expertise and competence. Prasser and Tracey caution that an inquiry can "produce poor quality advice, which the government then feels bound to follow".[14] This is possibly even more the case with inquisitorial royal commissions. Some, indeed many, policy areas are complex and quite specialist. It is not necessarily the case that a retired judge has the requisite expertise to develop policy in the area under investigation, especially if their main focus has been on the more adversarial, investigative aspects of an issue.[15] Relatedly, "the court-like approach ... has the ability both to instil high levels of public confidence in the integrity and robustness of the process and to create inflexibilities which make the development of policy-related recommendations more difficult".[16]

A more subtle or nuanced aspect of this criticism is that the policy process is also complex, not just the substantive issue at hand. It is commonly recognised that to achieve successful policy reform usually needs the support of key stakeholders, including service funders, providers and users. Increasingly, a co-design process is used – and this may be beyond the ability or the terms of reference of a royal commission.

Relatedly, it makes a difference how the commissioners themselves see their role. For example, Commissioner Lynelle Briggs explicitly considered that "the *Royal Commission into Aged Care Quality and Safety* is a policy commission".[17] It was not clear that her fellow Commissioner did, or at least not to the same extent.[18]

Furthermore, and somewhat unusually, these two commissioners disagreed on a small number of crucial recommendations. This allowed government to 'pick and choose' its preferred course of action – and, it could be argued, put the policy issues back to the department, where it had been before the royal commission was called.[19]

Another potential problem may be that the terms of reference of a royal commission may limit its ability to consider the wider implications of its recommendations, such as how they may impinge on other policy areas or conflict with other policy objectives of government. These can range from the relatively simple (but highly significant) matter of budgetary constraints (eg the fiscal implications of the aged care recommendations) to potentially negative impacts of new regulatory impositions on bank lending, for example, as a result of the recommendations of the banking royal commission.[20] The latitude provided to royal commissions in conducting their investigations and in providing recommendations means there is always a chance that they may go beyond their initial remit, and move into policy areas that government is not necessarily ready, willing or able to commit to.[21]

Sometimes, the apparent advantages of a royal commission can also be their downside. For example, the time-consuming nature of a royal commission may suit a government that wishes to delay action on an important issue, by 'kicking the can down the road' for another government or minister to deal with, in the hope that it will appease media and public critics in the short term. The focus on the issue may well have passed by the time the royal commission reports. While this may meet the government's political objectives, it may also mean the 'policy window' for meaningful action may have shut, leaving real policy issues unaddressed even if the final report and recommendations of the royal commission are soundly constructed.

Of course, these criticisms may also be levelled at any policy inquiry, not just a royal commission. It can be argued in return that by calling a royal commission, given their greater prestige and visibility, governments are more likely to have to respond eventually, rather than being able to simply ignore them. Indeed "it is seldom politically feasible to refuse to wholesale adopt recommendations".[22] The comprehensive nature of royal commissions can also have costs as well as benefits. One obvious one is that it prolongs the length of the inquiry. Another, related one, is its significant financial expense. A third is that the royal commission's recommendations may be 'all or nothing' in character, which may lead to 'nothing much' being done. Many policy issues and problems are complex, wicked even, with interlocking elements. A royal commission may demand wholesale changes to several areas that are likely to invite opposition from key actors or require reform in areas unrelated to the royal commission or by other actors, or significant time and resources to be realised. Kerr notes that the "sheer size and scope of royal commissions ... may lead to difficulties down the track ... in terms of absorbing and implementing their recommendations".[23]

Furthermore, the apparent 'failure' to implement all the recommendations (which can sometimes be very numerous) may give a misleading impression that no progress is occurring and reduce public confidence in how government is dealing with an issue. Gourley, in discussing the Coombs *Royal Commission into Australian Government Administration* (RCAGA), argues that "large reports, containing numerous and often inter-related recommendations with a good number couched in general terms requiring further development before implementation, may take many years for their proposals to be realised".[24] Nevertheless, he also points out that many reforms subsequently undertaken by governments could be traced back to that royal commission.

In sum, while incrementalism has its problems, it is often a surer way to progress an issue. Royal commissions and their advocates may run the risk of 'the perfect becoming the enemy of the good'.

The focusing event (eg the natural disaster or scandal) upon which many royal commissions are asked to investigate may also be misleading in providing lessons for future policy making. Eburn and Dovers have suggested that royal commissions are inevitably backward-looking, trying to understand past disasters that were unique events. The 'lessons' we may learn from them may not be useful, or the most appropriate, for preparing for the next disaster. This may be especially the case in an age of climate change, where the new threats may be of a magnitude or type that past processes and policies are unprepared for – even if they were carried out properly.[25]

By contrast, Stark has argued that analysts often take too narrow and simplistic an approach to 'lesson learning'. He argues that the range of actors influenced by royal commissions (and their recommendations) goes beyond governments to include a wide range of stakeholders. In addition, the learning that takes place can include "cognitive organisational learning", as well as the more typical instrumental learning associated with policy inquiries and their recommendations.[26]

Alternatives

As noted in the introduction, governments long ago moved beyond a reliance on royal commissions as a primary source of policy advice and development. In addition to run of the mill independent policy inquiries, governments of course have their own public service bureaucracy, including specialist government-funded policy agencies such as the Productivity Commission, Australian Institute of Health and Welfare, and the Australian Law Reform Commission. Parliamentary committees can also be important sources of policy analysis. Beyond government, there is now a highly contested 'policy advice' environment in which numerous groups and organisations conduct policy-related research and advocacy.[27] These include:

- independent think tanks initially funded by government, such as the Australian Strategic Policy Institute and the Grattan Institute.
- other think tanks aligned to certain interests and ideologies but which retain at least the perception of independence. These include the Institute of Public Affairs, Centre for Independent Studies, Australia Institute, and the Centre for Policy Development.
- think tanks expressly linked to a sponsoring political party, including the McKell Institute (Labor), Menzies Research

Centre (Liberal) and Page Research Centre (Nationals).
- university research institutes and centres.
- industry peak bodies and lobbyists.
- consultants, including accountancy-based firms.
- not-for-profit groups.
- trade unions.
- the media.

Two contributors to policy development that have received less attention but that might also be considered are auditors general and parallel inquiries.

Auditors-general have a long history of monitoring government expenditure and programs and reporting to parliament (and hence the public) on the use and misuse of public funds. A less appreciated aspect of their work is the performance audit[28], which involves a more forensic analysis of the effectiveness and efficiency of government programs or agencies. These sorts of audits can often be hard-hitting and provide important pointers to or actual policy advice – at a fraction of the cost of a royal commission. Admittedly, they tend to not get anywhere near the same publicity and their recommendations may be more easily ignored or played down by governments. However, whilst the choice of topics and their scope is not set by the executive, their contribution should be considered.

A second option would be to consider whether the role of royal commissions should sometimes be restricted to the identification of wrongdoing, with their broader policy-development role being explicitly assigned to another process or inquiry type. Eburn and Dovers, in their analysis of 50 years of inquiries into disasters, suggest a model along these lines. They argue that

> Rather than appoint a commission … to review all aspects of an event, consideration should be given to establishing an independent inquiry panel, similar to the current royal commission model, supplemented by specialist panels to investigate issues

that are raised by the particular event; for example issues of communications, inter-agency coordination, local government capacity, warning systems, land management, infrastructure management, policy and management failure, and the adequacy of the response, all of which are distinctly different issues requiring quite different forms of skills and investigative processes.[29]

The potential of this sort of approach is illustrated by the Western Australian *Royal Commission into Commercial Activities of Government and Other Matters*.[30] While it primarily focused on wrongdoing, it also provided a framework for reforms, making 40 recommendations in 1992 in relation to the latter.

One of these recommendations was the establishment of a Commission on Government (COG) as an umbrella body, and another seven referred specific matters to this proposed body. The COG was then created under a separate act of parliament, the *Commission on Government Act 1994*, and was required to inquire into 24 specified matters including issues in relation to parliament, electoral arrangements, statutory officials and public administration. The COG consulted widely and acted openly, releasing discussion papers and seeking submissions from the public. A member of COG, Frank Harman, later reflected on its impact and concluded that several reforms to policy and legislation had resulted from COG's work.[31]

A two-stage approach that separates investigating wrongdoing from formulation of policy advice is something that should be considered routinely, along with more research into policy implementation that can assist inquiries to maximise the likelihood that their recommendations will not just be accepted but also implemented in a way that achieves the intended benefits.

Conclusion

As Prasser and others have noted, royal commissions are creations of the executive, and can be established for many different reasons, from the worthy pursuit of truth and policy options, to deflecting criticism of government inaction, to the more openly political commissions set up to damage political opponents.

As vehicles for developing and advocating policy, they have both strengths and weaknesses, some of which are one and the same, ie their comprehensive nature and the significant time and resources at their disposal. Faster, less expensive and potentially more suitable alternatives exist but are seldom used when contentious and high public profile issues are confronting the executive.

Royal commissions are likely to remain an option for governments responding to problems and crises. Our hope is that books and chapters like this will inform thoughtful politicians and their policy advisors and assist them in reflecting upon the utility and implications of royal commissions as policy vehicles.

Public inquiries mentioned in this chapter[32]

Commonwealth inquiries

Royal Commission into Australian Government Administration (Coombs, 1974)
Royal Commission into the Activities of the Federated Ship Painters' and Dockers' Union (Costigan, 1980)[33]
Royal Commission into Aged Care Quality and Safety (Briggs and Pagone, 2018)

State inquiries

Royal Commission into Commercial Activities of Government and Other Matters, Western Australia (Kennedy, 2001)
Nuclear Fuel Cycle Royal Commission (Scarce, 2015)

Notes

1   Scott Prasser, *Royal Commissions and Public Inquiries in Australia,* 2nd ed, Lex-
    isNexis, Chatswood, 2021, p. 29. See also Australian Law Reform Commis-
    sion, *Royal Commissions and Official Inquiries,* Discussion Paper 75, Common-
    wealth of Australia, Sydney, 2009, pp. 49-54.

2   At State level, South Australia is a notable exception. Labor Premier Jay
    Weatherill established the *Nuclear Fuel Cycle Royal Commission* in 2015, which
    reported in 2016. Labor Premier Peter Malinauskis, elected in March 2022,
    has promised to establish a Royal Commission into Education Services for
    South Australian Children, focused on early childhood education and out of
    school hours care.

3   Prasser, *Royal Commissions and Public Inquiries,* p. 29.

4   This form of words can be found in the *Letters Patent* for the Child Abuse,
    Aged Care, Natural Disasters, and Disability royal commissions.

5   Christian Kerr, "Royal commissions and the press – seagulls at the lawyers
    picnic", in Scott Prasser and Helen Tracey, (eds), *Royal Commissions and Public
    Inquiries: Practice and Potential,* Connor Court Publishing, Ballarat, 2014, p. 283.

6   Institute of Public Administration Australia, *Public Policy Drift: Why govern-
    ments must replace 'policy on the run' and 'policy by fiat' with a 'business case' approach
    to regain confidence,* IPAA Public Policy Discussion Paper, 4 April 2012. Avail-
    able at https://www.ipaa.org.au/wp-content/uploads/2019/06/Public-Poli-
    cy-Drift-policy-paper.pdf

7   Brian Head, "Evidence-based policymaking – Speaking truth to power?",
    Australian Journal of Public Administration, Vol 72, No 4, December 2010, pp.
    397-403.

8   Prasser, *Royal Commissions and Public Inquiries,* p. 33.

9   Dominique Hogan-Doran SC, "Lessons for Government Reform from Re-
    cent Royal Commissions and Public Inquiries", Paper presented to the Law
    Society of New South Wales Government Solicitors' Conference, Sydney, 3
    September 2019, p. 3.

10 Scott Prasser and Helen Tracey, "Public inquiries – living up to their poten-
    tial", in Prasser and Tracey, *Royal Commissions and Public Inquiries,* p. 375.

11 John Kingdon, *Agendas, alternatives, and public policies,* (3rd ed), Little, Brown &
    Company, Boston, 1984/2011. Also see Michael Mintrom, Deidre O'Neill,
    and Ruby O'Connor, "Royal commissions and policy influence", *Australian
    Journal of Public Administration,* Vol 80, No 1, March 2021, pp. 80-96.

12 Hogan-Doran, "Lessons for Government Reform", p. 5.

13 Mintrom, O'Neill and O'Connor, "Royal commissions and policy influence."

14 Prasser and Tracey, *Royal Commissions and Public Inquiries,* p. 385.

15 Hogan-Doran, "Lessons for Government Reform", p. 17.

16 Susan Pascoe, "The 2009 Victorian Bushfires Royal Commission: Lessons
    for the Conduct of Inquiries in Australia", *Australian Journal of Public Admin-
    istration,* Vol 69, No 4, December 2010, p. 398.

17 Lynelle Briggs, (Co-Chair), Royal Commission into Aged Care Quality and
    Safety, "Care, Dignity and Respect – An Overview,", in, *Final Report: Care,
    Dignity and Respect, Volume 1: Summary and recommendations,* Commonwealth of
    Australia, Canberra, 2021, pp. 23-60.

18 Tony Pagone, (Co-Chair), "Chair's Preface," in Royal Commission into Aged

Care Quality and Safety, *Final Report: Care, Dignity and Respect. Volume 1: Summary and recommendations*, Commonwealth of Australia, Canberra, 2021, p. 1.

19 Stephen Duckett and Anika Stobart, "4 key takeaways from the aged care royal commission's final report", *The Conversation*, 1 March 2021

20 An example of the criticism can be found in Andrew Mohl, "Hayne's $65b shock to Australia," *Australian Financial Review*, 13 December 2019, p. 38. It should be noted that Commissioner Hayne disputed this view as having no supportive evidence. See Kenneth M Hayne, (Chair), Royal Commission into Misconduct in the Banking, Superannuation and Financial Services Industry, *Final Report*, Commonwealth of Australia, Canberra, 2019, p. 4.

21 The clearest example of this is the Costigan *Royal Commission into the Activities of the Federated Ship Painters' and Dockers' Union*, established in 1980 by Commonwealth and Victorian coalition governments with the aim of targeting a powerful trade union with Labor Party links. It ended up uncovering serious tax avoidance and money laundering which implicated many wealthy individuals, some with links to the government itself and led to legislative changes which were opposed by some people within the coalition.

22 Hogan-Doran, "Lessons for Government Reform", p. 17.

23 Kerr, "Royal commissions and the press", p. 284.

24 Paddy Gourley, "Inquiries into government administration," in Prasser and Tracey, *Royal Commissions and Public Inquiries*, p. 219.

25 Michael Eburn and Stephen Dovers, "Learning Lessons from Disasters: Alternatives to Royal Commissions and Other Quasi-Judicial Inquiries," *Australian Journal of Public Administration*, Vol 74, No 4, December 2015, p. 501.

26 Alistair Stark, "Policy learning and the public inquiry," *Policy Sciences*, Vol 52, No 3, September 2019, pp. 397-417.

27 See the chapters devoted to each of these policy organisations in Brian Head and Kate Crowley, (eds), *Policy Analysis in Australia*, Policy Press, Bristol, 2015.

28 Jeremy Lonsdale, Peter Wilkins and Tom Ling, (eds), *Performance auditing: Contributing to accountability in democratic government*, Edward Elgar, Cheltenham, 2011.

29 Eburn and Dovers, "Learning Lessons from Disasters," p. 504.

30 *Report of the Royal Commission into the Commercial Activities of Government and Other Matters*, Perth, Western Australia, 1992.

31 Frank Harman, "The Recommendations of the Commission on Government: Did Anyone Take Notice?", in Allan Peachment, (ed), *The Years of Scandal: Commissions of Inquiry in Western Australia 1991-2014*, University of Western Australia Press, Crawley, 2006, pp. 67-91.

32 List refers to name of inquiry, its chair and date of appointment.

33 This was a joint Commonwealth-State (Victorian) inquiry.

Section 4: Other countries' inquiries – experiences and lessons

Introduction

Scott Prasser

Most political systems, and indeed rulers, while relying primarily on advice from within government – such as the permanent bureaucracy, or from those close to them, like special advisers, or from ministerial staff, have also long sought views from external advisory mechanisms. International trends suggest that seeking views from outside advisory mechanisms is becoming more prevalent.[1] There are many reasons for this: the increasing complexity of issues; greater government involvement in society; the limits of expertise within government caused by a variety of factors;[2] decline in trust in existing government institutions; the need for more open decision making; and the importance of more and more public consultation to procure support for policy change.

Of course, one of the most important mechanisms that can be observed across many different jurisdictions, is the public inquiry, as defined in this volume (see Introduction). This section examines the use of the public inquiry instrument across the United Kingdom (UK), New Zealand and Nordic countries. The following chapters identify the numbers, forms, roles and trends of public inquiries in those different countries, and some emerging controversies.

While there is some common heritage across the UK, New Zealand and to a lesser extent, the United States, there has long been considerable differences in how public inquiries have developed in each of these jurisdictions. This has also been noted in relation to our legislative systems, including the Westminster ones. Craft and Halligan summed it up this way:

> Despite common lineage – the historical forms used in the United Kingdom – and diffusion of principles and approaches to inquiries among Anglophone countries, contextual factors still matter, and variations in terminology and practice abound ...it is something of a quagmire, the most universal observation being that it is impossible to have clarity over the different types of inquiry.[3]

So, while comparison across the United Kingdom, Australia and New Zealand is interesting enough with the United States as a useful addition, it was decided to broaden the comparison and examine the use of inquiries in a very different system – namely across Nordic countries. There were reasons for this. Although they have a different political system and culture to Westminster countries and that of the United States, Nordic countries have a long history of appointing public inquiries. Moreover, they have appointed a lot. Between 1990-2015 the Swedish Cabinet appointed between 68 and 134 commissions of inquiry each year. In Norway, from 1972 to 2016 it has been estimated that some 1500 commissions were established. In addition, these public inquiries have a distinctiveness in their role and functions that reflect Nordic culture and political systems with its neo-corporatist "managed pluralism"[4] approach which make them different to their Westminster counterparts. Further, Nordic political systems have been "characterised as technocratic, with a strong emphasis on the finding of rational solutions to policy problems based on relevant knowledge and through investigation".[5] Such features reflect many of the perceived positive attributes of public inquiries used to explain their appointment in our and related systems, thus making them especially appealing to study and to compare.

Turning to the chapters in this section we begin logically with Cooper and Thomas' study of the United Kingdom (**Chapter 14**) given the UK's particular relevance to Australia and New Zealand. Cooper and Thomas provide a brief historical development of UK public inquiries, highlight the distinctions between statutory and non-statutory inquiries and then focus on issues concerning several recent inquiries. These inquiries have investigated many areas similar to those in Australia, New Zealand and to some extent those in the US – scandals, disasters, and calamities and a host of policy issues. Cooper and Thomas share similar concerns expressed in previous chapters about inquiry capabilities, their expertise, adversarial and legalistic processes, high costs and lengthy deliberations. As in Australia and New Zealand there have also been some important legislative changes in the UK with the passing of the *Inquiries Act 2005*. At the same time certain important differences are highlighted. For instance, in the UK royal commissions have become largely defunct; and the UK persists in appointing sitting judges to chair inquiries and calling them "judicial inquiries". In Australia, there has been an increasing reluctance by sitting members of the judiciary to chair public inquiries[6] while the term "judicial inquiry" is unacceptable in the Australian context given its written constitution and the separation of powers.[7]

Moving to New Zealand, Wendy McGuinness (**Chapter 15**) explains the country's constitutional and legal developments that led to the new *Inquiries Act 2013*. It reflects recommendations by the New Zealand Law Commission which were similar to those made shortly later by the Australian Law Reform Commission and which have now become embodied in the new Victorian *Inquiries Act 2014* (see **Chapter 4**). That new legislation lays down criteria of when an inquiry is to be designated a "royal commission", and includes stipulations on timeframes, extensions and costs. Though New Zealand royal commission numbers have been trending downwards during the last decade, some very important ones have been appointed along with a host of other policy and ministerial public inquiries. The Chapter discusses the future of inquiries, possible topics they could explore and the processes that need to be attended to so that public support in this worthwhile instrument can be retained. Several historical case studies such as the 1919 royal commission into Spanish Flu are discussed in relation to the recent appointment of the *Royal Commission of Inquiry (COVID-19 Lessons)*.

Ken Kitts in **Chapter 16** reviews US presidential commissions. Perhaps more than any other jurisdiction covered in this volume, such inquiries cannot be appreciated unless the system of which they are a part is also understood. The US may have a very stable and straightforward constitutional framework, but its advisory system of which presidential commissions are but one small part, is large, complex, disjointed and entangled. The strong separation of powers between the legislature and executive combined with the federal system results in a host of advisory mechanisms each vying for attention and claiming prestige and status. There is some confusion as to what constitutes a 'public inquiry' or even a 'presidential commission'. The levels, of what Kitts calls, "commission politics" between the President and Congress concerning the appointment, membership, terms of references and powers of presidential commissions needs to be appreciated to understand the role and impact of these bodies, and their value in the American political system. Despite these characteristics, Kitt guides readers through this advisory maze so that key presidential commissions are identified, the politics explained, their value assessed and their future possible roles suggested.

Chapter 17 by Kira Pronin covers the Nordic countries of Sweden, Norway, Denmark and Finland – a large sweep. Certainly, as noted previously, there are several contrasting features about the Nordic countries' public inquiries compared to those in the Westminster and US systems. This includes their large numbers, integration into the decision-making process, wide membership, and role in building consensus for policy change in Nordic countries' corporatist decision making environment. While Nordic inquiries have generally been seen as successful there have been criticisms of late, some of which echo complaints heard in other jurisdictions. For instance, too many inquiries were being appointed, there were long gestation periods in their final reporting, and many of their recommendations were costly and even impractical. Consequently, although such inquiries are still employed, Pronin highlights some recent developments such as a tapering off in their numbers, changes in the composition of their membership, and in some cases, greater executive government control of their appointments. The Nordic countries increasing engagement with the European Union (EU) is also affecting how governments respond to inquiry recommendations and is another driver of change. Nevertheless, Pronin argues public inquiries continue to serve an important role in these countries and will continue to do so in the future.

In summary, this international comparison across similar and different political systems shows the continuing use and need of the public inquiry instrument, the many guises and forms it can take, and how local conditions affect inquiry operations and impacts. These issues will be explored in more detail in the concluding **Chapter 18**.

Notes

1   John Craft and John Halligan, *Advising Governments in the Westminster Tradition: Policy Advisory Systems in Australia, Britain, Canada and New Zealand*, Cambridge University Press, Cambridge, 2020.

2   Kate Crowley, Jenny Stewart and Brian Head, *Reconsidering Policy: Complexity, Governments and the State*, Policy Press, Bristol, 2021, pp. 97-9.

3   Ibid., p. 116.

4   Hugh Heclo and Henrik Madsen, *Policy and Politics in Sweden: Principled Pragmatism*, Temple University, Philadelphia, 1987, p. 6.

5   Johan Christensen and Stine Hesstvdet, "Expertisation and greater representation: Evidence from Norwegian advisory commissions", *European Politics and Society*, Vol 20, No 1, 2019, p. 94.

6   Scott Prasser, *Royal Commissions and Public Inquiries in Australia*, 2nd ed, LexisNexis, Chatswood, 2021, pp. 117-20.

7   Nicholas Aroney, "The constitutional first principles of royal

commissions", in Scott Prasser and Helen Tracey, (eds), *Royal Commissions and Public Inquiries: Practice and Potential*, Connor Court Publishing, Ballarat, 2014, pp. 23-35

14

Judge-led public inquiries in the United Kingdom: The gold standard?

Sarah Cooper and Owen Thomas

Introduction

In an atmosphere of palpable societal concern, government initiation of a public inquiry in the aftermath of a crisis, disaster, or even wrongdoing, is a common feature of the United Kingdom's (UK) political system. The inevitability of this probing instrument into public sector preparedness to tackle COVID-19, for example, was mooted even in the early stages of the pandemic in 2020. This creeping presence in the popular lexicon and acute public outcry for its establishment is indicative of the significance it holds in finding accountability, with 32 public inquiries appointed since the UK's *Inquiries Act 2005*, of which are 15 currently ongoing. These full statutory versions, ranging from the *Edinburgh Tram Inquiry* to the *Death of Dawn Sturgess*, are joined on the review roundabout by less formal, ad hoc investigations including non-statutory inquiries, independent panels, and royal commissions. This latter measure was historically much more in the favour of the decision makers with almost 400 exercised between 1830 and 1900. This number drastically declined to a point at which only 3 have been set up since the 1990s; in contrast to its Australian and New Zealand counterparts, the reduced popularity of this weaker form of investigatory power appears to be the victim of a creeping predominance of judicial type measures.

In 2019, however, both the Conservative and Labour manifestos promised royal commissions across the criminal justice system, substance abuse, and health and safety legislation. Although quickly criticised as outdated and ineffective in consensus building, their unlikely resurrection does not easily disband with a wider discussion on the utility of statutory public inquiries. A tendency to adopt forensic style investigations, with enforcement of the production of evidence readily backed by the courts, that proliferate a judicial tone of seeking blame, threatens to overshadow the important understanding of more deep-rooted societal issues. The extent to which non-statutory inquiry types can now escape these litigious tendencies, however, remains dubious.

This chapter provides an overview of the development of public inquiries in the UK. It continues to detail the habitual patterns of behaviour concerning truth-seeking and accountability that have emanated in the statutory process, and the associated weaknesses in accommodating broader processes of social change[1] and/or complex cultural matters[2] – unpacked here through the examples of racism and social housing. Concerns with the popularity of the statutory approach are extended into 'adversarialism' seemingly catalysed by Section 21's legal disclosure measures, with limits on the privilege of self-incrimination of witnesses played out in the cases of the Manchester Arena Bombing, and Bloody Sunday and Ladbroke Grove inquiries. Against the backdrop of the ongoing COVID-19 inquiry, a consideration that judicial capture drives a reluctance of individuals to aid these truth-seeking activities for fear of personal consequences is submitted.

Types of inquiry

Public inquiries are often appointed in the wake of a crisis.[3] They arise from public anxiety about harm, inequality, or injustice; uncertainty or disagreement about the reality, nature, and resolution of such crises; and they follow from an impetus that 'something must be done'. They are institutions of last resort, instigated when there is widespread suspicion that relevant state authorities lack the requisite powers and independence necessary to investigate or that, worse still, those authorities may be complicit in the alleged wrongdoing.[4] As **Table 1** shows below, the frequency of inquiries, into a range of social issues, has increased significantly since the 1990s.[5] This may reflect a broadening of public outrage into areas of social risk such as child abuse and medical malpractice.[6] It may also demonstrate a growing tendency by the government to use inquiries as part of a blame avoidance strategy: the appointment of an inquiry can be a short-term cost for government ministers (of acknowledging that something has gone wrong), but once this short-term cost is paid, an inquiry becomes a venue-shifting strategy that allows governments and ministers to refrain from addressing the issue for as long as the investigation continues – which could last years.[7]

Table 1: List of United Kingdom public inquiries, 1990 - 2022

Inquiry	Dates	Type	Investigation
Piper Alpha	1988-1990	Statutory	Fire that killed 167 people on Piper Alpha oil platform
Hillsborough	1989-1990	Non-Statutory	Deaths of 96 people at Hillsborough Football Stadium
Bingham	1991-1992	Non-Statutory	Collapse of a bank
Mirror Group	1992- 2001	Statutory	Alleged abuse of its pension funds
Scott	1992-1996	Non-Statutory	Approval of arms exports to Iraq

Allitt	1993-1994	Statutory	Deaths and injuries of 13 children caused by a nurse
Dunblane	1996	Statutory	Shooting of 18 people at Dunblane Primary School
North Wales Child Abuse	1996-2000	Statutory	Child sexual abuse in Welsh care homes
Pennington Group	1996-1997	Non-Statutory	Outbreak of E. coli
Ashworth Special Hospital	1997-1999	Statutory	Abuses in a mental health unit
Stephen Lawrence	1997-1999	Statutory	Death of Stephen Lawrence and the police response
Southall Rail	1997-2000	Statutory	Southall rail crash
BSE	1997-2000	Non-Statutory	UK's response to BSE outbreak
Bloody Sunday	1998-2010	Statutory	Deaths of civilians killed by British soldiers in Northern Ireland
Sierra Leone	1998	Non-Statutory	Ministerial involvement in the sale of arms
Bristol Royal Infirmary	1998-2001	Statutory	Care of children receiving cardiac surgery
MV Derbyshire	1998-2000	Statutory	Sinking of MV Derbyshire with a loss of 44 lives
FV Gaul	1999-2004	Statutory	Sinking of FV Gaul with a loss of 36 lives
Thames Safety	1999-2000	Non-Statutory	Safety on the River Thames
Ladbroke Grove	1999-2001	Statutory	Railway crash
Train Protection	1999-2001	Statutory	Rail safety
Royal Liverpool	1999-2001	Statutory	Post-mortems and handling human tissue/organs
Marchioness–Bowbell	2000-2001	Non-Statutory	Collision between the pleasure steamer and dredger
Victim Identification	2000-2001	Non-Statutory	Establishing victim identities after transport accidents
Shipman	2000-2005	Statutory	Murders by Dr Harold Shipman
Hammond	2001	Non-Statutory	Ministers granting a visa
Victoria Climbié		Statutory	Death of Victoria Climbié and failures in care

"Three Inquiries"	2001-2005	Statutory	Hospital patient safeguarding measures
Foot and Mouth	2001-2002	Non-Statutory	Foot and mouth disease outbreak
Equitable Life	2001-2004	Non-Statutory	Financial crisis at the Equitable Life Assurance Society
Holyrood	2003-2004	Non-Statutory	Construction costs of the Scottish Parliament building
Hutton	2003-2004	Non-Statutory	Death of Dr David Kelly
Soham Murders	2003-2004	Non-Statutory	Child protection measures in Police
Butler	2004	Non-Statutory	Use of intelligence which led to the Iraq War
Zahid Mubarek	2004-2006	Non-Statutory	Murder of Zahid Mubarek in custody
Rosemary Nelson	2004-2011	Statutory	Murder of Rosemary Nelson and the police response
Robert Hamill	2004-2011	Statutory	Death of Robert Hamill and police investigation
Billy Wright	2005-2010	Statutory	Murder of Billy Wright's inside a prison
2005 outbreak of E. coli	2005-2009	Statutory	Outbreak of E. coli
Redfern	2007-2010	Non-Statutory	Unsanctioned removal of human organs
ICL	2008-2009	Statutory	Factory explosion that killed 9 people and injured 45
Fingerprint	2008-2011	Statutory	Procedures used to verify fingerprint evidence
Penrose	2008-2015	Statutory	HIV/hepatitis C infections from transfused blood
Baha Mousa	2008-2011	Statutory	Death of Baha Mousa, detained by the UK Army
Northern Trusts	2008-2011	Statutory	C. difficile outbreak
Bernard Lodge	2009	Statutory	Death in custody
Vale of Leven Hospital	2009-2014	Statutory	Outbreak of C. difficile
Iraq	2009-2016	Non-Statutory	Govt. decisions/actions before and during Iraq War

FV Trident	2009-2011	Statutory	Sinking of FV Trident with a loss of seven lives
Al-Sweady	2009-2014	Statutory	Detention and death of Iraqi nationals
Azelle Rodney	2010-2013	Statutory	Death of Azelle Rodney, who was shot by the police
Mid Staffordshire NHS Foundation Trust	2010-2013	Statutory	Serious failings in standards of hospital care
Detainee	2010-2013	Non-Statutory	Mistreatment of detainees after 9/11
Leveson	2011-2012	Statutory	Ethics of the press and phone hacking
Historical Institutional Abuse	2012-2017	Statutory	Systemic institutional failures of care of children
Morecambe Bay	2013-2015	Non-Statutory	Maternity and neonatal care
Harris Review	2014-2015	Non-Statutory	Self-inflicted deaths of youths in custody
Edinburgh Tram	2014 –	Statutory	Delay and cost of Edinburgh Trams project
Litvinenko	2014-2016	Statutory	Death of Alexander Litvinenko
Scottish Child Abuse	2014 –	Statutory	Historical cases of child abuse by care institutions
Child Sexual Abuse	2015 –	Statutory	Failure by major institutions to protect children
Undercover Policing	2015 –	Statutory	Use of of undercover police operations
Anthony Grainger	2016 –	Statutory	Death of Anthony Grainger, who was shot by police
Renewable Heat Incentive	2017 –	Statutory	Political scandal related to renewable energy scheme
Grenfell	2017-	Statutory	Fire in Grenfell Tower, which caused 71 deaths
Blood Contamination	2017-	Non-Statutory	HIV/hepatitis C infections from contaminated blood
Manchester Arena	2019-	Statutory	2017 Manchester Arena terror attack
Brook House	2019-	Statutory	Mistreatment at Immigration Removal Centre

Sheku Bayoh	2019-	Statutory	Death of Sheku Bayoh, policy response and racism
Jermaine Baker	2020-	Statutory	Death of Jermaine Baker, shot by police
Muckamore Abbey	2020-	Statutory	Abuse of patients at Muckamore Abbey Hospital
Coronavirus (UK)	2021-	Statutory	UK's response to Covid-19 pandemic
Post Office Horizon IT	2021-	Statutory	Implementation and failings of Post Office IT system
Coronavirus (Scotland)	2021-	Statutory	Scotland's response to Covid-19 pandemic
Death of Dawn Sturgess	2021-	Statutory	Death of Sturgess, exposed to nerve agent Novichok

Proponents often identify functionalist, democratic purposes for an inquiry such as: establishing the facts and causes of what happened; learning lessons to prevent recurrences; facilitating public catharsis that could enable reconciliation; rebuild public trust by providing a reassurance that the issues have been properly investigated; hold actors and institutions to account; and allowing a government to demonstrate that "something is being done".[8] Yet a significant body of the existing scholarly literature is critical of the ability of inquiries to perform truth-seeking and accountability functions. Instead, it is argued that inquiries often close down the space for scrutiny and accountability, particularly of systemic or structural harms and inequalities.[9] From either this functionalist or critical perspective, the ultimate function of an inquiry is the same: to demonstrate that the failure can be dealt with or that there has been no failure at all.[10]

Inquiries can vary widely in their appearance, but they all share some basic features. They are ad hoc institutions created to investigate a specific event or issue and dissolved once its task is concluded); they are independent of the executive and other public bodies (such as the police); they are established by the government; they are discretionary, which means that there is no requirement to have an inquiry (and many inquiries are called for but never created, unlike a legally mandated inquest[11]); they are concerned with the past; and they are expected to allow public scrutiny of the facts (for instance, via public hearings, declassified evidence or a public report). This last point on publicness is critical to an inquiry's purpose: offering some symbolic reassurance of "an open, transparent society where, if a disaster arises, the voices of the powerless are not ignored and the powerful are held to account".[12]

There are two broad categories of inquiries: *non-statutory* inquiries and *statutory* inquiries. Each has advantages and disadvantages in fact-finding and accountability-seeking. Non-statutory inquiries lack legal powers and rely on the cooperation of those involved. They are also not required to hold public hearings (though many do). As we discussed below, they can facilitate a more inquisitorial, less adversarial approach, and enable sensitive evidence to be given in camera.[13] Statutory inquiries, by contrast, have a format defined and underpinned by law (most often, this is the 2005 *Inquiries Act*). This means, for example, that public inquiries possess powers to take evidence under oath and compel the production of witnesses and evidence. But the law also imposes duties: statutory inquiries are also legally obligated to ensure that the public can watch the inquiry and view the evidence.

A further distinction can be made between inquiries led by a current or retired judge and those that are led by senior figures from other professions that tend to command a high degree of public trust, such as civil servants, scientists, professors, doctors, and engineers.[14] Statutory inquiries are almost always led by a judge (which is unsurprising given that the chair must navigate and employ legal process). While non-statutory inquiries vary, governments have still tended to appoint a judge. Out of 76 inquiries undertaken since 1990, 53 were chaired by current or retired judges.[15] When inquiries are not led by a judge, they are often criticised as a lesser form of investigation. In 2009, the *Iraq 'Chilcot' Inquiry* – a non-statutory inquiry led by a panel of retired civil servants, diplomats and historians to investigate Britain's participation in the 2003 Iraq War – was criticised for not being led by a judge and for its legal powers to require evidence under oath, and its desire not to focus explicitly apportioning individual blame. The late MP Michael Meacher argued that the inquiry was "in keeping with this insidious culture of nonculpability".[16] The judicial style of inquiry is regarded as the 'gold standard' of investigation. This preference for judicial expertise is based on a long-standing perception, held by both elites and popular culture, that the legal method is the most rigorous and objective means of determining facts.[17] Moreover, the juridical method is perceived to be independent, neutral and without prejudice. In part, this perception is a result of the decline of public trust in government and parliament, whose conduct may be the subject of an inquiry.[18] Even quasi-judicial inquiry provides 'symbolic reassurance' to the public because the judiciary has a long tradition of independence from government.[19] This preference varies across other parts of the Commonwealth. In Australia, for example, in addition to a preference for royal commissions (which have fallen out of favour in the UK, as we note above), there is a convention against sitting judges leading such investigations.

Despite their popularity, statutory inquiries have some weaknesses. Firstly, statutory inquiries are usually the most lengthy and expensive. For example, only five inquiries have cost over £15m and all were statutory: the *Harold Shipman Inquiry* (£21m over four years), the Billy Wright Inquiry (£30.5m over six years), the *Robert Hamill Inquiry* (£33m over seven years), the *Rosemary Nelson Inquiry* (£46.5m over six and a half years), and the *Bloody Sunday inquiry* (a striking £191.5m over twelve and a half years). The retention of legal counsel can be a significant part of such costs. Secondly, and more fundamentally, judicial inquiries often employ *juridical* epistemology. That is, they produce knowledge according to the philosophical and methodological foundations of legal thinking. This juridical approach is well-suited to investigate fine-grained behaviour in a discrete event but less capable of addressing complex sociological and structural pathologies.[20] This is a limit well understood by legal practitioners. One senior judicial figure noted that such inquiries are less helpful where "issues of social or economic policy with political implications are involved".[21]

Of course, many inquiries are appointed precisely because the nature of the controversy involves such issues. As such, governments often ask judges to "take the hard decisions" even when judges may not be able to do so.[22] This is not a problem limited to the UK. The proliferation of royal commissions in Australia has been described as an addiction caused by a "disillusionment with conventional methods of politics...and the belief that only an expensive retired judge-led royal commission with deliver justice".[23] Yet such investigations are often appointed to consider (and perhaps delay)[24] knotty political problems for which judicial expertise is ill-suited. As we describe below, judge-led inquiries are often, at best, reluctant to engage with sweeping policy problems or, at worst, they explicitly exclude them from the investigation.

The limits of juridical thinking

A good illustration of the limits of the juridical approach is Lord Macpherson's 1997 *Inquiry into the Death of Stephen Lawrence.* The black British teenager had been murdered while waiting for a London bus in 1993. Macpherson's report was ground-breaking because it identified a serious failure to identify and prevent "institutional racism" in the Metropolitan Police Service, the Civil Service, the National Health Service (NHS) and the judiciary.[25] This broke with previous accounts (notably Scarman's *Inquiry into the 1981 Brixton Riots*) that denied the existence of institutional racism. Macpherson found a "collective failure" of state institutions to provide services to people "because of their colour, culture or ethnic origin".[26] For the first time in official discourse, the institutions of the state were complicit in racism and the perpetuation of social disadvantage Macpherson wrote that this racism took the form of "...lack of understanding, ignorance or mistaken beliefs... unfamiliarity with the behaviour or cultural traditions of people or families from minority ethnic communities... stereotyping of black people as potential criminals and troublemakers".[27] Macpherson's account of institutional racism was limited, however, because he did not delve into the question of what created the discourse of knowledge upon which the unwitting racism relied.[28] Put simply, where do these beliefs come from? How did they emerge and where are they reproduced? The capacity of *Macpherson's Inquiry* for fact-finding and lesson-learning was therefore fundamentally limited because the roots of racism were unaddressed; at worst, racism could be understood as an entirely accidental phenomenon for which a governmental response was not required.

Full statutory inquiries are well suited to address troubling events that have discrete timelines and where fact-finding rests on the forensic tracing of individual knowledge and behaviours. This, in turn, facilitates the attribution of responsibility and the identification of regulations that might prevent future occurrences. Some troubling events, however, are partly caused by complex sociological phenomena with an extensive history. Juridically-minded inquiries are often reluctant to engage with such concerns through "restraint", that is, determining that some matters lie outside of the expertise of the juridical inquiry, and "deference", that is, deciding that some matters such as whether the correct ethical or political policy was followed, should be left to elected politicians.[29] From 2011 to 2012, the *Leveson Inquiry (Inquiries into the culture, practice and ethics of the press)* examined unethical practices in the media. Leveson's inquiry – with its cross-examination of politicians, journalists and other figures – was very effective at unravelling a linear, forensic account of how the press used practices such as phone-hacking. However, the inquiry was far less comfortable when witnesses complained of a wider journalistic and societal culture that encouraged the journalistic trivialisation and sexualisation of violence against women, or a "sense of impunity" held by some parts of the press due to their concentrated economic and social power. Leveson concluded that his inquiry was not the place to address the "sociological factors" behind such social pathologies, and he "doubt[ed] whether [the inquiry] would have had the expertise" to undertake such an analysis.[30]

A similar concern has been raised about the *Grenfell Tower Inquiry*, appointed to investigate the fire in a London housing block that killed 72 people. This inquiry is well suited to its terms of reference to investigate the immediate causes of the fire, decisions relating to the design and construction of the building, the suitability of safety regulations, and the actions of authorities on the night of, and before the fire. These terms of reference, however, do not easily accommodate wider questions about the role of race, religion and social class in the provision and maintenance of social housing; neoliberal economic reforms, or the political culture of deregulation.[31] This hinders a wider analysis of inequality and social housing in Britain.[32] Nevertheless, a strict adherence to clearly defined legislative steps is embedded in the very fibre of the *Inquiries Act 2005*, to be explored next.

The problem of 'adversarialism'

The growing reliance on courts and judicial means for addressing a broader array of "moral predicaments public policy questions, and political controversies" is helpfully categorised by Hirschl into three interrelated streams: (1) the spread of legal discourse into the political sphere, (2) the ability of courts and judges to determine public policy outcomes, and (3) an emerging deference to courts and judges to deal with issues of "mega-politics".[33] This process of "judicialisation" in British politics has gained traction amongst scholars, with extension to the use of judicial review,[34] European Community (EC) membership,[35] and a rise in litigation of government.[36] Though supposedly not adversarial in the manner of courtroom drama in which there will be a winner and loser, a clear trend of such combative means can also be extrapolated from the development of judge-led public inquiries, and specifically the statutory measures of legal disclosure provided by the *Inquiries Act 2005*. Though the act specifically states that no inquiry panel has the power to determine any person's civil or criminal liability, it does not preclude the inferring of liability in the course of the procedure and encourages that no panel be inhibited by this possibility (Section 2). This ethos drives the entrenchment of powers of compulsion in the act and stipulates that evidence may be taken on oath, and individuals compelled to do so, by notice of the chairman of the inquiry (Section 21), with enforcement of this provision by the High Court or Court of Session by virtue of Section 36 not shied away from (*Inquiry into the Death of Billy Wright*). In tandem with this, although undertaking from the Attorney General can engage the privilege against self-incrimination, the enforcement power and sanction housed in Section 35 are still of concern to witnesses. These legal measures will be explored further here, and their impact on the pursuit of truth-finding discussed and unpacked through the example of COVID-19.

Section 21 of the *Inquiries Act 2005* outlines the power of the chairman in the course of proceedings. The legislation stipulates that this may take the form of the insistence of attendance at a time and place stipulated in the notice to give evidence or produce documents relating to the matter in question, or indeed the submission of a written statement and associated materials. Despite the failure to comply with this notice bearing the risk of 51 weeks imprisonment as outlined in Section 35, refusal to give evidence has recently come to the attention of the media in the inquiry into the Manchester Arena bombing,[37] in which the terms of reference included an investigation into the radicalisation of Salmen Abedi. A notice to the respondent to attend proceedings was issued to Abedi's older brother, who subsequently left the UK and failed to arrive on the stipulated date. In *Chairman of the Manchester Arena Inquiry v Romdhan [2021] EWHC 3274 (Admin)* a bench warrant was thus sought by virtue of section 36 (1) (a) of the Inquiries Act. During the proceedings, the defence contended that the purpose of Section 36, and the true intention of Parliament at the time of drafting, was to secure compliance with Section 21 and the quest for evidence; in that sense, they continued, the legislative intention was the obtaining of information, rather than the punishment of an individual. Though noting its extreme nature, the judge disagreed that a warrant would discourage the respondent from returning to the jurisdiction and therefore undermine this purpose, and permitted its issue based on its necessary and proportionate means.

Barriers to truth-finding again raise their head, however, when an acknowledgement is given to Section 22 and the caveat that no compulsion to give evidence can be made if they would not be permitted in civil proceedings. Section 14 of the *Civil Evidence Act 1968* proffers the mechanism of privilege against self-incrimination, outlining a person's right to refuse to answer a question or produce evidence that might evoke proceedings for an offence or the recovery of a penalty. An undertaking from the Attorney-General is oftentimes a measure sought within a public inquiry to circumvent this issue – a clear example of this being the 1995 *Bloody Sunday Inquiry (Bloody Sunday Tribunal of Inquiry)*. Stressing the need to uncover the truth concerning the demonstration in Londonderry on 30 January 1972, and the absence of charge to decide whether or not prosecution should be brought against individuals from the British Army who opened fire on Catholic civil rights supporters, all legitimate and proper means to remove the hindrance of self-incrimination was considered to access valuable information. Lord Saville expressed that in fact without such an undertaking, a witness could bear the additional burden of inference of criminal behaviour should they decline to answer questions or produce documents.[38] An important note about the scope of the privilege here, however, is that absolute immunity from prosecution cannot be assumed. Here we again return to the example of the *Stephen Lawrence Inquiry*. The five individuals who had previously faced prosecution for the teenager's murder, but whose cases had either subsequently been discontinued by the Crown Prosecution Service (CPS), or had secured acquittal through private prosecution, declined to give evidence. The Attorney-General undertaking established that no evidence in the course of the inquiry would be used against them in criminal proceedings, except "where he or she is charged with having given false evidence in the course of this Inquiry or with having conspired with or procured others to do so".[39] Two of the five were subsequently convicted of Stephen Lawrence's murder. A similar situation arose in the *Ladbroke Grove Inquiry*, convened in the wake of the death of 31 people following a collision between a Thames Train commuter train and a high-speed First Great Western train. In addition to the caveat of false evidence above, the undertaking asserted that the privilege did not cover "any other manifestation of the documents, whether retained originals or any copies, which the police or other investigators were able to obtain".[40] Network Rail Infrastructure Ltd. was later prosecuted by the CPS for health and safety offences.[41] Furthermore, the evidence used against that person by an employer in separate disciplinary proceedings also does not fall under the breadth of the privilege, as discussed in the *Undercover Policing Inquiry*.[42]

If the purpose of these powers of compulsion is thus to aid truth-finding, the adverse impact of such judicial tools on the reluctance of individuals to take part for fear of personal consequence must be considered. In the course of the aforementioned *Billy Wright Inquiry*, for example, the refusal of witness Mr Paisley to provide information concerning the police officer who had disclosed information around the destruction of files for money resulted in a fine of £5,000, and an order to pay a contribution of £3,000 to the cost of the inquiry.[43] This very tangible punishment, coupled with the sort of reputational damage that surfaced for tabloids post-Leveson Inquiry,[44] creates a palpable tension with the pursuit of a robust understanding of the situation at hand. Certainly, the attrition between holding individuals and organisations to account and the objective of lesson learning has been discussed in the context of the pandemic.[45]

One former inquiry member, Sir Lawrence Freedman, has argued against having a Covid inquiry that is judge-led precisely because that will not be the most effective way to uncover the facts of what happened in government during the pandemic. Reflecting on his own experience as a member of the *Iraq 'Chilcot' Inquiry,* Freedman recalled how they were advised against a judicial approach:

> Everybody lawyers up if you've got a judge, every witness will come with their own lawyer, the bereaved families will want to bring their lawyers who will want a right to cross-examine, and it will go on and on. You have to have witnesses feeling that they can respond to the questions…we didn't find that a problem in Chilcot…one of our witnesses said, "actually, with you, I'll say what I think," He was involved with another judge-led inquiry, and said, "there I was told that must say: 'yes', 'no', or 'I can't remember'". You don't want that; you want people to feel able to unload themselves…for many of the witnesses, for whom this will be a very traumatic and memorable experience, this is an opportunity for them to get it out: what they went through, what they saw at the time.[46]

Indeed, Freedman goes further to say that "interrogating witnesses may provide the spectacle, but in this case, most of the evidence can be gathered away from hearings".[45] The key to an effective coronavirus inquiry will be a range of expertise – such as public health, medicine, statistics, epidemiology, economics, and policy-making – who can uncover facts from archival evidence. The popular cultural desire to put the government 'in the dock' would, in this case, be counterproductive.

Conclusion: Back to the future for public inquiries?

Public inquiries are important instruments for fact-finding, accountability-seeking, and lesson-learning. Whether viewed positively or sceptically, they perform a crucial function in drawing a line and moving on from events that provoke widespread public concern. Inquiries are used frequently and focus on a wide range of social and political issues. As we have shown, the dominant approach for a public inquiry is the judge-led, statutory model. This demonstrates the considerable public trust enjoyed by the courts and senior legal practitioners and shows the cultural belief that the juridical method is one of the most effective ways of learning the facts of an event. Yet, judicially led and juridically minded inquiries have important limitations: they are reluctant to investigate widespread, historically embedded social issues such as racism or gendered inequalities, and the courtroom style of investigation can lead to 'adversarialism' that impedes openness and candour. There is also a serious risk to this overreliance on the judiciary to address policy problems and political issues that could be dealt with by governments, parliaments or even non-judicial inquiries. Relying on the judiciary and upon juridical methods to address social and political issues – such as institutional prejudice or systemic inequality – will at best lead to disappointment, as judges will freely admit that such questions exceed their competence. At worst, it can facilitate a populist backlash against the judiciary as out-of-touch elites who appear unable to engage in the issues that matter. Overreliance on the judge-led inquiry, therefore, risks undermining faith in the rule of law and, specifically, a profession that has historically been one of the most trusted.[48] Fortunately, there are alternative inquiry models available.

Practitioners and researchers are exploring alternative models of inquiry that could be used to complement or in place of judicial style inquiries. For example, "independent panels" can provide a different style of investigation. Rather than holding hearings, panels gather archival information and produce a wide-ranging historical account. Panels have been used in this way to investigate the Hillsborough tragedy and the 2011 riots. Untroubled by the problem of reluctant witnesses and the need to find fault, this type of inquiry can satisfy public expectations differently.[49] The return of the royal commission has also been considered. Commonplace in the 19th Century, these have fallen entirely into disuse in recent decades (the last one, examining reform of the House of Lords, finished in 2000). Unlike most inquiries, royal commissions focus on widespread policy problems rather than discrete events. They could complement other public inquiries by providing a system within which to examine the complex and deeply policy challenges – such as institutional racism, misogyny or wealth inequality – that arise out of concerning events.[50]

Finally, it is being recognised that inquiries need more diversity. Inquiry members are often old, white and male. Simply in terms of gender diversity, between 1990 and 2017, there were just six inquiries with a female chair – which is the same as the number of inquiries led by someone called Brian and fewer than the number of inquiries chaired by someone called either Anthony or William.[51] Moving beyond the lure of the inquiry led by the wise old judge, toward some of the instruments of the past, could be an important development in preventing and learning lessons from the most worrying problems of the twenty-first century.

Public inquiries mentioned in this chapter[52]

Edinburgh Tram Inquiry (Hardie, 2014)

Dawn Sturgess Inquiry (Hughes, 2022)

The Iraq Inquiry (Chilcot, 2009)

The Stephen Lawrence Inquiry (Macpherson, 1997)

Inquiry by Lord Scarman in the matter of Section 32 of the Police Act 1964 and in the matter of a local inquiry into the Brixton disturbances 10-12 April 1981 – The Scarman Report (Scarman, 1981)

The Leveson Inquiry: Culture, Practices and Ethics of the Press (Leveson, 2011)

Grenfell Tower Inquiry (Moore-Bick, 2017)

The Billy Wright Inquiry (MacLean, 2004)

The Bloody Sunday Inquiry (Saville, 1998)

The Ladbroke Grove Rail Inquiry (Cullen, 1999)

Undercover Policing Inquiry (Mitting, previously Pitchford, 2015)

Notes

1. Nigel Parton, "From Maria Colwell to Victoria Climbié: reflections on public inquiries into child abuse a generation apart". *Child Abuse Review: Journal of the British Association for the Study and Prevention of Child Abuse and Neglect*, Vol 13, No 2, 2004, pp. 80-94.
2. Owen Thomas and Sarah Cooper, "Understanding issue salience, social inequality and the (non) appointment of UK public inquiries: a new research agenda", *Public Money & Management*, Vol 40, No 6, 2020, pp. 457-67.
3. Adam Burgess, "The changing character of public inquiries in the (risk) regulatory state", *British Politics*, Vol 6, No 1, 2011, pp. 3-29.
4. Phil Scraton, "From Deceit to Disclosure: The Politics of Official Inquiries in the United Kingdom", in George Gilligan and John Pratt, (eds), *Crime, Truth and Justice: Official Inquiry, Discourse, Knowledge*, Willan, Cullompton, 2004, pp. 46-69.
5. Emma Norris and Marcus Shepheard, *How public inquiries can lead to change. Institute for Government*, Institute for Government, London, December 2017.
6. Burgess, "The changing character of public inquiries in the (risk) regulatory state", pp. 3-29.
7. Raanan Sulitzeanu-Kenan, "Reflection in the shadow of blame: When do politicians appoint commissions of inquiry?", *British Journal of Political Science*, Vol 40, No 3, 2010, pp. 613-34.
8. Kieran Walshe and Joan Higgins, "The use and impact of inquiries in the NHS", *British Medical Journal*, Vol 325, No 7369, 2002, pp. 895-900; see also Stuart Farson and Mark Phythian, *Commissions of Inquiry and National Security: Comparative Approaches*, Praeger, Santa Barbara, 2011; Alastair Stark, *Public inquiries, policy learning, and the threat of future crises*, Oxford University Press, Oxford, 2019.
9. Andrew D Brown, "Authoritative sensemaking in a public inquiry report", *Organization Studies*, Vol 25, No 1, 2004, pp. 95-112; Bill Rolston and Phil Scraton, "In the full glare of English politics: Ireland, inquiries and the British state", *British Journal of Criminology*, Vol 45, No 4, 2005, pp. 547-64; Andrew Williams, "The Iraq abuse allegations and the limits of UK law", *Public Law*, Vol 461, July 2018, pp. 461-81.
10. Frank Burton and Pat Carlen, *Official Discourse: On Discourse Analysis, Government Publications, Ideology and the State*, Routledge, London, 1979, p. 48.
11. There are various investigatory tools that can be performed by permanent bodies, which do not fit these "exceptional" features of a public inquiry. They are not ad hoc or necessarily established by a government. Although investigating past events, they may not be required to hold public hearings or publish evidence. Inquests, for instance, are legally mandated following an unexplained or unnatural death (eg the inquests into the deaths of four soldiers at Deepcut Barracks). Similarly, the Department of Transport has

several accident investigation branches legally mandated to investigate serious transport incidents. Whilst quick and cheap, such investigations can only examine the circumstances strictly related to the immediate causes of death; scrutiny of broader concerns requires the appointment of another tool (eg when the inquest into the death of Alexander Litvinenko was converted into a statutory inquiry to investigate the role of the Russian state).

12 Adam Burgess, "The changing character of public inquiries in the (risk) regulatory state," *British Politics*, Vol 6, No 1, 2011, p. 7.

13 UK Cabinet Office, *Inquiries Guidance: Guidance for Inquiry Chairs and Secretaries, Sponsor Department* - available at: https://www.parliament.uk/documents/lords-committees/Inquiries-Act-2005/caboffguide.pdf

14 For an overview of public trust in professions, see the Ipsos MORI Veracity Index, available at: https://www.ipsos.com/en-uk/ipsos-mori-veracity-index-trust-police-drops-second-year-row (accessed 04 March 2022)

15 Norris and Shepherd, *How public inquiries can lead to change.*

16 Michael Meacher, "Chilcot's Unfinished Business", *The Guardian*, 3 April 2010.

17 Walshe and Higgins, "The use and impact of inquiries in the NHS", pp. 895-900; Public Administration Select Committee, *Government by Inquiry*, The Stationery Office, London, 2005.

18 Chris Hanretty, "Leveson Inquiry: Letting the Judges Take the Hard Decisions?", *Political Insight*, Vol 4 , 2013, pp. 8-11.

19 House of Commons, Public Administration Select Committee, *Government by Inquiry*, First Report of Session 2004-5, Vol 1, 27 January 2005, p. 20.

20 Owen D Thomas, "Good faith and (dis)honest mistakes? Learning from Britain's Iraq War Inquiry", *Politics*, Vol 37, No 4, 2017, pp. 371-85.

21 Jack Beatson, "Should Judges conduct public inquiries?", *Law Quarterly Review*, Vol 37, 2005, p. 253.

22 Chris Hanretty, "Leveson Inquiry: Letting the Judges Take the Hard Decisions?", *Political Insight*, Vol 4, 2013, pp. 8-11.

23 Paul Kelly, "The cult that won false hopes in 2020", *The Australian*, 23 December 2020; see also Kenneth Hayne, "On Royal Commissions", Address, Centre for Comparative Studies Conference, Melbourne Law School, 26 July 2019.

24 As Sulitzeanu-Kenan argues, inquiries are an effective political tactic for blame avoidance and delaying difficulty policy decisions see Sulitzeanu-Kenan, "Reflection in the shadow of blame", pp. 613-34.

25 William MacPherson, (Chair), *The Stephen Lawrence Inquiry*, The Stationery Office, London, 1999.

26 Ibid., 17.

27 Ibid.

28 Colin Wight, "The agent–structure problem and institutional racism", *Political Studies*, Vol 51, 2003, pp. 706-21; Owen D Thomas, "Blind to Complicity? Official Truth and the Hidden Role of Methods", in Michael Neu, Robin Dunford and Afxentis Afxentiou, (eds), *Exploring complicity: Concept, cases and critique*, Rowman & Littlefield, London, 2016, pp. 161-78

29 Andrew Williams, "The Iraq abuse allegations and the limits of UK law", *Public Law*, Vol 461, July, 2018, pp. 461-81.

30 Brian Leveson, (Chair), *An inquiry into the culture, practices and ethics of the press*, The Stationery Office, London, 2012, p. 719; see also Deirdre O'Neill, "Will Leveson see off sexist coverage in the Press?", in John Mair, (ed), *After Leveson*, Abramis, Bury St Edmunds, 2013, pp. 108-16.

31 Patricia Tuitt, "Law, Justice and the Public Inquiry into the Grenfell Tower Fire," in Dan Bulley, Jenny Edkins, and Nadine El-Enany, (eds), *After Grenfell:*

Violence, Resistance and Response, Pluto Press, London, 2019, pp. 119-29; Brenna Bhandar, "Theft in Broad Daylight: Racism and Neoliberal Legality", *Law and Critique*, Vol 32, No 3, 2021, pp. 285-99.

32   Martin McKee, "Grenfell Tower fire: why we cannot ignore the political determinants of health", *British Medical Journal*, Vol 8111, 2017, p. 357.

33   Ran Hirschl, "The judicialization of mega-politics and the rise of political courts", *Annual Review Political Science*, Vol. 11, 2008, pp. 93-118.

34   Maurice Sunkin, "Judicialization of politics in the United Kingdom", *International Political Science Review*, 1994, Vol. 15, No. 2, pp. 125-33.

35   Danny Nichol, *EC Membership and the Judicialization of British Politics*, Oxford University Press, Oxford.

36   Mathew Williams, "The judicialisation of politics: why do governments face more litigation, and why do they lose more often?, *LSE British Politics and Policy, 8th March 2008*. Available at: https://blogs.lse.ac.uk/politicsandpolicy/the-judicialisation-of-politics/(accessed 26.5.2022).

37   Lizzie Dearden, "Manchester Arena bomber's brother leaves UK despite being ordered to give evidence at public inquiry", *The Independent*, 19 October 2021.

38   Lord Saville of Newdigate, *Report of the Bloody Sunday Inquiry*, Stationery Office, London, 2010.

39   William MacPherson, *The Stephen Lawrence Inquiry*, Stationery Office, London, 1999.

40   Lord W. Douglas Cullen, *The Ladbroke Grove Rail Inquiry: Part 1 Report*, HSE Books, London, 2001.

41   James Meikle, "Potters Bar train crash: Network Rail and Javis Rail to be Prosecuted", *The Guardian*, 10 November 2020.

42   Jonathan Hall QC.

43   Lord L. MacLean, *The Billy Wright Inquiry-Report*, Vol 431, The Stationery Office, London, 2010.

44   Josh Halliday, "Mail claims tabloids will be 'damaged' by anonymous Leveson evidence" *The Guardian*, 13 Jan 2012. Available at: https://www.theguardian.com/media/2012/jan/13/leveson-inquiry-anonymous-evidence(accessed 26.05.2022).

45   Christoph Meyer, Nikki Ikani, Mauricio Avendano Pabon and Ann Kelly, "Learning the Right Lessons for the Next Pandemic: How to Design Public Inquiries into the UK Government's Handling of COVID-19", King's College London, 2020.

46   Lawrence Freedman, *How to run a successful Covid 19 inquiry*, Institute for Government, available at: https://www.instituteforgovernment.org.uk/events/covid-19-inquiry (accessed: 20 March 2022).

47   Lawrence Freedman, "We will need a new kind of public inquiry to adequately reckon with this tragedy", *Prospect Magazine*, available at: https://www.prospectmagazine.co.uk/politics/covid-19-coronavirus-public-inquiry-iraq-chilcot (accessed 25 April 2022).

48   Judges have been amongst the most trusted professions in the UK, but there is evidence to suggest a decline. Between 2020 and 2021, judges slipped from the fifth to eight most trusted professions in the Ipsos MORI Veracity Index, available at: https://www.ipsos.com/en-uk/ipsos-mori-veracity-index-trust-police-drops-second-year-row (accessed 04 March 2022)

49   Norris and Shepheard, *How public inquiries can lead to change*.

50   Ibid.

51   Ibid.

52   List refers to name of inquiry, its chair and date of appointment.

15

Learning through hindsight: New Zealand's statutory inquiries[1]

Wendy McGuinness

Introduction

The New Zealand *Cabinet Manual 2017* sets out the basis upon which New Zealand inquiries are conducted. Although the title implies that it is a manual for Cabinet, it is much more than this. To appreciate its role is to understand that New Zealand's constitution is not found in one document. The Governor-General's website states that our constitution "has a number of sources, including crucial pieces of legislation, several legal documents, common law derived from court decisions as well as established constitutional practices known as conventions".[2] It also notes New Zealand's constitution increasingly reflects the Treaty of Waitangi as a founding document of government and must increasingly have regard to international obligations and standards.[3]

The *Cabinet Manual 2017* describes how each of these sources work together to form New Zealand's constitution. Paragraphs 4.74 to 4.110 of the *Manual* explain how our current system of inquiries operates in practice and provide specific guidance on the three different types of inquiry: (i) statutory inquiries; (ii) non-statutory ministerial inquiries; and (iii) standing statutory bodies with powers of inquiry.

This chapter focuses on the history of statutory inquiries, in particular those that include the term 'royal'. 'Royal' is used generally to denote a higher level of independence from government and is therefore "typically reserved for the most serious matters of public importance".[4] The chapter then describes a few selected commissions in detail, followed by a few suggestions on future inquiries and lastly a few observations on the process.

Historical context

First commissions of inquiry

Commissions of inquiry come in a range of different shapes and sizes; however, they are always temporary in nature. The first known commission was established in 1855, when the Nelson Provisional Council appointed commissioners to enquire into a system of secular primary education.[5]

The first time the government appointed commissioners was in 1864, to enquire into the location of the Seat of Government; New Zealand Governor Sir George Grey reported "that the Legislature has decided that the seat of government should be placed in a more central position – that is to say, somewhere in Cook's Straits".[6]

The term 'royal commission' was used for the first time in 1868, when the commissioners were asked to:

> Enquire into the provisions and operation of the laws and regulations now in force relative to prisons and gaols in the Colony, and into the treatment and management of prisoners, and into the condition and state of such prisons and gaols, and into the more effective provision for their regulation, and for the custody and treatment of prisoners, especially those convicted of serious crimes and sentenced to long periods of imprisonment; and to report whether any and, if any, what alteration is desirable, and

whether it would be desirable that a General Penal Establishment should be instituted for the Colony, and if so, on the best mode of instituting such establishment.[7]

Statutory commissions

Statutory commissions were originally introduced under the *Commissioners' Powers Act 1867*[8] (see, for example, the 1868 Royal Commission mentioned above). This Act enabled commission members (appointed by the Governor-in-Council) to examine witnesses under oath. The 1867 Act stated:

> It shall be lawful for any board or commission appointed or issued or to be appointed or issued by the Governor-in-Council to summon by writing under the hand of the chairman or any commissioner or member of the board any person whose *evidence* shall in the judgment of the said board or commission or any member thereof be material to the *subject matter* of the inquiry to be made by such board or commission to attend the said board or commission at such place and time as shall be specified therein and such person may be required by such summons to bring any books papers writings deeds and documents of which any court of law might compel the production and any member of such board or commission may *examine* such person *upon oath* touching the matter to be *inquired into* by such board or commission. [italics added]

This 1867 Act contains three key characteristics that continue to shape the law 155 years later. The Act makes it clear that commissioners appointed under law must be: cognisant of and stay within the scope of the subject matter; able to request documents and call and interview witnesses under oath; and required to examine the evidence. Two other characteristics that are inferred from this early legislation are that the commissioners are required to be independent of government (and therefore their recommendations are suggestions only) and their written report is able to be read and understood by the general public, not only setting out their conclusions, but describing the actions and processes they undertook to reach those conclusions.

After 1867, the *Commissioners' Powers Act 1867* was further amended with the passing of the *Commissioners' Powers Act 1867 Amendment Act* and the *Commissioners Powers Act 1867 Amendment Act 1872*.[9] It was then replaced by the *Commissioners Act 1903*[10] (and shortly afterwards amended by the *Commissioners Act Amendment Act 1905*).[11] In 1908, the legislation was again replaced, with the *Commissions of Inquiry Act 1908*; however, this time it has stayed relevant, remaining part of our current legislation to this day. Since its enactment, the 1908 Act has been amended seven times;[12] however, the changes were relatively minor, extending the rights and responsibilities of commissioners and specifying in more detail how a commission might be established. Hence, the overall framework has remained relatively stable for 155 years.

The birth of the Inquiries Act 2013

In 2007 and 2008, the New Zealand Law Commission undertook a review of the 1908 legislation and made recommendations on how the legislation could be improved.[13] Its terms of reference were to "review and update the law relating to public inquiries in New Zealand. This review will include inquiries established as royal commissions and other commissions established under the *Commissions of Inquiry Act 1908*, ministerial inquiries, ad hoc inquiries under specific statutes, and departmental inquiries".[14]

The Law Commission examined: "the role public inquiries have played (i) as fact-finders, (ii) as tools for developing policy and legislation, (iii) as an independent check on executive action and (iv) as a form of participatory government". It concluded that "formal commissions have been used in New Zealand for a very wide variety of reasons".[15] It also considered the influence of the growth of other inquiries (see excerpt below); delays in commissions reporting; and their costs. It found that while cost containment was an issue, "if [inquiries] are properly used and set up, they should be seen as a relatively inexpensive means of getting to the heart of an issue". Lastly, the composition of formal commissions was also considered. The review noted that: "Ministers may have been deterred from formal inquiries because of their predominantly judicial make-up and because of concern that they will become overly legalistic".[16]

The Law Commission found that fewer formal royal commissions were being appointed, while other types of inquiries had become more numerous. It concluded that there had been:

> considerable growth in the number of inquiries held by other bodies with inquisitorial functions. In particular, since the introduction of the Public Audit Act 2001, the number of inquiries undertaken by the Auditor-General has significantly expanded … Many other bodies have policy or inquiry functions, many of which were established in the 1980s (for example, the Commissioner for the Environment and Law Commission). Furthermore, in 1985 parliamentary select committees were given a general power to initiate inquiries themselves. Standing order 190(2) now enables them to initiate inquiries into any matters that fall within their defined subject portfolios. Since the introduction of MMP in 1996, the lack of a clear government majority on many select committees means they have had far more freedom to exercise this power.[17]

The Law Commission's findings are supported by the McGuinness Institute's subsequent research (published in March 2021).[18] Unlike the Law Commission's analysis, the McGuinness Institute's focus was solely on royal commissions (where the term 'royal' was either used in the title or in the text of the published report). **Figure 1** shows a shift away from the use of royal commissions in New Zealand, particularly since 1990.

Figure 2 illustrates the type of the subject matter covered by 130 royal commissions since 1868. **Figure 3** shows the number of royal commissions that could not be found in the public arena in 2020, suggesting more could be done to keep a better historical record of past inquiries.

The Law Commission believes the shift away from royal commissions has been caused by their high costs, delays in completing their reports, their excessive legal formality and adversarial processes. It is for these reasons they believe the more informal ministerial inquiries have become more common. The Law Commission also noted the limitations of these ministerial inquiries that "have little law governing them and no coercive powers at all. Neither do those conducting such inquiries enjoy any legal immunities. This situation can lead to significant limitations on the effectiveness of some such inquiries – they may not be able to get to the bottom of a matter because they cannot uncover the facts".[19]

Given these assessments, it was not surprising that the Law Commission recommended a new act (the *Inquiries Act 2013*), one that provided more legal rigour for the conduct of ministerial inquiries. In particular, it noted, "[w]e hope that by recognising the current constitutional reality and practice, our recommendations will coax ministerial inquiries into a proper legal framework".[20]

The Inquiries Act 2013

Today the *Commissions of Inquiry Act 1908* and the *Inquiries Act 2013* are both administered by the Department of Internal Affairs. Put succinctly, the 2013 Act elevated the term 'inquiry', and demoted the term 'commission'. However, the new Act did distinguish between types of commissions (see section 6: Types of inquiry, below). The Act also makes clear that all previous royal commissions are now to be treated as if they are public inquiries (see section 6 (1)(a)).

Prior to the 2013 Act, the Governor-General established all commissions. Hence the only way to know whether a commission was indeed a 'royal commission' was whether the term 'royal' was used in the terms of reference, the title, the resulting report, or (in a few cases) in newspapers of the time. For example, in the 1919 *Influenza Epidemic Commission*, the term 'royal' was never used, so it is treated as a normal commission (not a royal commission). **Figures 1–3** show all the royal commissions that have been identified under this protocol.

The 2013 Act also made it possible for statutory inquiries to be established by a party other than the Governor-General, in this case a minister. Two types of statutory inquiry operate under the Act; section 6 of the 2013 Act states:

> Types of inquiry
>
> (2) The Governor-General may, by Order in Council, establish a **public inquiry** for the purpose of inquiring into, and reporting on, any matter of public importance.
>
> (3) One or more Ministers may, by notice in the *Gazette*, establish a **government inquiry** for the purpose of inquiring into, and reporting on, any matter of public importance. [bold added]

Section 2 of the 1908 Act states:

> **Appointment of Commissions of Inquiry**
> The Governor-General may, by Order in Council, appoint any person or persons to be a Commission to inquire into and report upon any question arising out of or concerning–
>
> (a)   The administration of the Government; or
> (b)   The working of any existing law; or
> (c)   The necessity or expediency of any legislation; or
> (d)   The conduct of any officer in the service of the Crown; or
> (e)   Any disaster or accident (whether due to natural causes or otherwise) in which members of the public were killed or injured or were or might have been exposed to risk of death or injury; or

(f)   Any other matter of public importance.

The Law Commission was not able to recommend that the old 1908 Act be replaced by a new statute, as the 1908 Act was relied upon by a wide range of diverse bodies and mentioned in an assortment of legislation. Hence the Law Commission recommended that these diverse bodies continue to operate under the 1908 Act until each statute was individually reviewed "to determine how it should conduct its proceedings or inquiries in the future".[21] Examples given include the Waitangi Tribunal, the Social Security Appeal Authority and inquiries under the *Soil Conservation and Rivers Control Act 1941*.[22] For this reason the Law Commission recommended that the 2013 legislation include a review clause, suggesting "consideration be given to the 55 or so statutes that give statutory bodies the powers of a commission of inquiry" (see full list in Schedule 1 of the 2013 Act).[23] This became section 36 of the *Inquiries Act 2013*.

The review is being undertaken by the Department of Internal Affairs (DIA). In April 2022, DIA advised that the review is still in progress and that the next step in the process is to establish options for the entities listed in Schedule 1 of the *Inquiries Act 2013* (given they still require specific inquiry powers). They hope to complete the review by 2025, outlining options for the repeal of the 1908 Act for ministers to consider.[24]

The reporting process

Statutory inquiries are permitted under the new *Inquiries Act 2013* to inquire into, and report on, any matter of public importance. As one would expect, the commissioners' report containing the findings and the recommendations is first presented to the party that established the statutory inquiry. However, whether the report is the result of a public inquiry or a government inquiry, it must then be presented by the Speaker or a Minister to the House of Representatives.[25] This is essential, as the Governor-General must be seen to be independent of Parliament.

Importantly, the findings of a statutory inquiry bind no-one – they are only recommendations; it is up to the government and Parliament to decide how to respond, if at all.[26] However, if government were to ignore the findings completely, this might create voter disapproval and possibly result in public distrust.[27]

Many royal commission reports provide scholars and historians with detailed information on New Zealand's past. A classic example is the *Royal Commission on the Electoral System*, which was reported in 1986. It was more than just another inquiry report. It proposed a new electoral system, provided future generations with a detailed chronological history of the birth of democracy and set out, in a transparent, evidence-based and concise manner, its "proposals for good government and for a better democracy".[28]

Other royal commissions have provided New Zealand society with much needed clarity and truth in times of tragedy, such as the *Royal Commission of Inquiry into the terrorist attack on Christchurch masjidain on 15 March 2019*; the 2010 *Royal Commission on the Pike River Coal Mine Tragedy*; and the 1980 *Royal Commission to Inquire Into and Report Upon the Crash on Mount Erebus, Antarctica, of a DC10 Aircraft operated by Air New Zealand Limited.*[29] A full list of royal commission reports may be found on the Governor-General's website.[30]

Figure 1: Royal commission reports by decade, since 1860[31]

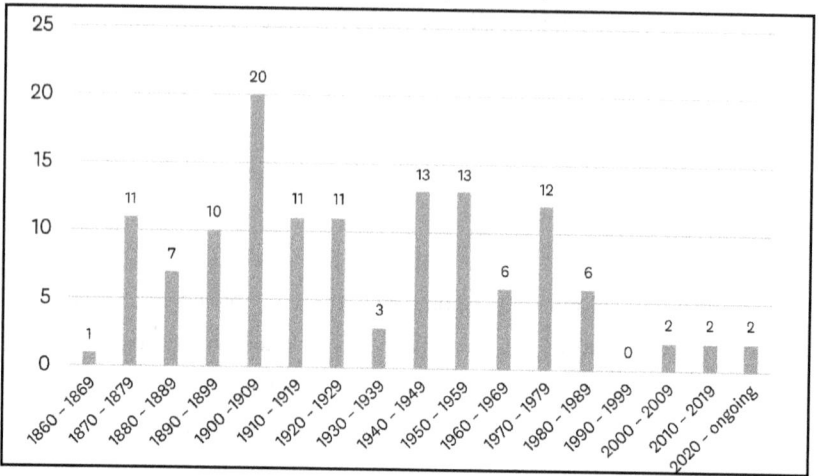

Figure 2: Royal commission reports by subject matter, since 1860[32]

Figure 2: Royal Commissions by subject matter, since 1860 [130]

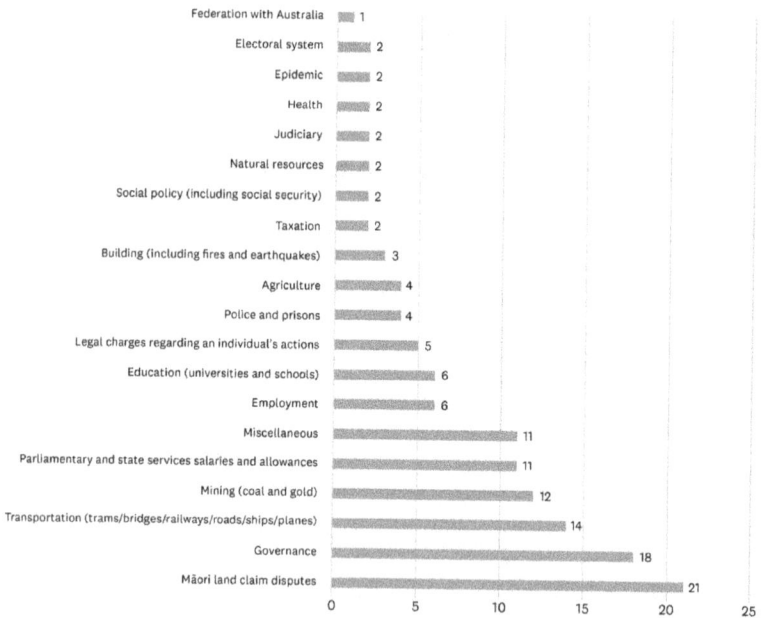

Figure 3: Royal Commission reports not found online in 2020, by decade, since 1860[33]

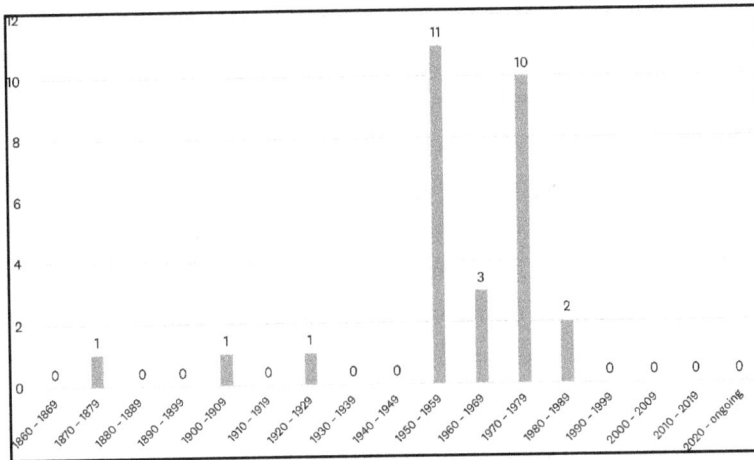

The inquiries continuum

In practice, a continuum of inquiries exist, which is able to inquire into matters of public importance or public interest. At one end is a group of statutory bodies able to undertake their own inquiries by reference to the 1908 Act. For example, the Auditor-General is separate from the ministers of the Crown, which loosely, by definition, include the Governor-General. As noted earlier, the Law Commission found that the number of inquiries being undertaken by the Auditor-General is increasing. Inquiries by the Auditor-General are arguably among the most independent of the political system, because the subject matter and timing is at the Auditor-General's discretion.[34] However, High Court Judge Matthew Palmer and Associate Law Professor Dean Knight note in their study that in recent years, "the Auditor-General has been careful about when to undertake an inquiry".[35]

At the other end of the continuum are inquiries undertaken by the House of Representatives, usually through a parliamentary select committee, "to inquire into any matter that it considers needs investigation in the public interest. [This] was a power possessed and exercised by the United Kingdom House of Commons on 1 January 1865 (as it still is), and it is therefore confirmed as attaching also to the House of Representatives as a legal power" set out in section 8 (1) of the *Parliamentary Privilege Act 2014.*[36] Although the key function of a select committee is to hold the executive to account for its priorities, policy formulation and legislative design,[37] in practice the political party or parties in power can block a potential inquiry or even prevent experts coming before the committee. This occurred recently, where Labour MPs voted down a March 2022 request to have the Police Commissioner brief the Justice Select Committee on the anti-vaccine- mandate occupation at Parliament.[38]

Public and government inquiries under the *Inquiries Act 2013* sit somewhere in between. Once established by government they are required to operate independently of government; section 10 of the 2013 Act states that "each of its members must act independently, impartially, and fairly".

Future statutory inquiries

Section 7 of the *Inquiries Act 2013* states the establishment instrument must, among other things, "specify the matter of public importance that is the subject of the inquiry". However, the term "public importance" is not defined in the Act. Clearly what is important to the public may differ from what is important to politicians; protests and petitions demonstrate the public's concerns, and therefore arguably illustrate topics of public importance. When issues are not well resolved by political and wider government processes, public inquiries can help move the country forward.

Issues that deserve serious consideration for a public inquiry might, for instance, include: an inquiry into New Zealand's response to COVID-19 (including the occupation of New Zealand Parliament by anti-vaccination-mandate protesters during this period); co-governance options under Te Tiriti o Waitangi (the Treaty of Waitangi); redesigning the dairy industry; and governing a climate-isolated New Zealand. These are now briefly considered.

New Zealand's response to COVID-19 – lessons from the 1918-19 pandemic and commission of inquiry

Pandemics are not uncommon. The COVID-19 pandemic is the fifth global pandemic in just over a century (in addition to the 1918 pandemic, later pandemics occurred in 1957, 1968 and 2009). When looking back over time, pandemics can be seen as part of the normal cycle of events, what the McGuinness Institute calls "The Long Normal".[39] In this context, taking the time to reflect on New Zealand's performance to date may reduce further health-care shocks during this pandemic and also help the country prepare for the next. Arguably the economic impacts on talent retention and supply chain issues will have a long-term impact on New Zealand's economic resilience.[40]

New Zealand undertook a commission inquiring into the flu pandemic in 1919 – the *Influenza Epidemic Commission*. It also held two earlier royal commissions related to epidemics: one in 1874 regarding the ship *Scimitar* (due to scarlet fever and measles) and another in 1880 regarding the ship *Oxford* (typhoid fever).

New Zealand health historian Geoffrey Rice wrote that "[h]ealth systems the world over were rudely shaken by the 1918 influenza pandemic. Even those in medically advanced industrial societies were made to look hopelessly inadequate by the unprecedented mortality of 'the great flu', which may have killed 22 million people worldwide", although the final figures are often disputed.[41,42] This included approximately 9,000 New Zealanders and 15,000 Australians.[43,44,45] As in the current COVID-19 pandemic, the flu swept through communities in two or more waves, often with gaps of only months between different countries. These gaps were surprisingly small given the limited numbers of people travelling in 1918-19.

One hundred years later, by August 2022 the COVID-19 pandemic had killed approximately 6.5 million people worldwide (30% of global fatalities in the 1918 epidemic), with 2,679 fatalities as at 22 August 2022 reported in New Zealand (30% of New Zealand fatalities in the 1918 epidemic).[46,47,48] In 2019, there were approximately 965 staff at the Ministry of Health in Wellington (in 1911, there were 12 staff).[49] In 2021, this figure had increased to 1,388 (a 31% increase in staff over a two-year period).[50]

The 1918-19 pandemic was clearly more deadly. There is no doubt lessons learned during that pandemic and from the 1919 *Influenza Epidemic Commission* report that helped put in place better resources and processes for later pandemics. There is now another opportunity to chronicle, record, reflect, inquire into and report on New Zealand's current response in order to deliver a better, more robust health-care system for future generations.

In light of the COVID-19 pandemic, many, including the ACT party and former prime minister Helen Clark, argued it was timely for a royal commission of inquiry into the Government's response.[51,52] Clark co-chaired an independent inquiry into whether the World Health Organization failed to adequately warn of the COVID-19 pandemic. The resulting May 2021 report recommended that "[a]ll national governments ... update their national preparedness plans against the targets and benchmarks set by WHO within six months, ensuring that whole-of-government and whole-of-society co-ordination is in place and that there are appropriate and relevant skills, logistics and funding available to cope with future health crises". The report, *COVID-19: Make it the Last Pandemic*, advocates for countries to prepare for future pandemics.[53]

Many countries are currently working on ways to improve overall preparedness for current and future epidemics and pandemics. One such tool is the Global Health Security Index (GHS Index), which ranks the capacities of 195 countries across six categories and

37 indicators. Associate Professor Siouxsie Wiles, an infectious diseases expert and advisor to New Zealand Prime Minister Jacinda Ardern in the early days of the COVID-19 pandemic, has said applying the GHS Index report "really saved us".[54] By 2020, New Zealand had undergone a Joint External Evaluation with WHO, which led to New Zealand moving up the GHS Index, from 35th to 13th place (out of 195 countries).[55,56] In addition, organisations and committees within countries have also undertaken a range of specific reviews. For example, in New Zealand, the Auditor-General has undertaken a number of specific inquiries into aspects of the pandemic response, but these have been narrow in focus and short in length.[57]

A number of countries (eg the United Kingdom and Sweden) have appointed public inquiries into their COVID-19 response.[58,59,60,61] Of note, on 7 April 2022, the Australian Senate Select Committee on COVID-19 tabled its final report, making 19 recommendations. Recommendation 17 is "that a Royal Commission be established to examine Australia's response to the COVID-19 pandemic to inform preparedness for future COVID-19 waves and future pandemics".[62]

On 5 December 2022, the New Zealand Government announced a *Royal Commission of Inquiry into its COVID-19 response* A summary of the terms of reference states: "The purpose of the inquiry is to strengthen Aotearoa New Zealand's preparedness for, and response to, any future pandemic by identifying those lessons learned from New Zealand's response to COVID-19 that should be applied in preparation for any future pandemic. … The inquiry should consider the strategies, settings, and measures identified above as they existed or operated between February 2020 and October 2022, and not outside those dates."[63] When compared with other inquiry terms of references, it is unusual for a number of reasons. The summary terms set out a detailed list of procedures and processes, and contains a long list of areas "outside the scope of the inquiry".[64] The terms will therefore constrain the Commissioners, both in terms of scope and procedures.[65] The Commission will be chaired by Australia-based epidemiologist Tony Blakely, former Cabinet Minister Hekia Parata, and former Treasury Secretary John Whitehead.[66]

There has been growing pressure on the Government to undertake an independent inquiry. In the months leading up to the announcement (February–December 2022), three major key events occurred: firstly, the 23-day occupation of Parliament in February–March 2022 by protesters against the vaccine mandates. Even though the Independent Police Conduct Authority (IPCA) is undertaking an investigation/review of the policing of the protest, it is narrow in scope, and a deeper inquiry beyond policing has been argued for. The IPCA report is due in April 2023.[67,68,] Secondly, in March 2022 the governing Labour Party blocked a select committee from questioning the Police Commissioner over the occupation of Parliament, a move the opposition National Party suggested indicates that the Government is not interested in a wider inquiry.[69] Lastly, three top health chiefs resigned in April 2022 (leaving major gaps in the country's institutional memory).[70] In addition to these key events, criticism over New Zealand's lack of preparedness for COVID-19, combined with the declining popularity of the Labour Government leading up to the 2024 election, may have contributed to the announcement of the royal commission of inquiry.[71]

Interestingly, COVID-19 Response Minister Ayesha Verrall said one of the lessons was that having a prescriptive pandemic plan, like New Zealand's influenza-based plan, is not the best way forward. Verrall said, "I imagine [the lesson] has been learnt that just looking at the characteristics of one bug isn't going to cut it and you need to think much more broadly".[72] The commissioners must deliver their report by 26 June 2024.[73]

Co-governance options under Te Tiriti o Waitangi

Peter Dunne, a retired New Zealand politician, recently suggested New Zealand needs what is arguably a royal commission (or at least a public inquiry) on co-governance:

An independent external group, comprising distinguished and respected New Zealanders, and no current or former politicians, to shape and lead the consultation process, to educate and inform as necessary, to correct inaccurate statements, and to ensure every group has a reasonable opportunity to have its say and be heard. At the end of the engagement and consultation process, it should be the group's responsibility to produce a full report setting out future options for consideration. The report should be released publicly when completed, without being sanitised by the government filter. To ensure that, it should first be submitted to the Governor-General and then released to the Government and the public at the same time.

In particular, he noted:

The lesson that arises, which is of acute relevance to the co-governance debate, is that reasonable public consideration of important issues will not take place if it is constrained by a framework constructed by politicians. All that ensures is that the outcome of any such consultation is shaped and ultimately decided according to the partisan political lines dominant at the time.[73]

Dairy-farming industry in New Zealand

Another contender for a public inquiry is the dairy industry, which some argue pollutes New Zealand's waterways with nitrates and our atmosphere with carbon, as well as eroding soil. Progress has been slow to address this issue given the now defunct 2003 Dairying and Clean Streams Accord (between Fonterra Co-operative, Group Regional Councils, the Ministry for the Environment and the Ministry of Agriculture and Forestry) failed to deliver in "reducing the impacts of dairying on the quality of New Zealand streams, rivers, lakes, ground water and wetlands".[74] It seems timely for a broad inquiry into the dairy-farming industry, like the comprehensive 1949 *Royal Commission to Inquire into and Report upon the*

Sheep-Farming Industry in New Zealand.[75] Such an inquiry could undertake a review of legislation (in particular the *Dairy Industry Restructuring Act 2001*); explore the impacts of the existing business model and identify and assess other business model options; identify ownership, funding, resourcing and staffing opportunities; traverse pollution, climate change, water quality and land use; and most importantly look at ways New Zealand might pivot to a more carbon-friendly farming model – for example, will we need to pay dairy farmers not to farm dairy cows?

A climate-isolated New Zealand

Air New Zealand's latest annual report makes clear that in terms of air travel, New Zealand will become increasingly isolated. It notes in its climate-related disclosures section that there will be "[i]ncreasing frequency of extreme weather events resulting in greater disruption to flights and the wider network" and that "[s]ea level rise and coastal intrusion [are likely to cause risks such as] network disruption, loss of access to airports, other aviation support facilities, critical infrastructure and supply chains".[76]

Recent research into rogue waves indicates New Zealand may become more isolated by sea, as well. A study published in the journal *Science Advances* in June 2020 suggested that extreme wave conditions may increase by 15 per cent. The research states that "high-latitude regions of both hemispheres are projected to have an increase in extreme significant wave height, while lower latitudes generally see a decrease" and "[t]he southern tip of South America is projected to experience an increase of approximately 20 per cent, with the west coast of New Zealand and Tasmania experiencing an increase of 10 to 15 per cent".[77] Although the research is still tentative, the implications for our economy, in particular our supply chain, are such that New Zealand needs to consider how to become more antifragile in the face of these risks.

Suggestions to improve existing public inquiry processes in New Zealand

There are several suggestions for how the New Zealand inquiry system could be improved, which would build on the existing legal and legislative framework. These include:

Provide broader (rather than narrower) terms of reference

Public and government inquiries clearly work well when the terms of reference are tight enough in scope to allow the commissioners to focus on a key problem, but not so tight as to prevent them from looking at how the problem fits within the larger system. Often those setting the terms of reference do so with little understanding of why the issue exists in the first place; hence the terms of reference should be broad enough to enable the commissioners to follow their curiosity and be creative with their recommendations.

Appoint, support and guide commissioners fit for purpose

There is a need to create an effective independent inquiry system that enables commissioners to pause, reflect and learn lessons, including interviewing experts and members of the public under oath in order to gain a deep understanding of the matter at hand. New Zealand will increasingly need to call on independent commissioners (with the necessary time, expertise, resources and independence) to inquire into a wide range of complex problems. However, there is arguably no guidance in the public arena for those selecting commissioners or reporting on progress (such as a financial report on costs), and no guidance for commissioners appointed to undertake an inquiry.

Given the level of public investment and public importance, the government could establish an independent inquiry secretariat for statutory inquiries. The resulting organisation could operate in a similar way to the New Zealand Productivity Commission, possibly supported by a board of Supreme Court judges and ex-prime ministers. The purpose would be to systemise inquiries, including managing, supporting and publishing inquiry reports. Ideally it would also be required to publish an annual report, including information on costs, progress to date and any changes in terms of references and extensions of time on all statutory inquiries established under the *Inquiries Act 2013*.

Improve implementation through reviews

One of the key issues about public inquiries across all jurisdictions, as discussed in this volume, is what happens to their reports and recommendations. Once a report has been tabled in Parliament, the inquiry commissioners generally make no further comment on the subject matter. The report is left for government to consider and respond to as it deems necessary. While some see this as the appropriate process, others argue that this is a lost opportunity, given the knowledge and expertise that commissioners may have acquired during their investigations. Therefore, it is suggested that former inquiry members should be part of a review mechanism to assess progress in the implementation of the inquiry's recommendations. This would make the cost and investment in the inquiry more worthwhile. Furthermore, some issues will re-emerge, and it will be useful to know what recommendations were implemented and what were not. A review would be very useful, particularly where a package of recommendations was crafted to resolve a complex and challenging issue. This review process could also provide an opportunity for commissioners to share any additional observations or thoughts.

An example where a public inquiry's recommendations were not fully implemented is the 2001 *Royal Commission on Genetic Modification*.[78] This was a new area of science and the terms of reference reflected this by giving the commissioners a wide scope of inquiry. The final report made 49 recommendations. However, there was no subsequent review of the implementation of these recommendations, many of which were quite specific and designed as an integrated package to deliver a level of safety and range of options for current and future generations. Given the level of public interest at the time (which included government putting in place a moratorium, GE-free hīkoi [marches], and numerous other petitions and protests), it was a surprise that once the report was delivered and the commissioners dispersed that the public conversation and national dialogue came largely to a close. The McGuiness Institute's subsequent review eight years later found there had been limited implementation of the 49 recommendations.[79] This example highlights that the temporary nature of inquiries and their members may explain why inquiry recommendations are not always implemented or reviewed.

Improve record keeping and organisational memory

Having improved clarity over who owns and is responsible for an inquiry report once released is also important. There is no doubt that many public servants and business leaders read the 1919 *Influenza Epidemic Commission* report during 2020 to learn more about the impacts of a pandemic (fortunately a copy could be found on the National Library of New Zealand website).[80] However, as a general rule, records of inquiry reports have not been well-maintained. For example, the McGuinness Institute's study could not locate the remaining 29 royal commission reports on any website (see **Figure 3** above). Nor could it locate a credible comprehensive list (other than a few tentative lists prepared by scholars over time). Given this, it was gratifying to learn that the Rt Hon Dame Patsy Reddy had arranged for all available royal commission reports to be uploaded to the Governor-General's website. This is an important start but more work needs to be done. In addition to finding and uploading the missing 29 royal commission reports, all the other non-royal public inquiries and other government inquiries should also be published and maintained on a public register. In the interests of effective stewardship, accountability and transparency, government inquiry reports should be accessible on the New Zealand Parliament's website (as they are established by the Crown and tabled by a minister in the House of Representatives).

This would ensure the reports are easy to find, assess, debate and review and would improve public trust in the processes of government. Although the Department of Internal Affairs is responsible for the administration of public and government inquiries,[81] these are in practice not departmental reports and it may be more appropriate if all public inquiries were made available on the Governor-General's website and government inquiries on the New Zealand Parliament website.

Maintaining a public register not only helps those interested in certain subject matter but should also assist those preparing terms of reference for future inquiries. We need to use every opportunity to seek out wisdom and expertise so that we learn not only how to solve the existing matter under consideration, but also how to improve our processes for subjects that might call for an inquiry in the future.

Focus long but engage early

There are arguably three types of sight: hindsight, insight and foresight. Public inquiries should use all three types of sight when considering the subject matter before them. Futurists aim to engage early with complex problems. Professor Leon Feurth, a former diplomat and futurist who served as national security adviser to former US Vice-President Al Gore, developed the term 'forward engagement'.[82] Public inquiries should aim to do just that: to forward engage with a specific subject to inform current and future generations on ways to prevent a future disaster or enable the country to manage a possible opportunity or threat.

Identifying emerging issues that may become significant in the future (ie weak signals) is an essential part of the broader process of inquiry and improvement. A new instrument that might help contribute to identifying issues early is the long-term insights briefing. The *Public Service Act 2020*[83] introduces a new requirement for departmental chief executives to publish a long-term insights briefing (LTIB) at least once every three years. The purpose of the briefings is to make available to the public "information about medium and long-term trends, risks and opportunities that affect or may affect New Zealand and New Zealand society" and "information and impartial analysis, including policy options for responding to these matters".[84] The LTIBs should result in better problem definition for upcoming inquiries or enable officials to engage early so inquiries are not needed.

Conclusions

Public and government inquiries are special. They are the ultimate tool for reviewing complex issues and getting to the truth. A well-resourced and highly skilled commissioner or group of commissioners working under a broad terms of reference can help inform the public on what they have learned and what they think the government, and others in society, should do. Without such an advisory mechanism, democracy is weakened.

Public and government inquiries deserve our care and consideration. Society needs to have confidence that the resulting reports are independent of party politics, comprehensive, accurate and accessible to current and future generations. Provided government continues to review and improve New Zealand's system of statutory inquiries, public and government inquiries will continue to be important tools in maintaining and building the public's trust in existing democratic processes and decision-making.

Inquiries mentioned in this chapter[85]

The Removal of the Seat of Government to Cook's Straits (Murphy, Docker & Gunn, 1864)

Prisons (Johnston, 1868)

Influenza Epidemic Commission (Denniston, 1919)

Royal Commission to Inquire into and Report upon the Sheep-Farming Industry in

New Zealand (White, 1949)

Royal Commission to Inquire Into and Report Upon the Crash on Mount Erebus, Antarctica, of a DC10 Aircraft operated by Air New Zealand Limited (Mahon, 1980)

Royal Commission on the Electoral System (Wallace, 1986)

Royal Commission on Genetic Modification (Eichelbaum, 2000)

Royal Commission on the Pike River Coal Mine Tragedy (Pankhurst, 2010)
Royal Commission of Inquiry into the terrorist attack on Christchurch masjidain on 15 March 2019 (Young, 2019)

Royal Commission of Inquiry (Covid-19 Lessons), (Blakely, 2022)

Notes

1 The author gives special thanks for the hard work of Isabella Smith, Lucy Witkowski and Arne Larsen, who researched and prepared the list of royal commissions. All three co-authored *Working Paper 2020/10 – A List of Royal Commissions since 1868.* This work contributed to the comprehensive list now found on the Governor-General's website.
2 See The Governor-General, "New Zealand's Constitution."
3 See The Governor-General, "The Constitution of New Zealand."
4 See *Cabinet Manual 2017,* para 4.81: "They are appointed by the Governor-General, in the name of the Sovereign and on the advice of the Executive Council, under clause X of the Letters Patent Constituting the Office of Governor-General of New Zealand 1983," Cabinet Office, *Cabinet Manual 2017,* para 4.81.
5 See Alan Simpson, "Commissions of inquiry – Functions, power and legal status," Te Ara – the Encyclopedia of New Zealand, 2012.
6 See T. Gore Browne, "Papers Relative to The Removal of the Seat of Government to Cook's Straits", *Appendices to the Journals of the House of Representatives,* Enclosure to No 13, D-02, 1864.
7 See G. Grey, "Reports of the Royal Commission on Prisons," *Appendix to the Journals of the House of Representatives of New Zealand,* 1868, Session 1, A-No.12.
8 See *The Commissioners Powers Act 1867.*
9 See *Commissioners Powers Act 1867 Amendment Act 1872.*
10 See *Commissioners Act 1903,* No 20.
11 See *Commissioners Act Amendment Act 1905,* No 13.
12 See Law Commission, *A New Inquiries Act,* Law Commission, Wellington, 2008, R102, p. 5.

13 See Law Commission, *The Role of Public Inquiries*, Law Commission, Wellington, 2007, *IP1*; Law Commission, *Public Inquiries: Draft Report*, Law Commission, Wellington, 2007; Law Commission, *A New Inquiries Act*, Law Commission, Wellington, 2008, R102.

14 See Law Commission, *The Role of Public Inquiries*, Law Commission, Wellington, 2007, *IP1*, p. 5.

15 Ibid., pp. 11, 17.

16 Ibid., pp. 19, 20.

17 Ibid., *IP1*, p. 19.

18 See McGuinness Institute, *Working Paper 2020/10 – A List of Royal Commissions since 1868* (last updated 26 April 2022), pp. 5, 14.

19 See Law Commission, *A New Inquiries Act*, Law Commission, Wellington, 2008, R102, p. 4.

20 Ibid., p. 5.

21 Ibid., R102, p. 6.

22 Ibid., in particular paragraph 15.9, pp. 186–190.

23 Ibid., p. 6.

24 Personal communication with Anita Balakrishnan, Department of Internal Affairs, 20 April 2022, Official Information Act [email].

25 See New Zealand Parliament, "Presenting Papers to the House of Representatives," 30 August 2021.

26 Law Commission, *A New Inquiries Act*, Law Commission, Wellington, 2008, R102, p. 5.

27 See Alan Simpson, "Commissions of inquiry – Functions, power and legal status," *Te Ara – The Encyclopedia of New Zealand*, 2012.

28 See *Report of the Royal Commission on the Electoral System: Towards a better democracy*, 1986, p. 293.

29 The Governor-General's website contains a list of all royal commissions; see The Governor-General, "Royal Commission Reports."

30 Ibid.

31 See McGuinness Institute, *Working Paper 2020/10 – A List of Royal Commissions since 1868* (last updated 26 April 2022), p. 5.

32 Ibid., p. 14.

33 Ibid.

34 Although the Auditor-General's primary function is to carry out annual audits, they also have the power to inquire into issues of concern. This inquiries function is completely discretionary; the scope of the inquiry can be large or small. Many take weeks or even months to complete. See Office of the Auditor-General, "Inquiries," 7 April 2021.

35 See Matthew Palmer and Dean R. Knight, *The Constitution of New Zealand: A Contextual Analysis*, Hart Publishing, Bloomsbury Publishing, Great Britain, 2022, p. 180.

36 See David McGee, "Chapter 29: Inquiries." in Mary Harris and David Wilson, *Parliamentary Practice in New Zealand*, 4th ed, Oratia Books, Auckland, 2017.

37 See Palmer and Knight, *The Constitution of New Zealand: A Contextual Analysis*, p. 123.

38 See Newshub, "National demands more scrutiny over Parliament protest as Labour blocks select committee from questioning Police Commissioner,"

17 March 2022.

39 See Wendy McGuinness, *The Long Normal: Preparing the National Reserve Supply (NRS) for pandemic cycles*, McGuinness Institute, Think Piece 33, April 2020.

40 See Roger Dennis, Wendy McGuinness and Rick Boven, *Lessons From the West African Ebola Outbreak in Relation to New Zealand's Supply Chain Resilience*, 7 May 2015, pp. 51-52.

41 See G. W. Rice, "The Making of New Zealand's 1920 Health Act," *National Library of Medicine*, Vol 22, No 1, 1988, p. 1.

42 See Ferris Jabr, "Covid-19 Is Not the Spanish Flu," Wired, 13 March 2020.

43 See NZ History, "The 1918 influenza pandemic: Page 1 – Introduction."

44 See The National Museum of Australia, "Influenza Pandemic," 6 September 2021.

45 See Ministry of Health, *New Zealand Influenza Pandemic Plan: A framework for action* (2nd edn), 2017, p. 4.

46 See World Health Organization, "WHO Coronavirus (COVID-19) Dashboard.".

47 See World Health Organization, "New Zealand." Retrieved 22 August 2022, Ministry of Health, "COVID-19: Current cases."

48 See Jamie Morton, "Covid-19: Everything we know (and don't) about NZ's 516 deaths," *New Zealand Herald*, 12 April 2022.

49 See Ministry of Health, *Annual Report for the Year Ended 30 June 2019*, Wellington, 2019, p. 147.

50 See Ministry of Health, *Annual Report for the Year Ended 30 June 2021*, Wellington, 2021, p. 42.

51 See ACT, "We need a Royal Commission on the COVID-19 response," 2020.

52 See Tim Murphy, "Coronavirus: Helen Clark wants full inquiry into NZ's Covid-19 response," *Stuff*, 6 August 2020.

53 See The Independent Panel For Pandemic Preparedness and Response, "COVID-19: Make it the Last Pandemic," 2022, pp. 50-51.

54 See Jessica A. Bell and Jennifer B. Nuzzo, *GHS Index: Global Health Security Index – Advancing Collective Action and Accountability Amid Global Crisis*, December 2021, p. 44.

55 See Elizabeth E. Cameron, Jennifer B. Nuzzo and Jessica A. Bell, *GHS Index: Global Health Security Index – Building Collective Action and Accountability*, October 2019, p. 240.

56 See Jessica A. Bell and Jennifer B. Nuzzo, *GHS Index: Global Health Security Index – Advancing Collective Action and Accountability Amid Global Crisis*, December 2021, p. 188.

57 See McGuinness Institute's list: Table 3: Independent Reviews on the Government's Response to COVID-19.

58 See Doug Faulkner, "Covid inquiry's public hearings to begin in 2023," BBC, 11 March 2022.

59 See Robert Booth and Ian Sample, "Pressure mounts on Boris Johnson to launch coronavirus inquiry," *Guardian*, 16 March 2021.

60 See Scott Prasser, "Brits beat us to an independent pandemic inquiry," *Canberra Times*, 7 January 2022.

61 See Nick Wilson, Jennifer Summers, George Thomson, Amanda Kvalsvig, Matt Boyd and Michael Baker, "Five Key Reasons why NZ Should have an Official Inquiry into the Response to the COVID-19 Pandemic," Public Health Expert blog, University of Otago, 11 June 2020.

62 See Parliament of Australia, *The Senate: Select Committee on COVID-19 – Final Report*, Commonwealth of Australia, Senate, Canberra, April 2022. See RNZ, "Jacinda Ardern, Ayesha Verrall announce Royal Commission of Inquiry into Covid-19 response," 5 December 2022.

63 See Beehive, Summary of the terms of reference for the Royal Commission of Inquiry into Lessons Learned from Aotearoa New Zealand's Response to COVID-19 That Should Be Applied in Preparation for a Future Pandemic, December 2022, p. 1.

64 See Scott Prasser, "Is New Zealand's royal commission into the pandemic response best practice?," Online Opinion, 13 December 2022.

65 See RNZ, "Jacinda Ardern, Ayesha Verrall announce Royal Commission of Inquiry into Covid-19 response," 5 December 2022.

66 See Jane Patterson, "Where are the promised inquiries into the Parliament protest?," RNZ, 21 March 2022.

67 See Independent Police Conduct Authority, "Scope of Investigation and Review," n.d.

68 See Newshub, "National demands more scrutiny over Parliament protest as Labour blocks select committee from questioning Police Commissioner," 17 March 2022.

69 See "More leading Ministry of Health officials resign," RNZ, 6 April 2022.

70 See Scott Prasser, "Is New Zealand's royal commission into the pandemic response best practice?," Online Opinion, 13 December 2022.

71 See Beehive, Post-Cabinet Press Conference: Monday, 5 December 2022 Hansard Transcript, 5 December 2022.

72 See Beehive, Summary of the terms of reference for the Royal Commission of Inquiry into Lessons Learned from Aotearoa New Zealand's Response to COVID-19 That Should Be Applied in Preparation for a Future Pandemic, December 2022, p. 2.

73 See Peter Dunne, "Māori co-governance deserves better than a bitter and divisive public debate," *Newsroom*, 7 April 2022.

74 The purpose of the Accord was to provide "a statement of intent and framework for actions to promote sustainable dairy farming in New Zealand. It focuses on reducing the impacts of dairying on the quality of New Zealand streams, rivers, lakes, ground water and wetlands." See "Dairying and Clean Streams ACCORD between Fonterra Co-operative Group, Regional Councils, Ministry for the Environment, and Ministry of Agriculture and Forestry," 2003, p. 1.

75 See R.E. Owen, "Royal Commission to Inquire into and Report upon the Sheep-Farming Industry in New Zealand," *Appendix to the Journals of the House of Representatives of New Zealand*, H–46A, March 1949.

76 See Air New Zealand, *Annual Financial Results*, 2021, p. 66.

77 See Alberto Meucci, Ian R. Young, Mark Hemer, Ebru Kirezci and Roshanka Ranasinghe, "Projected 21st century changes in extreme wind-wave events," *Science Advances*, Vol 6, No 24, 10 June 2020.

78 See the terms of reference. Marian Hobbs, "Royal Commission On Genetic Modification," Beehive, 17 April 2000. Retrieved 13 April 2022.

79 See Sustainable Future Institute (now McGuinness Institute), "The Review of the Forty-nine Recommendations of the Royal Commission on Genetic Modification," 2008. This paper provides background material for a Project 2058 report, titled *Report 16 – An Overview of Genetic Modification in New Zealand 1973-*

2013: The first forty years.

80 See the 1919 report here: John Edward Denniston, Edward Mitchelson and David McLaren, "Report of the Influenza Epidemic Commission," *Appendix to the Journals of the House of Representatives of New Zealand*, 1919, H-31a, p.16.

81 See Department of Internal Affairs, "Public and Government Inquiries," which currently provides a brief summary of the legal framework and contains links to 16 recent inquiries.

82 See Wendy McGuinness, "Creating Intelligent Countries through Forward Engagement," *The Futurist*, November–December 2010, p. 49.

83 See Schedule 6, clauses 8 and 9 of the *Public Service Act 2020*.

84 See Department of the Prime Minister and Cabinet, "Long-term Insights Briefings," 9 April 2021.

85 List refers to name of inquiry, its chair and the date of appointment.

16

US Presidential Commissions: An update

Kenneth Kitts

Introduction

The question of how to address controversies, crises, or traumas of national scope is certainly not unique to the government of the United States of America. Indeed, social contract theory posits that the primary purpose of all governments is to provide law and order. When disruptions or threats emerge that threaten that order, it is normal for the public to demand answers and accountability. The task for those in power is to find the appropriate mechanism with which to respond. In the United States (US), these calls for action and accountability are processed by and through the Madisonian system of separated powers. It is a cumbersome system by design.

The framers of the US Constitution were products of their time. They wrote the document in 1787, soon after gaining independence from Great Britain, and consequently were as concerned with guarding against excessive governmental power as they were with creating an efficient system for advancing the public good. James Madison captured these competing objectives brilliantly in Federalist 51:

> If men were angels, no government would be necessary. If angels were to govern men, neither external nor internal controls on government would be necessary. In framing a government which is to be administered by men over men, the great difficulty lies in this: you must first enable the government to control the

governed; and in the next place oblige it to control itself.[1]

In drafting the Constitution, Madison's solution to this dilemma was to disperse governmental power along the lines of executive, legislative, and judicial authority, and then to ensure that each "department" would have the means to "resist encroachments of the others." "Ambition," he wrote, "must be made to counteract ambition".[2]

Well over two hundred and thirty years have elapsed since this constitutional order came into being. Even so, Madison and company cast a long shadow, and the dispersion of power the framers created continues to be the defining characteristic of American politics. This is the context in which US presidential commissions operate. It is an essential frame of reference for interpreting commission politics and the development of public inquiries in the US system of government.

The universe of US advisory commissions

Presidential commissions are only one type of ad hoc committee that exist within the universe of federal advisory bodies in the U.S. Other bodies created within the executive branch are actually departmental committees, reporting not to the president but to a cabinet secretary or agency supervisor. These bodies typically deal with mundane, procedural questions far removed from matters that command national interest. Still others are interagency groups created to enhance policy coordination between two or more bureaucratic entities.

The complexity of the system is compounded by legislative involvement in public inquiries. Sometimes this takes the form of a special investigation conducted by a standing or select committee of Congress. The 1975 Church Committee hearings, so named for Senator Frank Church, into US intelligence activities stand as a good example of this type of probe.[3]

But these investigations are very political and frequently protracted.

Even within Congress, this leads to calls to go outside normal channels in the search for answers to the most pressing questions on the public agenda. The result is that Congress has occasionally appointed its own blue-ribbon commissions. Perhaps the best-known examples of this type of group were the two *Hoover Commissions on the Organization of the Executive Branch* in 1947-49 and 1953-55.[4]

Some critics find congressional commissions to be objectionable on grounds that lawmakers should be expected to perform the very tasks – policy evaluation and oversight of agency performance -- that are often delegated to the ad hoc body.[5] Others find value in the practice of asking "disinterested men of the highest probity" for assistance in dealing with issues "which congressional committees have neither the time nor the detachment to handle wisely and fairly".[6]

Because of this fragmentation, it remains exceedingly difficult to classify or even count federal advisory committees with precision. "No one knows," states a report by the General Accounting Office (GAO), "exactly how many miscellaneous boards, committees, and commissions exist at any given time".[7] Nor does GAO offer much hope that greater clarity will be forthcoming:

> It is always helpful at the outset to define your universe. In this instance, however, we have been unable to discover or devise a satisfactory definition... Advisory committees are only one type of these miscellaneous bodies, albeit the largest. The impossibility of crafting a useful definition becomes apparent upon considering the key elements of function, creation, membership, and duration.[8]

President Bill Clinton's *Task Force on National Health Care Reform* provides an excellent example of how difficult it can be to classify panels. The Task Force found itself at the center of a federal court case in 1993. At issue was the legal status of committee chair Hillary Rodham Clinton. The duties of a First Lady, the court decided, made Clinton a de facto government employee. That decision, coupled with the fact that all other members of the panel were also executive branch officers, meant that the panel did not constitute a "public" advisory committee under statutory guidelines.[9]

When the departmental, interagency, and congressional panels are pared from the list of federal advisory bodies, there remain a small number – typically less than five percent of the total in any given year - that may be loosely classified as presidential commissions.[10] And loosely is indeed the operative word! Some groups are easy to classify as presidential by dint of being created by executive order, comprising members chosen by the president, and reporting only to the White House. Other panels present more of an analytical challenge.

To aid in the process of classification, scholars have crafted a number of definitions to help identify the essential ingredients of a "true" presidential commission.[11] Some widely accepted attributes are that the panel must be temporary in nature and must include at least one member from outside the executive branch, or the federal rolls generally, depending on the definition. But here the consensus ends.

Thomas Wolanin wrote in 1975 that a commission should not be considered presidential unless *all members* are appointed directly by the president.[12] However, that degree of White House control over commissions has become less common over time. The 1994-95 *Commission on the Roles and Capabilities of the U.S. Intelligence Community* is indicative of the change. Of the seventeen members appointed to that panel, President Clinton selected only nine.[13] Along these lines, recent studies account for the growing number of "national" or "presidential-congressional" panels that feature varying degrees of legislative input.[14]

Table 1 provides a listing of some of the most important investigative commissions in the U.S. from World War Two to present. It is by no means an exhaustive list, but the common thread is that each entry is tied to a major scandal or crisis that that garnered sufficient national attention to warrant a response outside of normal bureaucratic or legislative channels.

Table 1 SELECTED US INVESTIGATIVE COMMISSIONS				
Crisis/Event	President	Commission	Authorization	Structure and Duration
Japanese Attack on Pearl Harbor (1941)	F. Roosevelt	Commission to Investigate the Japanese Attack of December 7, 1941 *Owen Roberts, chair*	Executive Order 8983 December 1941	5 Members (all appointed by president) Subpoena Power = Yes Final Report January 1942
Assassination of President Kennedy (1963)	Johnson	President's Commission on the Assassination of President Kennedy *Earl Warren, chair*	Executive Order 11130 November 1963	7 Members (all appointed by president) Subpoena Power = Yes Final Report September 1964
Urban Unrest (1965-1967)	Johnson	National Advisory Commission on Civil Disorders *Otto Kerner, chair*	Executive Order 11365 July 1967	11 members (all appointed by president) Subpoena Power = Yes Final Report February 1968
Revelation of CIA Domestic Spying (1974-1975)	Ford	Commission on CIA Activities Within the United States *Nelson Rockefeller, chair*	Executive Order 11828 January 1975	8 members (all appointed by president) Subpoena Power = No Final Report June 1975
Three Mile Island Nuclear Accident (1979)	Carter	President's Commission on the Accident at Three Mile Island *John Kemeny, chair*	Executive Order 12130 April 1979	12 Members (all appointed by president) Subpoena Power = Yes Final Report October 1979
Explosion of Space Shuttle Challenger (1986)	Reagan	Presidential Commission on the Space Shuttle Challenger Accident *William Rogers chair*	Executive Order 12546 February 1986	13 Members (all appointed by president) Subpoena Power = No Final Report June 1986

Iran-Contra Scandal (1986)	Reagan	President's Special Review Board *John Tower, chair*	Executive Order 12575 December 1986	3 Members (all appointed by president) Subpoena Power = No Final Report February 1987
9/11 Terrorist Attacks (2001)	G. W. Bush	National Commission on Terrorist Attacks Upon the United States *Thomas Kean, chair*	Public Law 107-306 November 2002	10 Members (9 appointed by congressional leaders, 1 by president) Subpoena Power = Yes Final Report July 2004
Explosion of Space Shuttle Columbia (2003)	G.W. Bush	Columbia Accident Investigation Board *Harold Gehman, chair*	Directive by NASA Administrator February 2003	13 Members (all appointed by NASA Administrator) Subpoena Power = No Final Report August 2003
Financial Crisis (2007)	G. W. Bush	Financial Crisis Inquiry Commission *Phil Angelides, chair*	Public Law 111-21 May 2009	10 Members (all appointed by congressional leaders) Subpoena Power = Yes Final Report January 2011
Gulf of Mexico Oil Spill (2010)	Obama	National Commission on the BP Deepwater Horizon Oil Spill and Offshore Drilling *Bob Graham and William Reilly co-chairs*	Executive Order 13543 May 2010	7 Members (all appointed by president) Subpoena Power = No Final Report January 2011

The great diversity of responses to these controversies underscores that variety is the order of the day when it comes to public inquiries in the US. Here we see groups empaneled by the president, groups empaneled by Congress, and groups empaneled by joint action of the two branches. We even see a high-profile board of inquiry appointed by an agency director. Significantly, the overview also provides an opportunity to compare how two very similar tragedies – the loss of two space shuttles, both to explosions, one in 1986 and the other in 2003 – gave rise to very different types of inquiries. This demonstrates that the emergence and trajectory of a public inquiry is situational. Politics, partisanship, and presidential preference play a large role in determining the contours of a blue-ribbon probe.

Presidential commissions as public inquiries

"Public inquiry" is not a commonly used term of reference in the US political system. Instead, commission-based investigations in the US are normally referred to as just that – commissions – with the press sometimes applying its own explanatory modifiers such as "board of inquiry" or "blue-ribbon probe." In most instances these references bear little or no relation to the panel's official designation, nor are they especially useful in helping to differentiate between various types of panels. Definitional chaos is still the order of the day when it comes to commission-based inquiries in the US.

While commissions come in all shapes and sizes, **Table 1** does suggest that presidential-variant commissions have predominated when it comes to the most high-profile events and investigations. The Japanese attack on Pearl Harbor and the Kennedy assassination gave rise to inquiries of this type, as did the Space Shuttle Challenger disaster and the incident at Three Mile Island nuclear facility.

To be sure, there are important exceptions to this investigatory rule. Significantly, the stock market crash of October 1929 did *not* give rise to a presidential commission, instead becoming the focus of a probe by Senate-appointed attorney Ferdinand Pecora.[15] Congress also took the lead with the inquiry into the causes of the 2007-2008 economic convulsion by creating its own *Financial Crisis Inquiry Commission*.[16]

Still more recently, President Joseph Biden rejected calls from members of his own party to appoint a presidential panel to look into the January 6, 2021, attacks on the US Capitol. Biden's Press Secretary made the point that, since Congress itself was attacked on

January 6, "Congress has a unique role and ability to carry out that investigation."[17] The US House of Representatives ultimately voted to empanel a select committee composed of members from within its own ranks to lead that inquiry.[18]

The inquiry created to deal with the terrorist attacks of September 11, 2001, deserves special mention due to the magnitude of that event and the politics that determined the course of the investigation. The day after the attacks, a prominent Democratic lawmaker stood on the floor of the US Senate and challenged President Bush to "form a board of general inquiry to review the actions of the US intelligence community and the failures which led to this massive loss of life and compromise of national security".[19] But as the days and weeks passed, Bush made no effort to empanel an inquiry.

The break with tradition was not lost on everyone. David Rosenbaum of the *New York Times* noted that the president's stance represented a "reversal of normal form...usually, after a calamitous event of a political embarrassment, it is the White House that seeks a commission to investigate".[20]

The reasons for Bush's obstinacy are debatable. Initially, the president and his lieutenants argued that a special investigation would tie up key officials and divert attention from the emerging war on terror.[21] They soon brought forth a second argument that focused on protecting confidential information. Vice President Dick Cheney suggested that an inquiry would "multiply potential sources of leaks" of sensitive intelligence and thus compromise the very security that it was intended to enhance.[22] But any objective assessment of this question must also consider the fact that Bush's refusal to act was in line with his penchant for secrecy and determination to resist any development that could limit executive authority.

If Bush was the seemingly immovable object in this drama, the 9/11 families emerged as the irresistible will. The widows, parents, and children of the victims found their voice, organised themselves, and mounted an effective lobbying campaign to get an inquiry established.[23] Congress took up the charge in the fall of 2002 and began to make plans for a commission of its own design.[24]

For Bush, the only thing worse than having to field questions from a group of his own creation would be to endure the same inquisition by a group of luminaries appointed by Congress. He thus reluctantly embraced the idea of a mixed national commission, for which he would share responsibility with Congress, in order to avoid being completely sidelined in the effort and to be able to exert some control over the commission's membership and mandate. Bush signed the National Commission on Terrorist Attacks Upon the United States into law on November 27, 2002 – fourteen months and sixteen days after the worst terrorist attack in American history.

Although President Bush succeeded in achieving that influence, his delay carried a political price. Had he acted more expeditiously, he could have ended up with a far more compliant panel. He also could have avoided the suspicion and ill will caused by his yearlong fight to prevent a blue-ribbon probe. Once the investigation was underway, Bush's attitude ranged from indifferent to defiant.[25] He risked any number of political confrontations with the commission. Conversely, the commission did not hesitate to confront the White House in public.

President Bush learned a hard lesson in commission politics with the 9/11 Inquiry. And learn he did. In early 2004, when questions arose regarding the absence of weapons of mass destruction in Iraq, he showed greater skill in handling calls for an investigation. He acted quickly to defuse the issue by appointing a more traditional, executive-dominated panel to examine the WMD question.

The panel had no subpoena power, and all ten members were selected by the president without input from opposition leaders. Moreover,

Bush granted the panel a generous period of thirteen months to conduct its investigation. Critics noted that the schedule was politically convenient since the commission would not issue its report until well after the 2004 presidential election.[26] In the end, the panel cited poor intelligence work, and not political interference from administration officials, as the main cause of the WMD failure.[27] It was exactly the finding Bush needed to make the troublesome issue go away.

Commission politics and executive-legislative tensions

As mentioned in the introduction, commission politics in the US must be understood in the context of the Madisonian system of separated powers. The tension between the executive and legislative branches of government is exacerbated during periods of divided government, when the normal contest of wills between the branches is heightened by an overlay of partisan pressures.[28] In the first half of the twentieth century, the president's party controlled both chambers of Congress over 80% of the time. Since 1950, however, divided government has become the rule rather than the exception with one party control occurring less than 40% of the time.[29]

Partisan and inter-branch bickering over commissions has resulted in a standoff of sorts. Congress does not like being excluded from decisions when a presidentially-appointed inquiry takes shape, yet there is nothing lawmakers can do to stop the president from using his star power to give a probe instant visibility. Conversely, presidents are free to use executive orders to launch blue-ribbon probes, yet they do not have the power to compel Congress to recognise the panel's legitimacy or to equip it with the legal powers necessary to conduct a thorough investigation.

In this environment, the political fight over commissions has, in recent years, moved to surrogate issues through which the two branches can continue to push for investigative primacy. Two of the more important issues with which to illustrate this dynamic are subpoena power and compliance with the *Federal Advisory Committee Act*.

The most common instrument by which presidents create investigatory commissions is the executive order. With an executive order, the president can set the panel's mandate, describe its composition, and set a timeline for completion of the probe and issuance of the final report. The president can even use his authority to require the cooperation of executive branch officials with the investigation.[30] What is *not* within the scope of his authority is to equip the commission with the power to issue subpoenas. That decision rests with Congress.

Subpoena power gives the commission the legal authority to compel attendance and testimony of witnesses and to require the production of documents or other material evidence that could have a bearing on the investigation. Most presidential commissions are not so-equipped. Partly this is due to the fact that many inquiries of this type focus on comparatively non-controversial matters of policy or administrative organisation.[31] But even for commissions with a more investigative orientation, the conferral of subpoena power is dependent upon two separate steps: the president must ask, and Congress must grant.

The first condition is absolute. There is no case in the historical record of Congress forcing subpoena power on a presidential commission over a president's objection. The most obvious barrier to such a move is that the president could exercise veto over that legislative action. But a greater concern is that it can be challenging to secure congressional support for subpoena power even when the president is behind the idea. Absent his push, it simply does not happen.

It is difficult to understand the logic by which a president would create a public inquiry and then cripple it by not petitioning Congress for subpoena power. Yet this does happen from time to time. President Ronald Reagan did not request subpoena power for the Tower Commission probe of the Iran-Contra scandal in 1986-1987.[32]

Similarly, President George W. Bush did not seek subpoena power for his 2004 *Commission on the Intelligence Capabilities of the United States Regarding Weapons of Mass Destruction.* It is likely that both presidents could have prevailed on the measure had they asked. In the case of the latter panel, Bush was even challenged on his silence by commission member and prominent Republican Senator John McCain.[33]

In cases where presidents do endorse a petition for subpoena power, the congressional response depends on the political winds of the time. In 1975, President Gerald Ford asked Congress to grant subpoena power to a commission of his creation on domestic spying by the Central Intelligence Agency. Representative Peter Rodino, Chairman of the House Judiciary Committee, cited the lack of congressional input on the panel as a point of friction and fought successfully to deny the request.[34] In 2010, a vote to give subpoena power to a presidential commission on the oil spill in the Gulf of Mexico sailed through the House by vote of 420-1 before being derailed by Senate Republicans.[35] By contrast, the commissions that dealt with the Pearl Harbor attack and the Kennedy assassination both obtained subpoena power easily, with the latter panel enjoying the additional power of being able to grant immunity to reluctant witnesses.[36]

A second surrogate issue for executive-legislative sparring over commissions is that of presidential compliance with the *Federal Advisory Committee Act* (FACA). FACA dates to the early 1970s and was put in place by Congress to check the growth in the number of federal advisory panels and reign in the executive role in commission-based inquiries. Among other things, FACA requires that commissions have a clearly articulated mandate, that meetings be made public, that commission actions be duly recorded and communicated, and that commission membership be balanced with respect to differing political perspectives.

Coming as it did in an era when fears of an "imperial presidency" were beginning to manifest, the FACA legislation carried a subtle commentary that presidents could not be trusted to mount inquiries without explicit statutory requirements for openness and accountability.[37] Presidents from both political parties have bristled at these provisions.

Presidents Bill Clinton and George W. Bush prevailed in court when challenged to defend advisory boards they had established that, by their declaration, existed outside of FACA coverage.[38] President Barack Obama moved with great care in December 2012 to create a "task force," led by then Vice President Joseph Biden, to look into the mass school shooting that occurred in Newtown, Connecticut. He went out of his way to stress that his creation was "not some Washington commission," then proceeded to structure an inquiry that, on technical grounds, stayed just beyond the boundaries of FACA.[39]

As with Clinton and Bush before him, Obama was challenged in federal court on his panel's non-compliance with the provisions of the Act.[40] Whatever the legalities of his strategy, his actions in the wake of the shooting made perfectly good political sense. Avoiding FACA permitted him to move much faster and more nimbly than would otherwise have been the case. He was able to get the group up and running without having to go through a formal chartering process. He did not have to worry about including representatives from the gun lobby on the task force. And, when convenient, his delegates to the task force could simply exclude the press from selected committee meetings.[41]

The issue of compliance with FACA surfaced again during the presidency of Donald Trump in the form of a challenge to his *Presidential Advisory Commission on Election Integrity*. Established in May 2017, the panel quickly became enmeshed in the controversy around Trump's claims that widespread fraud had prevented him from winning the popular vote in the 2016 presidential election. One of the Democratic Party representatives on the Commission went public with a complaint that the commission staff was withholding key documents.[42] He eventually filed suit against the commission on that basis. When a federal judge held for the plaintiff on FACA grounds, Trump opted to dissolve the commission rather than comply with the order.[43]

Conclusion

The presidential scholar Harold Laski once observed: "The processes of government are very like an iceberg: what appears on the surface may be but a small part of the reality beneath".[44] Laski's observation is as true of presidential commissions as it is of the larger practice of government in the United States of America. There is more to these curiously small and ad hoc bodies than meets the eye. The external face of a public inquiry can only hint at the amount of activity that takes place before the panel is established and, later, behind the scenes of the investigation.

Presidential commissions must be viewed through a political lens in order to understand these dynamics. The political pressures that swirl around commissions can be frustrating for those on the inside. But they nonetheless add richness to the story of American public inquiries. They also make it likely that scholars will continue to debate the extent to which public inquiries can perform effectively as agents of fact-finding and analysis. Whatever the outcome of that debate, presidential commissions and related types of inquiries are here to stay. They serve a useful role in allowing American leaders to respond when crises and political deadlock give rise to public demands for answers, accountability, and action.

Notes

1 Alexander Hamilton, John Jay, and James Madison, *The Federalist Papers,* Cosimo, New York, 2006, p. 337.

2 Ibid.

3 Loch Johnson, *A Season of Inquiry: Congress and Intelligence,* Dorsey Press, Chicago, IL., 1988; and Frank Smist, *Congress Oversees the United States Intelligence Community: 1947-1989,* University of Tennessee Press, Knoxville, TN, 1990.

4 William R. Divine, "The Second Hoover Commission Reports: An Analysis", *Public Administration Review,* Vol 15, No 4, Autumn 1955, pp. 263-69.

5 Colton Campbell, *Discharging Congress: Government by Commission,* Praeger, Westport, CT, 2002, p. xv.

6 Alan Barth, *Government by Investigation,* Viking Press, New York, 1955, p. 215.

7 *Principles of Federal Appropriations Law,* General Accounting Office, Government Printing Office, Washington, DC, 1991, p. 17-6.

8 Ibid., p. 17-5.

9 *Association of American Physicians and Surgeons v. Clinton,* 997 F.2d 898, D.C. Cir., 1993.

10 The best comparative data on this point comes through the Annual Comprehensive Review conducted by the federal government's Committee Management Secretariat. For the period FY 2010 to FY 2020, the number of presidentially-appointed panels stayed below five percent of the total number of advisory committees tracked by the Secretariat. See *Annual Comprehensive Review,* Committee Management Secretariat, General Services Administration, Washington, DC, available at https://www.facadatabase.gov.

11 Thomas Wolanin, *Presidential Advisory Commissions: Truman to Nixon,* University of Wisconsin Press, Madison, WI, 1975, pp. 7-9; Terrence Tutchings, *Rhetoric and Reality: Presidential Commissions and the Making of Public Policy,* Westview, Boulder, CO, 1979, pp. 11-12; Steven Zink, *Guide to the Presidential Advisory Commissions, 1973-1984,* Chawyck-Healey, Alexandria, VA, 1987, p. xiii; and Amy Zegart, "Blue Ribbons, Black Boxes: Toward a Better Understanding of Presidential Commissions," *Presidential Studies Quarterly,* Vol 34 No 2, June 2004, pp. 369-70.

12 Wolanin, p. 7.

13 Statement on Appointments to the Commission on Roles and Capabilities of the U.S. Intelligence Community, 6 February 1995, *Public Papers of the Presidents, William J. Clinton,* Office of the Federal Register, National Archives and Records Administration, Washington, DC, p. 155.

14 Zegart, p. 369.

15 Michael Perino, *Hellhound of Wall Street: How Ferdinand Pecora's Investigation of the Great Crash Forever Changed American Finance,* Penguin Press, New York, 2010.

16 Fraud Enforcement and Recovery Act of 2009, Pub. L. No. 111-21, 123 Stat. 1616, 2009.

17 Hans Nichols, "Biden Opposes a Presidential Commission for January 6", *Axios,* 3 June 2021.

18 "Pelosi Names Members to Select Committee to Investigate January 6th Attack on the U.S. Capitol" (Press Release), 1 July 2021, Speaker of the US House of Representatives.

19 Remarks by Senator Robert Torricelli, 12 September 2001, US Senate,

Congressional Record, Vol 107, No 118, p. S9312.

20   David Rosenbaum, "Bush Bucks Tradition on Investigation", *New York Times,* 26 May 2002, p. 18.

21   Andrew Jacobs, "Traces of Terror", *New York Times,* 12 June 2002, p. A25.

22   Larry King, Interview with Vice President Richard Cheney, *CNN Transcripts,* 22 May 2002, available at http://www.cnn.com/TRANSCRIPTS/0205/22/lkl.00.html.

23   Kristen Breitweiser, *Wake-Up Call: The Political Education of a 9/11 Widow,* Hachette Books, New York, 2006, pp. 100-37.

24   The bill that eventually made it into law was one of seven legislative proposals to create a board of inquiry to examine the 9-11 attacks. See Kenneth Kitts, *Presidential Commissions and National Security: The Politics of Damage Control,* Lynne Rienner, Boulder, CO, 2006, p. 133.

25   Ibid., pp. 143-150.

26   Mike Allen, "Bush Names Panel on Iraq Data", 8 February 2004, *Washington Post,* p. A1.

27   Commission on the Intelligence Capabilities of the United States Regarding Weapons of Mass Destruction, *Report to the President,* Government Printing Office, Washington, DC, available at http://www.gpo.gov/fdsys/pkg/GPO-WMD.

28   Morris P. Fiorina, "An Era of Divided Government," *Political Science Quarterly,* Vol 107, No 3, Autumn 1992, pp. 387-410.

29   Katherine Schaeffer, "Single-Party Control in Washington is Common at the Beginning of a New Presidency, But Tends Not to Last Long", *Pew Research Center,* 3 February 2021.

30   Reagan's executive order creating a "Special Review Board" to examine the Iran-Contra affair directed all executive departments and agencies to provide, on request, "such information as it may require for purposes of carrying out its functions. See Ronald Reagan, Executive Order 12575, President's Special Review Board Online by Gerhard Peters and John T. Woolley, The American Presidency Project, available at https://www.presidency.ucsb.edu. Even so, six executive branch officers refused to testify on their role in the Iran-Contra scheme, a list that included National Security Council staffer Oliver North and former National Security Advisor John Poindexter. Commission chair John Tower tried several different ways to secure their cooperation but each time was met with resistance. Reagan refused to push the issue. See Kitts, p. 110.

31   The US General Services Administration maintains an online database of advisory committees that operate under the provisions of FACA. A review of those listed as "presidential" in origin reveals that case-specific investigations are the exception rather than the rule. US General Services Administration, Federal Advisory Committee Act Database, https://www.facadatabase.gov.

32   The President's Special Review Board (Iran-Contra) noted the lack of subpoena authority in its final report. Even so, the commissioners maintained that the limitation "did not prevent the Board from assembling sufficient information to form a basis for its fundamental judgments." John Tower, Edmund Muskie, and Brent Scowcroft, The *Tower Commission Report: Full Text of the Report of the President's Special Review Board,* New York Times Edition, Random House, NY, 1987, p. 16.

33   Katherine Shrader, "Latest Panel Foregoes Subpoena Power", *Daily Herald* (Everett, WA), 4 May 2004.

34   Charles Leppert, C. Memo to Max Friedersdorf, 21 January 1975, Folder CIA Investigation, Box 10, Max Friedersdorf Files. Gerald R. Ford Presidential Library, Ann Arbor, MI.

35   Darren Goode, "Senate Panel Approves Creation of Competing Gulf Oil Spill Commission", *The Hill*, 30 June 2010.

36   It can be difficult to enforce compliance with subpoenas, especially given the tight time schedule on which most inquiries operate. Commissions generally are reliant on federal courts to assist when parties are non-compliant. Lance Cole, "Special National Investigative Commissions: Essential Powers and Procedures (Some Lessons from the Pearl Harbor, Warren Commission, and 9/11 Commission Investigations", *McGeorge Law Review*, Vol 41 No 1, 2009, p. 35.

37   Arthur Schlesinger, *The Imperial Presidency*, Houghton-Mifflin, Boston, MA, 1973.

38   Michael Mongan, "Fixing FACA: The Case for Exempting Presidential Advisory Committees from Judicial Review Under the Federal Advisory Committee Act", *Stanford Law Review*, Vol 58 No 3, December 2005, pp. 914-920.

39   Remarks by the President in a Press Conference (Press Release), 19 December 2012, The White House, archived at https://obamawhitehouse.archives.gov.

40   Bill Thompson, B. "Justice Department Fights Suit Filed in Ocala Challenging Obama's Gun Action," *Ocala Star Banner*, 8 March 2013.

41   Remarks by the Vice President at a Meeting with Law Enforcement Leaders (Press Release), 20 December 2012, The White House, archived at https://obamawhitehouse.archives.gov.

42   Secretary Dunlap Files Lawsuit Seeking Access to Elections Commission Correspondence, Information (Press Release), 9 November 2017, State of Maine, Department of the Secretary of State.

43   Josh Gerstein and Matthew Nussbaum, "Trump Disbands Voter Fraud Commission", *Politico*, 3 January 2018.

44   Harold Laski, *The American Presidency: An Interpretation*, Transaction: Piscataway, NJ, 1980, p. 2.

17

Commissions of inquiry in the Nordic countries

Kira Pronin

Introduction: The central role of commissions in Nordic policy-making

In the Nordic countries, commissions of inquiry (also known as ad hoc advisory commissions or state committees) have played an unusually central role in the governmental policy-making process. They have not been reserved only for the most controversial or significant policy issues, or for investigations of political scandals, large scale accidents, and controversial government actions. Instead, they have routinely been appointed to provide policy advice on both ordinary and significant legislative initiatives, administrative changes, and policy reforms. Examples include Swedish commissions investigating social service reform (S 2017:03)[1] and municipal economic equalization (Fi 2008:07).[2] This extensive use of ad hoc commissions in policy preparation has been considered one of the key elements of the Nordic model of government.[3]

Nordic commissions of inquiry are often broadly representative and include academic experts, representatives of interest groups, civil servants, and other types of bureaucrats. Confederations of the main labor unions and employer and industry associations are typically included, as are members of other peak interest groups, as appropriate. Commissions may also contain judges, and other types of professionals such as teachers and doctors. In Sweden, commissions with representatives from all main parliamentary parties (called *parliamentary commissions*) have been especially common. However, governments also appoint expert commissions with only a few civil servants or academic experts. These typically focus on more narrow technocratic or policy implementation issues.

The legal ordinances governing commissions of inquiry in the Nordic countries draw a distinction between large-scale, broadly representative commissions of inquiry and more narrow expert commissions. For example, the Swedish government ordinance regulating commissions (SFS 1998:1474)[4] distinguishes between parliamentary commissions and *special investigator* inquiries. Parliamentary commissions, which are the closest analogue to British royal commissions, consist of a chairperson and several commissioners (normally, politicians from the main parliamentary parties), various types of experts, and representatives of interest groups as well as one or more secretaries. Special investigator inquiries, which are more common, are led by a special investigator (*särskild utredare*), usually a judge or a high-ranking civil servant, supported by one or more experts and secretaries. Furthermore, parliamentary commissions allow for two types of dissent, reservations and dissenting opinions (although reservations can only be entered by commissioners), while special investigator inquiries allow only dissenting opinions. In practice, there are various types of commissions which are a mixture of these two types. For example, some otherwise broadly representative commissions lack parliamentary representation. There can also be an external reference group of parliamentarians attached to the commission or special investigator inquiry.[5] Such external reference groups are purely consultative.

In Finland, before the dissolution of the commission system in 2002, there was the same type of distinction between broad-based policy preparation commissions and special investigators. In Norway, advisory commissions are divided into policy preparation commissions, which provide recommendations on policy, and law-drafting commissions (*lovutvalg*), whose primary task is to draft legislative texts.

Regardless of the institutional differences among the Nordic countries, the procedure to initiate a public inquiry is typically as follows. The government issues a commission directive with the commission's terms of reference and expected time of completion. The appointing ministry then selects the chairperson or a lead investigator and assigns a budget to the commission. The commission then performs its research and deliberates on policy. It may also hold public consultations or consult with interest groups, government agencies, and other relevant parties. When the inquiry is completed, the commission issues a report of its findings and recommendations. In Sweden and Norway, the reports are published in a special report series (SOU in Sweden, NOU in Norway). The report is often sent for one or more rounds of formal public comments by government agencies, interest groups and local government authorities before the government uses the results to draft a bill or take other action based on the findings.

Another distinguishing characteristic of Nordic commissions of inquiry is their interest settlement function. By including interest groups from both sides of a policy issue as well as politicians from the main parliamentary parties, commissions have functioned as a platform for negotiation among organised interests, political parties, and the government. This distinguishes Nordic commissions of inquiry from British commissions, which have been expected to perform their duties in a disinterested manner.[6]

Dating back to the 17th century, commissions of inquiry have played a central role in state building and consolidation of the Nordic states, as well as in the implementation of the welfare state and other large reforms. In Sweden, hardly any major societal change in the 20th century has taken place without their input,[7] and their recommendations have generally passed with only minor modifications.[8] This chapter describes their role in Nordic policymaking, their historical development, and recent trends in their membership composition and appointment.

Nordic governments also appoint commissions of inquiry to investigate large-scale accidents, threats to national security, and controversial historical events. These types of commissions are rare compared with commissions providing policy advice, but their recommendations have also been influential. There are also advisory councils and agencies which began as ad hoc commissions and evolved into permanent or semi-permanent institutions. An example is the Swedish National Council for Nuclear Waste (formerly KASAM), which was established in 1985 to provide independent advice in nuclear policy matters and disposal of radioactive waste. However, the focus in this chapter is on ad hoc commissions advising the government during the policy formulation stage of the legislative process.

The historical development of commissions in the Nordic countries

The prominent role of ad hoc commissions in the Nordic policy-making process has deep historical roots. Starting in the 1660s, the Kingdom of Sweden (which at the time encompassed parts of modern-day Finland and Norway) began to consolidate its administrative structures and set up royal commissions to plan large-scale reforms of the judiciary, the army, schools, and other basic institutions of state.[9] These reforms led to the consolidation of the king's power over the landed nobility and created a political alliance between the king and the landowning peasantry, who were invited to participate in the work of the royal commissions. This participation paved the way for later state-civil society cooperation.[10]

The latter half of the 19th century and the first decades of the 20th century was another time of rapid societal change. Nordic governments again appointed commissions of inquiry in large numbers to address the challenges of modernisation and industrialisation. For example, between 1855 and 1904 the Swedish *Riksdag* and government appointed 531 commissions.[11] It also became common to recruit subject matter experts, such as academics, from outside the state bureaucracy. The recruitment of outside experts allowed for temporary expansion of the state's knowledge capacity.

As commissions increasingly focused on issues relating to social and industrial life, they also began to incorporate workers familiar with labour and factory conditions. By the 1910s, organised labour and capital had gained a prominent position in the formulation of Swedish labour market policy.[12] In Sweden and Finland (an autonomous part of the Russian empire between 1809 and 1917), commissions with parliamentary representation also substituted for parliamentarism before its formal institutionalisation in early 1900s.[13]

As labour unions and industry associations were consolidated into national confederations, the tradition of accommodating different societal interests led to the development of a tripartite policy-making structure involving negotiations between business, labour, and state in matters of labour and industrial policy. Similar arrangements were formed between the state and agricultural interests in agricultural policy. Within this tripartite structure, politicians and parties decided the overall policy goals in collaboration with leaders of main interest groups. The government then appointed commissions of inquiry to conduct policy analysis and to negotiate consensus with the relevant political actors. Interest groups were also represented on the boards of government agencies responsible for policy implementation. Eventually, such corporatist arrangements came to be used in a large number of policy areas such as education, health, and environmental protection, reaching a peak during the 1960s and 1970s.[14] Scholars have described this system of interest intermediation in terms of corporatist exchange, in which the state allowed interest groups influence over the political agenda and political and administrative decisions. In exchange, the government received policy-relevant expertise and political support for their policies.[15]

At the height of Nordic interest group corporatism in the 1960s and 1970s, there could be 100 to 200 commissions operating simultaneously in Sweden, Finland and Denmark in a given year. In Norway, there were 35 policy preparation commissions appointed per year, on average, between 1972 and 2016.[16]

Apart from corporatism and the historical-institutional development of the administrative state in the Nordic countries, the extensive use of policy preparation commissions can be explained by the relatively small size of ministries (in Sweden),[17] and the prevalence of minority governments which has made it necessary to seek consensus across the political aisle.[18] For example, in the politically tumultuous 1920s when there was no stable majority in the Swedish *Riksdag*, Swedish governments used parliamentary commissions to negotiate agreement with the opposition parties to avoid legislative gridlock.[19] In study of commissions in Norway and Denmark between 1971 and 2017, scholars found that minority and coalition governments have been more likely to appoint commissions than majority governments.[20] Swedish governments have also been more likely to appoint broadly representative commissions when parliamentary parties have been ideologically polarised.[21]

For the most part, Nordic commissions of inquiry have been regarded as successful both in terms of the quality of their recommendations and their influence on policy. They have also been regarded as a key contributor to the rational and consensual Nordic policy-making style.[22] As far as the mechanisms behind their success, scholars have argued that commissions with representatives from opposition parties are better at solving policy problems and provide an opportunity for political negotiation at the early stages of the policy process. This prevents conflict during the later stages of the legislative process. The inclusion of experts recognised by all parties also helps establish a common understanding of the policy issue[23], and the involvement of organized interests generates support and legitimacy for state policy and induces interest organisations to moderate their demands.[24]

The critics of Nordic commissions of inquiry, on the other hand, have characterised them as slow, ineffective, and being prone to making costly or unrealistic policy recommendations.[25] These concerns have led to several administrative changes, such as limiting inquiry lengths and requiring commissions to provide budget calculations for their recommendations. For example, in 1982, the Swedish Government restricted inquiry length to two years. A study by the Swedish National Audit Agency (*Riksrevisionen*) shows that between 1982 and 1995, the average duration of inquiries decreased from 4 years to 1 year; in 2002, the average duration was one year and 8 months.

Recent trends

Recent studies of Nordic commissions document an overall decline in the number of large, broadly representative commissions, and divergent trends in their overall membership composition and other characteristics.

In a sample of 2,087 Swedish commissions and special investigator inquiries between 1990 and 2016, the share of broadly representative parliamentary commissions decreased from 19.7 to 2.9% from 1990 to 2016, and the share of less representative special investigator inquiries increased from 70.9 to 92.9%.[26] (recall that there are hybrid types of commissions and inquiries, which account for the remaining percentage). To put these numbers in context, the share of parliamentary commissions hovered around 50% for the first half of the 20th century and for several decades after World War Two[27]. Since the 1980s, parliamentary commissions have become less common, but their share of public inquiries remained above 20% through the 1980s.[28]

During the same time period, the share of bureaucrats (in particular, civil servants employed by ministries) increased from 49.7 to 60 %. By contrast, the share of politicians decreased from 11.4% to less than 2%, and the share of academics from 8.4 to 5.1%. The share of interest groups remained relatively stable at around 6% of the overall membership.

The data do not show statistically significant trends in the shares of different types of interest groups. Overall, the largest category are NGOs ranging from large pensioners' organisations to small organisations representing religious and ethnic minorities (24.67% of all interest groups in new public inquiry appointments between 1990 and 2016 in the study sample). The single most frequent interest group is the Swedish Association of Local Authorities and Regions (SALAR) (24.04% of all interest groups), followed by employer and industry organizations such as the Confederation of Swedish Enterprise (16.92%), professional associations such as the Swedish Medical Association (14.94%), and the three main confederations of Swedish labour unions (LO, TCO, and SACO) (14.49%).

The decreasing share of politicians has meant that there are fewer reservations and dissenting opinions in commission reports, as politicians are most likely to dissent. In 1990, 25.6% of inquiries had at least one reservation, and 42.2 % least one dissenting opinion. In 2016, these numbers were 5.5% and 27.5%. The decline may indicate a diminishing use of commissions for conflict resolution and suggests that Swedish governments may have increased their political control over public inquiries.

In a sample of 1,530 Norwegian policy preparation commissions appointed between 1972 and 2016, the yearly number of commissions decreased from 44 to 17 from 1972 to 2020.[29] However, in contrast to trends in the membership composition of Swedish commissions, the share of academics increased from 7% in the 1970s to 26% in 2010s, and the share of civil servants decreased from between 40% and 50%

in the 1970s–1990s to around 30% in the 2000s and 2010s. The share of interest groups shows a more mixed picture, with a decrease during the general decline of democratic corporatism from 1980s onwards, and an increase during the resurgence of stakeholder participation in the 2010s. These numbers may reflect an increased reliance on experts in the policy formulation process.

In a sample of Danish policy preparation commissions between 1965 and 2005, there is a similar downward trend. In 1965, there were 298 commissions, 311 in 1975, 168 in 1985, 79 in 1990, 85 in 1995, 90 in 2000, and 45 in 2005.[30] In 1980, Danish interest organisations were represented in 70% of the commissions; in 2005 the corresponding figure was 87%. Another sample shows a drop of 27% in the number of policy preparation and implementation commissions with interest group representation between 1975 (considered the height of Danish group corporatism) and 2010 (from 374 to 273). Moreover, in 2010, only three of the committees were tasked with policy preparation, while the rest were devoted to policy implementation or other tasks[31] (recall that Nordic commissions range from broadly representative commissions investigating and deliberating particularly controversial or significant policy topics to ones performing more mundane and routine tasks).

The most dramatic change in the use of commissions has occurred in Finland, however. In the 1960s and 1970s, there were around 100-200 ad hoc commissions each year, in addition to several permanent commissions. Starting in the 1980s and 1990s, policy preparation was increasingly delegated to ministerial staff, broad-based working groups, and special investigators appointed by ministries.[32] In 2002, after commissions had largely fallen into disuse for a decade, a government decree abolished the commission system (A 1040/2002). Another development particularly peculiar to Finland has been the increasing use of consulting firms for policy preparation, a development which critics have dubbed "consultant democracy".[33]

Causes and consequences of recent changes to Nordic commissions of inquiry

What has caused the decline of the traditional, broadly representative commissions of inquiry in the Nordic countries? Many scholars have pointed to the overall decline of interest group corporatism since the 1980s as a contributing factor.[34] These arguments center on the fact that the base of the corporatist exchange between the state and peak interest groups has weakened since the height of democratic corporatism in the 1960s and 1970s. In particular, peak interest groups no longer control the resources which made them attractive negotiation partners, such as their ability to deliver political support of a large number of constituents. On the other hand, increased budget constraints have forced governments to contract existing welfare programs, and it has become more difficult to use economic distribution as a bargaining chip to gain support for policy.

Governments are also more limited in the policy concessions they can make because of increased Europeanisation of policy-making following Sweden's, Finland's and Denmark's accession to the European Union (EU). There has also been an overall trend of interest groups shifting towards lobbying elected representatives directly,[35] and the emergence of new participatory mechanisms and informal networks within the government.[36] These developments have shifted focus of policy influence away from commissions of inquiry towards other avenues. The decline of interest group corporatism has not proceeded at the same pace in all the Nordic countries, however, and in the case of Denmark, corporatist arrangements are still common.

In the case of Finland, another factor that led to the abolishment of the commission system were increasing complaints that commissions were slow and ineffective. At the same time, new, more flexible types of policy preparation venues such as working groups also emerged. Political leaders and ministries also wished to increase their control over policy preparation and its results, and the relative autonomy of the commissions had become a problem for the increasingly strong government.[37]

Some political commentators have argued that the decline in broadly representative commissions has reduced the quality of policy preparation. These claims frequently surface in newspaper editorials and opinion pieces, but have not been formally investigated.

What is perhaps clearer is that the reduced use of commissions with representatives from the major political parties has diminished the government's ability to identify and resolve dissent at the early stages of the policy formulation process. Reservations and dissenting opinions in commission reports grow out of fundamental differences in outlook and should be expected in a properly functioning democracy.[38] Therefore, the exclusion of potential dissenting voices from the early stages of the policy formulating process is problematic. At the least, it means that political conflicts are not resolved at the early stages of the legislative process and are instead postponed to later stages of the legislative process when party positions have already hardened.

This may increase legislative gridlock and reduce policy stability. These problems may be exacerbated by the expansion in the number of parties in the Nordic party systems. The current party system in Sweden, for example, includes eight parties, up from five before 1988, and the party system is also one of the most fragmented in Western Europe.[39] The shift to more informal policy networks from the more predictable, well-structured and transparent commission process may also diminish policy legitimacy and the democratic quality of governmental policy-making in the long run.[40]

The 2016 welfare inquiry (Fi 2015:01) appointed by the Löfven I red-green cabinet in Sweden is a good example of potential consequences of excluding dissenting voices from the early stages of the policy formulation process. The purpose of the inquiry was to recommend a new regulatory framework for public financing of privately performed health and welfare services. Previous inquiries in the same policy area had almost invariably been sent to broadly representative parliamentary commissions with academic experts and representative from both the public health sector and private industry. The policy issue was highly contentious and significant---changes to the regulatory framework would affect not only regional and municipal health care services but also ordinary Swedish citizens and the 4,500 health care businesses providing services through the existing framework.

Despite these considerations, the Löfven I cabinet appointed a municipal commissioner, Ilmar Reepalu, as a special investigator to lead the inquiry. He was assisted by seventeen experts from various ministries and governmental agencies, three subject matter specialists from the Ministry of Finance, and one representative from the Swedish Association of Local Authorities and Regions. The inquiry had two external reference groups representing the education and health care sectors, but these did not participate in the decision-making or in drafting the report, nor were any politicians from the parliamentary parties or academic researchers included in the inquiry.

The inquiry published its interim report in November 2016 and its final report in May 2017. Neither contained any dissenting opinions. The interim report concluded that private providers of public health care services had excessive profit margins and recommended a profit margin cap of 7% plus the current government interest rate. The report received immediate criticism from the opposition parties, policy researchers, governmental agencies, and the health care industry. The opposition parties accused the special investigator of having an ideological predisposition against privately provided health services. The Swedish Democrats disagreed with the proposal in general, while the centre-right alliance of the Centre Party, the Moderates, the Christian Democrats, and the Liberals was prepared to agree with the general framework, but only if the requirement for the profit margin cap was dropped. Various experts from the academe, the Stockholm

District Court, and the National Audit Office argued that the special investigator had failed to assess the potential consequences of the profit margin cap and to ensure that the proposed framework was consistent with existing Swedish and EU regulations. In a debate article published in *Svenska Dagbladet*, a representative of the Confederation of Swedish Enterprise, an employers' organisation representing 60,000 private companies with more than 1.6 million employees, argued that the new profit margin cap would bankrupt many small for-profit businesses providing health and welfare services. In another newspaper article, a representative of the Association of Private Care Providers, an association for 2,000 companies providing private care services in Sweden, called the inquiry "a fiasco". Eventually, the government implemented a different policy, which incorporated some of the criticisms received by the inquiry.

The future of commissions in the new policy environment

What is the future of Nordic commissions of inquiry? Will they ever be as strong as they were at the peak of interest group corporatism in the 1960s and 1970s, or are they an institution that belongs to the past? What is their potential in the current political and economic environment, and what are some challenges that future governments wishing to use commissions for policy preparation will likely face?

Commissions of inquiry have several advantages that speak for their continued use, at least in the Nordic context.

First, they have a long pedigree in producing high quality policy recommendations on a wide variety of policy issues in vastly different political contexts. Second, interest groups still widely perceive them as a legitimate and important policy-making institution.[41] Third, their ability to build consensus across the political aisle is remarkable: considering that Swedish parliamentary commissions have representatives from all major parliamentary parties, 43% of commission reports contain no reservations or dissenting opinions.[42] Fourth, the present political environment in many democracies resembles the politically turbulent period of the 1920s, which was characterised by political polarisation, political extremism, and high economic inequality.[43] During this time, Swedish minority governments (which had extremely low levels of parliamentary support) successfully used parliamentary commissions to get different political parties to agree on policy and to avoid gridlock. Fifth, both formal and informal procedures surrounding commission appointments, membership composition, and output are firmly established and transparent from the public's point of view, which is important for policy legitimacy.

On the other hand, several political and economic developments in recent decades present challenges for governments wishing to use commissions as a platform for negotiating agreement. First, it is possible that effective use of commissions presupposes a highly organised interest group structure and a policy environment where most policy issues can be reduced to a single left-right economic dimension. If there are too many political parties with platforms scattered across multiple dimensions, bargaining in commissions may lead to policy instability (due to McKelvey's famous result),[44] or simply be unworkable. Historically, party competition in the Nordic countries has been structured on the economic left-right dimension[45], and new dimensions, such as European integration, have generally been absorbed into the left–right dimension. However, in the last decade there has been an emergence of new dimensions of conflict over immigration and multicultural values. These dimensions may not be reducible to a left-right economic dimension or lend themselves to easy compromises. The Europeanisation and globalisation of policy-making and the ever-shrinking public budgets present another challenge to commissions of inquiry, which have historically focused on economic redistribution.

Recall also that from early 1930s to the 1980s, perhaps the golden age for Nordic commissions of inquiry, Nordic policy-making system was characterized by two equally matched powers: a strong administrative state and highly organised and centralised interest group structure. During this time, virtually all social interests of any significance were organized into local, regional, and national associations, and the most important interests (labor and industry) were organised into national confederations representing a majority of the labor force and industries.[46] Politicians and parties decided the overall policy goals in collaboration with leaders of main interest groups. The government then appointed commissions of inquiry to conduct policy analysis and to seek consensus on policy with the relevant political actors. In other words, there was a more limited number of policy actors, and peak interest groups were both more hierarchically organised and encompassed a much larger share of population than today. While the system of commissions of inquiry in the Nordic countries does show signs of adapting to an environment with a proliferation of new types of interest groups and a less hierarchical interest group structure, the sheer number and diversity of policy actors may pose a problem for negotiating agreement.

Finally, new technologies have opened up emerging avenues of accessing and disseminating policy expertise, which did not exist during the peak of Nordic corporatism. The information-gathering function of traditional Nordic commissions with significant academic representation may therefore be replaced by new types of policy preparation. However, the interest negotiation function of commissions still holds promise for the future, despite the present-day challenges.

Notes

1 https://lagen.nu/sou/2018:32 (Commission report)
2 https://lagen.nu/sou/2011:39 (Commission report)
3 David Arter, *Scandinavian Politics Today*, 2nd ed., Manchester University Press, New York, 2008.
4 https://www.riksdagen.se/sv/dokument-lagar/dokument/svensk-forfat-tningssamling/kommitteforordning-19981474_sfs-1998-1474

5   Carl Dahlström, Erik Lundberg and Kira Pronin, "No More Compromise? Swedish Commissions of Inquiry, 1990-2016", *Scandinavian Political Studies*, Vol 44, 2021, pp. 416-40.

6   Rune Premfors, "Governmental Commissions in Sweden", *American Behavioral Scientist*, Vol 26, 1983, pp. 623-642.

7   Lars Trägårdh, "Democratic Governance and The Creation of Social Capital in Sweden: The Discreet Charm of the Governmental Commission", in *State and Civil Society in Northern Europe*, Berghahn Books, New York/Oxford, 2007, pp. 254-70.

8   Jörgen Hermansson, *Politik som intressekamp* [Politics as Conflict of Interests], Norstedts, Stockholm, 1993, pp. 663.

9   Gunnar Hesslén, *Det svenska kommittéväsendet intill år 1905: dess uppkomst, ställning och betydelse [The Swedish Commission System until year 1905: Its Origins, Position, and Importance]*, Uppsala, 1927; Kaarlo Tuori, *Suomen komitealaitos* [The Finnish Commission System], Valtiovarainministeriön järjestelyosasto, 1976, pp. 191-203,318-219; Johanna Rainio-Niemi, "State Committees in Finland in a Comparative Perspective", in Risto Alapuro and Henrik Stenius (eds), *Nordic Associations in a European Perspective*, Connor Court Publishing, 2010, pp. 241–69.

10   Rainio-Niemi, 2010.

11   Hesslén, 1927.

12   Rainio-Niemi, 2010.

13   Hans Meijer, *Kommittépolitik och kommittéarbetet: det statliga kommittéväsendets utvecklingslinjer 1905-1954 samt nuvarande funktion och arbetsformer* [Commission Politics and Commission Work: Development of the Governmental Commission System 1905-1954 and Its Current Function and Working Methods], Gleerup, 1956; Tuori, 1976.

14   Leif Lewin, "Majoritarian and Consensus Democracy: The Swedish Experience," *Scandinavian Political Studies*, Vol 21, 1998, pp. 195-206; Peter Munk Christiansen, Asbjørn Sonne Nørgaard, Hilmar Rommetwedt, Torsten Svensson, Gunnar Thesen, and PerOla Ola Öberg, "Varieties of Democracy: Interest Groups and Corporatist Committees in Scandinavian Policy Making", *Voluntas*, Vol 21, 2010, pp. 22-40.

15   Anne Skorkjær Binderkrantz and Peter Munk Christiansen, "From Classic to Modern Corporatism: Interest Group Representation in Danish Public Committees in 1975 and 2010", *Journal of European Public Policy*, Vol 22, 2015, pp. 1022–39.

16   Johan Christensen and Stine Hesstvedt, "Expertisation or Greater Representation? Evidence from Norwegian Advisory Commissions," *European Politics and Society*, Vol 20, 2019, 83-100.

17   Premfors, 1983.

18   Johannes Lindvall, Hanna Bäck, Carl Dahlström, Elin Naurin and Jan Teorell, "Sweden's Parliamentary Democracy at 100", *Parliamentary Affairs*, Vol 73, 2020.

19   Herbert Tingsten, "Problemi svensk demokrati I: Vår parlamentarism" [Problems in the Swedish Democracy I: Our Parliamentarianism], *Tiden*, Vol 32, 1940, pp. 25-32; Meijer, 1956; Kent Zetterberg, "Det statliga kommittéväsendet" [The Governmental Commission System] in *Att Styra Riket*, Allmänna förlaget, Stockholm, 1990.

20 Stine Hesstvedt and Peter Munck Christiansen, "The Politics of Policy Inquiry Commissions: Denmark and Norway, 1971-2017", *West European Politics*, Vol 45, 2022, pp. 430-54.

21 Kira Pronin, *A Voice without a Veto: Consensus-building through Inclusion of Stakeholders*, Ph.D. thesis, University of Pittsburgh, 2020.

22 Olof Petersson, "Rational Politics: Commissions of Inquiry and the Referral System in Sweden", in Jon Pierre, (ed), *Oxford Handbook of Swedish Politics*, Oxford University Press, 2016, pp. 650-62.

23 Lindvall, Bäck, Dahlström, Naurin, Teorell, "Sweden's Parliamentary Democracy at 100".

24 PerOla Öberg, Peter Munk Christiansen, Asbjørn Sonne Nørgaard, Hilmar Rommetvedt, Gunnar Thesen, Torsten Svensson, "Disrupted Exchange and Declining Corporatism: Government Authority and Interest Group Capability in Scandinavia", *Government and Opposition*, Vol 46, 2011, pp. 365-91.

25 Jens Blom-Hansen, "Still Corporatism in Scandinavia? A Survey of Recent Empirical Findings", *Scandinavian Political Studies*, Vol 23, 2000, pp. 157-81.

26 Dahlström, Lundberg, Pronin, 2021.

27 Hans Meijer, "Bureaucracy and Policy Formulation in Sweden", *Scandinavian Political Studies*, Vol 4, 1969, pp. 103-16; Petersson, 2016.

28 Jan Johansson, *Det statliga kommittéväsendet: kunnskap, kontroll, konsensus* [The Governmental Commission System: Knowledge, Control, Consensus], Ph.D. thesis, University of Stockholm, 1992; Petersson, ibid.

29 Christensen Hesstvedt, "Expertisation or Greater Representation? Evidence from Norwegian Advisory Commissions".

30 Christiansen, Nørgaard, Rommetvedt, Svensson, Thesen, Öberg, 2010.

31 Binderkrantz, Christiansen, 2015.

32 Voitto Helander and Jan Johansson, *Det statliga kommittepväsendet. En jämförelse mellan Sverige och Finland. Meddelanden från ekonomisk-statsvetenskapliga fakulteten vid Åbo Akademi.* [The Governmental Commission System: A Comparison between Sweden and Finland. Proceedings from the Faculty of Economics and Political Science at Åbo Akademi], *Vol A:490*, Åbo Akademi, Turku, 1998; Anna Maria Holli and Saara Turkka, "The Changing role of science in corporatist policy advice. A Longitudinal Study of the Inclusion of Researchers in Finnish Policy Preparatory Working Groups in 1980-2018", *Politiikka*, Vol 63, 2021, pp. 101-22.

33 Hanna Kuusela and Matti Ylönen, *Konsulttidemokratia: Miten valtiosta tehdään tyhmä ja tehoton* [Consultancy Democracy: How to Make the State Dumb and Ineffective], Gaudeamus, Helsinki, 2013.

34 Öberg, Christiansen, Nørgaard, Rommetvedt, Thesen, Svensson, 2011.

35 Hilmar Rommetvedt, Gunnar Thesen, Peter Munk Christiansen and Asbjørn Sonne Nørgaard, "Coping with Corporatism in Decline and the Revival of Parliament: Interest Group Lobbyism in Denmark and Norway, 1980-2005", *Comparative Political Studies*, Vol 46, 2012, pp. 457-85.

36 Erik Hysing and Erik Lundberg, "Making Governance Networks More Democratic: Lessons from the Swedish Governmental Commissions", *Critical Policy Studies*, Vol 10, 2016, pp. 21-38.

37 Anna Maria Holli and Saara Turkka, 2021.

38 Harold F. Gosnell, "British Royal Commissions of inquiry", *Political Science Quarterly*, Vol 49, No 1, 1934, pp. 84-118.

39 Lindvall, Bäck, Dahlström, Naurin, Teorell, "Sweden's Parliamentary Democracy at 100".

40 Hysing, Lundberg, 2016.

41 Erik Lundberg, "Injured but Not Yet Dead: A Bottom-Up Perspective on the Swedish Governmental Commissions", *International Journal of Public Administration*, Vol 38, 2015, pp. 346-54.

42 Petersson, 2016.

43 Johannes Lindvall, Hanna Bäck, Carl Dahlström, Elin Naurin and Jan Teorell, *Samverkan och strid i den parlamentariska demokratin* [Cooperation and Conflict in Parliamentary Democracy], SNS Förlag, Stockholm, 2017.

44 Richard D. McKelvey, "Intransitivities in Multidimensional Voting Models and Some Implications for Agenda Control", *Journal of Economic Theory*, Vol 12, 1976, pp. 472–82.

45 Lindvall, Bäck, Dahlström, Naurin, Teorell, "Sweden's Parliamentary Democracy at 100".

46 Thomas J. Anton, "Policy-Making and Political Culture in Sweden", *Scandinavian Political Studies*, Vol 4, 1969, pp. 88-102.

Section 5: Conclusion: Where to next for public inquiries?

18

So where to next for public inquiries?

Scott Prasser

Introduction

This volume has highlighted the continuing roles and importance of the public inquiry instrument, as defined in **Chapter 1**, in performing a variety of functions across different Australian and international jurisdictions. Key issues concerning public inquiries have been covered: their historical roots; reasons for appointment; processes; collection of evidence; powers; legislative backing; effectiveness; impacts; and their limitations. In addition, the other issues addressed in this volume concerned whether inquiries are being used differently than previously, whether they are still needed, and by whom.

So, what are the conclusions from this volume about public inquiries?

Some key lessons

Public inquiries are distinct from other permanent policy advisory and investigatory mechanisms

First, public inquiries have a distinct recognisable, organisational form across all the jurisdictions and examples covered in this volume. Indeed, there is considerable congruence across jurisdictions as to what is accepted as a public inquiry. They are temporary, ad hoc bodies, with members mostly from outside government and which operate in the public arena in their collection of evidence and reporting arrangements. Public inquiries are distinguishable from other more permanent advisory bodies such as government departments and the more narrowly focussed permanent expert policy advisory bodies.[1] They are also quite distinctive from the partisan ministerial staff whose numbers have grown dramatically across most countries, especially in Australia.[2] They are also different from the permanent anti-corruption bodies that have developed across all Australian States and Territories since the 1980s following numerous royal commissions into scandals and corruption.[3] Although these bodies have similar powers to a royal commission (as do other bodies like the ombudsman), and are often referred to by their proponents as "permanent royal commission"[4] they have been assessed to be different and in several ways inferior to ad hoc, inquisitorial royal commissions.[5]

Public inquiries keep being appointed

Second, this volume highlights that despite the development of other advisory institutions close to and around executive government, public inquiries continue to be appointed in considerable numbers. **Chapter 1** explains this in the Australian historical context, but it is largely a feature across all the jurisdictions. In the United Kingdom (UK) (**Chapter 14**) there has been a flourish of inquiry activity especially since the new legislation, the *Inquiries Act 2005*, was passed. This has clarified their powers, roles and relationship to executive government. While there has been a moderation in royal commission numbers in New Zealand, they are still being appointed for major national issues along with a host of other inquiries now covered by new legislation (**Chapter 15**). Across the Nordic countries there has been a slight decline in numbers, but inquiries keep being appointed and are predicted to continue to be used in the future (**Chapter 17**).

Public inquiries have become an accepted and durable part of modern government

Third, public inquiries although temporary, ad hoc bodies and often lacking any formal constitutional standing have become a durable part of the architecture of modern government. The repeated public demand for public inquiries, and governments ready agreement, reinforces this sense of durability. Public inquiries have become an accepted part of government. Once overlooked in studies of policy advisory systems they are now recognised as being an integral part of the advisory system. This is being reinforced in some Australian jurisdictions like Victoria and soon South Australia as in Canada and New Zealand (**Chapter 15**) where all forms of public inquiries, not just royal commissions, are now being covered by legislation (**Chapter 4**). This reflects the recognition of public inquiries as a distinct and durable part of government. The studies in this volume highlight this. When there is a public scandal or a calamitous event, appoint a public inquiry to investigate. When there is a new policy issue to address, establish an inquiry to obtain advice. When some program or agency is in need for renovation (or abolition) governments so often turn to a public inquiry to conduct the review. When there is a pressing political problem the default position is to appoint an inquiry. Over and over only a public inquiry will do both for the government that appoints them and for the public who demand them. This is despite, as we are reminded in **Chapter 13,** that there are many existing institutions, like auditors-general, anti-corruption bodies, ombudsmen and think-tanks with the competence, and in some cases the same powers, to conduct such reviews.

Public inquiries have traits that make them unique and indispensable in modern government

Fourth, such proliferation in inquiry numbers and their durability, begs the question – why is this so? What do public inquiries bring to the advisory table that executive government finds so attractive and –

just as importantly – the public so often wants?

The chapters and examples in this volume provide several explanations.

Their bespoke nature means their form can be tailored by executive government to suit the task required. In the many examples discussed, public inquiries operate in a wide range of guises – some are statutory based with coercive powers, others are not. Some have just a single member, others employ panels and reference groups involving key stakeholders that assist in negotiating acceptable solutions. Some adopt formal public hearings and use coercive powers to enforce participation and to procure information. Others operate more informally, sometimes using innovative means to engage with interest groups and the general public. Some employ extensive research staff and pioneer new methodologies that expose corruption in high places or bring together analysis that makes the case for policy reform overwhelming.

Further, because public inquiries are often chaired by experts, recognised leaders in their field, and current or former members of the judiciary,[6] they carry considerable prestige. This, combined with their very temporary roles, allows them to cut through organisational and political barriers, protocols and sensitivities that more permanent institutions and staff cannot easily do.

Furthermore, as public inquiries are discrete, separate bodies with clear terms of reference and a specific focus, they can avoid the day-to-day distractions that afflict ministers, their staff, and the public service, from what has been described by one senior Commonwealth official as the "tyranny of the current"[7] (see **Chapters 3** and **10**).

The open processes of inquiries and the way they collect and release evidence (**Chapters 4** and **5**), their public consultation processes, what has been described as their 'publicness', stands in stark contrast to the way many perceive, rightly or wrongly, how politics and policy are done these days – an insiders' game for elites.[8] In other words, public inquiries are seen as being independent from executive government, even though appointed by executive government.

In short, all these characteristics make public inquiries a unique institution of government and thus an 'institution of last resort' which governments so often turn to and which the public demand.

Inquiries have impacts – but it is not as straightforward as some think

Fifth, inquiries, contrary to the cliche that they are "generally appointed, not so much for digging up the truth but for digging it in"[9] can have impacts that promote needed policy adjustments and institutional renewal. The issue, as highlighted in several of the chapters is how are impacts gauged and measured and over what time period (**Chapters 9-13**). Sometimes impact is immediate and direct. At other times, as seen with many of the royal commissions appointed by the Bruce-Page Government during the 1920s, implementation was a slow process with many other factors other than government indolence to blame for delays (**Chapter 2**). So often, inquiries, separate and independent from government have been able to market test and promote new ideas, without the debate being closed down. Taxation, welfare and other reforms have been assisted by the fresh insights, clear evidence and sound arguments which public inquiries so often bring to the public arena (**Chapters 3, 5, 10**). International experiences tell the same story (**Chapters 14-17**).

Public inquiries are not without flaws

Sixth, although an increasingly accepted and durable part of the political system, public inquiries are not without their flaws. Across the examples in this volume there is an echo of common complaints. Some inquiries are too slow, costly, adversarial, and legalistic (**Chapters 6 and 14**). Others misread their roles as being advocates for a particular policy or group rather than clarifying the facts and proposing workable solutions (**Chapter 11**). Some lack the expertise to provide the advice government needs or to sort out complex technical issues (**Chapters 6** and **13**). Inquiries may produce reports that are regarded as being of poor quality and vacuous (**Chapter 7**). Certain types of inquiries, like royal commissions can too often get bogged down in legalistic and adversarial processes undermining their effectiveness (**Chapters 10** and **14**). For other inquiries their very independence, prestige and distance from the areas they are reviewing make their recommendations "directed to the macro level of policy" thus missing the nuances of on-the-ground service delivery issues (**Chapter 12**). And yes, some inquiries are appointed for politically expedient reasons to justify government decisions already made (**Chapter 8**).

Do we still need public inquiries?

Yehezkel Dror, the famous political scientist, once wrote that rulers needed advice that was close enough to be heard, expert enough to have real insights into complex problems, but was also practical, strategic and independent. It was important for advisory bodies not to get lost in administrative detail, nor the immediate crises confronting a government, nor be embroiled in partisan wars.[10] This is a difficult set of criteria to meet. Dror focussed almost wholly on internal advisory processes and overlooked the value of the external public inquiry instrument. Several contributors to this volume too, have shown how some of the public inquiries they studied have been overlooked as being an important part of the policy advisory system.

That is now changing. Craft and Halligan in their international survey concluded that although permanent advisory systems are becoming more complex and sophisticated:

> ... the use of 'independent' inquiries will remain popular because they are flexible and short-term, satisfy expectations about cross-boundary collaboration, allow outsiders to be inserted and (depending on how they are constituted) are politically controllable.[11]

Their latter point is perhaps contestable, because public inquiries, as discussed in this volume and elsewhere, can often go their own way regardless of the constraints governments have sought to impose, including restricted terms of reference, tight reporting timeframes, limited resources, and specially selected members.

The issue today, is that public inquiries, despite their limitations as discussed in this volume, should no longer be seen as just some loose appendage of government. Rather, because of a host of other factors and trends it is harder for governments to gain any agreement on even minor overdue reforms, and to have legislation passed.[12] Consequently, it is no longer an issue of whether governments should appoint an inquiry, but whether they can afford not to, given their potential to overcome public distrust and to promote support for policy change. Furthermore, the criticism about the lack of implementation of inquiry recommendations is being increasingly challenged by new research (including by some of the contributors to this volume as noted above – see **Chapter 9**).[13]

Conclusions

The challenge for governments, especially in Westminster systems, is how to better integrate ad hoc public inquiries into the policy process so that their use is less sporadic, and their findings have more opportunities to be absorbed into a government's organisational memory.[14] This might allow more effective policy learning, moderate the repeated use of inquiries often within short timeframes into the same issues, and lead to more timely policy changes.[15]

John Dawkins when Australian Federal Minister for Finance in the Hawke Labor Government, was frustrated with the daily grind of politics and the reactive nature of so much policy development with its hit and miss approach of seeking the latest research to tackle current and long-term problems. He thought that public inquiries could overcome some of these issues if they were better integrated into the normal routines of government policy development:

> What we need to be able to do is to work out means whereby the results of policy analysis can be better integrated and made use of in the critical policy formulation processes of government. We must be able to find ways of fully and properly taking account of, for example, the work and reports of committees and commissions of inquiry that are too often used not as a means of solving a difficult policy issue but of putting it off.[16]

No Australian government, however, has attempted to use public inquiries in such a strategic way. Instead, they have continued to be appointed mostly as ad hoc responses to meet urgent problems. While Labor Prime Minister Gough Whitlam (1972-75) (**Chapter 1**) sought to provide a comprehensive rationale for his government's increase in public inquiry numbers much of this was more post hoc justification than any grand plan. Moreover, the appointment of so many inquiries with their externally recruited members reflected other motives such as being seen to "do something" and perhaps also finding roles for Labor supporters and sympathisers. Subsequent governments have done little to place or define more clearly the role of public inquiries. They remain an ad hoc affair – as unpredictable in their appointment as they are in the quality of their reports. Nevertheless, no modern government can now do without them. They fill too many gaps in the existing institutional arrangements and they meet too many growing public expectations, to be discarded in the future. Indeed, if trust in government and fragmentation in the modern body politic continues, then public inquiries will continue to be in demand into the future. They will be both wanted, and, it seems, increasingly needed.

Notes

1   Jenny Stewart and Scott Prasser, "Expert policy advisory bodies", in Brian Head and Kate Crowley, (eds), *Policy Analysis in Australia*, Policy Press, Bristol, 2015, pp. 151-66. In Australia, the federal Productivity Commission is an example of an EPAB. In Canada the Economic Advisory Council is another.

2   For an international overview see: Richard Shaw and Chris Eichbaum, (eds), *Ministers, Minders and Mandarins*, Edgar Elgar, Cheltenham, 2018; For the Australian scene see Maria Maley, "Understanding the divergent development of the ministerial office in Australia and the UK", *Australian Journal of Political Science*, Vol 53, No 3, 2018, pp. 320-35.

3   Rod Tiffen, *Scandals: Media, Politics and Corruption in Contemporary Australia*, UNSW Press, Sydney, 1999.

4   Gary Sturgess, "Corruption – Evolution of an Idea", in Scott Prasser, Rae Wear and JR Nethercote, (eds), *Corruption and Reform: The Fitzgerald Vision*, University of Queensland Press, St Lucia, 1990, pp. 19-20.

5   See ABC RMIT Fact Check, 10 February 20211 – see www.abc.net.au/fact-check.

6   In Australia sitting members of the judiciary are now generally unwilling to join public inquiries – see Scott Prasser, *Royal Commissions and Public Inquiries in Australia*, 2nd ed, Lexis Nexis, Chatswood, 2021, pp. 117-20, however this is not the case in the UK (see Chapter 14).

7   Peter Varghese, "Reflections of a most fortunate life", Address to Institute of Public Administration, (ACT Division), 9 June 2016 (retiring Secretary, Commonwealth Department of Foreign Affairs and Trade).

8   Gerry Stoker, *Why Politics Matters: Making Democracy Work*, 2nd ed, Palgrave, London, 2017, see pp. 7-15.

9   Alan P. Herbert, *Anything But Action?" A study of the uses and abuses of committees of inquiry*, Institute of Economic Affairs, London, 1960, p. 17.

10   Yehezkel Dror, "Policy analysis for advising rulers", in Rolfe Tomlinson and Istvan Kiss, (eds), *Research and System Analysis*, Pergamon, Oxford, 1984, pp. 79-123.

11   Jonathan Craft and John Halligan, *Advising Governments in the Westminster Tradition*, Cambridge University Press, Cambridge, 2020, p. 207.

12   See Ian Marsh, "Why politicians can't sell big reforms anymore", *Australian Financial Review*, 28 May 2014; Tom Dusevic, "Political paralysis endangers prosperity", *The Australian*, 20 July 2021.

13   Alastair Stark, (see also Chapter 9), has an Australian Research Council (ARC) Discovery Project for assessing the impact of Commonwealth royal commissions from 2000 through to 2018.

14   Alastair Stark, "Explaining institutional amnesia in government", *Governance*, Vol 32, 2019, pp. 143-58.

15   It has been estimated that between 1979 to 2008 there had been 101 public and parliamentary inquiries into teacher education – with little impact – see Bill Louden, "'101 Damnations': The persistence of criticism and absence of evidence about teacher education in Australia", *Teachers and Teaching: Theory and Practice*, Vol 14, No 4, 2008, pp. 357-68.

16   John Dawkins, Finance Minister, "Reforms in the Canberra System of Public Administration", Sir Robert Garran Oration, 15 November 1984, reported in *Commonwealth Record*, 12-18 November 1984, p. 2320.

About the Authors

Robert Carling is a retired senior Commonwealth and New South Wales Treasury official and is currently Senior Fellow at the Centre for Independent Studies, Sydney, NSW. He writes regularly in the national media on economic and budget issues.

Dr Margaret Cook is a Research Fellow at the Australian Rivers Institute, Griffith University, and holds a PhD in history from the University of Queensland. She is a member of the Professional Historians Association and has written on environmental issues, social history and heritage conservation. Her publications include *A River with a City Problem: A History of Brisbane Floods* (UQP 2019) and *Cities in a Sunburnt Country* (Cambridge 2022).

Sarah G.L. Cooper is a Lecturer in Politics at the University of Exeter. She works predominately in the field of gender public policy with a particular interest in how this is represented in inquiries, having been the editor of Public Money and Management's 'Equality in an Uncertain Public Sector' Special Issue (2020), and giving oral evidence to British-Irish Parliamentary Assembly Committee inquiry on cross-jurisdictional implications of abortion policy (2018). Her previous works include the monograph *Regulating Women* (Rowman and Littlefield, 2016). She was Co-Chair of the Council for European Studies' Gender and Sexuality Research Network from 2018-2021.

Dominic Elliott is Executive Dean of the School of Business at Dublin City University and has written on crisis management and on the impacts of public inquiries. Prior to joining DCU Dominic was at the University of the West of Scotland. He previously had the *Paul Roy* Professor of Strategy (2002-2018) at the University of Liverpool, where he was interim Dean of the Management School (2015-16) and

Dean of School of the Arts (2016-2018). In his research Dominic has published widely in the fields of crisis and strategic management and has interests in organisational learning from crisis and business continuity management. Dominic was a founding Editor of the Academic Journal - *Risk Management: An International Journal*, a position he held for ten years, and remains as an associate editor. The second edition of his co-authored book *Business Continuity Management: A Crisis Management Approach* was recently published. He has published many academic articles.

Paddy Gourley was employed by the Commonwealth Public Service Board and also worked in the departments of Employment of Industrial relations and Defence from 1969 to 2000. Since then, he has served on the boards of the Sydney Airport Corporation, the Great Energy Alliance Corporation and the Loy Yang Marketing and Management Company.

Ken Kitts became President of the University of North Alabama in 2015. Prior to joining UNA, Dr Kitts served in various academic and administrative positions at universities in North Carolina and South Carolina. Ken gained his BA, MA and PhD degrees in political science and his post-graduate certificate from Harvard University's Institute for Educational Management. His academic interests include the American presidency, national security and executive advisory systems. He is the author of an award-winning book on presidential commissions, *Presidential Commissions and National Security* and has published widely on a variety of related topics.

Marlene Krasovitsky has extensive experience with public inquiries. Marlene was the Director of *Willing to Work, the National Inquiry into Employment Discrimination Against Older Australians and Australians with Disability* with the Australian Human Rights Commission (AHRC). She was also the Research Director with the AHRC's *Review into the Treatment of Women in the Australian Defence Force*. Marlene was part of the *NSW Special Commission of Inquiry into Child Protection in NSW*. These inquiries sparked Marlene's interest in the role and impact of public inquiries and royal commissions which became the subject of her PhD thesis, *Putting the 'Public' back into Inquiries: Assessing the Success of Public Inquiries in Australia.* Marlene is currently the Co-Chair and Director of EveryAGE Counts, Australia's national coalition to end ageism. Marlene has also worked in Commonwealth and State governments in executive, policy and operational roles. Marlene has an Executive Masters of Public Administration (ANZSOG), a Master of Business Administration (University of Technology, Sydney) and is a registered psychologist.

David Lee is Associate Professor, School of Humanities and Social Sciences, University of New South Wales, Canberra, having been Director of the Historical Publications and Information Section, Department of Foreign Affairs and Trade, from 1997 to 2019. His research interests include the history of Australian politics and public administration, economic, business and mining history, Australian biography, and the history of Australian diplomacy and strategic policy. His publications include *Stanley Melbourne Bruce: Australian Internationalist* (2010), *The Second Rush: Mining and the Transformation of Australia*, and *Stanley Melbourne Bruce: Institution Builder* (2020) and *John Curtin* (2022). He is the Chair of the Commonwealth Working Party of the Australian Dictionary of Biography.

Wendy McGuinness is the Chief Executive of the McGuinness Institute, which she established in 2004 as a way of contributing to New Zealand's long-term future. The McGuinness Institute is a non-partisan think tank that applies hindsight, insight and foresight to explore challenges and opportunities facing New Zealand. Wendy has worked in both the public and private sectors specialising in public sector reporting, risk management and future studies. She continues to be fascinated by the development and implementation of public policy, in particular how New Zealand might secure its future in the long term and in doing so, how it might become an exemplar for the world. Her research into royal commissions and inquiries stems from her interest in learning lessons and processes from the past in order to enable decision-makers and citizens to develop effective instruments and processes for the future.

Anita Mackay is a Senior Lecturer at La Trobe Law School at La Trobe University, Melbourne. Dr Mackay's research evaluates inquiry processes, such as royal commissions and parliamentary committees. In researching this area, she draws on her experience as a legal researcher for a Victorian parliamentary committee, and extensive experience developing government responses to inquiry recommendations from within the public service.

John Phillimore has been Executive Director of The John Curtin Institute of Public Policy at Curtin University since 2007. John has published on Australian public policy, politics, public administration, political economy, health regulation, and social policy. He has done contract research for many government agencies and other public, private and not-for-profit organisations. He is a regular media commentator on Australian and Western Australian politics and public policy and has worked at senior levels in the Western Australian Government.

Scott Prasser has worked in federal and state governments in senior policy and research roles and in addition has held senior academic positions across several Australian universities. His latest publication is *Royal Commissions and Public Inquiries in Australia* (2nd ed) was released in 2021. Scott has written extensively on federal and state politics and public policy.

Kira Pronin is a Postdoctoral Research Associate in Experimental Political Economy in the Political Science Department. She earned her PhD in Political Science from University of Pittsburgh (2020-2021). Her research focuses on deliberation and consensus-building within legislative and policy-making institutions. Her dissertation, which uses the Empirical Implications of Theoretical Models (EITM) method and hand-collected data on 2,705 Swedish advisory commissions between 1990 to 2018, examines whether governments can build broad consensus on policy by soliciting advice from independent commissions of experts and stakeholders.

Dr Sue Regan joined Volunteering Australia in February 2020 and is a Visiting Fellow at the Crawford School of Public Policy, at the Australian National University. Sue is Vice President of the Australian Social Policy Association. Formerly, Sue was Program Director at the Institute of Public Administration Australia and Program Lead (Social Policy) at the HC Coombs Policy Forum. Sue has an MA in Economics and a PhD in Public Policy (ANU). Her thesis was on *Evidence and Policy Judgement in Public Inquiries*.

Alastair Stark is a Reader in Public Policy at the University of Queensland and specialises in the study of crisis management. Alastair has published widely in high-ranking international journals and is the recipient of the Henry Mayer Prize (best paper in the Australian Journal of Political Science) and the Harold Lasswell Prize (best paper in policy sciences). He has authored two books that addressed crisis and risk management in the public sector and policy learning and public inquiries. Alastair's current research examines three areas: the role that institutional amnesia plays in terms of policy learning, deliberative democracy and policy design, and the implementation of royal commissions in Australia.

Owen D. Thomas is a Senior Lecturer in Politics and International Relations at the University of Exeter, UK. He has a broad interest in how inquiries and other forms of investigation are used to seek truth and accountability in the wake of outrage and scandal. His previous research has included extensive work on British inquiries (especially on the 2003 Iraq War), freedom of information, secrecy studies and 'scandalogy'. He is a member of the "Secrecy, Power and Ignorance Research Network" (https://secrecyresearch.com/) and leads a Leverhulme Research Project on, "Warnings from the Archive: A Century of British Intervention in the Middle East" (https://warningsfromthearchive.exeter.ac.uk/).

Paul Tilley was an economic policy adviser to governments for 30 years, working mainly in Treasury but also in the Prime Minister and Cabinet, the Treasurer's office and the OECD. He has since published a book on the history of the Treasury, *Changing Fortunes: A History of* *the Australian Treasury*. Paul is a Visiting Fellow at the ANU's Tax and Transfer Policy Institute and a Senior Fellow at the Melbourne Law School. He is currently writing a book on the history of tax reform in Australia.

Andrea Wallace is a Lecturer at the School of Business, University of New England. Andrea holds undergraduate and postgraduate qualifications in politics, history and economics from the University of Canterbury, New Zealand, and the University of New England, Australia. She completed her PhD focusing on local government structural reform in 2019. In addition to her on-going research in local government, other current research interests include public policy, and social and economic issues.

Peter Wilkins is an Adjunct Professor at The John Curtin Institute of Public Policy at Curtin University. He served as Western Australia's Deputy Ombudsman. and prior to this had been WA Assistant Auditor General Performance Review. He has diverse work experience in Australia, England, Malaysia and Canada including roles as an engineer, researcher, consultant and thirty years as a public sector manager. He is a National Fellow and Western Australian Fellow of the Institute of Public Administration Australia.

www.ingramcontent.com/pod-product-compliance
Lightning Source LLC
Chambersburg PA
CBHW061615220326
41598CB00026BA/3772